THE MODERN RESEARCHER

FOURTH EDITION

THE MODERN RESEARCHER

FOURTH EDITION

BY JACQUES BARZUN AND HENRY F. GRAFF

HARCOURT BRACE JOVANOVICH, PUBLISHERS

San Diego   *New York*   *London*

Requests for permission to make copies of any part of the work should be mailed to: Permissions, Harcourt Brace Jovanovich, Publishers, Orlando, Florida 32887.

ISBN: 0-15-562512-8 (paperback)
ISBN: 0-15-161479-2 (hardbound)   ISBN: 0-15-661483-9 (trade paperback)

Library of Congress Catalog Card Number: 85-60646

Printed in the United States of America

The authors wish to thank the following copyright holders for the privilege of quoting from or reproducing selections from their works:

Figure 1—cartoon reprinted from *Through History with J. Wesley Smith*, by Burr Shafer, by permission of the publisher, Vanguard Press, Inc. Copyright © 1950 by Burr Shafer, copyright © 1977 renewed by Evelyn Lanning Shafer.

Figure 2—*left, The Columbia-Viking Desk Encyclopedia*, copyright © 1953, published by Columbia University Press; *right, Dictionary of Clocks and Watches* by Eric Bruton, copyright © 1963, published by Archer House.

Figure 7—cartoon by LEA reprinted courtesy of *Moneysworth*, copyright © 1983.

Figure 9—*left, Poole's Index to Literature* by William F. Poole and William I. Fletcher, published by Houghton Mifflin Company; *right, Readers' Guide to Periodical Literature*, published by H. W. Wilson Company.

Figure 10—cartoon from *Basic Programming* by Donald Spencer, copyright © 1983 by Camelot Publishing Company Inc. Reprinted with the permission of Charles Scribner's Sons.

Figure 12—*left, Uncommon Law* by A. P. Herbert, copyright © 1935, Methuen & Company Ltd., London, by permission of Lady Herbert; *right*, column by Phyllis Battelle reprinted with special permission of King Features Syndicate, Inc., copyright © 1975.

Pp. 272–273—passage from *English Literature at the Close of the Middle Ages* by Edmund K. Chambers, copyright © 1945, published by Oxford University Press, Clarendon Press. Reprinted by permission of the publisher.

Figure 20—*left, Hubert Humphrey: A Political Biography* by Carl Solberg, copyright © 1984, published by W. W. Norton & Company; *right, A Stroll with William James* by Jacques Barzun, copyright © 1983, published by Harper & Row.

Figure 22—cartoon by Eli Stein from the *Wall Street Journal*, permission from the Cartoon Features Syndicate, copyright © 1984.

Figure 25—proofsheet from Balzac's *Eugénie Grandet*. Reprinted courtesy of the Pierpont Morgan Library.

P. 419—passage from Robert Latham, "Pepys and His Letters," *Journal of the Royal Society of Arts*, 132, no. 5334 (May 1984).

Every one of you gentlemen, every thinking man generally, is always searching for sources and is a pragmatic historian. There is no other way to understand the events that take place before your eyes. Every business man who handles a complicated transaction, every lawyer who studies a case, is a searcher for sources and a pragmatic historian.

—THEODOR MOMMSEN
Rectorial Address at the
University of Berlin, 1874

Preface

This book is for anyone who is or will be engaged in research and report-writing, regardless of his or her field of interest. The work is planned on original lines because the authors have found in their experience as teachers and editors that the needs of writers and researchers—whether in college or graduate school, in business or the professions—are met neither by the usual "Introduction to Research" nor by the usual "How to Write" book. Rather, the need is for a new view of the single subject, Research-and-Report, which the ordinary manuals split apart. In academic life, the fallacy of the split is expressed in the impatient outcry: "Why doesn't the English Department teach them how to write?"

The authors are historians who sympathize equally with the English Department, with the universal demand for better writing, and with all those who, soon or late in their education, try to master at once the techniques of research and the art of expression. What such persons need is a manual designed to give not so much a set of rules as an insight into what the mind is about when it searches for facts in library books and prepares a report on its findings for the inspection of others.

To carry out its purpose, this book concentrates on principles of thought and the analysis of difficulties. It illustrates both theory and practice by examples from many fields, and it shows how methods of investigation and expression follow from the obvious features of typical problems. These methods are of course the general ones of scholarship, not the particular ones of statistical and mathematical work, or the laboratory and field techniques of testing and interviewing. The present book, in short, aims at imparting the fundamentals of informed exposition.

The scheme of the work is simple. Any researcher's first question is: What kinds of aids—indexes, bibliographies, dictionaries, catalogues, monographs—are there accessible to me? And the next is: How can I make them yield just so much of their information as I want? The technique for satisfying these wants is universal and it is learnable.

The digging and delving once done, the next step is to verify and assemble the data; after which we are led to ask: What is the value of the "story" we recover from records? How far can we trust our sources? What is the effect of bias? the mechanism of causation? the relevance of philosophic systems? If every researcher produces a different picture from the same sources, and if on large subjects rival interpretations continue to flourish, how can the reader of any history or biography escape confusion and ultimate skepticism?

Such ideas as these may not cross the mind of the researcher as he or she works at a limited project for an immediate purpose—a report on the operation of a business or an army camp, a study of divorce statistics or of consumer tastes. But at some time or other the query "What is truth?" will occur to any seeker after facts or will be put to anyone who reports "what happened."

Well before such a writer or speaker is challenged he or she will have run into the problem of exposition. The facts *never* speak for themselves. They must be selected, marshaled, linked together, and given a voice. Obviously, research is not an end in itself. The day comes when the pleasures and the drudgery of the detective hunt are over and the report must be written. At that point, fit expression no longer appears as a mere frill added to one's accumulation of knowledge. The expression *is* the knowledge. What is not properly presented is simply *not present*—and its purely potential existence is useless.

Except in the rare cases where formulas and graphs can stand alone by virtue of being well-known periodic reports in themselves, the sole carriers of information are words; and these, as everybody knows, are hard to handle. Not only is it difficult to make words agreeable to read and impressive enough to remember; it is also difficult to make them reveal the exact contours of the facts and thoughts one has unearthed.

This book does not profess to make good writers by rule and precept, but it does attempt to show how skillful expression is connected throughout with the technique of research and the art of thought. Understanding a text and taking notes on it require the same attention to words and meanings as preparing and polishing a report. Whoever attains skill at the one and is a good researcher can develop the skill at the other and become a good report-writer. And with a little added effort he or she can learn how to shape the material so as to produce an interesting speech. Here then are detailed the systematic ways in which the student, the government expert, the lawyer, the journalist, the business executive, the editorial assistant, the club secretary, the scientist, as well as the professional scholar or the scholar by necessity can all equally criticize and improve their writing and make their reports or lectures come closer to the reality they have discovered by research.

Note on The Fourth Edition

It is thirty years since the text of this book was dispatched to the publisher, after having been "taught" and "revised" for three years in a graduate course given by the authors at Columbia University. In that third of a century a generation of researchers, professional and other, has made use of the examples, precepts, and references here offered. At intervals, these have been changed to keep up with the changing realities of the time, which include the proliferation and the perfecting of both the means of research and the facilities for imparting its results.

This fourth edition follows precedent. It presents new examples from recent events, titles of new reference books, new uses of old methods, and old uses of new devices such as computers, word processors, and data banks. It tries, as before, to describe the merits and limitations, the convenience and the snares of every type of research instrument.

In addition, owing to what may be called the democratization of research and the popularization of interest in relics, anniversaries, docudramas, and other historical bits and pieces, sections have been added on the shifting attitudes toward documentation, on revisionism, on the typology of error, and on kindred topics made relevant by current developments in our culture.

Finally, the alterations brought about in the idea of biography and history by social preoccupations in behalf of ethnic and class groupings justified the addition of a chapter devoted to the place and function in the contemporary mind of psycho-history, quantified history, and the vast literature of retrospective sociology. Whether consciously or not, these modes of thought affect every researcher, whatever his or her immediate subject may be—business or the law, medicine or sports. Research and reporting are inescapably influenced by the tendency of general assumptions and public opinion.

We take pleasure in renewing here our warm thanks for suggestions from our readers and our colleagues. Especial gratitude goes to our friend Eugene P. Sheehy for his faithful scrutiny of our bibliographic recommendations and to Julia Stair for preparing the materials used in making the Index.

At our publishers' we met, as usual, the most attentive help, notably from Drake Bush and his aides, as well as from the art department, Merilyn Britt in particular.

Note on the Third Edition

Between the present and previous editions of this book a good deal has happened to the mechanics and facilities of research and report-writing, though the fundamental principles, of course, remain what they were. Accordingly, we have maintained the plan and the outlook which we originally embodied in the book, and which have commended themselves to its many users for over two decades.

Even so, we have felt it necessary to subject the text to a thorough verbal revision amounting for certain sections and chapters to a complete rewriting. Changes of connotation in words and of perspective in the authors required corresponding changes of emphasis, as well as the fresh characterization of familiar things. The result, we hope, is a book that will afford up-to-date counsel and guidance to the ever-enlarging group of persons in every part of society who engage in research and writing.

As for the "mechanics and facilities" of that research, the art of exploiting the full resources of present-day libraries has become more demanding as the adjuncts to books on shelves—data banks, joint repositories, microcollections, and the like—have grown in number and variety. Catalogues, too, and reference works have multiplied and required changes in the classification and numbering systems. Whether one wants to tap an electronic bibliography giving quick but not fully selective access to large bodies of periodical literature or to consult the "union lists" for interlibrary loan, or discover whether a microfiche series exists on one's subject, one needs ahead of time something like a map and a forecast of possibilities. Our chapter on Fact-Finding gives the reader an idea of the planning needed, as well as many time-saving directions to carry it out successfully.

The enlarged and reshaped Bibliography supplements that chapter by adding to it the titles of numerous works, not previously available, which are themselves specialized and comprehensive guides to subjects of academic, technical, and practical research.

The book has widened its range in still other ways through added sections and new illustrative matter. The former deal with such topics as rumor and fraud, and supply guidelines on lecturing. The latter make visually clear some of the precepts we offer, such as the use of a perpetual calendar.

Finally, the most recent tendencies in method and the vogue of novel disciplines—from the use of computers for cliometrics to the doctrines of psycho-history—have engaged our critical attention. Two new chapters replace our earlier discussions of American and European history and of the historical sciences. Reviewed in the light of the innovations just mentioned, these topics remain of great importance to all researchers, and indeed to the general reader who wants to keep in touch with the thought of his own times. Accordingly, we deal with these three subjects, particularly in relation to our undiminished concern for accuracy of fact, solidity of evidence, fullness of verification, and quality of exposition—the essence, in short, of "research and report," which it has been our endeavor to set forth in theory and connect with the best means of practice.

For the help and encouragement given us by colleagues and others in the making of the first and second *Modern Researcher* we continue to feel a deep obligation. The names of those generous friends—some, alas, now departed—were set down in the previous editions. In preparing this latest one, we again record our gratitude and extend it to several other persons, including a number of correspondents, whose approval and queries have served as a welcome spur to our efforts. We are particularly indebted to Alden T.

Vaughan, of the History Department of Columbia University, for his perceptive observations derived from teaching the book.

On a number of technical matters we have drawn on the expert knowledge of our academic associates. We value especially the advice of Eugene P. Sheehy, Head of the Reference Department of the Columbia University Libraries and that of his fellow librarians in the University.

Contents

List of Figures

THE MODERN RESEARCHER

FOURTH EDITION

PART I

First Principles

1

Research and Report as Historian's Work

The Report: A Fundamental Form

In a once-famous book on the Middle East, the English archeologist Layard printed a letter in which a Turkish official answered an Englishman's question. It begins:

My Illustrious Friend and Joy of My Liver!
     The thing you asked of me is both difficult and useless. Although I have passed all my days in this place, I have neither counted the houses nor have I inquired into the number of the inhabitants; and as to what one person loads on his mules and the other stows away in the bottom of his ship, that is no business of mine. But, above all, as to the previous history of this city, God only knows the amount of dirt and confusion that the infidels may have eaten before the coming of the sword of Islam. It were unprofitable for us to inquire into it. O my soul! O my lamb! Seek not after the things which concern thee not. Thou camest unto us and we welcomed thee: go in peace.[1]

This unruffled public servant obviously made no annual report—those were the good old days. It is interesting to note the three things

[1]Austen H. Layard, *Discoveries in the Ruins of Nineveh and Babylon . . .* , London, 1853, 663.

he so courteously declined to provide: vital statistics, business reports, and history. Life as we know it today would stop if information of these three kinds were not readily available on every sort of subject. All over the globe, every moment of the day, someone is being asked to make a search and write a report on some state of fact, or else to read and analyze one, so that action may be taken. Reports are the means by which we try to substitute intelligence for routine and knowledge for guesswork.

This characteristic behavior of modern man makes "the report" fundamental in the conduct of affairs. It has become a familiar form, like the business letter or the sonnet.

Every report implies previous research, whether by the reporter or by someone else. Thousands of persons not connected with academic life are thus turned into more or less able scholars. The Turkish official of today has dropped his hookah, leaped from his cushion, and is busy counting the houses for the Ministry of the Interior. The figures he gathers are then published as government statistics, which other researchers will use for still other reports— from the university student writing a paper on modern Turkey to the foreign businessman who wants to trade in that country.

Among the many useful documents that may strictly or loosely be classed as reports there is no essential difference of outlook or method. The student writing a book report for a Freshman English course is doing on a small scale and with a single source the same thing as the president of a corporation who prepares his annual report to the stockholders, or as the President of the United States when he reports to the people on the state of the Union. The general form and the devices employed in preparation are identical in all three.

What is common to all these tasks is the need to investigate and to report findings, that is to say, face the problems of research and exposition, which—it turns out—are solved in similar ways. The writers of reports use the common tongue and draw upon the same vast reservoir of information. Apart from the fresh facts that, to pursue the examples above, the treasurer of a corporation or the Secretary of State supply to their respective presidents, the written sources for the millions of words uttered in reports are the familiar ones—newspapers, learned journals, histories, statistical abstracts, law cases, state papers, and so on through the many categories of books found in large libraries. This huge accumulation is what the researcher must learn to use in order to satisfy his or her particular need. And as the conditions of the search are the same for researchers, it is possible to discuss research and reporting apart from their occasion or subject.

The Historical Attitude Underlies Research *and* Report

To regard the report as a form is further justified by the fact that the attitude and technique of the report-writer are derived directly from one of the great literary and academic disciplines—History. It is from historical scholarship—originating with the antiquarian—that the world has taken the apparatus of footnotes, source references, bibliography, and so on, which have become commonplace devices. It is from the historical study of texts by philologists and historians that writers at large have learned to sift evidence, balance testimony, and demand verified assertions. ·

It might seem as if, in spite of what has just been said, a great difference separated the scholar's interest from that of the ordinary report-writer. The former seeks to know the past; the latter is concerned with the present, generally with a view to plotting the future; hence their outlooks must differ. This difference is more striking than significant. Whatever its purpose, a report is invariably historical, it deals with recent events, perhaps, but they too are in the past. Recorded opinions obviously belong to what has gone before, to history. Suppose a study of American foreign policy designed solely to change future action. It can do so only by discussing principles or personnel: but to do this its arguments must lean on the evidence of what has been happening—on what is past, recorded, and beyond the reach of change. What else is this but a piece of history?

The same holds true when a report is, as we say, "purely fact-finding," for example, a survey of the conditions of the public schools in a certain town. This description of "the present" is actually a description of the past—last year or last week, it is all the same, a backward glance. Only events already gone by can disclose the prevailing state of things. Even the unassuming book report is a record of the past. It records, to begin with, what the student thought and felt at 2 A.M. the day it was due. It is also part autobiography, part criticism, and part literary history. The book was probably read earlier and compared with still older experiences; and the words of the book, which the report may quote, refer to a yet more remote past. Whatever else it is, every report is historical and cannot avoid being so.

Historical Writing in Daily Life

A few examples of the generality just advanced will show how frequently in ordinary life we are asked to give our attention to fragments of historical writing in the midst of our activities. These fragments of course are not necessarily *good* historical writing. They and the reports in which they occur may be inaccurate, biased, fanciful, or downright fraudulent. That is not the point. The point is that the workaday world cannot do without historical materials put in historical form. "In a certain sense," said Carlyle, "all men are historians. . . . Most men . . . speak only to narrate." Here, for example, is part of a bimonthly business report.

> The International Monetary Fund created the SDR in 1968 as an asset that countries would hold and use in settling their international accounts.[2] The idea was that the stock of SDRs would be managed so that world reserves would grow in line with world commerce. The SDR was created in a world of fixed exchange rates that reflected fixed par values of currencies. . . . Two subsequent devaluations of the dollar brought the gold price to $42.22 per ounce. . . . In early 1973, the fixed exchange rate system gave way to generally floating rates determined in the market.

These words, dates, explanations are business history, obviously. From it, a future archeologist could draw conclusions about twentieth-century America.

In science, which most often seems timeless, and in social science, which wants comparisons through time-series, dates are of

[2]SDR stands for Special Drawing Rights.

fundamental importance. The meteorologist occasionally reports to the public: "Last April and May [1980] saw the driest weather in England and Wales since 1896, followed by the wettest June since 1879, but the year before suffered the wettest March to May since 1727."

One does not usually consider advertisers great champions of Fact, yet they too want to find out what's what. Here is a New York agency making known through an advertisement its philosophy of research. The heading runs, "First, Get the Facts."

More business mistakes are due to faulty facts than to faulty judgment. As used by us, research takes many forms: motivation studies, copy testing, leadership surveys, consumer opinion research, store audits, consumer panel surveys, and dealer surveys. . . . In innumerable instances, research has provided a foundation for building a more efficient advertising program and taking the guesswork out of future planning.

One can imagine the endless reports arising from all these panels and surveys, the steady repetition of "It was found that . . ." and the scholarly comparisons, with dates and percentages, between the devotees of tooth paste and the partisans of tooth powder.

Like advertising, journalism has adapted to its use the ways of historical research and popularized its externals. Magazines such as *Time* and *Newsweek* employ corps of persons who bear the title of Researcher and whose function is to verify every statement made in the stories turned in by those whose title is Reporter.

As a final example of the varied forms that historical writing may take—this time on the geological scale—consider these few sentences from an issue of a journal of popular science:

The element uranium changes gradually, through a series of transition products—the most important of which is radium—into its inactive end-product, the lead isotope with an atomic weight of 206. The transformation rate is extremely small; in any uranium mineral, only 1 percent of a given amount of uranium is transformed in 65 million years. . . . Similarly, but even more slowly, thorium is transformed. . . . The older methods of geologic age determination were based on the determination of the lead and helium content of uranium and thorium minerals.

History the Great Catch-All

It should now be clear that History is not simply an academic subject among others but one of the ways in which we think. Every use of the past tense—"I was there." "He did it"—is a bit of history. True, false, or mistaken, it expresses our historical habit of mind. We have newspapers because we are interested in the previous day's history. We correspond with our friends to tell them what has happened to us since the last time we wrote and to hear their story in return. People keep diaries to preserve their memories or to impart their doings to posterity; or again, they delve into their genealogies to nourish their pride and enhance their feeling of "belonging." The physician arrives at a diagnosis after asking for the patient's history—previous illnesses and those of the parents. Every institution, club, and committee keeps minutes and other records, not merely as proofs of achievement but as stores of experience: What did we do last year? How did we answer when the question first came up? Lawyers and judges also think with the aid of precedents, and their thought is our law. And our most popular form of literature, the novel, apes the form of genuine history in order to bestow an air of reality on imaginary events.

All this remembering and recording is conveyed by the written word. But other kinds of signs are also historical. As a critic and museum director reminds us:

> There is one point which must always be kept in mind in thinking about contemporary painting and sculpture: that a work of art is truly contemporary only to the artist while he is actually producing it. Once he lays down his brush or chisel on the completion of his work it is already history—yesterday's work.

Independently, a distinguished musician confirms the art critic while making a further point as to the role of history:

> One of the principal tasks of musicology has always been to discover what meanings notational symbols had in their own time and to transcribe the music into symbols generally understood at the date of transcription. In this, musicology directly serves, of course, the performing, "practical" musician. . . . The two activities—performance and scholarly investigation—are aspects of the same search.

Out of all that survives of these portions of history—true or imaginary, written or composed, painted or carved, intimate or public, curious or practical—the formal narratives of an age or of a person's life are fashioned. The letter that carried news or affection becomes a documentary source; the public official's diary, written for self-communing or self-protection, throws light on governmental secrets; the broken pottery or the cave painting tells of a vanished people, as the modern novel and daily paper variously reveal the temper of the age.

Thus does "history proper" intertwine with our speech, our beliefs, our passions, and our institutions. Theoretically, everything we can think of has its history and belongs to History: not only kings and battles and economic forces, but costume and courtship, railroading and the game of chess, mathematics and the meanings of words, military strategy and old silver, the migration of continents and the surface of the moon.

Nor are these subjects separate; all are part of the history of man, even the history of stars; for, as the philosopher William James pointed out, history is the great humanizer:

> You can give humanistic value to almost anything by teaching it historically. Geology, economics, mechanics, are humanities when taught with reference to the successive achievements of the geniuses to which these sciences owe their being. Not taught thus, literature remains grammar, art a catalogue, history a list of dates, and natural science a sheet of formulas and weights and measures.

Lacking as we do the time to study every subject in this historical way, we tend to learn the history of what most deeply interests us; doing so extends and solidifies our experience: the baseball fan quickly becomes an amateur historian of the game. But what enriches the individual's life is to the group a necessity. For a whole society to lose its sense of history would be tantamount to giving up its civilization. We live and are moved by historical ideas and images, and our national existence goes on by reproducing them. We put the faces of our great men and women on our stamps or coins, we make symbols of historic places and objects—Monticello, Plymouth Rock, the Liberty Bell—and we take pains every year to relive historical events and translate them into visual forms. And like banks, colleges, and married pairs, we celebrate anniversaries. The words "Established 1877" on shop front or stationery suggest that no financial panic since then has been able to unseat the firm, just as the nation making 1976 the Bicentennial Year and selling replicas of Washington's inaugural sword is a sign that a set of ideas still has living force, and their embodiment in institutions continuous existence.

The same motive of preserving memories finds expression in much of our architecture—the restoration of a part of a town at Williamsburg, or the Gateway Arch on the Mississippi at St. Louis, which symbolizes the westward movement of a whole people. Congress has established the National Trust for Historic Preservation in the United States, whose object is "to halt the wanton destruction of historic buildings, homes, and sites." "Historic" in this context means, in addition to its literal sense, valuable as a stimulus to the emotions of unity and pride.

An angry group of Scottish patriots scolded Queen Elizabeth II . . . because [she] had called herself "Queen of England" and referred to the first Queen Elizabeth as her forebear. The reference . . . is "entirely inaccurate. Queen Elizabeth of England died unmarried and childless. The ancestor and forebear of our noble Queen was Scotland's contemporary monarch—Mary Queen of Scots—not Elizabeth of England. The council also urges that the words Britain, Britons, and British shall be used at all times when Britain or the British nation and peoples [i.e., England, Scotland, and Wales] are referred to."

When the thought of the past can arouse so much feeling, it is not surprising that it can also satisfy mankind's insatiable curiosity, afford readers elevated pleasure, and, by simply showing how anything came to be what it is, furnish every man a unique kind of reassurance. The excitement caused by new accounts of old stories is seemingly inexhaustible. Books about Lincoln, Caesar, Mary Queen of Scots, Captain Bligh, Marie Antoinette, Lewis and Clark, Lord Byron, Joan of Arc, and dozens of other familiar figures are always sure of a large audience, almost irrespective of the merit of the work. The naive interest in small detail is what often carries the reader along. Thus in *The Day Lincoln Was Shot,* Jim Bishop, a newspaper reporter and not a professional historian, made the search into such details a formula. He read 7 million words of contemporary testimony to glean curious scraps. He shows, in addition, our modern zeal for numerical accuracy: "I traveled the escape route of Booth in an Oldsmobile and checked it to the tenth of a mile."

Making a fetish of fact goes with the notion that all records whatever should be saved to form "archives." The result is overcrowding—and desperate disposal: some 500 pounds of New York State papers were caught on their way to a pulping mill in Canada, and boxes of records of the City of New York were discovered in cavities within the framework of Brooklyn Bridge. One never knows, of course, when a remote and nearly forgotten fact can be useful. Until recently, students of the special problems of arid lands neglected history. But Paul B. Sears of Yale made the point that "We can do no better in some places than find out where the ancients had their irrigation systems" as a prelude to reclamation.

Finally, the "argument from history" is a commonplace of domestic politics. When the late Adlai Stevenson was put forward for the presidency a second time, the public argued pro or con from precedent; a writer to the letters column of a newspaper cited Jefferson, John Quincy Adams, Andrew Jackson, William Henry Harrison, and Grover Cleveland as having lost and then won. Only four men ran twice and were never elected, and it was suggested that "even a cursory glance at a reliable reporting of history will illustrate why."

So much for the excitement and the practical utility of history. The solution of mysteries is no less important for our pleasure and peace of mind. People are still bothered by such questions as: Who was the Man in the Iron Mask? Who wrote the "Letters of Junius"? What did Napoleon die of?[3] Who erased part of the Nixon tapes? Speaking of a famous modern crime and the alarm it caused, the English writer Rebecca West pointed out:

> The position of man is obviously extremely insecure unless he can find out what is happening around him. That is why historians publicly pretend

[3]Until recently, Malta fever and cancer of the stomach were the rival hypotheses. In 1982, a thoroughly documented and well-written work appeared, setting forth evidence that he was deliberately poisoned by arsenic. See *The Murder of Napoleon* by Ben Weider and David Hapgood, New York, 1982.

that they can give an exact account of events in the past, though they privately know that all the past will let us know about events above a certain degree of importance is a bunch of alternative hypotheses.

The remark may be right about man's insecurity without history; it is quite wrong about the historian's "public" versus "private views." This is a point we shall return to.

FIGURE 1   *History as Visual Symbols and Associations*

"Don't anybody leave—where's that gold spike?"

The two locomotives facing on a single track in the presence of top-hatted dignitaries call up automatically the celebrated completion of the first transcontinental railroad (Promontory, Utah, 1869). The best-known gold object in American history is the Last Spike, set in place on that occasion. The humor obviously draws on the instinctive question that generations of students have asked: "Is the spike still there?" (It was removed almost immediately for safekeeping.) The scene and the remark suffice to evoke the event.

A parallel of even greater magnitude is found in the prolonged controversy over the assassination of President Kennedy, about which a sense of mystery persists. Historical truth, ancient or recent, is always complex and always difficult to ascertain. Eyewitnesses are generally few, hard to find and question, and they often prove untrustworthy. And so the secret of a crime done in private is more likely to remain hidden than the truth of a great public event, but not absolutely so, as the murder of Kennedy suggests.

History's Home and Foreign Relations

Though we are not yet ready to list the kinds of resources available to the historical researcher, we may point out that the all-pervasiveness of history connects him or her with nearly every other branch of learning and makes the person a "generalist" as well as a specialist. Take this eye-catching paragraph from the announcement of a scholarly work: "The year *The Communist Manifesto* appeared, gold was discovered in California, *Vanity Fair* was published, Metternich resigned, the new French Republic elected Louis Napoleon president, Emperor Ferdinand abdicated." What these remarks are supposed to do is transport us back to 1848. In order to report intelligently about those six events (out of many more) an historian must be prepared to write about the following subjects, among others:

For *The Communist Manifesto*:   about Marx and Marxism, the history of economic thought, and Utopian Socialism.

For the discovery of gold: about California geology, geography, and settlement; the history of exploration and of western expansion.

For *Vanity Fair*:   about Thackeray and the English and Continental novel.

For Metternich: about the Congress of Vienna, the Holy Alliance, Nationalism, and Friedrich Gentz.

For Louis Napoleon: about Napoleon Bonaparte, his empire, his brothers, their fate and their descendants. Also: the genesis of the Second French Republic, its constitution, parties, and problems.

For Emperor Ferdinand: about the house of Hapsburg, the Austrian Empire in the nineteenth century, its national and linguistic
minorities, and the rise of Liberalism.

By this point our historian has become something of an economist, a geographer, a literary critic, a sociologist, an anthropologist,
and a political theorist, as well as a student of military campaigns,
diplomacy, constitutional law, and philosophical systems. Besides
which, he or she has to be a wide-ranging biographer, hence acquainted in some measure with all the unpredictable matters that
human lives contain.

It is obvious that the historian cannot be all these things in full.
Life is too short to master so many extensive disciplines. But he must
know how to use the results supplied by others in their studies (called
monographs) upon the related topics that he encounters while pur-
suing his own.

What he himself contributes is twofold. First: the results of his
own search for facts as yet unknown, or possibly ill handled by a
previous worker.[4] Second: the organizing principles, narrative skill,
and conclusions or explanations that make of the disconnected facts
"a history." In his first capacity the work of the historian may be
loosely likened to a science. In the second, it may be considered an
art. Actually, these two functions are not separable except in thought;
the historian is an exact reporter working in the realm where the
concrete and the imponderable meet.

The Research Scholar and Writer

It is now possible to draw conclusions about the identity of the
historian's techniques with those of the researcher-at-large preparing
a report. Both have recourse to the same infinite range of materials,
find their way among books by the same devices, gather and test
facts according to the same rules, exhibit their results in the same order and spirit, and hope to impress others' minds by the same
literary means.

[4]See Chapter 4 and Chapter 15, p. 367.

The difference is chiefly one of scale and aim. One thinks of an historian as treating in lasting fashion a large slice of the past, and of the maker of a report as bent over a narrow set of facts whose interest is momentary. But this is not invariably so. Alexander Hamilton's *Report on Manufactures* was a political document by a public official, yet it is a more valuable piece of research and writing than the *Life of George Washington* by the itinerant preacher Parson Weems, who launched the best-known fabrication in American history, the cherry-tree story. To repeat once more, the obvious and important difference between the professional student of history and the unpretentious reporter of contemporary matters does not affect the similarity of their problems and instruments of work. Neither does the quality of the results they produce nor the subject matter they take up.

2

The ABC of Technique

The Prime Difficulty: What Is My Subject?

Any account, report, or other piece of historical writing is intended to take effect on someone at some time. It must consequently meet that someone's demands. Those demands can for convenience be summed up in a pair of questions: Is the account true, reliable, complete? Is it clear, orderly, easy to grasp and remember? All the devices and methods that the researcher combines under the name of technique exist to satisfy these inescapable requirements.

This in turn means that the researcher must first ask the questions of himself, and not only at the end, when the finished typescript is being neatly clamped in attractive folders, but at many points between the beginning and the end. It is evident that in order to be able to answer Yes to each part of the two questions, the writer must be sure of what his subject is. If he does not know, how can he tell whether the treatment is complete? If he does not know, how can he expect a reader to find his paper clear? If he does not know, what yardstick can he use for including and omitting, and how can he proceed in orderly fashion from opening to conclusion? If he does not know, how can he test reliability? For reliability only means "These words fairly represent certain things outside (facts, events, ideas) that are naturally linked to form 'a subject.'"

Now a writer always starts with *some* idea of what his or her subject is, even if that idea is contained in a single term—Blimps or Fish or Alexander the Great. But the discovery of the true, whittled-down subject that the essay will propose to the reader and that will inevitably determine the writer's demands is a task that begins with the first steps of research and ends only when the last word has been written and revised.

The truth of this abstract statement you will experience the moment you tackle *your* subject. Between the first notion of it and the final draft you will probably modify your conception more than once. It does not greatly matter if in doing your research you pick up a number of facts or ideas that you later discard as irrelevant. But it is obvious that if you take time to collect nearly everything that some-how clings to any part of your topic, you will have a library on your hands, and not the materials with which to work up a report on "a subject." Fortunately, as you proceed, your judgment grows more and more assured about what belongs and what does not, and soon you begin to *see your subject*. From then on you must not take your eyes off it. You must keep seeing it at every moment of fact-gathering and of composition.

The reason for this constant attention is that a subject does not let itself be carved away from neighboring subjects as if by a butcher carving off one chop from the next. A subject is always trying to merge itself again into the great mass of associated facts and ideas. Take a small book like Rachel Carson's *The Sea Around Us*. Before starting, the author undoubtedly had the general notion of writing for laymen about certain facts relating to the sea. She could hardly have chosen a more difficult *notion* to turn into a *subject*. The sea is immense. Its action and effects, its form, substance, and inhabitants furnish matter for thousands of monographs. Yet the writer could not choose for her book a few of these matters at random and then stop. The result would have been the same as that produced by the amateur writer who called up a publisher and asked: "How long is the average novel nowadays?"

"Oh, between seventy-five and ninety thousand words."

"Well then, I've finished!"

The anecdote illustrates by a negative example the principle that to make any lasting impression there must be unity and completeness in the works of the human mind. In order to perceive what is necessary to completeness, that is, what the subject requires, you must first know the projected size of its treatment. Suppose a stranger to Western civilization asks you: "What does 'Roman Empire' mean?" You can answer him in a sentence, in a paragraph, or in a page. You can refer him to an essay, a book, or Gibbon's six volumes. All these forms determine by their scale what is and what is not part of the subject; for if you have but one sentence at your disposal you will certainly not mention the geese that saved the Capitol, or even the three wars against Carthage; and if you have six volumes at your disposal you will nowhere find it necessary to give a one-sentence definition of the whole.

In other words, your subject is defined by *that group of associated facts and ideas which, when clearly presented in a prescribed amount of space, leave no questions unanswered* WITHIN *the presentation, even though many questions could be asked* OUTSIDE *it.* For example, if you defined the Roman Empire as "an ancient power which sprang from a city-state in central Italy to cover ultimately both shores of the Mediterranean, and which between 100 B.C. and A.D. 476 transmitted to the West the cultures it had conquered to the East," you would have, not indeed a *perfect* definition, but one that is complete as far as it goes. In any longer account, the added detail must sustain the impression of closeness to the central idea and of even distribution around it.

Without unity and completeness, details make, as we say, "no sense." Even a reader ignorant of your subject will notice something wrong if you give a page to the legend of Romulus and Remus suckled by a she-wolf and later on dispose of Caesar's murder in one sentence. Nor can you at the last page leave a dozen questions hanging in the air. The reader knows from experience that things written about exhibit a logical structure. Time, place, and meaning give things their connectedness, which must come out again in a report upon them. And once subjects have been made distinct by an appropriate treatment they will not readily mix again. This is the point of Dickens's joke about Mr. Pott, the journalist in *Pickwick Papers*, whose colleague had written an article about Chinese Metaphysics, though he knew nothing of the subject. He used the encyclopedia, said Mr. Pott, and "read for metaphysics under the letter M, and for China under the letter C, and combined his information."

To test the relevance of any one or more ideas within a large subject and as it were to draw a circle around whatever should be in it, the researcher will find that an expanded title often helps. This is one reason why reports of factual investigation generally carry long and explicit titles. Books used to be titled in this same descriptive fashion, for example, Malthus's *Essay on the Principle of Population, as it affects the future improvement of Society: with remarks on the Speculations of Mr. Godwin, M. Condorcet, and other writers* (1798). The title not only gives fair warning about the contents; it also sets limits. It makes a kind of contract with the reader as to what he or she will get, and the contract helps the writer to fulfill the bargain. In this regard such a title is at the opposite extreme from the modern style shown in *The Sea Around Us*, which could encompass anything and everything.

Note that a seemingly clear, sharply defined subject like "The American Presidency" actually conceals a multitude of separate subjects. Would a book on the Presidents from 1789 to the present take up their private lives and their careers before election? If so, to what extent? And what about their characters, their wives, their illnesses? We can think at once of instances in which any of these topics would be immediately relevant to the central theme—if we knew what that theme was. "The American Presidency—The Conflicts Between the Executive and Congress" is a different book from "The American Presidency—A Study in Personal Power." Lengthening the title to narrow the limits has the effect of driving doubts into a corner. There your mind can grapple with them and decide the recurring issue of relevance: is this particular incident a case of personal power, Yes or No? does it duplicate or amplify a previous instance, Yes or No? and so on until you have finished deciding In or Out.

These difficulties are inseparable from research. They illustrate the general truth that reading, writing, *and thinking* are the three activities of research. As a student naively but truthfully remarked in discussing the matter in an examination, "thinking about one's subject should be a frequent process, whether or not one is reading or writing."

Though painful, the delimiting of the subject has one advantage—and this is a thought in which the weary researcher, struggling with his notes and ideas like someone filling a featherbed, can take comfort—a writer cannot "tell all." No one wants him to. The writer will often wonder, "Do I need to mention this?" And he can and must frequently answer: "They don't want to hear about *that!*"

To sum up, fashioning the subject may be likened to sculpturing in clay when working from visual memory. A sculptor shapes his work by adding and by taking away until the lump resembles the image he has carried in his mind's eye. He is aided by his general knowledge of how objects look, but he must use trial and error to achieve the desired likeness. The reason why research is like sculpturing *from memory* is that in neither is there a concrete visible subject to copy directly. The subject exists only when the object is finished.

"I Have All My Material"—But Have *You?*

The available material in research is the huge mass of words bearing on the innumerable topics and subtopics within the subject.[1] The invariable first step in carving out the substance of your report is to find out whether someone has already dealt with the subject in print—in an article or in a book. At this late date in the world's history very few subjects of research can be entirely original. Even the newest experiment in science has been led up to, and the report on the new work usually gives a bibliography, which is but a pointer to previous findings.

The record of earlier work in any field—known as its "literature"—is accessible in many ways, of which more will be said in Chapter 4. The fact to note here is that, barring exceptional cases, leads to your material exist, probably in abundance. Discovering them is a question of skill and patience—of technique.

Technique begins with learning how to use the catalogue of a library. Whatever the system, it is only an expanded form of the

---

[1]Field investigations and laboratory experiments are in part exceptions to this generality, though they too involve library research.

alphabetical order of an encyclopedia. A ready knowledge of the alphabet is therefore fundamental to all research.[2]

But it must be supplemented by alertness and imagination, for subjects frequently go by different names. For example, coin collecting is called Numismatics. More complicated is the way in which one who wants information about the theory of the divine right of kings arrives at the term "Monarchy." One might conceivably have reached the same result by looking up "Right, divine," or even possibly "Divine Right," if the library owns a book by that title or is fully cross-indexed. What is certain is that there is little chance of success if one looks up "King" and no hope at all if one looks up "Theory." In other words, one must from the very beginning *play* with the subject, take it apart and view it from various sides in order to seize on its outward connections.

Suppose that after some ingenuity and considerable tramping about the library you have found two articles and three books, all bearing clearly and largely on your topic; the temptation is now strong to consider that the search in research is pretty well over. You like to think that what remains is to read, take notes and arrange them, and write your essay. You probably announce that you "have all your material." In this error you are not far removed from the brash journalist who "combined his information." True, you may as well start reading, but research has not yet begun: the chances are that you have scarcely read more than a few pages in the second article when you discover between it and the first a discrepancy in date or name, which the books, when appealed to, do not resolve. You consult the nearest encyclopedia: it offers you a third variant. You are perplexed, yet you should feel a certain elation: research—as against *re*-search—is about to begin.

How far it will take you, no one can predict. By the time you have tracked down all uncertainties, followed up side lines to their dead ends, filled in gaps in logical or chronological sequence, and

[2]This remark may sound obvious to the point of foolishness; it is deliberately made as a hint to those people (including college and graduate students) more numerous than one would suppose, who are crippled in research by an inability to follow quickly and accurately the alphabetic order beyond the first or second letter of the key words.

FIGURE 2   *The Alphabetical Order*

Gleizes, Albert Léon (älběr′ lāő′ glěz′), 1881–, French cubist painter and illustrator.
Glencoe (glěn′kō), residential village (pop. 6,980), NE Ill., N suburb of Chicago.
Glencoe (glěnkō′), valley of Coe R., Argyllshire, Scotland, overhung by lofty mountains. Macdonald clan massacred here by the Campbells in 1692.
Glen Cove, city (pop. 15,130), SE N.Y., on N shore of Long Isl., in summer resort area; settled 1668. Mfg. of office supplies, clothing, and radios.
Glendale. 1 City (pop. 8,179), S central Ariz., NW of Phoenix. Agr. trade point in SALT RIVER VALLEY. **2** Suburban city (pop. 95,702), S Calif., N of Los Angeles; laid out 1886 on site of first Spanish land grant in Calif. Mfg. of petroleum products, aircraft, and glass. Has Forest Lawn Memorial Park, cemetery containing reproductions of great works of art.
Glendale, battle of: see SEVEN DAYS BATTLES.
Glendive (glen′dīv), city (pop. 5,254), E Mont., on Yellowstone R. and NE of Miles City. Center of farm, stock, and poultry area. Has railroad shops.

Frequency Comparison Meter Special meter used at electricity power stations to compare mains frequency with a MASTER CLOCK, so that SYNCHRONOUS CLOCKS are kept to MEAN TIME.

Friction Spring Spring acting as a clutch for hand setting; also one for taking up backlash of a CENTRE SECONDS HAND.

Frictional Rest Most ESCAPEMENTS release a tooth of the ESCAPE WHEEL for a fraction of a second and then hold it up. With some, like the CYLINDER ESCAPEMENT, the escape wheel tooth is held up by its resting against part of the moving BALANCE WHEEL. Such frictional rest interferes with the free swing of the balance wheel. The LEVER ESCAPEMENT locks an escape wheel tooth without touching the balance wheel, and is therefore free.

Fromanteel Famous family of clockmakers in London, which originated from Holland. They were named Ahasuerus, John and Abraham. John learned how to make HUYGENS pendulum clocks in Holland and the Fromanteels were the first to introduce them into England in 1658. Evelyn

---

Knowing the order of the letters of the alphabet is indispensable to anyone who wants to find or consult a book. Catalogues, indexes, and reference works are built on the alphabetical order. But within that order variations in the sequence of words will be encountered. The reason is this: single words can be arranged in only one way if the order of letters is followed: a*bac*us, a*bb*ot, a*bdi*cate, a*bdo*minal. But double or compounded words offer a choice. Suppose that your index includes the names *Glen Cove, Glen Ellyn, Glen Ridge, Glencoe,* and *Glendower.* You may choose to list first all the names in which *Glen* is separate before putting down the others. But you may also choose to arrange the names regardless of the break, and then *Glencoe* comes first, *Glen Ridge* last, and *Glendower* ahead of *Glen Ellyn*, as in the entries to the left above. The right-hand entries (from a *Dictionary of Clocks and Watches* by Eric Bruton) illustrate the alternative form by putting *Friction S . . .* ahead of *Friction a(l).* Note also that almost all indexes give the proper names that begin *M′, Mc,* and *Mac* ahead of those that begin *Ma.* This is done because of the difficulty of remembering which variant spelling of *Mac* belongs to the name sought.

reached solid conclusions of your own, you will have acquired a sizable amount of information, written matter, and technique. But you may still not be entitled to tell your inquiring friends, "I have all my material."

What you have done—to go back to our pair of fundamental questions—is to make sure that your report will be true and reliable. But there is one more test of completeness to be applied. Assuming that you have been working steadily with library resources and that in your single-mindedness you have perhaps neglected your ordinary routines, you must now remember that while you were so engaged the world has been moving on, newspapers have continued to come out, people have died, other researchers' work has been published. You must therefore make a last survey. Recent issues of periodicals will not have been indexed nor death dates recorded; you have to rely on your wits. To the very end of your work on the paper, you must keep an eye on events and publications for the latest relevant facts. At the worst, to neglect them may mean that you have overlooked something that knocks the props from under your results; at best, it may mean that you will be disconcerted in public or private when someone brings up a fact that everybody knows but you.

The Practical Imagination at Work

The nucleus of two articles and three books on your subject has expanded by addition and verification into material for an essay or report possibly twenty pages long. This report of yours will be no mere précis or résumé of what was in the nucleus. It should offer something not directly or fully treated in any one source. It will be a new arrangement consisting of tested facts and fresh thought. At the moment, the new arrangement does not exist, but only the materials for it. These so-called materials are in fact scribbles you have made on pieces of paper—notes taken as you pursued the elusive dates, the missing middle name, the descriptive detail, or the clinching piece of testimony supporting a conclusion.

But it is not possible to write a report direct from the sum total of the available materials. You can *compose* only from what you deliberately select from your notes, which bulk larger than your report will when done. It takes no argument to prove that this collection of notes you have taken can very soon become unmanageable. You must therefore adopt some system for creating order as you go, so that you may select intelligently later on. There is no one system to be preferred above all others, except that the system most congenial to you will probably give you the best results.

What you want to establish is a regular procedure that will enable you to turn to a given note without having to riffle through sheafs of stuff. At any time in research you may want to compare a quotation you took down a while ago with a new version you have just come across; or you may want to fill in a blank with a date that has turned up unexpectedly. Ultimately you will need to sort your notes into bunches, as preparation to writing your first draft.

For all these purposes, experience shows that you must take notes in a uniform manner, on paper or cards of uniform size. Some researchers favor notebooks, bound or looseleaf;[3] others prefer ruled or blank index cards—3 × 5 inches, or 4 × 6 or 5 × 8—but one size only for the main materials. Those who use notebooks, large or small, copy out facts or quotations as they come, regardless of subject. They leave a wide margin straight down one side to permit a key word or phrase to be put opposite each note as a guide to the eye in finding and classifying that note. It is also possible to write in notebooks in such a way that each note will fill no more than a given amount of space on the page. Then, when the book is filled, the pages can be cut into slips of uniform size and shuffled into groups.

The same principle underlies the use of small cards. Those who favor them make a point of noting down only a single item on any one card. Room is left in an upper corner for the key word by which related cards are later assembled. Advocates of the larger cards use them as do the users of notebooks. Other variations of these fundamental ways will suggest themselves. A distinguished English

---

[3] Many technicians throw up their hands in horror at the thought of notebooks, but great examples justify their use (Gibbon, Rhodes, A. F. Pollard, Oman). No doubt this older practice will continue to have its devotees. Certainly the researcher who has to travel is better off with notebooks than with stacks of cards.

physician of the early twentieth century, Sir Clifford Allbutt, recommended using slips of paper the size of a check and leaving a wide left-hand margin, partly for keying, partly for gathering under a snap clip. The notes for each section being held together provide the researcher with a series of small booklets that he or she leafs through thoughtfully when about to write.

The common feature of all these devices is clear: the information is extracted from all sources as it comes and is set down on one kind of card or paper. Before the miscellaneous collection becomes unwieldy, it is roughly keyed or indexed for ready reference after sorting. The single-fact-to-a-card system gives the most thorough index. But it has the drawback of producing very quickly a large, discouraging pile of cards, bulky to carry around and clumsy to handle when the time comes for writing. The notebook system is much less cumbrous but also less strictly organized. Which to choose? You should consult your taste and decide whether your temperament makes you want to have everything just so, or whether you can stand a certain amount of extra leafing through pages for the sake of having your materials more compact and portable.

The nature of the subject may also dictate a choice. For very large statistical surveys it may prove desirable to use punched cards and machines, which would be a nuisance, say, in writing a biography.[4] In deciding upon a notetaking method, there is no substitute for judgment. But no researcher, it goes without saying, should amass notes higgledy-piggledy on a variety of slips or notebook pages, leave them unkeyed, and then face the task of reducing the chaos to order. If at times you are unexpectedly forced to take down a reference on the back of an envelope, you should as soon as possible transfer it in proper form to the regular file.

The only sensible irregularities are those that have a purpose. For example, users of notebooks often find it convenient to make out a 3 × 5 card for each book and article they encounter, alphabetizing them by author as they proceed. Similarly, users of cards may keep a small notebook in which to list queries as they arise—points to look

---

[4]See the discussion of computers, pp. 101 ff.

up later in reference works or elsewhere. It is a saving of time to do these verifications in batches, rather than interrupt the train of thought while reading and notetaking. One can set aside for days of headache or indisposition the more mechanical tracking down of dates and the like, thus reversing one's best mind for study properly so-called.

In short, if you will have an eye to the obvious, foreseeable uses to which you are going to put your notes, and also observe your own preferences or peculiarities, you can put together a system that will suit you. Once you adopt it, stick to it, for it will serve you best from the moment you no longer think about it but use it automatically.

Again, if you do not discipline yourself to the habit of always writing down author, title, and page number each time you note a fact or copy a quotation, you will lose endless hours later in an irritating search for the exact reference. The same holds for clippings from newspapers: write the date and year of the issue, for the dateline of the news story may be several days before and the year is never given. Finally, there is in research one absolute rule that suffers no exception: NEVER WRITE ON BOTH SIDES OF ANYTHING. If you violate the rule and do it once, you will do it again; and if you do it from time to time you can never remember when you have done it; you thereby condemn yourself to a frequent frustrating hunt for "that note," which may be on the other side of some unidentifiable slip or card or page. You will go by it a dozen times without seeing it, turn over hundreds of pieces of paper to recover it.

A Note Is First a Thought

So much for the mechanical side of notetaking. The intellectual side cannot be as readily described or discussed. The advice "Don't take too many notes" is like the recipe in the cookbook that begins: "Take enough butter." How much is "enough"? Taking too many notes is tantamount to copying out your printed source in longhand. If you find yourself approaching this limit, even over the stretch of one page, halt and take stock. You might conceivably need a full page verbatim, but this is seldom true, apart from the need to reproduce letters, diary entries, and the like; in that case it is safer, because more accurate, to make photocopies from the book.[5]

Rather than try to gauge your notetaking skill by quantity, think of it in this way: am I simply doing clerk's work or am I assimilating new knowledge and putting down my own thoughts? To put down your own thoughts you must use your own words, not the author's. Make a conscious, steady effort to do this until it becomes second nature. For example, you read in your source the following passage:

> The early 1860's were the years of Garibaldi's greatest vogue and notoriety. The United States minister, Marsh, wrote home to his government in 1861 that, "though but a solitary and private individual, he is at this moment, in and of himself, one of the great Powers of the world."[6]

Out of this you may make the lazy man's note:

> 1860s _G's "greatest vogue and notoriety";
> Marsh, U.S. min., wrote home (1861) G. was
> "one of the great Powers of the world."

The *work* you have done on that passage is minimal. It is also negative, in that you have merely cut out connectives and fullness of expression. Such notetaking soon becomes absentminded. You do it while half thinking of other things; hence what you read leaves little trace in the memory. This lack will handicap you at the writing stage and will not be compensated by the fact that your notes will be a perpetual surprise to you—stranger's work. Suppose that instead of merely making a telegram out of the two sentences above, you recast the thought and the wording as you go:

[5]Because photocopying machines are easily accessible, some students like to make them do the work of taking notes—whole pages at a time. But although the accuracy of quotations is increased thereby, the saving of time hoped for is an illusion. Putting the substance of the notes through the mind, as described in the paragraphs that follow, cannot be eliminated; it is only postponed.

[6]Denis Mack Smith, *Garibaldi*, New York, 1956, 113.

THE ABC OF TECHNIQUE 29

*G. at peak of renown in 1860s. U. S.
Min.   Marsh called him in 1861 dispatch "one of the great Powers of the world."*

What you have accomplished is threefold: you have made an effort of thought, which has imprinted the information on your mind; you have practiced the art of writing by making a paraphrase; and you have at the same time taken a step toward your first draft, for here and now these are *your* words, not a piece of plagiarism thinly veiled by a page reference. The principle here applied is that of précis writing. As for the blank purposely left between Min. and Marsh, it is a reminder that you must look up Marsh's full name and dates of service in Italy. Why dates? Because your author may just possibly have written Marsh when he meant Mason or Morris or Masham, and the dates would disclose the error.[7]

If you are good at taking notes, you will have seen that the example just given does not show great compression. Four lines are reduced to three in either version. But with a longer original you can do much better than that. Whole paragraphs or sections can be summed up in a couple of sentences. This may be due to the original's being diffuse or badly written, as will be illustrated later on, or it may be because the detail in the source happens to be of no importance for your purpose. Here is where your notetaking grasp of the subject comes into play. You are aware that the book in front of you was written with a certain aim in view—say, to give the story of Garibaldi's life—whereas you, the researcher, are working on a study of American foreign policy. The two aims intersect, and only at the points of intersection do you make a note. You make it with *your* purpose in mind, leaving out what would be essential to another. You omit, for example, part of the quoted dispatch, which only elaborates the point. If the note taken shows signs of having passed through a mind, it is a good test of its relevance and adequacy.

---

[7]There is of course no error in the text quoted. The philologist George Perkins Marsh was the first U.S. Minister to the new Kingdom of Italy; he served from 1861 to 1882.

You will also have noticed that in order to make the note as short as possible abbreviations were used. This is legitimate, but subject to the general caution that abbreviating must not lead to confusion. If in your notes G. stands for Garibaldi, it must not also stand for Gladstone. Words as well as names can be shortened if, once again, you as notetaker are systematic. You must not only know what you are doing, but also imagine trouble ahead. At the moment it is taken down, the note speaks volumes and looks foolproof. But nothing grows colder more rapidly than notes. A week later that beautifully condensed and abbreviated statement may be utterly incomprehensible.

Even when the statement is clear and, at the time, pregnant with meaning, you may think it advisable to guide your later self by an additional remark—anything from "X says, but be sure cf. [compare] Z, *Hist. Italy*" to a full-fledged comment that might find a place in the finished paper. When such asides are put, quite rightly, next to the fact they refer to, it is advisable to mark off your addition by a special sign. A pair of slashes around the remark is convenient; it means: /I, the notetaker, am saying this, not the author I am transcribing./ Once adopted, the symbols for this or any other device must be invariable.

After taking notes on a book or two you begin to discern the large natural divisions of the subject—the main heads of your report. You are now ready to begin indexing the notes you have collected. If the report is planned to be of modest size—twenty to thirty pages— three or four divisions will suffice. If the work is to be larger, you should break the main heads down into subdivisions, giving each a provisional name or, if you like, a number.[8] In a biography, for instance, there might be Youth and Education; Adult Beginnings; Success as Lawyer; Politics; Early Character and Avocations; Crisis of 1889; Voluntary Exile; Last Years and Death; Estimate of Career; Bibliography.

These working titles, or their initials, or else Roman numerals corresponding to an outline on which the titles appear, form the key or index. The appropriate word or sign is written in the margin of the notebook opposite each note, reference, or quotation. If cards have been used, the key word or sign is entered in the chosen corner.

[8]See Chapter 11.

Misjudgments as to where a certain fact belongs are bound to occur. For this reason, it is best not to scrawl a large key word in the available space. You may have to cross it out and substitute another. Or again, a given fact may have two or more uses and need as many key words. It is likely, for instance, that some fact under Crisis of 1889 will come up again under Estimate of Career and be anticipated in Early Character.

This grouping of notes carries as yet no hint of detailed order and sequence, but it does show how much is still lacking for a balanced treatment. The category Politics may be bulging with notes while Youth and Education is thin and anemic. Since no relevant reference to other sources goes unnoted, the Bibliography group grows as fast as any and gives promise of supplying the lack of information disclosed by the indexing.

It should be unnecessary to point out that every one of the technical hints just given is readily transferable. The last example has been taken from biography because the life of a notable is a typical subject familiar to all. But the ways of notetaking, abstracting, indexing, and classifying are applicable to any subject of research. The sources need not even be books in the library sense. They can be manuscript letters or diaries, answers to questionnaires, a court record of testimony, or the books (in another sense) of a business firm. Wherever there is a multitude of facts and assertions to be selected, marshaled into kinds, and used as evidence of a state of affairs, the operations of the mind that guides the pen are fundamentally the same.

Knowledge for Whom?

The effort of research is so taxing and exciting that whoever has gone through it feels a natural desire to exhibit the results. Sometimes his audience is ready-made: he may have been commissioned to undertake the investigation, and interested people are waiting for his report. At other times the research has been entirely self-propelled. In either case the report-maker never knows exactly whom he is addressing. He knows only the general category of persons. Even a college student writing "for" his or her instructor may find a term paper being read to the whole group, or learn that it has been used as an anonymous example in another class. Similarly in the world of published research, it is impossible for the writer to foresee into whose hands his work will eventually fall.

These circumstances impose on the writer a double duty. He must write so as to inform his immediate colleagues, employers, or other familiar audience, and he must also discharge his obligation to the Unknown Reader. Though he may fondly expect his intimates or fellow workers to understand him regardless of his powers of expression, he knows that he cannot hold other readers' attention unless he is clear, orderly, and, if possible, agreeable to read. In truth, the difference between the two groups is an illusion. Neither the close nor the distant readers can be expected to see through a brick wall, to strain their wits as they grope for a meaning. Those steeped in your subject may manage to catch your drift; but they will not be grateful or admiring if they do it in spite of you. A writer who has some contribution to make must so put it that any interested reader will grasp it with only a normal effort of attention. The possibility of this result is what makes the report useful, what gives the measure of its value.

It follows that *the report-maker must write always as if addressing the whole educated community.* His yardstick is: Can another trained mind, not expert in my subject, understand what I am saying?

In using this standard of self-criticism, technical terms are of course left out of account. The assumption is that they will be used correctly, and they generally are. But a good reader needs no knowledge of such terms to tell at a glance whether a report outside his field is intelligible. He sees at once from the ordinary words whether he could understand the report if he took the trouble to learn the technical vocabulary. The failure of all "difficult" writing without exception lies elsewhere than in the technicalities.[9] In such writing it

---

[9]This statement is borne out by the efforts of scientific and other professional journals to coach their contributors in the craft of producing clear prose. In medicine, Dr. Lois DeBakey has devoted her life to holding seminars all over the country for physicians who publish research papers, and she contributes columns and articles on the subject to a wide variety of periodicals. Similar attempts to improve legal writing have produced such books as David Mellinkoff's *Legal Writing: Sense and Nonsense* (New York, 1981) and Henry Weihofen's *Legal Writing Style,* 2nd ed. (St. Paul, 1980).

is the common words that are misused, the sentence structure that is ramshackle, and the organization that is wild or nonexistent. And as we shall see, every one of these faults goes back to a fault in thinking. It follows that a fault in expression is a flaw in the knowledge that is supposedly being conveyed.

Let us take an example. When the original polio vaccine was first introduced, its merits and defects were of urgent concern to all Americans. Unexpectedly, deaths had occurred following its use. The United States Public Health Service accordingly issued a report on the vaccine supplied by the Cutter Laboratories, which was suspected of having caused instead of prevented the disease. That report exactly fits our double specification: the physicians who made it had to address their colleagues on a professional matter and at the same time inform the lay public. From either point of view the report could hardly have been more clumsily framed.

The organization was logical, for scientists are trained to follow a set form, but they are seldom trained to express themselves clearly and accurately, apart from the use of technical words.[10] Here is how the report in question dealt in paragraph eleven with a point of importance to every family:

There were ninety cases of poliomyelitis in household contacts occurring within forty-nine days after vaccination of a household associate with Cutter vaccine. In seventy-one of these cases the occurrence of the disease could be associated with specific distribution lots of vaccine.

It is difficult enough, even on a second reading, to grasp this short fragment; when twenty-five paragraphs in this style follow hard on one another the effect is very likely total bewilderment. The ordinary citizen modestly concludes that here is science too abstruse for him. He skips to the summary and this is what he finds:

The study produced nothing which pointed to contamination as a source of the live virus but it did produce data suggesting the combination of inadequacy of virus inactivation and failure of the safety tests as responsible for live virus remaining undetected in the finished vaccine.

[10]See Sam F. Trelease, *How to Write Scientific and Technical Papers*, Cambridge, Mass., 1969.

This conclusion is as murky as what went before. Let us see what might have been said if pains had been taken to communicate with the public as was evidently intended. The first passage meant to say,

> Ninety cases of poliomyelitis occurred within forty-nine days after another person in the same household had received the Cutter vaccine. In seventy-one of these cases a connection could be shown with particular lots of the vaccine.

Before going on to the "translation" of the second passage, the phrasing of the first is worth analyzing. In the original text the ninety cases occurred not in people but in "household contacts," an ambiguous phrase, which leaves unclear whether it was the disease or the contact that occurred "within forty-nine days." Throughout, phrases are run on in defiance of syntax, and the word "associate" is used in two senses oddly linked ("household associate with Cutter vaccine") ("associated with distribution lots"). The result is to destroy the plain connections of things: people associating with people, disease occurring in people, and investigation tracing the cause to a particular (*not* a "specific") group of substances. The report is confusing also by its continual repetition of "distribution lots," as if other lots of vaccine, undistributed, could have been involved.

In the summary the ideas presumably intended were these:

> The study brought out no facts to show that the live virus came into the vaccine by contamination. But the facts did suggest two reasons why the live virus was present in the finished vaccine. One was that the means used did not make the virus sufficiently inactive. The other was that the tests for safety failed to detect this.

When the meaning is brought out of the depths in this way, it is seen to be a good deal less imposing and perhaps even a little silly: since there *was* dangerously live virus in the vaccine, it is clear that it had not been deactivated and clear also that the safety tests had failed. These two alleged reasons follow from the one important fact that the live virus had not got in by contamination. Considered as a piece of historical writing—a report on a series of events—the document in question falls far below the standards that the conscientious report-writer must maintain (see Figure 3, p. 36).

It is but fair to add that the whole tendency of our civilization is to make clarity and precision of expression rare and difficult.[11] We rely on instruments, formulas, and technical vocabularies, believing that if those are correctly handled the rest will take care of itself, the rest being common words. But the rest does not take care of itself, and it is the rest that controls public opinion, that fills and shapes our minds, that forms the stuff of our inner lives. The national mistakes that we suffer from, like the private boredom and the painful struggle to understand, go back ultimately to some writer or speaker's careless thought and indifference to expression. This failure is of course not limited to scientists or technologists or to any other profession or class. For example, the *rapporteur* of a university-sponsored seminar on European unity conveyed the opinion of a distinguished participant:

> In summary, Mr. X noted that progress toward regional integration in the earlier period was the result of the perception of rewards from unity and the absence of divisive factors in the European system. Its later decline resulted from a decline in threat perception and the injection of divisive factors from outside the European system. He concluded by stating that of his four areas political cooperation is the most important since poor political relations in the short run can wipe out long-run gains in the other areas.[12]

And the writer of business reports, whether Chairman of the Board or outside auditor, is likely to spin out tautologies: "Our examination was made in accordance with generally accepted auditing standards, and accordingly included such tests of the accounting records and such other auditing procedures as we considered necessary in the circumstances." That is: "We audited."

---

[11]Even in European countries where literacy and secondary education are thought to remain of high quality, language has deteriorated. The forces of mass culture, the influence of "scientific" linguistics which advocates "hands off" all types of ignorance and error, and the example of modern literature, which plays freely with idiom, grammar, and syntax, have combined to lower precision in vocabulary and encourage distortion at the expense of clear communication (see pp. 295–297).

[12]The meaning is that when good political relations pay, they are maintained; when outsiders interfere, they break down, regardless of the benefits from cooperation.

FIGURE 3   *Writing Means Rewriting*

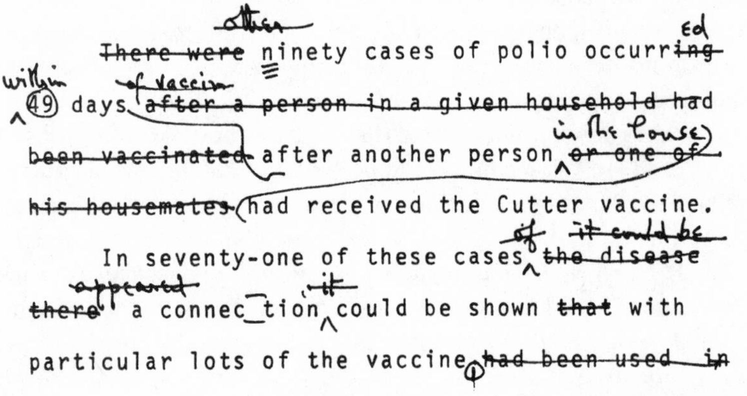

> ~~There were~~ ^other^ ninety cases of polio occurr~~ing~~ ^ed^
> ^within^ ^of vaccine^ ^(49)^ days ~~after a person in a given household had~~
> ~~been vaccinated~~ after another person ^in the house)^ ~~or one of~~
> ~~his housemates~~ (had received the Cutter vaccine.
> In seventy-one of these cases ^of it could be^ ~~the disease~~
> ~~there~~ ^appeared^ a connec_tion could be shown ~~that~~ with
> particular lots of the vaccine ~~had been used in~~

A satisfactory last draft cannot be achieved without the labor of revision, much of it a matter of trial and error. Note the elimination of the weak "There were" so as to begin with the true subject. The circle around the figure 49 tells the typist or printer to spell it out.

Hard Labor Makes Royal Roads

The point of these quotations is not to hold up the writers to ridicule or show superiority over them. Any of us might under certain conditions have written those sentences. They do no more than mirror the way the mind strings ideas together—in an endless, shapeless series. But having written such sentences, the person who is going to thrust a piece of prose on someone else's attention has a duty to make them more intelligible and attractive. He or she must try to read them with the eyes of a stranger, see their faults, and correct them. This obligation defines one of our principles: except for those who compose slowly in their heads before setting down a word, NO ONE, HOWEVER GIFTED, CAN PRODUCE A PASSABLE FIRST DRAFT. WRITING MEANS REWRITING.

The question is, how to go about it? Rewriting implies dissatisfaction with what was put down in the first grapple with an idea, dissatisfaction with diction (the choice of words), coherence (the linking of ideas), and logic (the validity of the reasoning). For your self-criticism to be rapid and effective, you must be alive to a great many distinct faults and master an equal number of corrective devices. The most important of them form the subject of Part 3 of this book.

What you must be persuaded of at this point is that care lavished on expression is not some optional embellishment bestowed upon your work; it is the means through which your work begins to exist. Your research turns up raw materials—very raw. Writing and rewriting make them into finished, usable products. Until brought out in full view by the best possible arrangement of words, your results remain incomplete, doubtful, hidden from every mind but your own. And your own, as your first draft shows, is none too clear.

Our attempt a moment ago to rewrite a few sentences from the official report on the Cutter vaccine showed what revision uncovers: it reveals errors and absurdities of thought. This is invariably true, as every experienced report-writer knows: the analysis of expression is nothing else than the analysis of thought. You are therefore thinking hardest and most searchingly about your subject when scanning successive drafts to make your words "clear, orderly, and easy to grasp and remember."

The best position from which to do this is that of an editor—the editor of a magazine or the person in a publisher's office who goes over every word of a manuscript for sense and style before sending it to the printer. To develop for your own work the sharp eye of an editor, it is best to let some days elapse between writing and revision. You will then find that you yourself cannot make out the meaning of a sentence that seemed perfectly clear when it was fresh. You will notice repetitions, illogicalities, circular arguments, tautologies, backtrackings, and all the other causes of confusion, from the vagueness of clichés to the ambiguity of pronouns with multiple antecedents.

Students, who in general resist the idea that their writing needs to be improved, are the first to complain when they are assigned readings in poorly written books. They call them "dry" or "dull" and imagine that the fault lies in the subject. But every subject can be made interesting, because every subject *is* interesting. It would never have aroused human curiosity if it were not. The trouble with the uninteresting assignment is that the interest has been blotted out. The book makes for heavy going because the ideas do not flow, because the sentences are off balance, because the syntax gives false cues that compel one to go back and read again, because the words do not say what they mean. Reading in that case is like wading in a swamp.

To illustrate this point a second time, and strengthen in the report-writer the passion for the clarity and order that ensure ease of reading, consider how even an acceptable fragment of prose can be edited into something still more desirable, because sharper, cleaner, and swifter:

> For a book like the one before us, consisting as it does of a mass of close on to a hundred and fifty heterogeneous documents, what seemed to be needed in the way of introduction was a short historical sketch to furnish some sort of explanatory background for the persons and events with which these documents have to do. Accordingly that is what we have here, far as it is from telling the whole story. It is hoped, however, that it may make a little plainer what kind of men took part and why certain things happened as they did in the first of the great international congresses of our history.

That opening paragraph was, at a guess, the writer's Draft No. 3 or 4; that is, he reread it three times, changing some details each time. Now compare what we shall call Draft No. 6:

> A book such as this, comprising nearly a hundred and fifty documents of various kinds, needs by way of introduction a brief historical sketch of the events and persons to which the documents refer. Such a sketch cannot, of course, tell the whole story. It is hoped, however, that this account may make a little plainer both the causes of events and the character of the men who took part in the first great international congress in our history.

It is not the mere saving of nearly a third of the words (79 in place of 111) that recommends this last version, though brevity in itself is a service to the reader. What is decisive is that the order and connection of ideas is now unmistakable. The mushrooming of secondary thoughts has been cut out and the reader is guided down a straight path instead of being distracted by a series of side signals leading nowhere. It is the waste of effort in responding to them that is wearisome in reading certain books, making them dry, dull, heavy. In other words, faulty expression maims the subject—which is the point we set out to prove.

Notice, from the numbering of the drafts as well as from Figure 3, that improved expression cannot be attained at one jump. Between the acceptable Draft No. 4 and the reasonably trim No. 6 there had to be two further attempts to reach adequacy. The moral of this—the last of the First Principles before we go more deeply into the substance and technique of research—is that there is no short cut to full expressiveness.

PART II

Research

3

The Searcher's Mind
and Virtues

History in Nature and Culture

In the opening chapter of this book we drew attention to the need universally felt for referring to the past and pointed out how many fragments of written history are thrust on our attention in the daily business of life. We did not then stop to define History or to retrace its development into a subject of formal study and a branch of literature. The examples sufficiently proved how familiar to everyone the idea of History is. The ordinary person takes the reality of History for granted, calls it "a force" or "a precious heritage," though probably never asking what is meant by those phrases; but the researcher, who is naturally subject to the same cultural influence, should become more conscious and more critical of this force and this heritage. And anyone engaged in work of the mind should at some time take a bird's-eye view of the large field of which he or she will cultivate a small patch. This is the journey we now invite the researcher to take.

Seeing how impossible it would be to uproot historical ideas and feelings from our lives, we are tempted to conclude that man is "by nature" an historical animal. He is a being who remembers his past, individual and collective. This observation holds true even when the

43

memory is vague, as it was in the example of the Turkish official who would not be bothered with fact-finding. Though he had no precise information about his birthplace, he did remember having lived there all his life and he would have been sure to notice any marked change in the look or character of the town. Without this developed sense of the self, and without words in which to record experiences, man would be doomed to live entirely from moment to moment, like a cow in a field.

The first thing to note about History, then, is that it has its origin in man's awareness of continuity. But this idea is at once modified by that of separateness—of moments, days, years, hours, centuries. Ideas and objects find their place in Time, or more exactly in recorded Time (which is History), with the aid of Before and After. This is why dates matter so much, though for reasons different from those parroted to schoolchildren. Periods, like centuries, are only arbitrary divisions for convenience, but that convenience is indispensable.

Though all mankind shares the perception of time, the very fact that we discuss and feel the need to define history shows that the awareness of the past in the larger sense can differ in degree. Our invaluable Turkish official offers the example of a man who knew just enough history to be aware that Mohammed had existed and laid down the precepts of the true religion; and perhaps on this account our Turk was not interested in past events of merely earthly import. This outlook has been shared by whole civilizations, notably India, though nearby China from early times supplied itself with historians and historical writings.

One concludes that having a deliberate and developed History is a cultural phenomenon. History is an invention, an art, probably due in the first instance to the thought of a genius whose novel idea others took up. In the Chinese language the original form of the character for "historian" represented a hand holding a receptacle used to contain tallies at archery contests. From recording this or similar matters of passionate interest, peoples nearly everywhere came to record other things—court ceremonies, religious sacrifices, and striking events. Ultimately a day-to-day record was kept—in China it was known as the *Spring and Autumn Annals* though it covered the entire year. But this rather dull chronicle (eighth century B.C.) had been preceded by a collection of notable sayings and moral injunctions to officials that is called *The Book of Documents* or *Book of History*. This earlier record was a more poetic and attractive work than the dry calendar of facts; it can be likened to a fanciful archive of state papers. The *Annals* were a sort of public diary. Both together would be, to us, materials for a true history.[1]

In Western culture the same sequence of interests and expression is found, with two important differences. If we take Homer's account of the Trojan War as paralleling the Chinese *Book of Documents*, we find in the Greek work a much richer, more highly organized piece of legendary history—a better work of art. And when we look for a Greek parallel to the Chinese *Annals* in Herodotus, who lived in the fifth century B.C., we find not only superb literary art once again, but also a deep curiosity about other peoples and *their* history—the Egyptians, Medes, Persians, and so on. The seamless fabric of History is thus extended beyond local limits and domestic concerns.

The curiosity that took Herodotus on his many travels in search of information was not confined to him alone. The Greeks, as traders and seafarers, were an active, bustling, wide-awake people who "wanted to know." Herodotus gave them what he called *historiai*, which means "researches." His book begins, "These are the researches of Herodotus of Halicarnassus"; and what follows is a series of reports for oral delivery. We know they were read by the researcher himself, in the open air, to any Athenian who cared to stop and listen. This was an added reason for making these *logoi*, or speeches, attractive little works of art. The fact that Herodotus was the first to weave his researches into a continuous and shapely narrative, ultimately for readers, is what justifies his ancient title of "Father of History." After Herodotus, written history is, in the West, an accepted art.

This tradition having remained unbroken, Western culture may be said to be the historical culture par excellence. Just as Herodotus

---

[1] See Burton De Witt Watson's translation of chapters of the *Shih-chi* (New York, 1969) and his life of the Grand Historian of China. *Ssu-ma Ch'ien* [145–190? B.C.] (New York, 1963).

went back in time to explain to the Greeks how the Persian invader came to be where he was, so we try to grasp our own situation with the aid of innumerable historical ideas. We are doing this right here and now by tracing back our daily historicism to an ancient Greek and calling him the "father" of one of our intellectual disciplines.

We recognize historical continuity by the way we refer to the various divisions of what we possessively call *our* civilization. We date one idea or custom from the Middle Ages, another from the Renaissance, and a third from modern times, but the joint product survives in ourselves. We explain our ideas and ways of life as continuous transformations through twenty-five hundred years and more—just as we explain the form and meaning of our commonest words, including the word History itself. All but a few European languages use derivatives of the word that the Greeks had for it: Latin and Spanish *historia*, French *histoire*, English *history*, Italian *storia*.

From this same root we have also the cognate noun "story," and as we pointed out before, the West is so accustomed to conceiving life historically that in the novel, the dominant literary form today, we enjoy seeing how fiction and imagination have been subdued to the critical control of fact. In pure history, naturally, it is understood that nothing is reported but verified fact. In other words—and this is our first definition—*History at its simplest is the story of past facts.*

Four Meanings of the Word History

A moment's thought, however, shows that we commonly use the word History in two senses, and perhaps more. In one use, as in the title *History of the Peloponnesian War*, we mean the story of what happened. In another use, as in "By that decision, the President made history," we mean the notable fact itself; not the story but the substance of what happened.[2] This ambiguity is inevitable and it turns

---

[2]The German word for History is *Geschichte*, which comes from the verb *geschehen*, "to happen"; and its other use—as "story"—parallels the practice of the other languages cited above. Going farther back into etymology, one finds that the root *his* in early Indo-European is related to *vid*, meaning to see, to understand. Compare *wit* and *idea*. History is thus linked with *vision* and one might say that historiography is a type of videogram.

out on reflection to be very instructive. For it records our belief that what is in the book exactly corresponds to what occurred in real life. When we read, "the story" is like witnessed History. We could say that a history (with a small *h*) deserves its name when it truly represents a portion of History (with a capital *H*). The aim of written history is realized when it achieves what Longinus, an ancient critic, said in praise of Herodotus: "He takes you along and turns hearing into sight."

Written history, then, holds its place in our civilization because we know that it reports things that actually took place. Civilized man has a passion for facts. This is so strong that Bernard Shaw, when giving advice to a beginner, made his cardinal precept: "Get your facts right first: that is the foundation of all style." Though the proposition is far from self-evident, we accept it because we connect factuality with honesty, honesty with sincerity, and sincerity with style.

The man who has got his facts right and is about to report on them may or may not think of himself as an historian; but if he does, the term History very likely has for him a third sense. He may say, for instance, "History requires the most painstaking research." It is clear that he means by History something halfway between the past events and his report, as yet incomplete. He means the *fashioning* of written history. This, he knows, requires method. The professional attitude makes certain demands and the art obeys certain rules. To refer to this disciplining of the mind it might be better to use the term Historiography, and henceforth in this book an attempt will be made to observe the distinction. Yet so close is the association in our minds between the event, the account of it, and the means by which the account is prepared that a consistent usage is difficult. The ideas overlap and prompt the speaker to use the most general term for the science, the art, and its substance: History.

Our position as latecomers in Time encourages this fusion of ideas. We in the West have for so long had access to abundant written sources, as well as to written histories based on these sources, that we take both for granted and think of them together as almost physically containing "our past." But in an age that lacked the printing press and was limited in literacy, or where the climate was adverse to keeping written records, oral communication was the dominant carrier of ideas. History must then have seemed more at the mercy of chance, more an accident of individual memory than a collective possession.

This feeling left its mark on Herodotus and Thucydides—indeed on all the historians in ancient times. They wrote like orators because whatever sounded right had the special merit of being more memorable. To us this form of presentation seems "unhistorical"; for Fact, we think, matters above all else. Yet we may be going to a dangerous extreme on the opposite side when we imagine that something set down on paper, no matter how, is history even if nobody reads it. Our national and other archives pile up documents by the cubic mile: in what sense are they history if no mind ever subjects them to the processes of historiography? And during those processes, what is the proper action of the reader's mind upon the substance of History? A soldier-scholar like Lawrence of Arabia scorned the squirrel-like habits of a Paper Age, and counseled a friend accordingly:

> You are retired to write your book about the Empire. Good. Remember that the manner is greater than the matter, as far as modern history is concerned. One of the ominous signs of the times is that the public can no longer read history. The historian is retired into a shell to study the whole truth; which means that he learns to attach insensate importance to documents. The documents are liars. No man ever yet tried to write down the entire truth of any action in which he has been engaged. All narrative is parti-pris. And to prefer an ancient written statement to the guiding of your instinct through the maze of related facts, is to encounter either banality or unreadableness. We know too much, and use too little knowledge. Cut away the top hamper.[3]

This "cuts away" too much. Documents are not all liars. But Lawrence has a sound point about the workings of the human mind, and he has the support of some distinguished professionals. At a meeting of a British learned society in the mid-1930s, the renowned scholar R. H. Tawney declared with some impatience: "What historians need is not more documents but stronger boots."[4] The implica-

[3] *The Letters of T. E. Lawrence*, ed. David Garnett, New York, 1939, 559.
[4] Quoted in W. K. Hancock, *Country and Calling*, London, 1954, 95.

tion, as another noted historian put it, is that "history, when it is written from documents alone, is dead stuff and probably more false than true."[5] Without the *experiencing mind*, the searcher after truth cannot bridge the gap between the lived occurrence and the dusty record.

If other human beings are to enjoy and use the knowledge gathered from records by the searcher's critical methods, the breath of life must be in the product. Otherwise, it is no more than the evidence digested and collected. It is a report, not on the events, but on the documents and the search. Or as the famous parody of history *1066 and All That* made plain by a brilliant exaggeration: "History is what you can remember. All other history defeats itself."[6] This was in fact the principle that the ancients believed in and acted on. In making up the speeches of ambassadors and generals as they *might* have been spoken, Thucydides knew that they would become what he hoped his whole history would be—lifelike and memorable: we still quote from his pages Pericles' Funeral Oration.

So we come, by way of the gravest problem of historiography, to yet another meaning of History: the recollection of the past in the minds of a whole people. This Popular or Folk History is of course not of uniform quality. It includes legends like that of Frederick Barbarossa asleep in his cave until he wakes to found a new German Empire; the virtuous deeds of national heroes; the biased interpretations that make all national wars noble and all drawn battles victories; and a mixed lot of names and dates, images and slogans, which rouse immediate emotion and serve as triggers to action: "No Entangling Alliances," "Fifty-four Forty or Fight," "The Big Stick," the covered wagon, John Brown's body, Pearl Harbor, the Great Society, the Right to Work. Every institution, every family has such catchwords and lives by them. In all new or old forms History is the past shaping the present and future, having first shaped the minds of the historian and his audience. To sum up, History-as-Event generates (through History-as-Hard-Work) History-as-Narrative, which in turn produces History-as-Maker-of-Future-History.

[5] *Ibid.*
[6] By W. C. Sellar and R. J. Yeatman, New York, 1931, vii.

The Changing Uses of a Changing Past

On the power of historical recollections rest the numerous arguments for the importance of historical studies. But each argument tends to make of history something different, and the researcher must distinguish, in himself and in others, what the authentic historical residue may be. There is the patriot's history. A nation being united by language, intermarriage, territory, and common historical traditions, its young in school study history in order to become true citizens. The adult population of democracies is told that it must read current history in order to understand the world it lives in and vote intelligently on national issues. Political leaders likewise profess to find history the best guide to action. The faith in the utility of history, though vague, is widespread.[7]

History also moves minds by what it inspires. According to President Harry Truman, the most formative book he read as a child was a compilation entitled *Great Men and Famous Women*—from Nebuchadnezzar to Sarah Bernhardt—and it is well known that Plutarch's *Lives* once exercised an incalculable influence on the minds of men. The most heroic careers of early modern times, the noblest passions of the French Revolution, followed the models in those short biographies drawn from the history of ancient Greece and Rome.

Prophets (and politicans too) tend to agree with Lamartine, the poet who was part historian and part statesman and who said that "History teaches everything including the future." But most professional historians refuse to predict. Many of them deplore the distortions brought about by "present-mindedness," the habit of reading into the past our own modern ideas and intentions. Yet some have not hesitated to admit their desire to influence events by "proving" the rightness or wrongness of a cause through showing its historical antecedents. And the makers of great historical systems, as we shall see, set out to discover the "laws" of history so that mankind may foretell the shape of things to come. Such men, of whom Karl Marx was the least deterred by doubts, believed that History itself was speaking through their mouths.

[7]See Chapter 6.

The laws, needless to say, have not yet been found, though the detailed knowledge of a particular culture or country often enables students to distinguish the constant from the fleeting, and thereby to guess intelligently at the outcome of a given situation. Thus in the middle of the Second World War nine American historians were brought together in Washington and "asked to predict, largely on the basis of what had already happened, the ability of the Nazi war machine and the German people to stand up under Allied pressure." The nine read secret documents, heard the testimony of scores of witnesses, and within three months made their report. When it was reviewed in the light of subsequent events it was found "a remarkably accurate forecast."[8]

The application of history to a purpose so sharply defined is rare. The benefit more usually expected is an enrichment of the imagination that promotes a quick and shrewd understanding of the actions of men in society. Hence the value of historical training to the student of any aspect of life and to the worker in any branch of social intelligence. The famous jurist Learned Hand, who called history the cornerstone of a liberal education, explained why the subject is a begetter of social wisdom.

> Most of the issues that mankind sets out to settle, it never does settle. They are not solved, because . . . they are incapable of solution properly speaking, being concerned with incommensurables. . . . The dispute fades into the past unsolved, though perhaps it may be renewed as history and fought over again. It disappears because it is replaced by some compromise that, although not wholly acceptable to either side, offers a tolerable substitute for victory; and he who would find the substitute needs an endowment as rich as possible in experience, an experience which makes the heart generous and provides the mind with an understanding of the hearts of others. The great moderates of history were more often than not men of that sort, steeped, like Montaigne and Erasmus, in knowledge of the past.[9]

But the diversity of searchers' minds remains. Lynn Thorndike, an early historian of science, pointed out that "for some, history is literature; for others, facts; for some, delving in archives; for others,

---

[8]*New York Times*, June 8, 1946.

[9]Address at the evening session of the 86th convocation of the University of the State of New York, Albany, October 24, 1952.

interpretations of the sources; for some, an art; for others, a science; for some, drudgery; for others, a romance; for some, an explanation of the present; for others, a revelation and a realization of the past."[10]

No one can tell another person what kind of historian to be, or can know, at the outset of a career, how research and reflection will ultimately dictate a view of the subject chosen. It is obvious that for many researchers the interest lies in the chase. Research is armchair detection par excellence. But its results furnish the mind with quantities of new and unexpected ideas, which it is a pleasure to contemplate and a challenge to fit into a communicable pattern. Then, too, such ideas permit one to generalize and to compare, until increasing familiarity with men and nations dead and gone, their words and their deeds, their costumes and their thoughts, ends by making the student feel thoroughly at home in the varieties of human life—as if he had traveled for years in strange lands and learned many languages.

In other words, whether the facts of history are put to use in the present, or simply garnered out of curiosity, or enjoyed as objects of contemplation, we can frame an inclusive definition by saying: *History is vicarious experience.*[11] Knowledge of history is like a second life extended indefinitely into the "dark backward and abysm of time." When history is described in these terms it is usual to add that history is an art, not a science. What this means is that history communicates "incommensurables," not formulas to be applied. It acts directly from mind to mind; it affects personality rather than policy; its power to change intellect and spirit is subtle, not overt.

This undoubted influence answers a question which puzzles many people and to which we shall return in Chapter 7. Historians are often asked, "How can History be of any value in use when what it tells us is so uncertain? Every historian differs from every other, and all discard their predecessors' views every generation. With such instability about the past, which manifestly cannot change or be changed, History seems hardly knowledge, only a serious kind of entertainment."

[10]Book review in *Journal of Modern History*, 9 (September 1937), 369.

[11]"Experience" here is to be taken literally as meaning the "actually lived"; it is merely imagined experience that we make our own in reading fiction or beholding a work of art.

Though we postpone discussing the reliability of history, we must take note here of the important fact that in its mutability history does not differ from science. Science too changes its interpretations every few years, and on its frontiers hypotheses conflict. Yet one could say of Nature as one says of the past that it is an unchanging reality that should allow no difference of opinion. The fact remains that both science and history are variable.

Some Varieties of Occidental History

One cause of the diversity in historical writing is temperament, as Lynn Thorndike suggested above. He might have gone on to say that in addition to his pairs of historians contrasted by temperament there were schools and periods and entire ages that cherished opposite conceptions of historiography. Until the advent of modern science, the two dominant conceptions of history were the moral and the political. Herodotus and Thucydides conveniently represent these two tendencies. Herodotus wants his history to give great men "their due meed of glory"; he believes that notable lives and deeds have permanent value as moral teachings. He has political and cultural interests too, zeal for knowing things simply in order to know them, and as we shall see more fully in Chapter 10, he is the first sociologist.

Thucydides repudiates this view. He considers both the idle curiosity and the moralizing intent irrelevant to his purpose, which is the practice of politics. His manner is impersonal and austere; he will not digress and would rather not entertain. He is a warrior and statesman writing for his peers.

With the coming of Christianity the moral concern of historiographers overwhelms every other interest. Saint Augustine and—with far less power—Orosius narrate great events like true historians, but they interpret catastrophes as God's chastisement. Events formerly taken to be under the rule of change or natural law are now interpreted as the working out of a divine plan. The Christian historian applies to the past a rigid moral standard enforced like a retroactive law, and his curiosity is modified by revelations, prophecies, and concern about the aftermath of Judgment Day.

To this intense moralism there was added in the Middle Ages a ready belief in the occurrence of the supernatural on earth, the miraculous intervention of Providence in human affairs. Chronicles and lives of saints continued to show that Western man cared about keeping records and writing biography, but these activities reflected even more the spiritual and theological preoccupations of the writers, who belonged for the most part to the clergy. Consequently, the reawakening of historiography in the ancient (and present-day) sense coincides with the secularization of life in early modern times. The rise of monarchies and nation-states, the passionate scholarship of the Renaissance humanists, the widening discussion of methods and results in physical science—all contributed to the reinstatement of the historical and critical virtues. Pierre Bayle's famous *Historical and Critical Dictionary* (1695–1697) summed up the results of the scholarly attitude that had been at work in Europe for two centuries: the word "critical" was a triumphant declaration of independence for research.

In the next generation Voltaire enlarged the scope of hitherto monarchical history by showing in his *Essay on the Manners and Customs of Nations* (1756) that aspects of civilized life other than battles and kings have importance and can interest the general public. Finally, in the nineteenth century, the upshot of two revolutions sealed the triumph of history as a subject of universal interest. One was the French Revolution of 1789, which set peoples on the thrones of kings and thus stimulated nations to rediscover their past from its beginnings after the Fall of Rome. With the same ardor, oppressed nationalities all over Europe founded their unity on the basis of their popular histories. It was this cultural nationalism that inspired Walter Scott to make Scotland as well as the Middle Ages live in his great creation, the historical novel. As Trevelyan said, the enormous popularity of Scott's works "taught Europe history."

His influence was reinforced by the gradual spread of the idea of Evolution. When the debate about it grew violent after 1860, a second cultural revolution occurred. It put physical science at the top of the tree of knowledge and affected the form of all traditional subjects. Thinkers borrowed the "genetic method" from evolutionary thought in biology. This stated that behind every phenomenon was a long chain of facts, which must be discovered before the fact in front of us could be understood. Not only individual and national life, but laws, customs, institutions, ideas, morals, religions, and even deities began to be studied genetically, which is to say historically. The modern Western mind was by now inescapably historical.

Accordingly, it has seemed to many that historiography must push beyond the old purposes of morality and political practice: history must be made scientific, on a par with geology, paleontology, and biology. Accumulation and verification must take precedence over literary skill, and encyclopedic thoroughness must become a commandment. To be scientific, a monograph must tell all about a single small subject, and what the work contains must aim at being definitive. Present-day historiography has abated some of its original scientific claims, though its attitudes, whether psychological or sociological, continue to imply certainty and predictive power, as in science. Meanwhile, in the workaday world, researchers of all kinds are at one with the public in acknowledging the sway of the genetic interpretation. Every speech, report, inquiry, or application begins with "the background"; nothing, it is thought, can be understood apart from a knowledge of what went before.

The Searcher's Virtues

Enough has been said of the nature and effect of our long "historicizing" tradition to enable the reader to form some idea of the mental habits a researcher will possess to start with. It remains to say something of the qualities he should develop in addition. Temperament and point of view cannot be legislated about; they are his affair; but the fundamental virtues can be prescribed and can be trained by exercise and self-control. It is in fact this possibility that justifies our giving to any branch of learning the name of discipline.

In speaking of "virtues," one is of course using the word as a piece of shorthand to suggest what impulses the researcher must curb or encourage. No doubt more qualities than the half-dozen about to be listed are called into play. But these are indispensable, and giving them names may not only help the researcher along his path, but also deepen his understanding of what this book attempts to teach him.

He should, after pondering the six virtues, go over the present chapter again and, by connecting them with the topics discussed, discover how inherited ideas affect the individual's curiosity about fact and his or her ability to find and interpret it.

1. The first virtue required is ACCURACY. No argument is needed to show why. If "History is the story of past facts" (our first definition), those facts must be *ascertained*. Making certain implies being accurate—steadily, religiously. To this end, train yourself to remember names and dates and titles of books with precision. Never say to yourself or to another: "It's in that book—you know—I forget what it's called and the man's name, but it has a green cover." Being precise means *attending* to the object when you first examine it and noting small differences instead of skipping over them: "Here is a volume on the Lincoln Memorial in Washington. It is edited by Edward Concklin, and the author spells his name with an added *c*." There is no profound significance in this fact, no imperative need to remember it, but if you do this kind of thing repeatedly, regularly, you will avoid a multitude of mistakes. Some few you are bound to make. Everybody is liable to them almost in proportion to the length of his work. But they can be kept to a minimum by the habit of unremitting attention. Do not fear that such details will clutter up your mind: they will lie dormant until needed, and often will suggest important links with other matters you would not otherwise have thought of.

2. Next comes the LOVE OF ORDER. There is in any piece of research so much to be read, noted down, compared, verified, indexed, grouped, organized, and recopied, that unless one is capable of adhering to a system the chances of error grow alarming, while the task itself turns into a perpetual panicky emergency—What did I do with those bibliographic notes? In what notebook did I list the dates I checked? Does this page belong to Draft 1 or Draft 2? And so on ad infinitum. Some people may overdo orderliness, but most of us underdo it, usually from groundless self-confidence. You may think you know what you are doing and have done. The fact is that as you get deeper into a subject you will know more and more about *it* and very likely less and less about your own movements and belongings.

Hence the value of the system, which keeps order for you. Sticking to it is never a loss of time, though it calls for the union of three minor virtues: calm, patience, and pertinacity.

3. It might be thought that orderliness would also imply LOGIC. In'practice it seems to do so to a negligible extent; the one is mechanical, the other intellectual. The logic considered here is not the formal art of the philosopher but its ready and practical application to the perplexities of library research. As will be shown in the next chapter, the researcher must quickly learn the schemes of innumerable reference books; if you are not adept at inference you will bog down or make mistakes. For example, in the *Thesaurus* of ancient Latin authors, which offers to the eye under each entry an unappetizing block of print, the punctuation is faint and confusing. If you do not reason correctly from the first or last quotation in each block, you will infallibly connect the one you look for with the wrong author.

The physical arrangement of books in any given library may present the same kind of problem: if over here we are in the *G*s and over there in the *K*s, the intervening books (including the *H*s, which I want) must be in some obvious but self-concealing place, such as the lower part of this large reference table, which has shelves—and here in fact they are. If you run to the librarian for the solution of every puzzle, mental or physical, trivial or important, you will be an old but *in*experienced researcher before you have finished.

4. Elsewhere HONESTY may be the best policy, but in research it is the only one. Unless you put down with complete candor what you find to be true, you are nullifying the very result you aim at, which is the discovery of the past as embedded in records. You may have a hypothesis that the new fact shatters, but that is what hypotheses are for—to be destroyed and remolded closer to the reality. The troublesome fact may go against your moral purpose or prejudice, but nothing is healthier for the mind than to have either challenged. You are a searcher after truth, which should reconcile you to every discovery. And even if you should decide to become an advocate for a cause, you had better know beforehand all the evidence your side will have to face. For if one fact is there obstructing your path, you may be fairly sure others to the same effect will be turned up, possibly by

your adversary. It is the nature of reality to be mixed, and the research scholar is the person on whom we rely to chart it. Accuracy about neutral details is of little worth if we cannot trust the writer's honesty about significant ones.

5. Some persons are honest as far as they can see, but they do not see far enough; in particular they do not see around themselves. They lack the virtue of SELF-AWARENESS. The searcher needs it, first, in order to make sure that he is not unwittingly dishonest and, second, in order to lessen the influence of bias by making his standards of judgment plain to the reader. Nobody can be a perfectly clear reflector of what he finds. There is always some flaw in the glass, whose effect may be so uniform as not to disclose itself. The only protection against this source of constant error is for the writer to make his assumptions clear. To invent an *outré* example, a fanatical teetotaler might in a biographical sketch of General Grant assert that here was a man of revolting and immoral habits. Given nothing else, the reader is inclined to trust the conclusions of the writer. But if the accusation reads: "Anyone who habitually drinks whiskey is a person of revolting moral character; therefore, General Grant, etc." The reader has a chance to dissent and judge for himself.

This simplified instance bears on two important realms of reporting: the description of cultures alien in time or space, and biography. In both, it is essential for the researcher to control his emotions as he finds evidence of behavior repugnant to him or to the standards of his age.[12] In such cases he must set forth (though more subtly than in the example above) what his criteria are before he passes judgment or describes by epithets. Failing this, the way is open to the meanest kind of libel and defamation of character.

6. Everybody is always urging everybody else to have IMAGINATION, and this is indeed good advice. But perhaps the hint should suggest not so much laying in a stock as releasing what we have. Convention and lazy habits often suppress the happy thought that, if let alone, would lead to the desired goal. In research this goal is double—practical and abstract. The researcher must again and again

---

[12]Notice that these standards may be those of laxity as easily as those of strictness—whence the frequent misjudgment of the Puritans as well as of the Victorians by our "enlightened" critics.

imagine the kind of source he would like to have before he can find it. To be sure, it may not exist; but if it does, its whereabouts must be presumed. By that ingenious balancing of wish and reason which is true imagination, the seeker can make his way from what he knows and possesses to what he must possess in order to know more. The two chapters following will give concrete instances. And the researcher must also perform these acrobatics of the mind around his abstract problems. For example, working upon a critical study of Henry James and noticing the novelist's persistent attempts in later life to become a playwright—a determination shown also in the dramatic tone and structure of the later novels—the critic begins to wonder what theatrical influences could have formed this taste. Is it possible that James as a child or youth attended the New York theaters, then famous for melodrama? The dates coincide, and behold, autobiographical evidence when sought confirms the inspired guess.

The historian's imagination has other uses that go far beyond this simple pulling of oneself up by the bootstraps. We have not said the last word on the subject. But the historical imagination of a genius cannot be asked of every modest worker. It is the modest imagination that is insisted on here as an implement that none can do without. Remember, too, that even with the lesser kind there is no law requiring it to be used in modest doses.

Let the researcher give free play to these six virtuous forms of energy and he is ready for his first foray into that *terra incognita*, the library.

4

Finding the Facts

The Detective and the Clues

What is tantalizing about the proverbial task of finding the needle in the haystack is that you are assured the needle is there. The space is restricted, the object is unique, it must be possible to find it. And no doubt, with enough care and patience it could be found with just a pair of eyes and a pair of hands. Of course, if the hay were to be packed in small cubes and a large magnet brought to bear as the contents of each were spread out, then the task would be made much easier—it would almost turn into a game.

This fairy-tale problem has its analogue in the researcher's hunt for the facts. The probability is great that any one fact he wants is in some printed work and the work in some library. To find it he has to find the right cube of hay—the book or periodical—and then use his magnetic intelligence to draw out the needlelike fact.

That "the library"—as yet unspecified—is the repository of by far the largest part of our recorded knowledge needs no demonstration. The author of an article on West Africa who reports that the annual rainfall in Fernando Po is 100 inches found this information in the library—in a book. It is most unlikely that he measured the rain himself. Aside from the direct knowledge of an event by an eyewitness, or a firsthand investigation on the scene through interviews, laboratory or field work, or the study of relics,[1] the shortest path to the facts is library research.

The library may be a small collection on a special subject, owned by a business firm and housed in a single room; it may be a college library designed to meet the needs of undergraduate courses; it may be a reference collection of moderate size for the researchers of a magazine such as *Forbes* or *American Heritage*; or it may be an "encyclopedic" library—properly a research library—that owns millions of old books and has a standing order with leading book distributors for most new ones. Unless the library accessible to you is specialized, the chances are that it contains something you want, if not for itself, then as a lead. If this something does not furnish sufficient information, it may prove negatively useful by enabling you to cross off what looked like a lead. In either case, there is no choice: into the library you must go. It is the researcher's first port of call.

It is natural enough for beginners to feel disconcerted—lost and lonely—in a strange library. You can quickly overcome this feeling by making up your mind to learn your library. Regardless of size, all libraries have common features that the experienced researcher looks for at once. After you have conquered a few of these strongholds you will realize that to master one library is to master them all.

What then do you look for in a library? First, the card catalogue—where is it? How do the tiers of drawers run, perhaps from one room to the next? Is the catalogue all one, or subdivided into Books (authors and subjects, in one or in separate sections) and Serials (periodicals)? The heading at the top of the cabinets will give you the answers. What is the cataloguing system in use? Open a drawer and see if the now-standard Library of Congress cards (with their characteristic call numbers) are there, or some other kind.[2] If the cards are of another size and pattern, denoting an older system, you will have to study it, perhaps with the help of the librarian.

In the simple days of not so long ago, the user of an unfamiliar library could step up to the catalogue with a fair degree of confidence. One would find cards in trays and the cards would bear a call number

---

[1]See Chapter 7.

[2]For a reproduction of a Library of Congress card with explanations of its contents, see Figure 4, p. 70.

in one of three systems: the Dewey decimal;[3] the Library of Congress; or a local one antedating these two, as in the Boston Athenaeum library. The overwhelming majority of places had adopted the Dewey system and all libraries used standard printed cards, on which one found the necessary and expected information in full.

Now all this is changing. Some libraries continue to use a card catalogue—one catalogue. Others, wishing to convert their Dewey numbers to the Library of Congress scheme, face the researcher with two sets of cards, separated by a cutoff date: all books published before 1972 are in one row of cases and bear Dewey numbers; after that date, the new numbers and cards are in another part of the room.

Presumably, after a time, all the cards, with the new call numbers, will be reunited in one set of trays and cabinets, and the user will be able to follow his familiar routine. Meanwhile, the student may have to look in two places to find what he wants. The word "presumably" above was meant to suggest a doubt. For in a number of large and important libraries other arrangements have recently been tried. In some, large volumes have replaced the cards, giving the same information, of course, but not with the same facility, for flipping cards is easier than turning pages and continually shifting one's eye level.

In other libraries (often at universities) the researcher is faced with a microfiche system. At several "posts" consisting of a table and chair, a machine "reader," and a revolving stand, the person who wants to find a book must first turn the panels hung on this stand until he comes to the one marked with the letters that include the initial of the author sought—say A to D for Byron. On the panel are pockets, and the mark on one of these will "cover" the letters *By*. From the pocket a thin plastic *fiche* is taken to the "reader" and the knob is turned until *Byron, George Gordon, Lord* appears magnified on the glass.

What shows up is a regular, printed library card that has been reduced to a point where hundreds of them can be crowded on one fiche. In other words, the whole library catalogue is transferred to these movable pieces of plastic and the space taken up by cabinets of

---

[3]See pp. 70ff.

trays is saved. There are obvious disadvantages: the user does not always replace the fiche in the right pocket; the fiche itself gets dog-eared by careless use; there is no room on the fiche to insert new acquisitions—a whole new fiche must be manufactured, thus precluding the convenient "temporary card" prepared by the local librarian used in the older card system.

Finally, some libraries have installed or are installing a computerized catalogue, the Online Public Access Catalog (OPAC). It reproduces the card in full on a screen. No difficulty there about inserting new entries in alphabetical order. But with computers and microfiche readers, the number of searchers for books is limited to the number of machines. How many terminals can a library afford to install? In the former catalogue room of a large research library, as many people could work simultaneously as they found physical room for their bodies: the number of trays will always be greater than the size of the crowd. But even with as many as fifty terminals, "book lines" like bread lines might develop at the Forty-second Street library in New York.

Besides, using the console requires a certain dexterity. The professional researcher will soon acquire it, no doubt, but the occasional reader will not. He or she will fumble and use up computer time as well as occupy the machine others are waiting for. In addition, if a system is not self-contained but "stores" its information in a distant place, the link by wire with that place will be subject to interruption; the library will have to announce that the computers are "down." And other accidents are possible, such as obtaining by chance or by guile information that should remain private—for instance that Borrower so-and-so, address such-and-such, owes unpaid fines in the amount of $42.50. For with a computer available, the library administration will exploit its facilities for registering other things than books—its purchases, running expenses, salaries of employees— every kind of useful data. The computer is a marvelous instrument whose value lies, not in itself, but in its use. It remains to be seen whether its use in cataloguing books will serve the researcher as well as it does the administrator and as well as the previous system of cards in trays.

The cost and complicatedness of putting the old catalogue cards on line—a process librarians label "retrospective conversion"—is so forbidding that for the foreseeable future researchers will have to consult the "frozen" (that is, closed to further entries) card catalogue of older books, as well as the OPAC. Arrangements will vary from one reference center to another: the old catalogue of the Library of Congress, for instance, is on microfilm and on fiche; that of the New York Public Library has been issued in book form; that of Columbia University will continue to be available in file drawers.

Turn now to the shelf or section of reference books. It will tell you roughly what kind of collection the library contains—its size and its specialization if any; for in these respects the reference shelf mirrors the rest of the library. Next discover or inquire whether you have access to the stacks: if a placard of stack floors and their contents is prominently displayed to the public, this doubtless means that you may go direct to the books. Make a mental or written note of the floors where books on your subject are housed. Then turn back to the catalogue.

We will assume that the cards, whether in drawers or in microform or on a computer, are the Library of Congress cards, or that you have worked out, alone or with help, the principle of some other type. All but a few systems are in the form of a continuous alphabet of cards, which give the reader at least this information: author's name, title of book, place and date of publication, indication of the spot where the book stands in the library. We will further assume that you have not stepped in merely to ascertain the annual rainfall on Fernando Po. You are looking for at least three or four books—that nucleus spoken of earlier. Fewer than this number are hardly likely to give you the materials for even a short paper or thorough book review. The catalogue holds the clue to the existence and whereabouts of those books.

Publishing has so greatly increased, the world over, that it is no longer possible simply to scan a few shelves and take down all the works you need. The expansion of the resources is as alarming as it is gratifying. Together the United States and the United Kingdom annually throw 65,000 new titles in English into the sea of printed literature. The libraries of the great institutions of learning double in size every sixteen to eighteen years. But there are various patterns of growth. Columbia University acquired its one-millionth volume in 1925—forty-two years after the consolidation of its separate collections. Its two-millionth volume arrived in 1946, and its three-millionth in 1960. The four-millionth was catalogued in 1969. In 1980, the five-millionth was received. The Library of Congress receives daily five times as many books as were in Thomas Jefferson's magnificent collection in 1815, when it became the foundation of that library. The principal book-producing countries publish well over 600,000 titles each year, the United States supplying more than 85,000 of them.

The rate of growth is not the only predicament. A huge and distressing problem confronting libraries—and consequently civilized society itself—is the gradual disintegration of millions of books and other documents all over the world. The cause is the process of papermaking that became almost universal in the nineteenth century. That process leaves a residue of acid in the paper which in the course of time destroys its cellulose fiber and makes it so brittle that it flakes into mere scraps. If catalogues are not to become mere fossil records of books that once existed, heroic measures are required, without delay, because centuries of printed matter are now in danger of being lost.

The Library of Congress, estimating that at least 6 million volumes in its collection may not survive much longer, has been preparing for a large-scale preservation program of deacidification to begin in 1986. The Library officials are hopeful that the chemical process their holdings undergo will extend the life of modern books from about 35 years to possibly 600 years. Meantime, the Council on Library Resources has undertaken a campaign to persuade publishers to use acid-free paper manufactured according to specifications set by the American National Standards Institute. This so-called permanent paper is expected to last "at least several hundred years without significant deterioration under normal library use and storage conditions."

The dream persists that books and other library resources can be preserved indefinitely and distributed broadcast through microreproduction. The most familiar of these microforms is microfilm. It provides on 35mm film a simple method of protecting and filing bulky, fragile documents like newspapers and collections of correspondence. A second microform now widely used is the microfiche—a file card in the form of film—on which as many as 300 pages can be reproduced. It is read through a table- or lap-viewer with moderate convenience, and a photocopier can be linked with the viewer to reproduce a desired page readily. Camera technology now makes possible the ultrafiche which can contain over 3,000 pages.[4]

Although the microforms should present no great difficulty for ordinary reading, for consulting and comparing they may prove somewhat less satisfactory than books. But it often happens that a book is not to be had, on loan or in any other way, because of distance, rarity, or disintegrating state. The microforms will prolong the life of the book and multiply its presence. University Microfilms, a pioneer distributor of micrographics, has shown how researchers can conveniently range far beyond the library that they make their base.

Whichever form of the book you seek, when you step up to a catalogue to begin your search, you should already have answered in your mind the question What am I hunting down? We shall make a number of alternative suppositions to show that "knowing what you want" depends on "knowing what you don't want." Thus you are looking for Louis Napoleon's early political ideas, but not necessarily for the latest biography of him; you want a detailed explanation of the Special Drawing Right, but will not be sidetracked to a general history of international finance; you want to know the origin of the use of firecrackers in patriotic celebrations, but will not need a history of the Declaration of Independence.

If by luck or cunning you already know the name of the author of a work on your subject, you simply go to the right alphabetical catalogue drawer, or press the correct keys on a terminal, and find what you want. You are launched on your research, for that one author's citations and bibliography will carry you forward a good distance.

If you cannot name the author, look up the title instead. You are an unusual person—almost a professional—if you have remembered it correctly. Most often you retain the sense of the title but uncon-

---

[4]Microfiche reproduction now covers many fields. *The Bell & Howell Micro Publishing Catalog* (1985) includes newspapers, foreign and domestic, and other periodicals. Even outside the realm of print, microfiche is being used, e.g. the monumental Index of American Design.

sciously change the wording. You want *The Origins of the American Revolution*, but you recall it as *The Causes of the Revolutionary War*. You must from now on make a point of remembering books by their authors. Not only does this knowledge help you to discriminate among the many books on the same subject, but it also offsets the inconvenient fact that on some topics all titles sound much alike. Sometimes, indeed, they are identical: at least four books about New York have been called *East Side, West Side*; three other books, on different subjects, are called *East of the Sun and West of the Moon*. Moreover, a garbled title is more difficult to straighten out than a garbled name, because librarians, like others who deal daily with books, tend to remember books by their authors rather than by their titles or the color of their bindings.

If neither the "author entry" nor the "title entry" in the catalogue brings you what you want, you have to look up the subject. When you are seeking information about a public figure this is easy. The biographies of Benjamin Franklin, as well as his works, are catalogued under "Franklin, Benjamin." Sometimes you have to know the birth and death dates in addition to the name, because the catalogue contains a number of people with the same names, for example, Samuel Butler.[5] Their dates are the readiest means of telling them apart. To work up a biographical sketch, then, all you need know to start with is that books *by* the individual come first, followed by books *about* him (or her), these last books being in the alphabetical order of their authors' names.

To find a subject other than a person, you must bring to bear on the problem a little more knowledge and imagination. As was shown in Chapter 2 with regard to the divine right of kings, you must guess under what word or words your subject has been catalogued. If it is "flying saucers" you want, you are not likely to go astray even though books and articles will call them UFOs—Unidentified Flying Objects. But for many topics you must know how the librarian thinks when classifying books. Not all librarians think alike. There is reason

---

[5]First names are essential: there are two poets named Pope in English literature. But there are not always first names to distinguish other pairs, e.g., the two famous Greeks named Thucydides. Here only dates help.

in their ways, yet small variations of words can create puzzles. If you are studying the opening of Japan, for example, you discover that some of the pertinent books are listed under "Japan Expedition of the American Squadron, 1852–1854"; others under "U.S. Japan Expedition of the American Squadron, 1852–1854"; and still others under "United States Naval Expedition to Japan, 1852–1854." Why is this so? Because books on this subject have been published for over a century now, and rules and fashions of cataloguing, like other rules and fashions, have changed with the years. Keeping this example in mind, form the habit of imagining synonyms and possible permutations of terms.

Moreover, odd as it may seem, new subjects are continually being created for which the old catalogue with its fixed subject entries must still serve. For example, until 1954 the word "desegregation" was seldom used to describe the movement to end Jim Crow. The researcher confronting the card catalogue will have to try a number of subject headings, such as "Negro," "Civil Rights," and "Afro-American(s)."[6] Finding these "cognate headings" is the first knack the researcher acquires. One learns one's way in libraries through learning the ways of librarians.

Cross-Questioning the Book

But there is more yet to be squeezed from the catalogue cards. Suppose the searcher has heard of a book called *Powers of Mind* by an Adam Smith, who is obviously not the eighteenth-century Scottish philosopher who wrote *The Wealth of Nations*. What does the searcher do? He or she goes to the card catalogue or its equivalent and looks up "Smith, Adam" and finds half a drawer of entries. Most of them read "Smith, Adam, 1723–1790," the works of the Scotsman or works about him. The only other "Smith, Adam"—and with no dates after his name—is a librettist whose book, a comic opera in three acts called *Nectarine*, was published in London in 1902. He can hardly be the man being sought. The searcher starts over again. It turns out that

[6]In many libraries a list of subject headings may be consulted at the reference desk.

FIGURE 4   *The Library Catalogue Card*

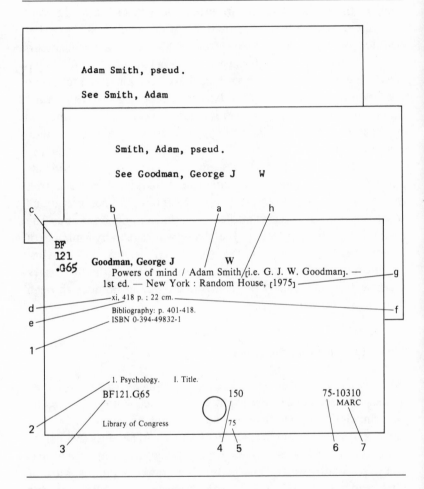

Cards like the one shown are printed and sold by the Library of Congress to many libraries throughout the world. You will probably find that such cards or similar ones make up the catalogue of the library you are using.

A Library of Congress card contains two types of information. One, occupying the upper portion of the card (marked here with letters), describes the characteristics of the book it stands for. The other sort of information, occupying the lower portion of the card (marked here with numbers), is addressed primarily to the librarian and the cataloguer.

ahead of all the cards in the drawer is one reading "Smith, Adam, pseud. See Goodman, George J W." The seeker regards it with lively interest and hope. The author, he muses, must have chosen the handy, well-known name for its striking quality.

Taking a good look at the resume that stands for your tentatively chosen books may save you the trouble of going to the shelves or waiting at the delivery desk for a work that is of no use to you. In many large libraries the shelves are not open to the public and you ask for books sight unseen; hence the value of knowing how to size up a book by rightly interpreting the "card." From the wording of the title in full—for example, its "jazziness"—you know it is not what you are after. Suppose you want an account of the military history of the Civil War. Among the titles you find James Street's *The Civil War.* The entry gives you its subtitle: "An Unvarnished Account of the Late But Still Lively Hostilities." This suggests either a jocular handling of the subject or a narrative by a contemporary. But this second alternative is ruled out by the author's date of birth, which is given as 1903.

The quality of a book is sometimes indicated by the publisher's name, which you learn to look for. The researcher soon comes to

---

a. Author's "literary name" (pseudonym) that appears on the book.
b. Author's real name.
c. Call number, used for finding book on shelf.
d. Number of prefatory pages.
e. Number of text pages.
f. Height of book in centimeters.
g. Year of publication (brackets show that date was inferred from copyright page).
h. Publisher, preceded by place of publication.

1. International Standard Book Number (0 stands for the United States, 349 identifies the publisher, the five-digit number is the publisher's book number, and the 1 is a computer-verification number).
2. Headings to be used in subject catalogue.
3. Library of Congress call number, same as c above.
4. Dewey classification number (see p. 73).
5. Year of publication of the card, present century implied.
6. Serial number of this Library of Congress card.
7. Indication that the information on this card has been put on the computer tape of the Library of Congress *MA*chine *R*eadable *C*ataloguing System.

know that, today at any rate, a privately printed work is one that was not able to enlist the interest of any established publisher. This may well be a clue to a book's reliability. Unlike the regular firms, a private printer almost never edits, criticizes, or recommends changes in the text he sets in type.

The size of the book also tells the reader what to expect of the work itself. A history of the steel industry in 16mo size,[7] or one only sixty-four pages long, is not likely to be the volume, rich in details, that you are looking for. Possibly it was a piece of corporate promotion. In general, books published by university presses are scholarly in form and treatment; books with indexes are more likely to be serious works than those without (though exceptions keep occurring); and books imported from England or translated from a foreign language may be supposed to justify this expense and effort. But all of this is only *presumable*.

The date of publication is a further sign that the inquirer should not overlook. Suppose you want to read a biography of Benjamin Harrison. Your search of the catalogue turns up one by Lew Wallace published in 1888. Since you once saw the movie of Wallace's *Ben Hur* on television, your first impulse may be to acquaint yourself with his writings through this work. But the fact that Harrison was elected to the Presidency in 1888 should occur to you at once and stay your hand. Obviously, Wallace's book is a "campaign biography," designed not so much to instruct and elevate your mind as to instruct the voters and elevate Harrison. In the date itself lies the hint to you that the work in question is partisan, incomplete (for Harrison was still alive), and written in haste.

No less important than the date of publication is the edition of the book. When Charles A. Beard brought out a new edition of his famous work *The Economic Basis of Politics* in 1945, he added a chapter that put his conception of the subject in an entirely new light. The researcher makes it his business to know whether the book he seeks has appeared in more than one edition and whether the new edition or editions were enlargements, abridgements, or some other form of revision. Depending on the problem he is studying, he will decide whether he must get all the editions for comparison or

---

[7] 16mo = sextodecimo; each page is 4½″ × 6¾″.

whether any one of them will do: to know what Darwin's *Origin of Species* really said, you must read all six editions.

Once you have found the titles you want and inferred their credentials from the catalogue, you mark down their call numbers. These are the figures and letters that appear in the upper left- or upper right-hand corners of the card (practice varies from one library to the next). They direct you to the books themselves. The system of numbering once most commonly used, known as the Dewey Decimal system, was devised by the late Melvil Dewey. It assigns to each subject category a fixed number, each author a fixed letter (almost always the initial of his last name), and each volume a volume number. As new fields of knowledge developed, the Dewey system proved to be not sufficiently flexible. It could not, for example, provide a range of numbers for all the new subdivisions of the social sciences. Consequently the system of classification most commonly used in large libraries today is that of the Library of Congress. In this system, categories have fixed letters or letters and numbers. You will soon learn that the category of United States history runs from E to F 999 and European history from D to DR. Economics is in the range HB to HJ, books about pure science are under Q, and technology is under T.[8] You need not memorize these and other designations; they will be posted in more than one place in any library and frequent use will make them or their like as familiar to you as your own address.

Though you need not learn the techniques of a cataloguer, you can profit from knowing a fact or two more about the way librarians have coped with the flood of books since the turn of the century. The Dewey and Library of Congress systems replaced by a many-branched subject classification the former alphabetization by author alone. Thus if you are seeking facts about the city of Paris in the nineteenth century, the call number for the anonymous work *An Englishman in Paris* will bring you to a shelf of books on France and her history, subsection "Paris."[9] The books in that group are in one way or another related to your subject. One may be Hilaire Belloc's

---

[8]In the Dewey system, American history begins with 973, European with 940, economics in the 300s, technology in the 600s, pure science in the 500s.

[9]That anonymous work, by the way, is a hoax perpetrated by the journalist Philip Vandam, but it is an excellent hoax; he had the instincts of an historian and made his work a fair reconstruction of a time he did not witness.

Paris, another Jules Ferry's pamphlet *Les Comptes Fantastiques d'Haussmann*. You never noticed the latter item in the card catalogue, very likely, because you were paying less attention to authors' names than to useful titles. Nevertheless, this is a book you want to look at; so in the same way that you carefully analyzed the catalogue cards before you, you now examine the shelfmates of the book you have come to find.

Cataloguers of course make mistakes like the rest of us and they may assign call numbers that cause books to appear in unexplained if not hostile company. In a large eastern library George Eliot's *Mill on the Floss* rested next to Mill *On Liberty* for many years before being sent back to "English Literature" where it belonged. Walter Bagehot's love letters were in the business school library of a great university because the author's *Lombard Street* rightly suggested that he was an economist.

These are some of the hazards with which the researcher must reckon. They are sometimes amusing, often irritating—as when the journal *Agricultural History* is filed close to periodicals dealing with soil chemistry—yet also understandable as part of the great need to organize books in such a way that people who do research can most readily organize knowledge. Since many books cross the boundary lines of any classification,[10] scanning the shelves is a great advantage. But because a book can be in only one place at a time, while duplicate cards in the catalogue can be filed in any number of places, the researcher must rely primarily upon the catalogue. Going to the likely shelf first and looking around casually is not the way of the professional.

The foregoing advice applies when a book on a subject is known or may reasonably be expected to exist. You will soon develop a sense of what subjects are unlikely to have been treated in a book. These are the subjects which embrace a multitude of facts that in their nature are only fitfully recorded; for example, the form and amount of the patronage given the arts in any century. Several lifetimes of random note-gathering would not suffice for such a study, though

[10]Where, for example, would you put Chaddock's *The Safety Fund Banking System in New York, 1829–1866*? It could be put with works on banking, or books on the Jackson era, or shelved with New York State history.

occasionally a work of this sort *is* written—a wonder of nature.[11] Norman Longmate's *King Cholera: the Biography of a Disease* is one such book, and, concerning a different but similarly disunified array of facts, so is Siegfried Giedion's *Mechanization Takes Command: A Contribution to Anonymous History.* The first is a history of epidemics. The second is a study of the evolution of tools and machines and their effects on modern civilization. Both subjects are so intertwined with the petty detail of life that to have extracted their histories from books about other subjects could only have been a labor of love and long patience. The researcher can never *assume* that subjects such as these have been written about.

At the other extreme is a type of book that one can confidently expect to find: political biography. Almost without exception, a biography exists for every head of state in the Western world during the last three centuries. Biographers rarely overlook any significant or picturesque figure. This has been especially true in recent years, with the great rush of Ph.D. candidates toward untouched subjects. In any case, a biography is the most predictable outcome of every political career. Despite Mrs. Warren G. Harding's destruction of all her husband's papers that she could find, she could not delay or deter biographers from their self-appointed task. The researcher who can make biography the starting point of his labors has a head start.

Professional Informers, or Reference Books

The forms and uses of the catalogue have been dwelt on at length, because the catalogue is for the researcher the typical guide to sources. Every other aid, in whatever form, is a catalogue, *is a list.* All but a few lists follow the alphabetic order, once the broad classifications by subjects or periods have been made. Until the researcher actually lays hands on the books he wants, he is consulting one or another sort of catalogue—once again, an alphabetical list of names and works.

---

[11] Yet two books on the subject have been written: Lillian B. Miller's *Patrons and Patriotism: the Encouragement of the Fine Arts in the United States, 1790–1860* (Chicago, 1966); and Francis H. Taylor's *The Taste of Angels* (Boston, 1948).

FIGURE 5   *General and Specialized Encyclopedias*

General

The New Columbia Encyclopedia (4th ed., 1975, the best one-volume compendium)

Kodansha Encyclopedia of Japan (in English)

The Great Soviet Encyclopedia (in English)

Grand Larousse Encyclopédique (in French)

Encyclopaedia Universalis (in French)

Allgemeine Enzyklopädie der Wissenschaften und Künste (in German)

Enciclopedia Barsa (in Spanish and also in Portuguese)

Enciclopedia Italiana (in Italian)

Specialized

The Reader's Encyclopedia (literary and historical)

The Reader's Encyclopedia of American Literature

The Encyclopedia of Philosophy

The Encyclopedia of Education

The Catholic Encyclopedia

The Encyclopedia Judaica

The Dictionary of the Middle Ages (up to vol. 6 by 1985)

The Dictionary of Scientific Biography (16 vols.)

McGraw-Hill Encyclopedia of Science and Technology (15 vols.)

Grzimek's Animal Life Encyclopedia (13 vols.)

Encyclopedia of American Foreign Policy (3 vols.)

The Harper Encyclopedia of Science (Newman, 4 vols.)

The Princeton Encyclopedia of Poetry and Poetics

An Encyclopedia of the Book (Glaister, 1 vol.)

The McGraw-Hill Encyclopedia of Russia and the Soviet Union (Florinsky, 1 vol.)

The Encyclopedia of the Social Sciences (both editions useful)

A Dictionary of Comparative Religion

Halliwell's Filmgoer's Companion

The physical form a list may take varies widely. It may be a many-volume printed catalogue, like that of the British Library (formerly the British Museum) or the Paris Bibliothèque Nationale; a variation on this, like the *National Union Catalog*, the successor to the catalogue of the Library of Congress; a single-volume handbook, such as Burke and Howe's *American Authors and Books: 1640 to the Present Day*; or a bibliography of a few pages appearing in one issue of a periodical or in an annual publication like the *Index Translationum*, the international bibliography of translations. In essence they are all one.

Nor does the subject pursued greatly affect the form of the listing. The researcher may be tracking down someone's portrait through the catalogue of paintings and engravings of the American Library Association,[12] or hoping to find the picture of a particular house or site or looking for autograph letters by going through the annual issues of British and American *Book Prices Current*. In all of these and a thousand more books of reference, only the divisions, the abbreviations, the symbols, the length and detail of each entry differ.

These different schemes themselves are codified, usually at the beginning, under a heading that says or signifies "How to Use This Book." Do not, then, open the book at random and merely follow the alphabet. If you do, you may fall in the section covering A.D. 1500–1800 instead of the one you want, earlier or later. Turn, rather, to the explanatory note or preface and master its instructions, using any nearby entry to follow what is being said. Nor should you let the seeming intricacy drain away your energy or scatter your attention. Remember the encouraging motto that the famous mathematician Sylvanus Thompson prefixed to his book on calculus: "What one fool can do, another can." Some reference books are better designed than others, but all are meant for people of ordinary intelligence, not clairvoyants: the sale of reference books is small enough as it is.

It follows from all this that the reference shelves of the library are the real training ground of the researcher. If he happens to be working in a library of limited size or scope, the catalogue may yield little or nothing to his purpose. In that case, instead of struggling with

---

[12]*A.L.A. Portrait Index*, ed. W. C. Lane and N. E. Browne, Washington, D.C., 1906. For guidance in finding pictures of all kinds and obtaining copies, see H. and M. Evans and A. Nelki, *Picture Researcher's Guide to Picture Sources* (New York, 1974). The work lists all the great collections here and abroad, indicating their scope and the procedure for consulting each. Students should also learn to use as needed Cuthbert Lee's *Portrait Register* (Asheville, N.C., 1968) and the *Allgemeiner Porträt-Katalog* (Hildesheim, West Germany, 1967) and its supplements, which locate 30,000 portraits covering the years 1600–1900.

the cards, his best move is to consult a bibliography on his subject and to draw from this his first list of books and articles. He then obtains these works by purchase, borrowing, or, if remote and out of copyright, by microfilming. Most bibliographies will not give the researcher the same broad survey as the large library catalogue, but the first few titles will enable him to break into the subject, and the bibliographies appended to these books will lead to others.

It is again to the reference shelves that he repairs, in any library, when he has to find a book whose existence he only suspects, when he requires information found only in periodicals,[13] or when he has no notion whatever of the existing literature. It is in the course of worming answers out of dumb books that he acquires the experience, the judgment, the facility that will shorten and make more assured the same operation the next time. Even then this part of research calls for the instinct of the gold prospector and the skill of the detective. Both abilities develop in proportion to the attention one pays to detail. It lies with the researcher whether he soon knows his way around or remains a permanent babe in the woods.

The questions that come up in research are never all of one kind. The researcher, as we said, must specialize in being a generalist; he must follow wherever his subject leads. He may have to discover Bismarck's religious opinions as a young man; a specimen of Martin Van Buren's signature to compare with an A.L.S.;[14] what was in the Lusitania's hold—gold or munitions or both—when she was sunk; or who was the first American to win the Nobel Prize for Literature. In such quandaries only reference books will serve.

One can of course apply to the reference librarian. But one cannot ask him or her to do one's work on the hundreds, the thousands, of questions that will arise in the writing of a book or report. One must be self-reliant.

To know almost automatically in what *kind* of book what *kind* of fact is recorded means knowing the scope of a great many types of books. But it also means knowing the scope of a particular work within each type. For example, if you are a student of Western

---

[13]In the physical sciences especially, long monographs go quickly out of date and the literature of value is mainly periodical.

[14]The abbreviation for "autograph letter signed."

culture, the biographical facts you need will be best found in biographical dictionaries of the national sort, *not* in encyclopedias. But to know that is not enough. If you are looking for, say, a nineteenth-century French figure, you must recall whether he flourished in the first or the second half of the century. The big work by Michaud, like that by Hoefer, hardly goes beyond the halfway mark. For later figures you must consult Larousse, Vapereau, or some other, each of which has characteristics that you take into account before you pull it off the shelf. Here memory is a great time-saver. You do not want to spend half-hours poring over an atlas when the fact you seek lies in a gazetteer, or riffling through a dictionary of dead authors when your subject is still alive.

For the beginner's convenience reference books can be grouped into the nine types that are listed with comments in Figure 6. Whatever your field of study, you may begin with the most general bibliography of bibliographies, namely the indispensable *Guide to Reference Books*, now under the editorship of Eugene P. Sheehy.[15] If you are a student of any portion of history, the first work to consult is the general historical bibliography in English, which the American Historical Association published under the learned editorship of a board headed by George Frederick Howe, although it is by now considerably out of date.[16]

The nine groups of books described in Figure 6 give only a rough idea of the vast territory they cover. The sciences, and more lately business and industry, have spawned a large number of specialized works of reference. Still other works swell the list of reference aids and serve very special concerns—for instance the several "Dickens Dictionaries," in which the author's multitudinous characters are treated biographically. Those in Balzac's *Comédie Humaine* have been similarly traced through the many stories in which they pursue their fictional lives. Such books, which are immensely useful for the rapid verification of allusions and quotations, are but a few of the works in any large library to which the eager beginner as well as the seasoned professional must repair again and again.

---

[15] 9th ed., Chicago, 1976.
[16] *American Historical Association Guide to Historical Literature*, New York, 1961.

FIGURE 6   *Types of Reference Books*

---

1. Encyclopedias (general, national, religious, and topical, e.g., the *International Encyclopedia of the Social Sciences*).

2. Biographical Dictionaries (national, in one or many volumes; regional; professional; topical, e.g., musical; contemporary, e.g., *Who's Who*; and current, e.g., *Contemporary Authors*).

3. Indexes to Periodicals (retrospective and current, e.g., *Poole's* and the *Readers' Guide*; also devoted to special literary forms, e.g., the *Book Review Digest*; to special subjects, e.g., *Chemical Abstracts*, which, as the name suggests, furnishes more than an index; and to single publications, such as newspapers, e.g., the *New York Times Index*, and journals, whose indexes are published annually in one of their issues and are sometimes cumulated every five or ten years).

4. Dictionaries of Quotations, and Concordances (e.g., of the Bible and of famous authors).

5. Atlases and Gazetteers. (Some atlases are historical, e.g., Shepherd's, whose latest edition appeared in 1964, or refer to particular matters such as languages, treaties, etc.)

6. Chronologies or Books of Dates (many kinds).

7. Language Dictionaries (many kinds; and note also *World Dictionaries in Print*).

8. Handbooks and Source Books (dictionaries, manuals, and anthologies, e.g., the *Oxford Classical Dictionary*; Commager's *Documents of American History*; and *Twentieth Century Literary Criticism*).

9. Bibliographies (national, topical, e.g., *Arts in America* [four volumes], current, i.e., the books of the month or year; and individual, e.g., Bengesco, *Bibliographie des Oeuvres de Voltaire* also in four volumes).

Which Do I Want?—A Series of Examples

So important is it for the neophyte to acquire seasoning that he should make mental and written notes of his discoveries among reference works: he makes up his own private "research manual." What goes into it? Chiefly details related to his line of inquiry.

Suppose that you are describing the emergence of characteristic institutional forms in modern American life, and you want to know by what date the supermarket had become a common phenomenon. The work entitled *Editor and Publisher's Market Guide* is a key to the economic life of almost every community in the United States. From it you learn how many drugstores there are in Atlanta, the resources of the banks in Spokane, and the quality of the tap water in Cheyenne. Having once consulted this annual, you will know how helpful back issues can be for social history, long after they have ceased to interest the advertisers and salesmen for whom they are compiled.[17]

Suppose again that you are working on the history of the French franc. Experience has taught you that unlike ourselves the French seldom thoroughly index their periodicals. But the Germans are diligent and they publish an excellent index to foreign periodicals— including the French—now called *Bibliographie der Internationale Zeitschriftenliteratur*. Your needs are met—provided that for the years before 1963 you know the name of your subject in German.

For handy use, the researchers will want to remember that the men and women whose lives are recorded in the *Dictionary of American Biography* are dead. This simple fact is the first that one notes about the *D.A.B.* The same rule applies to the *D.N.B.*, the *Dictionary of National Biography*, that great British compilation, which was said to add a new terror to death, and upon which the American was modeled. But the user of the *D.A.B.* should know further that not all of the original volumes were published at the same time. Volume 1 appeared in 1928 and volume 19 in 1936. Any important figure named, let us say, Adams, and who died in 1929, would be missing because the *As* were already done, but a notable Williams who died in 1934 would be included.

Encyclopedias should similarly be "learned" and not blindly used. The childhood faith in *the* encyclopedia that happened to be the one large book of knowledge in the house should be replaced by a discriminating acquaintance with others. Many Americans who were reared on the *Britannica* are not aware that the fourteenth edition

---

[17]In each field of study there may be a reference book which one uses so frequently that the researcher will want to own it; for example, students of urban history need the new *Biographical Dictionary of American Mayors, 1820–1980*.

was the first to cater to the Anglo-American audience and, among the earlier, that the ninth and eleventh have special virtues. The latest edition on a stunningly novel plan appeared in 1974 and justified the title, *The New Encyclopedia Britannica*. The chief English encyclopedia is the venerable *Chambers's*, which was entirely recast by 1950 and whose latest edition appeared in 1967.

Encyclopedias are useful for quick reference and confirmation of minor points—dates, titles, place names—but on main subjects their deliverances must be verified in detail, for several reasons: (1) scholarship is always ahead of any but a newly published encyclopedia; (2) the size and scope of an encyclopedia make error or ambiguity more likely than in a book; and (3) revisions and additions introduce discrepancies.

Here again it must be pointed out that latest does not automatically mean best;[18] your purpose—and your knowledge of the composition of the work—can make any edition the best. The *Century Dictionary and Cyclopedia*, last republished in 1913, defines "Communist" without reference to the Russian Revolution—naturally—but for that very reason it yields the researcher important historical information; on other subjects it will never be out of date, notably in its comprehensive dictionary of names. In many ways, the *Century* remains the finest work of its kind ever published in the United States. Among other standard encyclopedias up to date and worth consulting are the *Americana, Collier's, Compton's*, and the *World Book Encyclopedia*, plus the various "national" encyclopedias and similar works on special topics. See Figure 5.

You also know that in recent times some of the national encyclopedias have become the voice of the party in power rather than of disinterested scholarship. If you are studying cultural bias, that latest edition is for you the best; if such is not your subject, an older edition should take its place. On points of dogma, a religious encyclopedia is the best; on church history it may not be. Out of the many works bearing in English or foreign tongues the name "encyclopedia" ("cir-

---

[18]The word "latest" must take into account the fact that encyclopedia makers now keep their works up-to-date by "continuous revision," that is, by making certain indispensable changes every time they reprint the volume.

cle of all teachings") there is one that is best for every particular purpose.[19]

Sooner or later the researcher will have to turn to a dictionary and may require one that gives the histories of words. In English, Murray's *New English Dictionary*, commonly known as the *Oxford English Dictionary* (hence as the *O.E.D.* for short), is the most complete. Craigie and Hulbert's *Dictionary of American English on Historical Principles*, coupled with Mitford Mathews's *Dictionary of Americanisms*, corresponds to the great English model. For the slang and vulgarisms of all English-speaking peoples, Partridge's *Dictionary of Slang and Unconventional English* (and supplement) is standard, although students of American culture find value in Wentworth and Flexner's *Dictionary of American Slang*, which exists in a Second Supplemented edition.

Consider a moment the uses of these works for the writer of history: anyone studying the era of the American and French revolutions will frame a correct conception of that time only after he has learned how the late eighteenth century used such words as "liberty" and "authority." An historical dictionary will describe the shifts in meaning. American historians were once concerned with the question whether Andrew Jackson was really the friend of labor, or perhaps rather a spokesman for the small entrepreneur. This was a question of words. It hinged on the meaning of "workingman," which some argued meant "proletarian" while others insisted it meant the owner of an independent business. To settle the point, the first step should have been toward the historical dictionary.

Popular quotations, catchphrases, and allusions are also signs of the times and call for attention. What is the connection of "twenty-three, skidoo!" with the spirit of the 1890s? What is a "tandem" in

---

[19]Researchers should not be abashed at finding that the appropriate reference work for them is in a language they do not know. Let them turn to the article they need and see what they can make out. If they can read French, they should be able, with a dictionary at hand and a little patience, to muster enough "encyclopedia Spanish" or "encyclopedia Italian" to read what they require. Similarly, on the basis of German, they can make use of Dutch, Danish, and Swedish reference works. The reading is usually for the sake of a single point that, when found, is copied out verbatim for verified translation by a colleague. For lack of this venturesomeness, scholars working on Jefferson may miss the article on Philip Mazzei, the great Virginian's friend, in the *Enciclopedia Italiana*.

FIGURE 7   *The Difficult Art of Reading Books Has to Be Learned*

"How do you work this? There's no display screen."

the history of locomotion? What are "routs," "crushes," "kettle-drums," in the context of sociability? Who, exactly, belongs to the *demi-monde*, and when was the phrase first used? Finding origins and contexts is often as necessary as defining the single word.

A recent edition of the *Oxford Dictionary of Quotations* reports the dropping of 250 quotations that no longer seemed familiar. What does this signify about literary culture? The change of interest, which is not at all unusual, points once more to the utility of earlier editions of the book. Good librarians keep old issues, and the researcher seeks them out for "period work."

The Fruits of Experience

After these representative examples of the researcher in action, it hardly seems necessary to repeat that imagination, seconded by patience, is indispensable to success. These strengthening qualities among the half-dozen mentioned earlier go hand in hand with increasing one's stock of information. The more you know, the easier it is to imagine how and where to learn still more.

Some researchers seem to have an equivalent of the gardener's "green thumb." It is perhaps nothing more than a "well-read thumb," the researcher having his references at his fingertips. For the commonest kind of problem can seem the most hopeless if you do not know enough about seemingly trivial matters. How, for instance, do you answer the myriad-headed question Who is (or was) Who? Some persons are not important enough to have had a biographer. Others have not been dead long enough. Still others became prominent only a few months or weeks ago. Many are notable only in certain circles. Others *were* notables but are not so any longer. Some owe their place in history to mere position, inherited or acquired. Still others have multiple namesakes. How to begin?

First the researcher knows that most countries have (1) a general *Who's Who* of the living[20] and (2) a biographical dictionary of dead notables. Not so many countries, but some few, have (3) a "current" biography or its equivalent for newcomers to renown; (4) classified

[20] A number of current foreign *Who's Who*s are being issued in English under a variety of imprints. The same is true of specialized lists of professionals, notably the *World Who's Who in Science*, the *Directory of British Scientists*, and *American Men and Women of Science*, all in successive editions or supplements. The *International Authors and Writers Who's Who* and the *International Who's Who in Poetry* are now bound together in one volume.

lists of authors, physicians, scholars, actors, journalists, clergymen, etc.; and (5) directories of various kinds—the peerage and other social registers, city and parliamentary directories, and the like. There are in addition a small number of international lists, and an indefinite number of "vanity" lists, designed chiefly to be sold to those listed in them. Seldom reliable by themselves, they may give clues to a better source, even when they are as narrowly conceived as the *Who's Who Among Americans of Italian Descent in Connecticut* or as ambiguously defined as *Who's Who in Stained Glass*.

The researcher starts, then, with set categories within one or more of which his Unknown fits. A few points are worth keeping in mind:

1. The title of the general *Who's Who* in each country is usually that same phrase in the given language, followed by the name of the country. The exception is the British *Who's Who*, which stops short with those two words, apparently in the belief that anybody who is anybody is a British subject, but which actually includes a number of Americans and other foreigners.

2. *Who's Who in America* is published every two years. The publishers of the British *Who's Who* and of *Who's Who in America* select from among the recent dead certain names for their respective *Who Was Who*s. The publisher of *Who's Who in America* also issues four regional *Who's Who*s covering the East, the Midwest, the South and Southwest, and the West. It also produces *Who's Who in the World, Who's Who in Finance and Industry, Who's Who in Government, Who's Who in Religion, Who's Who of American Women*, and *Who's Who in American Law*. These are indexed together in a volume issued for the first time in 1974. And, drawing on the 90,000 sketches in the first six volumes of *Who Was Who in America*, it published in 1976 three volumes called *Who Was Who in American History*, one covering "Arts and Letters," another "The Military," and a third, "Science and Technology."

3. Remember such peculiarities of foreign biographical dictionaries in many volumes as were mentioned above (p. 79), and bear in mind that a French-looking name may be Belgian or Swiss; a German one, Austrian; and so on. Different nationals will be found in different works.

4. Some of these works have supplements (e.g., the *D.A.B.*) and also concise editions (e.g., the *D.N.B.* in one volume). Seven *D.A.B.* supplements have been published. An eighth containing biographies of people who died not later than the end of 1970 is in preparation.

5. Newspaper indexes, such as that of the *New York Times*, give clues to much biographical information. The semimonthly issues are made into a volume for each year, available a short time after its close. A rich source of biographical data not readily obtainable elsewhere is the *New York Times Obituaries Index*, containing over 350,000 listings of deaths reported on the obituary pages of the *New York Times* since 1858.[21] *Biography Index* refers you to printed sources in English that contain biographical data, without restriction of subject, time, or nationality.

6. For newcomers to renown, of whatever nationality, try *Current Biography*, issued monthly, which provides sketches and portraits of figures that have suddenly attained prominence—a new movie star, dictator, or Olympic champion. Writers will be found in *Contemporary Authors*. For work on the achievements of women, researchers should know the three-volume *Notable American Women, 1607–1950*, and its supplement, volume 4, *The Modern Period*.

Occasionally, one of these reference works will unwittingly mislead, as when *Who's Who in America* printed in good faith the "facts" (complete with a Heidelberg medical degree) about a drug manufacturer who was an ex-convict living under a false name.[22] Again, the nineteenth-century *Appleton's Cyclopaedia of American Biography* contained at least forty-seven sketches of persons invented by one or more unscrupulous contributors.[23] In this way there came into exis-

---

[21] A supplement published in 1980 covers the years 1969–1978 and contains 36,000 entries. The British counterpart, in three volumes, is *Obituaries from* The Times, covering the years 1951 to 1975. As well as being a name index, it includes selections from the obituaries themselves.

[22] Trusting researchers and editors were not the only people he fooled. For a full account see Charles Keats, *Magnificent Masquerade: The Strange Case of Dr. Coster and Mr. Musica*, New York, 1964.

[23] See Margaret Castle Schindler, "Fictitious Biography," *American Historical Review*, 42 (July 1937), 680–690.

tence an explorer named Bernhard Hühne, who was credited with discovering part of the California coast, and a French epidemiologist who battled cholera in South America fifty years before the disease appeared there. Such hoaxing is not a thing of the past. As recently as 1980, the monumental reworking of Grove's *Dictionary of Music and Musicians* was "enlivened" by one jaded contributor through the addition of half a dozen or more imaginary composers and performers.[24]

Because the data in most *Who's Who*s are supplied by the subject himself or herself, the sketches can sometimes be puzzling or revealing. The entry for Richard Nixon does not record his service with the Office of Price Administration during the Second World War, though it was an important phase of his development. Theodore Roosevelt omitted to state that he ran unsuccessfully for the presidency in 1912; and William Howard Taft unwittingly validated that omission by reporting that he had been defeated by Woodrow Wilson in that year, as if no other candidate had run against him or received more votes. But imposture and suppression are exceptional, and researchers will not be alone in their embarrassment if they are led astray.

A final suggestion: for steady use at or near the desk, *Webster's Biographical Dictionary* (Springfield, Mass., 1970) or *The New Century Cyclopedia of Names* (3 vols., New York, 1954) gives reliable aid and comfort to the researcher.

In seeking identities, it is well to remember that persons' names follow certain conventions. Knowing the conventions may shorten the search, and observing them in narrative will mark off the trained writer from the amateur. To begin with, names should be given as the bearers themselves used them. It is H. L. Mencken, A. P. Herbert, Calvin Coolidge, H. G. Wells—not Henry L., Alan Patrick, John Calvin, or Herbert George. Giving the full spread only confuses the reader who, in the case of Wells, will imagine a person different from the familiar H. G. Wells. With French names this distinction is

---

[24]It should be added that the *New Grove's* inadequate treatment of American music and musicians is being repaired by the projected publication of an additional volume exclusively American.

essential, because it is usual for parents to give their children two or more first names, often including their own in permutation. The bearers of these names usually choose to be known by only one: the full name of Chateaubriand, the historian and statesman, is François-René de Chateaubriand (all first names are hyphened into a single group). In life he used René; yet in a useful American anthology on Romanticism he appears as François Chateaubriand. Knowing the conventions would have prevented this error, as well as that of omitting the *de*.[25]

A different usage applies to pseudonyms: they are not separable into first and last names. *Mark Twain* is one unit, alphabetized under *M*. Nor do these made up names admit of titles. One does not write Dr. Mark Twain (after he got an Oxford degree) nor should the French cartoonist Caran d'Ache (Karandash, which is Russian for "pencil") be referred to as M. D'Ache.

Finally, there is a sort of tact applicable to persons whose names or titles changed during their lifetime.[26] Thus in writing about biographical matters, one might put down "Sir Arthur Conan Doyle," whereas it is more natural to refer to "Conan Doyle's Sherlock Holmes stories." The shorter form is more historical, too, since most of the tales were written before his knighthood; but the point is: the more famous, the less fuss about forms. We say Homer and Caesar and Shakespeare, disregarding any other nomenclature.

[25]French usage about *de* only seems to be complicated. *De* is invariably used when it is attached: *Robert Delattre* gives by itself *Delattre*; it never appears in any other form. All other names with separate *de*, fall into three classes: names of one syllable, names of more than one syllable, names of more than one syllable that begin with a vowel. All the names of one syllable must always have *de* before them: *De Thou, De Retz, De Mun*. All the longer names, unless they begin with the vowel, *must* drop the *de: Tocqueville says . . . ; Vigny's poems are austere; Gobineau was no racist*—and hence: *Maupassant* (not *de*) *wrote innumerable short stories*. But names longer than one syllable that begin with a vowel break the rule for long names and require *D': D'Argenson, D'Artagnan*. The simple aid to memory is: *De Gaulle, Tocqueville, D'Artagnan*. A further comfort: all the foregoing applies exclusively to *de*. *Du* and *des* are invariably used with the last name, short or long, voweled or not: *Des Brosses, Du Guesclin*. And when the first name is given there is again no problem: *Alexis de Tocqueville*. (See Follett's *Modern American Usage*, New York, 1966, 329.)

[26]A useful book of modest size, *Titles and Modes of Address* (London, A. and C. Black, various editions), will assist the American student who may be confused about English titles. It also gives the (unexpected) pronunciations of certain English names, many of which have importance for the historian.

All this is common knowledge, yet certain errors of naming are embedded in the common tongue, which it would be pedantic and impossible to correct, even if one were to give full time to the task. For example, "Joan of Arc" is a misnomer. Her name was not D'Arc, but Darc, which does not mean "from Arc." She was from Domrémy. But whereas no one will waste breath to point this out to playwrights who dramatize her life as Joan of Arc, any historical account of her should make use of her right name. Familiarity with such points will obviously direct—and shorten—the practical reader's search for names.

Chronology to the Rescue

No advance information saves more time for the researcher than the dates of certain guidebooks. He knows these dates by heart and he acquires more as he goes along. Each person makes up a list tailored to his needs. For example, 1802–1906—the years included in *Poole's Index to Periodical Literature.* Knowing this, one knows one will not find listed there any contemporary magazine article on either the guillotining of Marie Antoinette (1793) or the sinking of the *Titanic* (1912). Again, 1876–1909, and also 1913. The first pair are the inclusive dates of the *New York Daily Tribune Index*; the date 1913 standing alone marks the year when the *New York Times Index* first appeared in its present form.[27] One more date for good measure: 1873—the year when the *Congressional Record* begins; but remember that verbatim reporting begins in the *Congressional Globe* in 1851.

Speaking of Congress, it is convenient to have a ready way of computing when, let us say, the Forty-third Congress was elected. The facts of our history suggest the formula: double the number of

[27]The *New York Times* has issued a "Prior Series" covering 1851–1912 based on the newspaper's handwritten records. The current *New York Times Index* is naturally a work of increasing complexity, almost as difficult to find one's way in as the world that it mirrors. When the subject sought is steadily in the news ("Middle East," "Social Security") patience and ingenuity are needed to find the article one has previously read or is sure must have appeared. The subheads are themselves overflowed by the substance.

the Congress, add this sum to 1788, and subtract 2. The worker in European history will similarly want to know by heart how to translate "the year VIII" of the French Republic or the dates of New Style and Old Style as they affected Continental Christendom until October 5, 1582, the Germanies until 1700, England and the colonies until 1752, and Russia until 1918.

In making these changes in dating, it must be kept in mind that working out the correct date of an event that occurred in England when the Julian (Old Style) calendar was in force is not without pitfalls, as is shown by the arguments over the date of Newton's death. The inscription in Westminster Abbey gives the date as "20 March 1726." The year should be 1727 (as it is given in most handbooks and encyclopedias); but the day of the month should also be changed, to March 31, because in the shift to the Gregorian calendar in 1752, the date of September 2 was immediately followed by September 14.[28]

A good example of how these niggling details affect important statements is the frequent mention of the supposed coincidence between Galileo's death and Newton's birth: "both in the same year." The fact is that this conjunction holds only if one reckons in both calendars at once. For Galileo died on January 8, 1642, N.S. and Newton was born on December 25 O.S. If one makes the adjustment of putting Newton on the same calendar as his great predecessor, he turns out to have been born on January 4, 1643. A similar discrepancy prevents one from saying that Cervantes and Shakespeare died on the same day in 1616. Think of the annoyance of those who celebrate centenaries![29]

Long before you have assimilated some of these tricks of the trade you will have lost the bewildered feeling that assailed you when you first entered the library and faced the row upon row of tired volumes in buckram. Instead of being somewhat on the defensive, as if the catalogue and the books were in league to defeat you, you will

---

[28]In other words, the gap is eleven *days*, though subtracting the first *date* gives the answer twelve. In the Russian changeover during our own century the gap was thirteen *days*.

[29]The careful reader will note that whereas the gap for Newton's death (in the eighteenth century) was eleven days, that for his birth in the seventeenth was only ten.

have taken the offensive and be challenging them to show cause why they should not help you. More than that, you will have grown into habits of noting and collecting which, though as automatic as reflex action, nonetheless imply foresight and prudence.

For example, you will always carry a few 3 × 5 cards for jotting down facts and ideas casually encountered. You will clip articles, large or small, from newspapers or book dealers' catalogues. The telling modern instance or the unusual remark in an unpublished manuscript in private hands cannot be sought for, it comes of its own accord; to be useful it must come ahead of the need for it. Cards and clippings are classified "on arrival" in suitably marked folders.

Some research is impossible without maps and much of the rest can benefit from their use. For American subjects, *The National Atlas of the United States of America* has no competitor. For the geography of the world, consult *The International Atlas* and *The Times Atlas*. Descriptive matter on any geographical entity is to be found in *The Columbia-Lippincott Gazetteer* (1962). Governmental information as well as geographical is found in the *Political Handbook of the World*, issued annually.

Any piece of research, of course, can unexpectedly raise special questions. You may, for instance, want to compare the distribution of the population of England in 1750 with that of 1850, or measure the distance between two points on the Oregon Trail, or visualize the precise area of Africa into which European diplomats banned the import of arms and liquor in 1890. Only an historical atlas will give you such information. You will find a great variety of works that map the answers to questions of military or economic or Biblical or literary or other import, or else illustrate the salient facts about a stated region or period. For general use Palmer's *Atlas of World History* (1957) or the older Shepherd's *Historical Atlas* may be turned to first. For the United States, a handsome and comprehensive work is *The American Heritage Pictorial Atlas of United States History* (1966), but there is value still in the much older Paullin's *Atlas of the Historical Geography of the United States*.

It goes without saying that the student will miss no chance to add the name of reference volumes to his panoply, even if he sees no immediate use for it—for instance, the *Weekly Compilation of Pres-*

idential Documents (published every Monday) which contains statements, messages, and other matters issued by the White House during the preceding week. Another such source turns up as you read for another purpose an old issue of the *Mississippi Valley Historical Review* (now the *Journal of American History*), the chief periodical devoting itself exclusively to American history. That source is Herbert O. Brayer's "Preliminary Guide to Indexed Newspapers of the United States, 1850–1900," the value of which is self-evident. Another suggestion may strike the eye in a newspaper advertisement, or may come to you in the mail—perhaps an announcement that at last there is available the *Guide to Research Collections of Former United States Senators, 1789–1982*.

One by-product of reprint publishing is the emergence of specialized reference works which despite narrow coverage are indispensable. To take an example at random, the French list of books and drawings suppressed or prosecuted between 1814 and 1877, including such authors as Rabelais, Villon, Gautier, and Flaubert. This list, *Catalogue des ouvrages écrits et dessins de toute nature poursuivis supprimés ou condamnés depuis le 21 octobre 1814 jusqu'au 31 juillet 1877* (published in Paris, 1879, and reprinted in 1968 in Brussels by Gabriel Lebon in his series *Éditions Culture et Civilisation*), gives summaries of the legal proceedings and the names of participants following the titles and dates and constitutes a useful compendium for the historian of nineteenth-century culture.

Books Beyond Reach and the Lonely Fact

No researcher should feel constricted by the limitations of the library or libraries he works in: if he knows what he wants he can borrow by interlibrary loan from other institutions. The librarian will make the arrangements. If the books themselves cannot be borrowed, the relevant portions can be microfilmed or photocopied, subject to the rules of copyright.[30] The same is true of newspapers and journals,

---

[30]Congress in 1976 passed a comprehensive bill that went into effect in 1978 revising existing rules and guarantees. The standard introduction to the law of literary property is Donald F. Johnson, *Copyright Handbook*, 2nd ed., New York, 1982.

whose whereabouts are detailed in the invaluable "Union Lists" of American newspapers and of "serials." Microfilming is now so commonplace, convenient, and cheap that all but the most penurious library can obtain for you a replica of the Gutenberg Bible or a file of the *Emporia Gazette*. Moreover, in *Newspapers in Microform* you can find out what is available and where.

The Library of Congress is of course the great American repository of printed and manuscript materials that the researcher will resort to for remote sources. A Library of Congress card is prepared for the works it catalogues and these cards are published (together with cards for the holdings reported by 1,100 other libraries) as the *National Union Catalog*.[31] For other kinds of materials, the searcher will have to explore in the series of bibliographies that span our publishing history.[32]

It is evident that the only hopeless task is to look for a book that never existed. Yet modern students who want to be sure of the date, edition, and contents of an actual work unquestionably face a harder task than their predecessors of twenty-five years ago. The reason lies in the proliferation of reprints, paperback and other, which seldom

[31]The *National Union Catalog* is extended backward in time to cover the years up to 1956. This mammoth project, completed in 1981, is contained in 754 volumes.

[32]For books, pamphlets, and periodicals published in the United States through the year 1800, consult Charles Evans's *American Bibliography*, and know that a microprint edition is available for every item listed there, as well as an exhaustive two-volume index prepared by C. K. Shipton and J. E. Mooney. Overlapping in part, but extending in coverage to the latter half of the nineteenth century, is Joseph Sabin's *Dictionary of Books Relating to America*, which, like Evans's volume, usually indicates where copies of the items it lists may be found. (The period 1801–1871 is covered further, though somewhat unevenly, by R. R. Shaw and R. H. Shoemaker's *American Bibliography*, by O. A. Roorbach's *Bibliotheca Americana*, and by James Kelly's *American Catalogue*.) Sabin's work has been made immensely more useful by the author-title index to it compiled by J. E. Molnar. For the years since 1876 the field is well covererd by two series, the *American Catalogue* (1876–1910) and the *United States Catalog* with its supplement, the *Cumulative Book Index*, which has been published regularly since 1899.

For manuscript material in general see p. 124, n. 18. Diaries, the most elusive of manuscripts, are listed in William Matthews's *American Diaries in Manuscript, 1580–1954* (1974). References to published diaries and journals covering the years 1492 to 1980 are found in the new *American Diaries: An Annotated Bibliography*, ed. Laura Arskey, Nancy Pries, and Marcia Reed, 2 vols. (1983).

disclose their true or full natures, and which often escape systematic listing in catalogues and bibliographies.

As for nonexistent books, their birthplace—or at least their cradle—is someone's listing from which you copied the title. A volume of *Who Was Who in America* ascribes a biography of James Wilson, a signer of the Declaration of Independence, to Burton Alva Konkle, thus implying that the published book exists. The truth is that the book never appeared; it is a "ghost book." Such "books" are rare and not likely to turn up in your path any more often than forged documents, but you should be prepared for all contingencies.

Your adventures as a researcher in the library result, ordinarily, from your wanting to "get the facts." Very different is the task of finding "the fact," in the singular. If "the fact" is incidental or recondite, do not let it hold you up. You can write about the Republican campaign of 1860 now and postpone until later trying to find where Lincoln stayed during the convention, just as you can follow the career of Lord Byron without knowing which of his legs was deformed. If, however, you must prepare for a newsmagazine a complete list of the Presidents of the United States who have left the country during their terms of office, and give details of their trips, you obviously have nothing to postpone.

This kind of search can be anguishing beyond belief, and success correspondingly enthralling. Since "the fact" may turn up almost anywhere, you must be ready to spring in any direction. For American "facts" other than quotations, you can try *Scribner's Dictionary of American History* or Johnson's *Oxford Companion to American History*. For European facts, the compendium is William L. Langer's *Encyclopedia of World History* (an *n*th revision of the German original by Ploetz), supplemented by Alfred Mayer's *Annals of European Civilization: 1501–1900*. For historical facts not only about Europe but also about Africa, Asia, and Latin America, look at the *Harper Encyclopedia of the Modern World* edited by Richard B. Morris and Graham W. Irwin. An amazingly large number of facts, together with interpretation, are organized chronologically and topically in Richard and Jeffrey Morris's *Encyclopedia of American History*. If "the fact" is a name, past or present, a thing or person or place, fictional or legendary or mythological, begin with the three volumes of Barnhart's *New Century Cyclopedia of Names* (100,000 entries), or the earlier edition mentioned above.[33]

If "the fact" appeared in an article, or if the fact *is* an article, go to the various guides to periodicals we have listed. For all manner of numerical data, you should learn to use the *Historical Statistics of the United States* and the latest issue of the *Statistical Abstract of the United States*. Another compendium of great interest is B. R. Mitchell's *European Historical Statistics, 1750–1970*. For electoral data you should at once and confidently turn to the *Guide to U.S. Elections*, the series *America Votes*, and the annual *Almanac of American*

---

[33] If the fact is known to be American and historical and has been the subject of an article or book since 1902 (a safe guess is that it has been), consult *Writings on American History* (1902–1903; 1906–1940; 1948–1959), compiled by Grace Gardner Griffin and others. Each volume is exhaustively indexed, but all diggers should be aware that a meticulous cumulative index covering the years 1902 to 1940 has been issued (American Historical Association, 1957), making the series very convenient to use. This series was discontinued with the volume for 1961. A successor series now under the editorship of Cecelia J. Dadian is *Writings on American History: A Subject Bibliography of Articles*, published regularly, but lacks adequate indexing. All researchers should be familiar with the annual *America: History and Life*, which indexes bibliographies, article abstracts, and book reviews. It is online through DIALOG data base. For a much briefer bibliography on a subject in American history, the reader can turn to the *Harvard Guide to American History* (1974).

Every seeker after facts should know where to find those contained in United States government publications. Access seems at first complicated, but a little practice removes the difficulties. The collected edition of documents comprising House and Senate Journals, Documents, and Reports is known as the Serial Set, amounting now to about 15,000 "volumes." The puzzle is to find the serial number of the volume you need. For the years 1789–1909, use the *Checklist of United States Public Documents, 1789–1909*, if you know the number of the document or report you want. If you do not, turn to the chronological listing: B. P. Poore, *A Descriptive Catalogue of the Government Publications of the United States, September 5, 1774 to March 4, 1881*. This is followed by J. G. Ames, *Comprehensive Index to the Publications of the United States Government, 1881–1893*, which is arranged alphabetically by subject and contains also an index to proper names. For the years 1893 to 1940, use the "Document Catalog," a short title for the *Catalog of the Public Documents of the — Congress and of All Departments of the United States*. This is a dictionary catalogue listing documents in one alphabet under author, subject, and sometimes title. If you are delving for government publications issued since 1940, you must turn to the *Monthly Catalog of United States Government Publications*. Unfortunately, this does not list serial numbers, for which you must rely on *Numerical Lists and Schedule of Volumes of the Reports and Documents of the — Congress*. The *CIS* [Congressional Information Service] *U.S. Serial Set Index*, issued in 1976 and covering the years through 1969, usefully supplements the foregoing.

Politics. For national judicial history, the best single volume is the Congressional Quarterly's *Guide to the U.S. Supreme Court.* But unquestionably the most baffling queries are those about quotations and anecdotes. Try to find, for example, the circumstances in which Hamilton is supposed to have said, "Your people, sir, are a great beast." Or where Gouverneur Morris told how he greeted George Washington by a slap on the back and got in return for his exuberance a cold stare that he remembered for the rest of his days.

"Bartlett" is almost synonymous with "Quotations," but note that unlike the first eleven editions, which offered "classic" and famous quotations, the fifteenth (1980) introduces aphorisms from foreign cultures and lines from cowboy songs, sea chanteys, and spirituals. Other compilations include those by Burton E. Stevenson, H. L. Mencken, J. K. Hoyt, Rudolf Flesch, J. M. and M. J. Cohen (Penguin series), James B. Simpson, P. H. Dalbiac, and the editors of the Oxford Press. Foreign quotations are to be found at the back of Hoyt's *Cyclopedia* or in separate volumes by H.F.W. King, H. P. Jones, G. Büchmann, O. Guerlac, E. Genest, and many others. If the quotation is not in any of these books, your little problem has suddenly become a big one. If you do not believe this, wait until it happens to you, or else ask a friend who has been looking through all of Matthew Arnold's writings page by page for a sentence he knew must be there, but now thinks may be by Walter Pater after all.

To mention other "fact" books here would be futile, they are so numerous. Until you set out on your search you will not credit how many patient people have toiled weary hours to enable you to find in half a minute some isolated name, date, or utterance. The sum total of such books in all languages, no one knows; but the most prominent and promising you will find listed in Sheehy's *Guide to Reference Books* already cited. It describes most books in great detail and presents them in groups. On American politics, for example, you find three time-saving compendiums: Kirk H. Porter's *National Party Platforms, 1840–1972*; Thomas H. McKee's *National Conventions and Platforms, 1789–1905*; and Richard C. Bain's *Convention Decisions and Voting Records.* Sheehy's *Guide* will also assist those interested in "firsts" by referring them to such useful works as Patrick

FIGURE 8   *Dictionaries of Quotations and Special Terms*

Quotations, General
    Bartlett, *Familiar Quotations* (all editions from the 9th on)
    Benham, *A Book of Quotations*
    Dalbiac, *A Dictionary of Quotations*
    Gross, *The Oxford Book of Aphorisms*
    Hoyt, *Cyclopedia of Practical Quotations* (foreign and classi-
        cal section at the back)
    Mencken, *A New Dictionary of Quotations on Historical
        Principles*
    The Oxford Dictionary of Quotations
    Partridge, *A First Book of Quotations*
    The Penguin Dictionary of Quotations
    Stevenson, *The Home Book of Quotations*
    Stevenson, *The Home Book of Shakespeare Quotations*
    Tripp, *The International Thesaurus of Quotations*

Quotations, General, in Classical and Modern Foreign Languages
    Büchmann, *Geflügelte Worte* (in 9 languages, with German
        translations)
    Genest, *Dictionnaire des Citations Françaises*
    Guerlac, *Les Citations Françaises*
    Guterman, *A Book of French Quotations* (with English trans-
        lations)
    Jones, *Dictionary of Foreign Phrases and Classical Quota-
        tions* (with English translations)
    King, *Classical and Foreign Quotations* (with English)
    Larousse, *Dictionnaire des Citations Françaises*
    Riley, *A Dictionary of Latin and Greek Quotations* (with
        English translations)

Quotations, Specialized
    Esar, *The Dictionary of Humorous Quotations*
    MacKay, *Scientific Quotations*
    Oxford Book of Legal Anecdotes (in preparation, 1984)
    Oxford Book of Literary Anecdotes
    Strauss, *Familiar Medical Quotations* (many from general
        literature)

Terminology and Nomenclature
  Art and Architecture
    Adeline, *Art Dictionary* (translated from the French)
    Collett-Sandars, *Handbook of Architectural Styles*

Mayer, *The Artist's Handbook of Materials and Techniques*
O'Dwyer and LeMage, *A Glossary of Art Terms*
Parker, *Concise Glossary of Architecture*
Smith, *Dictionary of Greek and Roman Antiquities*

Language and Literature
The Barnhart Dictionary of New English Since 1963
Freeman, *A Dictionary of Fictional Characters*
Partridge, *A Dictionary of Catchphrases*
Pei, *Glossary of Linguistic Terminology*
Schur, *British Self-Taught* (differences between British and American usage)

Music
Smith, *A Dictionary of Musical Terms in Four Languages*
Wotton, *A Dictionary of Foreign Musical Terms and Handbook of Orchestral Instruments*

Science and Technology
Crispin, *Dictionary of Technical Terms* (definitions)
Flood and West, *An Elementary Scientific and Technical Dictionary*
Newmark, *Dictionary of Science and Technology* (equivalents in English, French, German, and Spanish)

Robertson's *The Book of Firsts* and Joseph N. Kane's *Famous First Facts* (3rd ed., 1964), which records when the zip fastener became reliable and who is the mother of Father's Day.

To be sure, running the eye down somebody's alphabetical list and pawing over pages till column 978a comes into view, or tossing thick tomes from hand to shelf and back again, is not the be-all and end-all of research. Far from it. But it is the inescapable prerequisite, and the demands that these activities make upon the mind are close kin to those that occur at the later and higher stages. The difference between a good researcher and a poor one is not decisively shown by their respective skill in using the library, but that skill is certainly a main ingredient of excellence. The writing of a report for a class assignment or the creation of a masterpiece of history both depend in the first instance on the ability to summon up the past that reposes in library books—forcing them, as it were, to yield their secrets.

FIGURE 9   *The Chief Indexes to Periodicals*

Woman Question. Canad. Mo. **15**: 568. **16**: 80–620. —
(E. Archard) Radical, **2**: 715. — Victoria, **18**: 261–
449. — (J. Weiss) Chr. Exam. **56**: 1. — (E. C. Stan-
ton) Radical, **3**: 18. — (L. G. Noble) Scrib. **3**: 483.
—(E. Benson) Galaxy, **2**: 751. — (C. A. Bristed)
Galaxy, **9**: 841. — (C. Kingsley) Ev. Sat. **8**: 556. —
(O. A. Brownson) Cath. World, **9**: 145. — Brown-
son, **22**: 508. — Mo. Rel. M. **18**: 234, 399. **19**: 65.
20: 225. **21**: 179. — (H. James) Putnam, **1**: 279.
— Bushnell on. (E. L. Godkin) Nation, **8**: 496.
— Essays on. (O. B. Frothingham) Nation, **9**: 342.
— Hopkins on. (C. C. Nott) Nation, **9**: 193.
— in Berlin. Victoria, **8**: 291.
— Ladies' War. Victoria, **21**: 225.
— Latest Crusade. Victoria, **11**: 193.
— Men and Women. Victoria, **26**: 149.
— Modern Moated Grange. Victoria, **20**: 401.
— Neglected Side of. (E. L. Godkin) Nation, **7**: 434.
— Reply to Parkman on. No. Am. **129**: 413.
— The Revolt and the Revolters. (M. Taylor) Victoria,
   17: 193.
— Sex in Politics. (E. L. Godkin) Nation, **12**: 270.
— Shall Womanhood be abolished? (C. W. Clapp) New
   Eng. **36**: 541.
— Something on, from Germany. Victoria, **8**: 195.
— Various Aspects of. (F. Sheldon) Atlan. **18**: 425.
— A Woman's Protest. Mo. Rel. M. **32**: 213.
— A Working-Woman's Statement. (L. E. Chollet) Na-
   tion, **4**: 155.
— Wrong and right. (G. H. Johnston) Mercersb. **25**: 524.
Woman Reformers. (J. R. Dennett) Nation, **9**: 479.
Womanhood. (H. T. Tuckerman) Chr. Exam. **68**: 157.
— and its Mission. Dub. Univ. **53**: 623, 696. Same art.
   Ecl. M. **47**: 349, 492.
— Christian, French Study of. Dub. R. **88**: 288.
— Ideal. (S. B. Cooper) Overland, **6**: 453. **7**: 69–535.
— in America. Mo. Rel. M. **17**: 46.
— New Ideal of. (A. M. Machar) Canad. Mo. **15**: 659.
— Old. Two Pictures of. (C. Lushington) Good Words,
   18: 476.
Womankind abroad. (W. L. Tiffany) Knick. **58**: 194, 487.
— in Western Europe. (T. Wright) Stud. & Intel. Obs.
   1: 21–445. **2**: 15–448. **3**: 11–444. **4**: 32, 120, 187.
Womanliness. Knick. **63**: 227. — Sharpe, **43**: 151. —
   N. Ecl. **7**: 451.

WOMEN as athletes
Barney, E. C. American sportswoman. Fortn
   62(ns 56):263-77 Ag '94
Kenealy, A. Woman as an athlete. 19th Cent
   45:636-45 Ap '99; Same. Liv Age 221:363-70
   My 6 '99; Reply. L. O. D. Chant. 19th Cent
   45:745-54 My '99; Same. Liv Age 221:799-806
   Je 24 '99; Rejoinder. 19th Cent 45:915-29
   Je '99; Same. Liv Age 222:201-13 Jl 22 '99
Sutphen, W. G. V. Golfing woman. il Out-
   look 62:249-57 Je 3 '99
WOMEN as authors
Cone, H. G. Woman in American literature.
   Cent 40(ns 18):921-30 O '90
DuBois, C. G. Femininity in literature. Critic
   23(ns 20):310 N 11 '93
Gardener, H. H. Immoral influence of women
   in literature. Arena 1:322-35 F '90
Green, A. S. A. S. Woman's place in the
   world of letters. 19th Cent 41:964-74 Je '97;
   Same. Liv Age 214:300-7 Jl 31 '97; Comment.
   Same. Liv Age 78:796-7 Je 5 '97
Lathrop, G. P. Audacity in women novelists.
   No Am 150:609-17 My '90. Discussion. 151:
   127-8 Jl '90
Noguchi, Y. Japanese women in literature.
   Poet Lore 15 no3:88-91 Jl 1904
O'Hagan, T. Some Canadian women writers.
   il Cath World 63:779-95 S '96
Rogers, A. Literary life of woman; does it
   interfere with her domestic life? Outlook
   52:666-7 O 26 '95
Sichel, E. H. Women as letter-writers. Corn-
   hill 79(s3 6):53-67 Ja '99; Same. Liv Age
   220:513-23 F 25 '99
Walford, L. B. Working women. Critic 16(ns
   13):159 Mr 29 '90
Williams, A. M. Our early female novelists.
   Cornhill 72(ns 25):588-600 D '95 (pub anon);
   Same. Liv Age 207:804-12 D 28 '95
   See also
Authors, Women
Women as journalists
Women as poets
WOMEN as farmers
Bradley, E. Agricultural brigade of the mon-
   strous regiment of women. Fortn 69(ns 63):
   334-7 F '98; Excerpt. R of Rs 17:346 Mr '98
Sykes, E. C. Simple life on a poultry-ranch
   in British Columbia. Cornhill 111(s3 38):
   214-22 F 1915
Women as stock-keepers. Spec 81:111-12 Jl
   23 '98
WOMEN as inventors
Woman as an inventor and manufacturer;
   review of O. T. Mason's Woman's share
   in primitive culture. il Pop Sci 47:92-103 My
   '95
Women inventors. Sci Am 81:123 Ag 19 '99

To the left, part of a column from *Poole's Index*; to the right, a sample
from the *Readers' Guide*. Notice the simpler but less informative citation in
the older work: *Poole's* gives the title of the magazine, the volume number,
and page. The lack of author entries, a great inconvenience since 1848 when
Poole's first appeared, was remedied at last by the publication of a cumulative author index in 1971.

The *Readers' Guide* gives the title of the magazine, the volume number,
and page; adds the month and year, and the date if appropriate. The user will
find at the beginning of the volume the explanation of the symbols by which
he may find out more about the character and contents of the article. The
Readers' Guide beginning with the issue for 1983 is online through the
Wilsonline data base.

The Computer: Bosom Friend or Occasional Aide?

It was inevitable that the advent of the computer in the science laboratory, the registrar's office, and the library should put ideas in the heads of scholars in neighboring buildings. The reputed feats of the machine, its speed and accuracy, its superficial comparability with the mind of man, and its taste for a fast life (obsolescence of each "generation" in ten years or less) all excited a natural wonder and desire to gain access to the controls, in hopes of lifting from scholarly shoulders the heavy burdens of drudgery and thought.[34] Yet in spite of the enormous amount of talk and publicity about computers, a great many educated people entertain incomplete and misleading ideas about them.

The name of the device is in part responsible: "compute" suggests numbers and hence mathematics. But although a computer can be used to calculate, it is not a mathematical machine but a logical one. The French name *ordinateur* expresses the fact more accurately: a computer "ordinates"—puts in the right order—a series of simple steps equivalent to yes or no, adding or subtracting. These taken together lead to a desired result that may be very complicated indeed. The familiar word "program" indicates the same thing; it is an *agenda*, which is the Latin for things to be done; a *program* is an agenda written in advance.

Other terms used in the computer jargon can be equally misleading. A computer does not think; it reacts to electrical impulses; it does not read but registers one of these reactions, essentially no different from that of switching a current on and off; it has no memory, but only storage space. In the words of an authority, "a computer does not do any thinking and cannot make unplanned decisions. . . . *Computers do not solve problems—people solve problems*. The computer carries out the solution as specified by people."[35]

The solutions or decisions planned in advance "by people" and the data on which they are based constitute the program for each computer problem. It is not the purpose here to teach programming,

<hr />

[34]Trends in computerized research are discussed in the journal *Computers and the Humanities*. See also A. Brier and I. Robinson, *Computers and the Social Sciences* (New York, 1974).

[35]Donald D. Spencer, *Basic Programming*, New York, 1984, 17, 19.

but an outline of the procedure may help the researcher to understand the ways in which a computer can or cannot aid his research. It is fatally easy to spend computer time at a high cost for unsatisfactory results.

Everything registered in a computer takes the form of sequences of binary numbers: *1*s and *0*s, each unique sequence corresponding to a particular word or number supplied as data. The computer's "expressions" are thus long and difficult to distinguish. For example, the first two bars of Beethoven's Fifth Symphony when converted to binary numbers for digital recording and printed out cover about three sheets of 8½ by 11-inch paper. No human eye could read them comfortably or intelligently, and it follows that, in reverse, nobody could write a program easily and accurately if it had to be couched in these binary numbers.[36]

Hence the creation of the so-called computer languages—Basic, Cobol, Pascal, Fortran. They are not languages, of course, but symbolic systems that make it relatively easy to list the steps for activating the computer—i.e. to design the program. It is first put together in one of these systems of symbols and then converted electronically into the binary numbers. The symbolic systems are called high-level languages, because they are closer to human modes of expression than the bewildering 0,1 level of the machine. It is a case of "the simpler the higher." Basic—perhaps the most widely used of the schemes—is quite simple and high level at the same time.[37]

Now for a little more jargon. The computer itself and its terminals make up what is called hardware. The program, in English or in Basic (or other high-level language), the documentation, any sample runs, and all associated materials are called "software." The sequence of steps in any program is called an algorithm or flow chart. In outline, it goes: start, read, compute, print, and stop. The middle section, "compute," is the complicated one. For example, to have the

---

[36]In contrast to a *digital* computer, which translates into set numbers, an *analog* uses directly measurable quantities (voltage, resistance) to carry out results. To suggest a comparison, the telegraph key uses Morse translation for words; a typewriter key spells them out direct.

[37]Do not confuse with *Basic English*, a vocabulary of 800 words devised by C. K. Ogden to help foreigners learn English.

computer bring forth the largest of three numbers takes six steps: Is A larger than B? If yes, then is it larger than C? If no, then . . . , etc., down to: Is the result larger than C? For these steps to be taken requires a series of "lines" to be entered in the computer, beginning with: Let A = (whatever the first of the three numbers is), Let B = . . . , Let C = . . . , after which come the questions above, followed by Read, Compute, Print, and End (or Stop).

Each numbered line contains only one item or demand, set forth in the conventional word or symbol and placed in the order of logic. In complex programs, "loops" permit the same section of a program to apply to different sets of data. What makes programming a challenging craft is this need to break down a question or problem into elements that can be most economically used; squeezing all desired consequences from all the data available.[38]

When a computer is used for counting, sorting, or indexing items, the data consist of the entire collection of items—for instance a whole book or set of documents. Suppose these are to be indexed. The task means selecting and alphabetizing certain words and entering their page numbers. Obviously, all the words must be put in the computer before instructions about them can be executed. Most book indexes include proper names, which are already distinguished in ordinary print by a capital letter. But if the instruction should call for all capitalized words, the computer would bring out all the words that begin a new sentence; it cannot tell *The* from *Shakespeare*. So in putting in the data, all proper names must be keyed by a symbol that singles them out—laborious but essentially simple.

What is more difficult is to key the common nouns that belong in the particular index, because many words have multiple meanings and trying to separate and key these distinct meanings ahead of time would be difficult and expensive. A lawyer who wanted a list of cases on eminent domain, as well as passing references to the subject, would key that central phrase and perhaps *compulsory sale, expropriate*, and *appropriate*. The printout would faithfully turn up all such references, but dozens of them would be to passages which used

[38]See the various handbooks by Donald D. Spencer such as *Problem-Solving with Basic*, (New York, 1983).

appropriate as an adjective, meaning suitable, which had nothing to do with eminent domain.

A statistical study of sharply defined purpose is, by contrast, well suited to computer work. Thus in 1984 the *Stockholm Studies in English*, using a sample of English and American prose, plus twenty novels, ascertained the frequency of use of *too* and *also*. The computer saved untold drudgery, eyesight, and error. In using data banks, the customer must be prepared for a large excess of information from which he must weed out what the literal-minded machine has brought forth that is not to the point. It is the great power and flexibility of human speech, especially in highly developed languages, that makes it impossible to use computers for translating from a foreign language. Expressions that a child readily understands in different senses are confused by the computer and make it produce nonsense.

The Limits of Computer Indexing

This same obstacle, which is not technological but logical, is found in indexing. The point is well illustrated by the experience of the publishers who brought out the remarkable and pioneering *Dictionary of Scientific Biography* in fifteen volumes. Highly competent programmers, as well as the leading manufacturer of computers, were consulted about the possibility of making the index with their aid. After studying the text it became clear to all that no amount of logical foresight could direct the computer to perform the task. To use a simplified example, the computer could spot the word *entropy* wherever it appeared, but it could not associate it with references to alternative terms—*thermodynamics, second law, heat death,* and possibly others. In science and the arts, where a rich variety of synonyms is used to begin with, and where historically terms for the same thing have changed repeatedly, indexing ideas by computer is not practicable.[39]

[39]The editor of the modern edition of Pepys' *Diary* confirms the difficulty: "I doubt in fact if a computer can be used for indexing a text like Pepys, in which there are so many indirect and submerged and ambiguous references. To have determined who he meant by 'my Uncle' or by 'the Duke' or by the unattached pronoun 'he', and so on, would have meant going back to the text" (*Journal of the Royal Society of Arts*, 132 [May 1984], 398). See the end of Chapter 16.

In the event, the index of the *Dictionary of Scientific Biography* (volume 16) was prepared by a team of persons with broad scientific training. They worked on each volume as it appeared and completed the task in ten years. To be sure, computers can save time and effort by recording what such workers would otherwise have written on 3 × 5 cards and pulled out again and again, then alphabetized. In these ways the computer is a handmaid, but it is not a mistress. Since a logical machine cannot exercise fresh judgment but reacts only when all decisions have been made, it is clear that the active verbs commonly used in dealing with computers—that they "think," "read," sort, and so on—are metaphors; they are anthropomorphic (and therefore unscientific) projections of our activities upon a wonderfully complex mechanism that is dependent upon our will and our imagination for its working.

For the researcher, these facts suggest what must be considered when deciding whether or not to use expensive computer time in a humanistic undertaking. For a straight index of proper names, for example, a computer printout may well be worth the expense. Names not relevant (place names or publishers' or names in footnotes) may be crossed out, leaving just what one wants. But in a book about ideas one wants references more subtle than those to single words or conventional names. For a study or an index, it will prove safer, cheaper, and easier to do the study or the index oneself—perhaps with a word processor to aid in the clerical part of the work. Note that even when indexing is delegated by the author to another intelligent person working under definite instructions, some of the same rigidities that characterize the computer will apply: the index will fail to include some items that one wants—for instance, the real name of a person cited in the text under his or her pseudonym or the different dates of two persons with identical names. In short, one cannot blindly rely on the results of any predetermining system.

There remains the possibility of counting items and interpreting totals. Properly programmed, a computer will supply with wonderful speed and accuracy any set of figures and their combinations and permutations: how many books were taken out of the library last year by how many users; the number of books overdue and fines paid and unpaid, with the names and addresses of those who still owe them and the titles of the books they have failed to return. This lavish spread of facts presupposes classification. In the example given the grouping is supplied by the record of self-defining acts—people take out books and return them, or don't, and then they owe fines.

But in more complex behavior classifying is more difficult. It is notorious that crime statistics are extremely hard to make reliable, because similar names cover different actions and vice versa. Taking a national census encounters endless obstacles of the same kind— interpreting the questions varies. In both cases the trouble is that which we all face when filling out a form—do we belong under "working" or "retired" when the fact is that we have retired and are still working? In the social and political, and even more in the intellectual and spiritual activities of mankind, classifications tend to be arbitrary; the necessary decisions are made more or less by fiat, owing to the impossibility of knowing the facts. In this way all college graduates will be deemed to belong to "the educated part of the population." Church attendance will be equated with religious belief. Divorce statistics will be taken as an index of the (dis)respect for the institution of marriage. The sales of a book are often regarded as a measure of its influence—and even of the number of its readers. The fallacy in each of these suppositions is plain, from which it follows that, on such topics, totals from computers are at best suggestive. In reporting them the classification must be closely scanned for rigor (assuming rigor to be at all approachable), and some sort of corrective (often very difficult to find) must be applied to the usual inference that A is an "indicator" of B—diploma indicates education.

Studying literary texts—or, as has been done, musical compositions—with the aid of computers entails the same uncertainty in an even higher degree. Some scholars believe that doubtful or unknown authorship can be ascertained by comparing frequency figures for given words and turns of phrase in a known work with corresponding figures in the questioned text. The assumption is that phrasing is an unchanging trait. It may or may not be; some authors do change their manner radically between youth and age (e.g., Henry James). And the chosen features may not be individual and unique. There is a period style, as well as clichés; and imitation, parody, and plagiarism are constant elements of literature.

FIGURE 10   *"Computer Language"*

"Hopkins, YR. ABRV. ENG. STMTS. LV. MCH. 2 B DSRD."

"Computer Language" is not a language at all, but sets of abbreviations and of made-up or ordinary words transferred to new uses. Some are ill-considered and confusing: a *byte* does not seize nor a *bus* carry anything or anybody.

In music, the attempt has been to study style by counting the recurrences of certain technical devices.[40] It is not clear why style cannot be studied direct, and perhaps more subtly without such computations; for it is recognized that a device in music as in any other art has different uses in different contexts and therefore a different stylistic significance, which the computer program is bound to overlook. Such ambitious efforts may show a misplaced desire to "prove" and perhaps also an impulse to use a fashionable machine, rather than leave it for jobs suited to its true possibilities.[41]

And here a further misconception must be noted in passing. There is a notion that data banks can or will replace books.[42] This hope (or fear) overlooks what actually happens when one goes to a book to learn about a subject—e.g. bridge building. What the reader finds is not merely the answer to the question How do those long ones hold up in the middle? He finds all the associated questions and problems which the writer has assembled for him in due order, and which the inquirer did not suspect existed. In other words, to use a data bank, one must already know much and want but little more; it gives scraps of information, not knowledge. Of course a whole book or essay can be put in and retrieved from a data bank, but then it serves only a preference for reading from a screen instead of a page; it does not fulfill the claim that the art of study has been revolutionized by electronics.

[40]A recent literary study of "themes" in Joyce's *Ulysses* revealed that their spacing and recurrence "showed a pleasing pattern." Many readers had found that out before.

[41]See Susan Hockey, *A Guide to Computer Applications in the Humanities*, Baltimore, 1983.

[42]The most widely used of them are MEDLINE (for medical information), LEXIS (for legal information), and NEXIS (for information in current newspapers and magazines).

5

Verification

How the Mind Seeks Truth

Every thinking person is continually brought face to face with the need to discriminate between what is true and what is false, what is probable and what is doubtful or impossible. These decisions rest on a combination of knowledge, skepticism, faith, common sense, and intelligent guessing. In one way or another, we decide whether the road to town is too icy for going by car, whether the child is telling the truth about seeing a burglar upstairs, whether the threatened layoff at the local plant will take place after all. All adults have acquired techniques for verifying a rumor or report so that they can take appropriate action. They supplement their experience and learning by recourse to special sources or items of information—the broadcast weather report on the state of the road; the child's known habit of fantasy; or the word of the plant manager who has access to firsthand knowledge.

Few of those who run their lives in this way stop to think that in the first case they trusted a technical report which, though not infallible, is the only authority on the subject; that in the second case, the ground for judgment was prior observation and inference; and that the third resort was to a competent witness. It is sometimes possible to use all three kinds of aids to judgment, and others besides, such as the opinions of neighbors and friends, to say nothing of trial and error. All but the most thoughtless and impulsive will use their minds before giving credence to others' say-so, and try to collect evidence before trusting their own surmises. The world is too full of chance and falsehood to make any other course mentally or physically safe.

The intelligent newspaper reader, for example, daily encounters "incredible" stories and tries automatically to "verify" them, first by "reading between the lines" and drawing what seems at the moment an acceptable conclusion, and later by looking for further reports. Limited as this effort is, one cannot always make it from an armchair.

Take the once-shocking news story that appeared under the headline "Clare Luce's Illness Is Traced to Arsenic Dust in Rome Villa."[1] According to the article, Mrs. Luce, at that time United States Ambassador to Italy, had in the summer of 1954 begun to experience symptoms of anemia and fatigue that disappeared when she was absent from her post in Rome, but recurred as soon as she returned to it. Hospital tests, it was said, disclosed that she was the victim of arsenic poisoning. Who was administering the poison? Investigation had brought out that "arsenic paint" on the roses adorning her bedroom ceiling was the source of the poison. Minute flakes of the paint were dislodged by people walking in the laundry above and drifted down, to be inhaled by the Ambassador or swallowed with her morning coffee. Skillful detection by the Central Intelligence Agency was credited with finding the cause of the trouble; and it was announced that steps had been taken to remove it.

The critical reader's immediate response to the story is amazement verging on incredulity—emotions which impel the mind toward the work of truth-seeking or verification. To begin with, one can think of no reason why the report should have been fabricated. Second, one notes that the events were first made known in a newsmagazine published by Mrs. Luce's husband: he had a double reason to protect his reputation for accuracy. Third, one reflects that since the announcement was made by Mrs. Luce just before returning to her post, the incident is almost certainly true. What patriotic person would want to embroil Italian-American relations by raising even the possibility of a plot to poison the American Ambassador?

[1]*New York Times*, July 17, 1956.

But offsetting these probabilities, the critical reader notes, is the absence of any corroborative statement from either the Department of State or the Central Intelligence Agency—or from any Italian source. It is difficult, moreover, to imagine the United States Ambassador living in a house where the paint is so old as to flake off, and where the washing is done on a floor above the bedrooms. If the reader has a smattering of medical knowledge, he is even more puzzled. Was the poison arsenic, which produces a particular set of bodily symptoms, or arsenate of lead, formerly a common ingredient of house paints, which produces different symptoms, those of lead poisoning? If it was arsenic, what was it doing in the paint? If arsenate of lead, why are people with scientific training miscalling it? When ordinary readers encounter a story of this kind and carry their speculation as far as we have supposed, they end by doing one of several things: (1) they accept it because it appeared in a periodical they trust; (2) they reject it because it does not square with what they think likely; (3) they suspend judgment until more information comes out;[2] or (4) they ignore the enigma altogether.

A judicious reader will adopt (3), though there is nothing downright foolish about the other choices. But the researcher and historical reporter has a greater responsibility, which denies him the right to any of the four solutions. He may indeed come to rest on (3), but not until he has done a great deal of work; and except under certain conditions, (1), (2), and (4) go against his professional training and obligations. As the student of past events tries to answer the question What *did* happen? he confronts the same uncertainties as the newspaper reader, but with this important difference: *the researcher must*

[2]Subsequent reports confused the original story beyond hope of armchair unraveling: first, the Ambassador herself cast doubt on the chronology by putting the poisoning back one year; and then the American physician who had been consulted at that time asserted that no tests for arsenic had been made (*New York Times*, July 22 and November 20, 1956). The episode continues to be mystifying. Mrs. Luce has stated that she plans to write her account of it (letter to Henry F. Graff, August 10, 1967); her secretary in Rome, Letitia Baldridge, has written about it in *Of Diamonds and Diplomats*, Boston, 1968, 75–80. Mrs. Luce is most recently reported to have said that she tried "to contain the arsenic report; that she told Eisenhower about it privately with a view to resigning quietly, and that Ike's press secretary . . . stuffed it into his next news briefing, and the deed was done" (Wilfrid Sheed, *Clare Boothe Luce*, New York, 1982, p. 122).

try to reach a decision and make it rationally convincing, not only to himself, but to others. The steps by which he performs this task constitute Verification.

Verification is required of the researcher on a multitude of points—from getting an author's first name correct to proving that a document is both genuine and authentic.[3] Verification is accordingly conducted on many planes, and its technique is not fixed. It relies on attention to detail, on common-sense reasoning, on a developed "feel" for history and chronology, on familiarity with human behavior, and on ever-enlarging stores of information. Many a "catch question" current among schoolchildren calls forth these powers in rudimentary form—for instance the tale about the beautiful Greek coin just discovered and "bearing the date 500 B.C." Here a second's historical reflection and reasoning are enough for verification: the "fact" is speedily rejected.

The first sort of verification consists in clearing up the simple obscurities that arise from one's own or somebody else's carelessness. A good example is found in the following account of a copy editor's search, as reported by the publishing house where she worked:

In the bibliography of a manuscript there appeared this item: "Landsborous, A., and Thompson, H.F.G., *Problems of Bird Migration.*" In the line of duty, the editor queried the spelling of Landsborous, but it was returned by the author without change or comment. Not satisfied, she searched in various bibliographies and in two history catalogues for the name. She could find neither it nor the title of the book. Then she began to look for "Thompson, H.F.G." but without success. Under the subject "Birds—Migration" she was referred to "Aves—Migration." There she found that an A. L. Thomson (without the "p") had written *Bird-Migration* (2nd ed.). Further research in the subject index of the British Museum Catalogue revealed that the first edition had indeed been entitled *Problems of Bird-Migration*. The proper entry then proved to be: "Thomson, Arthur Landsborough, *Problems of Bird-Migration.*" The initials following the name

---

[3]The two adjectives may seem synonymous but they are not: that is genuine which is not forged; and that is authentic which truthfully reports on its ostensible subject. Thus an art critic might write an account of an exhibition he had never visited; his manuscript would be genuine but not authentic. Conversely, an authentic report of an event by X might be copied by a forger and passed off as the original. It would then be authentic but not genuine.

"Thompson" in the original version continued to puzzle the editor until someone suggested that they might indicate an Honorary Fellowship in Geography. . . .[4]

Not all uncertainties can be so thoroughly grappled with and disposed of. Some are like prickly fruit: one does not know how to take hold of them. Others are plain enough but require enormous patience and tireless legwork. No interesting or important question, it is fair to say, can be settled without detailed knowledge, solid judgment, lively imagination, and great persistence. What to do and how to go about it comes with practice; to enumerate rules would be endless and of little use. The best way to show in what the practice consists is to describe in some detail a variety of typical operations that were gone through in actual research.

Collation, or Matching Copies with Sources

One of the fundamental ways of verifying complex facts is known as collation. This simply means "bringing together." Thus when a scholar has found a manuscript and prepares it for publication, he must collate the successive proofsheets with the original before he passes them for publication. Collating is best done with help: one person— the "copyholder"—reads the text, punctuation included, while the scholar—who is known in this role as the "editor"—follows the printed version.

Many rules govern the form in which this kind of transfer from manuscript to type is to be made. They need not concern us here. But the principle of collation should be what, on a small scale and apart from work with manuscripts, is called comparison. It is by rapid single-handed collation that you discover small discrepancies or oddities and are able to stop error.

Among examples of the longevity of error through endless repetition in print, none could be more striking than the presence of a

---

[4]Columbia University Press, *The Pleasures of Publishing*, 14 (June 30, 1947), 2. Landsborough's names and titles appeared correctly in his obituary, thirty years later (*New York Times*, June 11, 1977).

certain proper name in one of Edgar Allan Poe's best known stories. The name is La Bougive and it occurs in "The Purloined Letter," side by side with those of Machiavelli, La Rochefoucauld, and Campanella, all of whom Poe scorns for their shallow and specious notions of the human mind. La Bougive never existed; there is no use looking for him in any dictionaries or pseudonyma.[5] He is simply a misprint for La Bruyère, the French moralist and writer of maxims, who lived in the seventeenth century. Poe was fond of reading him, and in other stories and essays Poe spells the name correctly. But he missed the "typo" both in proof and in his own annotated copy of the *Tales* (1845). In the 1890s the editors of the Chicago edition made the proper guess and put in La Bruyère, but down to the present, new anthologies, both the cheap paperback and the would-be scholarly, go on faithfully reproducing the error.[6]

The basis of the necessary correction here is a knowledge of French literature and a sense of language in relation to proper names.

Rumor, Legend, and Fraud

It may seem more difficult to know when to be skeptical about small details in genuine documents than to doubt a legend or anecdote that sounds too pat to be true, but Verification may be as laborious in the one case as in the other.

The doubtful anecdote you recognize immediately; it bears a family likeness common to the many that you know to be apocryphal. One such famous story has for its hero Stephen A. Douglas, the Illinois Senator contemporary with Lincoln. Tradition has it that on September 1, 1854, a few months after reopening the slavery question by introducing the Kansas-Nebraska Bill, the "Little Giant" stood before a hostile crowd in Chicago and attempted to justify his action. Booed, jeered, and hissed, Douglas held his ground for over two

---

[5]See below, pp. 133 and 142–143.

[6]One of the authors of the present book made a survey of all English and American editions available in print or on library shelves and found fewer than one in four with the correct reading. See Jacques Barzun, "A Note on the Inadequacy of Poe as a Proofreader and of His Editors as French Scholars," *Romantic Review*, 61 (February 1970), 23–26.

hours, determined that he would be listened to. Finally, so the story goes, he pulled out his watch, which showed a quarter after twelve, and shouted: "It is now Sunday morning—I'll go to church and you may go to Hell."

How does the researcher verify his or her doubts of a "good story" of this kind? The steps taken by one scholar to establish or destroy this legend were as follows.[7] First, he searched through the Chicago newspapers of late August and early September 1854 for some account of Douglas's return from Washington. This, he found, had been regarded as a great event, impatiently awaited by the public and fully covered in the press. Next, he scanned the accounts of the meeting itself, looking for any reference to the scornful remark. He found none. Neither the newspapers nor the first biography of the Senator, which was published in 1860, reported the incident. So far the results of a good deal of work, being negative, seemed to justify the doubt.

Yet on the main issue the search turned up some positive though indirect evidence. Two papers, one in Chicago and one in Detroit, stated that Douglas had left the platform at ten-thirty. Moreover, the meeting had taken place on a Friday, not a Saturday night! In the absence of a dated newspaper, a perpetual calendar (see Figure 11) will quickly establish the day of the week on which a date fell or will fall in any year of the Christian era.[8] This is a fixed point: no doubt is possible that September 1, 1854, was a Friday.

But considering the simple ways of press reporting in that age, another possibility remains: perhaps in the uproar no newspaperman heard Douglas's emphatic remark. Of course, if we suppose this in order to support the story, we must also assume that Douglas was so rattled by the heckling of the crowd that he could neither read his watch correctly nor remember what day of the week it was. When the researcher finds himself multiplying hypotheses in order to cling to a belief, he had better heed the signal and drop the belief.

---

[7]Granville D. Davis, "Douglas and the Chicago Mob," *American Historical Review*, 54 (April 1949), 553–556. The definitive account of what actually happened is Robert W. Johannsen, *Stephen A. Douglas*, New York, 1973, 453f.

[8]Researchers will find it advisable to have a perpetual calendar within reach, even when they are away from their books, and they may need a book of tables for other datings than the modern era in the West. (For such a book, see p. 430.)

FIGURE 11   *Perpetual Calendar, A.D. 1753–2020*

Years	Jan (31)	Feb (28)	March (31)	April (30)	May (31)	June (30)	July (31)	Aug (31)	Sept (30)	Oct (31)	Nov (30)	Dec (31)
1761 1789 1801 1829 1857 1885 1903 1931 1959 1987 2009 / 1767 1795 1807 1835 1863 1891 1914 1942 1970 1998 2015 / 1778 1818 1846 1874 1925 1953 1981	D	G	G	C	E	A	C	F	B	D	G	B
1762 1790 1813 1841 1869 1897 1915 1943 1971 1993 2010 / 1773 1802 1819 1847 1875 1909 1926 1954 1982 1999 / 1779 1830 1858 1886 1937 1965	E	A	A	D	F	B	D	G	C	E	A	C
1757 1785 1803 1831 1859 1887 1910 1938 1966 1994 2005 / 1763 1791 1814 1842 1870 1898 1921 1949 1977 2011 / 1774 1825 1853 1881 1927 1955 1983	F	B	B	E	G	C	E	A	D	F	B	D
1754 1782 1822 1850 1878 1901 1918 1946 1974 2002 / 1765 1793 1805 1833 1861 1889 1907 1929 1957 1985 2013 / 1771 1799 1811 1839 1867 1895 1935 1963 1991 2019	B	E	E	A	C	F	A	D	G	B	E	G
1755 1783 1800 1823 1851 1879 1902 1930 1958 1986 2003 / 1766 1794 1806 1834 1862 1890 1913 1941 1969 1997 2014 / 1777 1817 1845 1873 1919 1947 1975	C	F	F	B	D	G	B	E	A	C	F	A
1758 1786 1809 1837 1865 1893 1905 1933 1961 1989 2006 / 1769 1797 1815 1843 1871 1899 1911 1939 1967 1995 2017 / 1775 1826 1854 1882 1922 1950 1978	G	C	C	F	A	D	F	B	E	G	C	E
1753 1781 1810 1838 1866 1894 1906 1934 1962 1990 2001 / 1759 1787 1821 1849 1877 1900 1917 1945 1973 2007 / 1770 1798 1827 1855 1883 1923 1951 1979 2018	A	D	D	G	B	E	G	C	F	A	D	F

▲ COMMON YEARS

LEAP YEARS ▼

Years	Jan	Feb	March	April	May	June	July	Aug	Sept	Oct	Nov	Dec
1764 1792 1804 1832 1860 1888 1928 1956 1984 2012	G	C	D	G	B	E	G	C	F	A	D	F
1768 1796 1808 1836 1864 1892 1904 1932 1960 1988 2016	E	A	B	E	G	C	E	A	D	F	B	D
1772 1812 1840 1868 1896 1908 1936 1964 1992 2020	C	F	G	C	E	A	C	F	B	D	G	B
1776 1816 1844 1872 1912 1940 1968 1996	A	D	E	A	C	F	A	D	G	B	E	G
1780 1820 1848 1876 1916 1944 1972 2000	F	B	C	F	A	D	F	B	E	G	C	E
1756 1784 1824 1852 1880 1920 1948 1976 2004	D	G	A	D	F	B	D	G	C	E	A	C
1760 1788 1828 1856 1884 1924 1952 1980 2008	B	E	F	B	D	G	B	E	A	C	F	A

A

Sun	Mon	Tues	Wed	Thur	Fri	Sat
	1	2	3	4	5	6
7	8	9	10	11	12	13
14	15	16	17	18	19	20
21	22	23	24	25	26	27
28	29	30	31			

B

Sun	Mon	Tues	Wed	Thur	Fri	Sat
		1	2	3	4	5
6	7	8	9	10	11	12
13	14	15	16	17	18	19
20	21	22	23	24	25	26
27	28	29	30	31		

C

Sun	Mon	Tues	Wed	Thur	Fri	Sat
			1	2	3	4
5	6	7	8	9	10	11
12	13	14	15	16	17	18
19	20	21	22	23	24	25
26	27	28	29	30	31	

D

Sun	Mon	Tues	Wed	Thur	Fri	Sat
				1	2	3
4	5	6	7	8	9	10
11	12	13	14	15	16	17
18	19	20	21	22	23	24
25	26	27	28	29	30	31

E

Sun	Mon	Tues	Wed	Thur	Fri	Sat
					1	2
3	4	5	6	7	8	9
10	11	12	13	14	15	16
17	18	19	20	21	22	23
24/31	25	26	27	28	29	30

F

Sun	Mon	Tues	Wed	Thur	Fri	Sat
						1
2	3	4	5	6	7	8
9	10	11	12	13	14	15
16	17	18	19	20	21	22
23/30	24/31	25	26	27	28	29

G

Sun	Mon	Tues	Wed	Thur	Fri	Sat
1	2	3	4	5	6	7
8	9	10	11	12	13	14
15	16	17	18	19	20	21
22	23	24	25	26	27	28
29	30	31				

To find the day of the week for, say, July 4, 1776, first find the year in the two-part block on the left. Then go to July in the list of months at middle right. These two points are each on a "row." Where the rows meet is a letter—in this case A—which tells you which of the seven calendars to use. There you find the fourth to have been a Thursday. In reverse, the process leads to more than one year. The right one is chosen with the aid of other known facts—century, lifespan, decade, etc.

Myths and "good stories" will of course persist despite the efforts of historians. What fits a character or the sound of a name acquires a life of its own which seems immortal.[9] But the varieties of legend and counterfeit deserve the verifier's attention, so that he can develop a connoisseur's instinct for the genre. Consider some examples. Situations of danger are likely to breed rumors. During the sinking of the *Andrea Doria* after a collision at sea, the word flew among the survivors that a baby had been born in one of the lifeboats. Again, a joke may unwittingly turn into a "fact." When the philosopher Diderot was visiting Catherine the Great in Moscow, some disgruntled courtiers arranged an incident in which the French philosopher was challenged in aggressive words:

$$\text{"Sir, } \frac{a + b^n}{z} = x. \text{ Therefore God exists. Reply."}$$

Diderot, suspecting a put-up job and sensing the hostility to his presence, did not reply. Told and retold, this supposed dumbfounding of the learned man grew into a tale of confrontation with the great Euler, the comment being that "all mathematics was Chinese" to Diderot.[10] The fact is that he had published mathematical papers that a recent authority has called "competent and original." Yet the fabrication survives in serious books down to our day, the latest (1983) using the tale both in the preface and on the book jacket to show how important it is to know something of mathematics.

The type of *ben trovato*, or aptly made-up story, includes Galileo's experiment of dropping weights from the Leaning Tower of Pisa, Newton's observing the fall of an apple (a less strenuous "experiment"), and the remark "Let them eat cake," attributed to Marie Antoinette. Even such a mind as John Dewey, educated and ex-

---

[9]For example, Captain Kidd stands in the popular imagination as the pirate par excellence, whereas it is quite likely that he did not commit the acts for which he was tried and which gave him his reputation. Likewise with Dr. Crippen, "the murderer" who was a physician but not a doctor, and who probably poisoned his wife accidentally with the then-unfamiliar soporific hyoscine.

[10]Compare H. L. Mencken's famous "bathtub hoax," to the effect that President Fillmore on taking office in 1850 instructed his Secretary of War to invite tenders for the construction of a bathtub in the White House—as if it were a recent invention. Lives of Fillmore and even guidebooks to the White House were repeating the "fact" decades after Mencken admitted authorship, ten years after the hoax. The article was first printed in the New York *Evening Mail* for December 18, 1917, and reprinted in *The Bathtub Hoax and other Blasts and Bravos*, New York, 1958.

acting, seems to have believed that Columbus was the first man to think the earth was round.[11] All these notions are false. The Marie Antoinette tale was a commonplace of eighteenth-century hostility toward rulers and is mentioned by Rousseau and others before Marie Antoinette was born.

When it becomes necessary to test the accuracy of a story of this kind, whether because a broad conclusion depends on it or because the legend affects character in a biography, the proof or denial presents uncommon difficulties. Most books on the subject—even the best—will be found to contain the anecdote or saying. The first step is to try to trace the tale to its origin.[12] Failing that, the search should establish the conditions that would have to be met if the suspected account were true. Thus it has been "well known" in French literary circles that Flaubert was the real father of Guy de Maupassant. The older novelist did encourage and coach the younger and showed and received from him warm affection: what more "obvious" than to explain these facts by the relation of father and son?

The biographer of both Flaubert and Maupassant, Francis Steegmuller, disposed of the story in the two ways mentioned above. He found the origin of the allegation in the *Journal* of the Brothers Goncourt (notorious gossips) under date of October 1, 1893. The known relationship other than literary, between Flaubert and Maupassant, is quite simple: Flaubert had a childhood friend whose sister married a Maupassant. Guy, the future writer and first son of that marriage, was born on August 5, 1850. What are the historical conditions required for Flaubert's paternity of that son?

---

[11]*How We Think*, New York, 1910, 5.

[12]But beginnings are notoriously hard to ascertain, unless someone happens to round up witnesses while memories are fresh and inconsistencies can be removed by questioning. Imagine trying to find out how the bikini swimsuit burst upon the unprepared universe. You might first consult fashion magazines or the family page of a great daily—provided you know roughly the date of the innovation. But has anything been written—article or book—on the subject by itself? There *is* a book entitled *Bikini Beach: The Wicked Riviera*, which gives a fairly complete history of the quasi garment. First designs of such a thing were made in 1945, but the real start was made in June 1946 when a Paris designer hit upon the now familiar name, because of the publicity given to the island just blasted by atomic tests. As often happens, the original form was not what we now see, but simply a two-piece swimsuit that exposed only the navel. It took from ten to fifteen years for women in various parts of the world to accept the current style. (Geoffrey Bocca, *Bikini Beach*, New York, 1962, 132.)

Obviously, in late 1849 Flaubert, then aged twenty-eight, must have been in the same city as the Maupassant couple, who lived much of the time in Normandy. In the stated year, Flaubert was in Paris between October 25 and October 29, preparing for a trip to Egypt with his friend Maxime du Camp. He did not return to France until June 1851. The possibility of his paternity is thus limited to five days—unlikely. And what more do we know? Flaubert kept a fairly full diary of those days and wrote at least once each day to his mother in the country. Nowhere does he mention seeing his childhood friend's sister Laure, who was intimately known to Flaubert's mother. For the rest, he was extremely busy and often accompanied by his traveling companion.

On the other side of the supposed affair, there is no evidence that Laure de Maupassant was in Paris, none that her husband or her son ever doubted the latter's legitimacy. It was not until Maupassant was seventeen that Flaubert met him, four years after a correspondence had begun between Flaubert and the young man's mother. Its tone makes it still more unlikely than the dates that the two ever had a love affair. So despite the reappearance from time to time of this old story, the conclusion must be that it is another legend made plausible by its aptness to literary purposes.

At the same time, not all discrepancies signalize a myth or a fraud. In autobiographies, for instance, one must be prepared to find errors in dates and names without necessarily inferring that the account is false. Unless written with the aid of a diary or a full correspondence file, memoirs are likely to embody the unconscious tricks that memory plays in everyone, the "short-circuiting" of associations. Thus the first use of the block-signal system on a railroad in the United States is credited to Ashbel Welch, vice-president of the Camden and Amboy. The installation was made in 1863. In memoirs written much later, Welch says that he was led to devise the system after a disastrous rear-end collision that killed many Civil War soldiers coming home on furlough. But that accident occurred on March 7, 1865. It would be absurd to disbelieve the main fact because the date is two years off. And the reason assigned is probably right, too—some rear-end collision that took lives, though not the one cited.

Falsification on the Increase

It should be borne in mind, however, that during the last fifty years, new modes of communication and entertainment have exploited in pseudo-historical fashion the recent and the remote past alike, and this popular (and profitable) enterprise has led to a noticeable weakening of the standards of evidence and truth-telling. In the so-called documentary film or broadcast and their more recent offshoot, the docudrama, a good deal of attention is paid to externals—the site, the costumes, the picturesque detail—but facts and their probability or even plausibility are steadily ignored. Thus in a British series about the life of the master spy Sidney Reilly, Sir Basil Zaharoff is shown shooting and killing one of his own aides with a revolver. Zaharoff, a millionaire arms dealer much valued by heads of state before and during the First World War, was called by his enemies a "merchant of death" and that label is apparently enough to justify depicting him as a cynical, indeed frivolous murderer.

For most people seeing is believing and a strong image such as this becomes historical truth. The "research mind" will resist, of course, but it faces other pitfalls of a new kind. For example, in the interests of "free speech," the libel laws in the United States have lately been modified in such a way that the press can without risk print fabrications—outright lies—provided no malice prompted the deed.[13] At the same time, the newspaper reporter is protected from having to disclose his source. In these conditions, few public figures will venture to start a suit—indefinitely long and expensive—in order to clear their good name. The researcher dependent on reports published in reputable journals will therefore find no corrective to the lie, as he would have when libel was still a serious matter.

To the same effect, it now appears that weekly journals, which employ researchers and thus guarantee factual if not intellectual accuracy, have been betrayed by some of their writers who—thinking of Thucydides, no doubt—invent speeches and persons and "telling"

---

[13]The test is "reckless disregard of the truth." If a reporter sincerely believes the lie he or she has been told, there is no malice in printing it. This acts as an encouragement to print after superficial inquiry, the writer "sincerely believing" what one or two have said "in confidence."

incidents. By a plain paradox, the state of veracity was sounder when no one expected a reporter to be strict about facts and no one verified them at the office.

To make a splash in the endless flood of publications, authors have found that scandal, accusations, shocking discoveries are virtually de rigueur. Books are therefore cobbled together about the recently dead (or barely alive) to launch one of these "charges" and get noticed—never mind if no scrap of evidence is available.[14] The public has become used to this avalanche of gossip gathered from surviving neighbors of the subject, from schoolmates, second cousins, and friends and enemies at every stage of life. Unless the author can say he has conducted hundreds of interviews and traveled thousands of cassette miles, he is thought not to have done his homework. That work is inquisitorial and does not stop even before the unknowable: as a reviewer complained not long ago, "We are not told exactly what went wrong between S—— and his second wife."

This frame of mind in both writer and reader destroys the proper taste for truth. It makes likelihood seem tame and bland. It tempts the researcher to throw the falsehoods into his text as interesting possibilities. He "takes no responsibility" but gains credit for industry, thoroughness, and a sense of what is "important and exciting." In these conditions, a balanced estimate of a situation, a true portrait in biography become rarities. That superb writer and judicious critic Harold Nicolson pointed out long ago how by "telling all" one falsifies. In his life of Lord Curzon, he said, he refrained from dwelling on Curzon's obsessive parsimony and frequent bouts of temper, because these traits would have overimpressed the reader and distorted—not filled out—the correct image of the man.

It should be clear that by definition, the whole man, the interesting man, is the one who performed actions worth remembering and recording, whether or not he suffered from *alopecia areata*. Besides, some of the traits and tics that can be giggled at or gloated over are liable to grave misinterpretation. Thus the late President Johnson's habit of taking another person's elbow and drawing close for a con-

---

[14]Reputable publishers have begun to ask authors for documentation when a thesis challenges probability too violently. See *New York Times*, August 2, 1984.

versation *à deux* was not "a sign of secretiveness"; it turns out the president was somewhat deaf.

In sum, the increasing overlap between history-writing and cheap journalism, both printed and broadcast, has been detrimental to the public mind. False reports spread and defy denial. The myth of "the Bermuda Triangle," for example, becomes an accepted fact; and the demand for evidence grows weaker and weaker, even when no partisanship interferes. Thus a publisher was found for a book that says Pope John Paul I was murdered and offers no proof, and a famous German magazine bought the "Hitler Diaries" and for weeks gulled both journalists and scholars into accepting them. It is a time for keeping one's head when all about you are losing theirs.

Attribution, or Putting a Name to a Source

The historian arrives at truth through probability. As we shall see in a later discussion,[15] this does not mean "a doubtful kind of truth" but a firm reliance on the likelihood that evidence which has been examined and found solid is veracious. If you receive a letter from a relative that bears what looks like her signature, that refers to family matters you and she commonly discuss, and that was postmarked in the city where she lives, the probability is very great that she wrote it. The contrary hypothesis would need at least as many opposing signs in order to take root in your mind—though the possibility of forgery, tampering, and substitution is always there.

As everybody knows, the number of signs that point to genuineness reinforce one another and vastly increase the total probability. If their force could be measured, it would amount not to their sum but to their product. In other words, with each added particle of truthfulness, it becomes far less likely that deception has been practiced or an error committed. Hence in cases where no direct sign is available, a concurrence of indirect signs will establish proof. The "circumstantial evidence" of the law courts is a familiar example of this type of mute testimony. It must always be received with caution and tested bit by

[15]Chapter 7, pp. 168–178.

bit, but when it survives analysis its probative value is fully as great as the testimony of witnesses—and often greater.

One type of difficulty that the researcher overcomes by looking for cumulative indirect proof is that of identifying the unsigned contributions in periodicals. The problem is a frequent one, for until about a century ago nearly all journalism was anonymous. Sometimes an account book survives to tell us who was paid for writing what.[16] But usually no resource is in sight except the researcher's sharp wits. Here is how one researcher arrived at an important identification.[17] In the early 1830s, the young writer John Stuart Mill was greatly interested in the work of the Saint-Simonians, a French socialist group. He met some of their emissaries in England and studied their ideas. So much is clear. Now on April 18, 1832, there appeared in *Le Globe*, which was the newspaper of the French society, a long letter signed "J." that purported to give an Englishman's opinion of the Saint-Simonian doctrines. The mind naturally jumps to the possibility that this letter was a translation of something written by Mill. But jumping is not proving. How do we make sure?

First, research discloses two earlier allusions by one of the editors of the paper to the effect that "one of the most powerful young thinkers in London" intended to write a series of open letters on the new ideas.

Second, there exists a letter to that same editor announcing the visit of a third party who would bring him, among other things, "the work of your young friend M." With the published "J." the "M." makes out a *prima facie* case for identifying the writer as John Mill; yet it needs strengthening.

Third, it was within three days of receiving the piece of news just recorded that the newspaper published the open letter of "an Englishman" who signed himself "J."

At this point the scholar whose researches we have followed remarks that "a cautious reader will still properly feel some reserva-

[16]This was the method used by Daniel C. Haskell in producing volume 2 of his *Indexes of Titles and Contributors of* The Nation . . . *1865–1917*, 2 vols., New York, 1951–1953.

[17]Hill Shine, "J. S. Mill and an Open Letter to the Saint-Simonian Society in 1832," *Journal of the History of Ideas*, 6 (January 1945), 102–108.

tions" about attributing the letter to Mill. He therefore continues the chase. "Two further bits of circumstantial evidence," he tells us, "seem decisive." They are, to pursue the enumeration:

Fourth, a letter of May 30 from Mill to his Saint-Simonian friends referring to "my letter which appeared in *Le Globe*"; and

Fifth, a footnote added to that private letter by the editor of Mill's correspondence, stating that Mill's public letter appeared on April 18, 1832.

At this point no further doubt is possible and the researcher can exclaim, like Euclid at the end of a theorem: "Q.E.D."

Explication, or Worming Secrets Out of Manuscripts

Young researchers who want to obtain their professional license by earning the Ph.D. often believe that the best indication of merit is to find a packet of letters in an attic. The implication is that professionals value above all else a new find of primary sources.[18] This is not so. But new evidence is always interesting and it may be extremely valuable. If it consists of manuscripts, it creates special problems for the verifier. Manuscripts often come in huge unsorted masses—the "papers" that are the bulky leftovers of busy lives. Of such papers, letters are perhaps the most difficult to subdue: they must be forced, in spite of slips of the pen, bad handwriting, or allusions to unidentified persons, to tell the exact story that the author intended and that the recipient probably understood.

In this kind of decoding and classifying no librarian can go very far in supplying help. It is an expert's job, and no one is an expert until he has made himself one. You learn your letter-writer's quirks

[18]In historiography, a primary source is distinguished from a secondary by the fact that the former gives the words of the witnesses or first recorders of an event—for example, the diaries of Count Ciano written under Mussolini's regime. The historian, using a number of such primary sources, produces a secondary source.

This brings up the important subject of the whereabouts of manuscripts. The two main books to consult are Philip M. Hamer, ed., *A Guide to Archives and Manuscripts in the United States* (New Haven, 1961), now computerized at the National Archives, and *The National Union Catalog of Manuscript Collections*. The latest aid is *The National Inventory of Documentary Sources* (1984). For work on official papers a knowledge of public archives and their holdings is required. Study Philip C. Brooks, *Research in Archives: the Use of Unpublished Primary Sources* (Chicago, 1969).

and foibles from what he or she wrote and said; you date and interpret the documents by internal and external clues. To do these things, you go back and forth between clear and obscure, dated and undated pieces, acquiring information by which to pull yourself forward until gaps are filled and contradictions become intelligible. Dumas Malone, for instance, learned from long familiarity with Jefferson's papers that his subject's vocabulary grew more "radical" in writing to younger men. This was a sign not so much of Jefferson's eagerness for a new revolution as of his desire to awaken the coming generation to its responsibility for progress. This fact, once observed, becomes a test for the literalness of some of Jefferson's most advanced proposals. The point of this example is that only an expert— one might even say only *the* expert—is in a position to make sound inferences from a given letter.

Dealing with letters, then, is not a sinecure. It requires an agile mind, or one made such by repeated bafflement and discovery. Consider the simplest of questions: When was this written and to whom? Unless the writer was a regular "dater," or the post office stamped the letter itself, or the envelope has been kept, or the recipient was a methodical person who endorsed each letter with the particulars of its date and bearing, the precious piece of paper may raise more questions than it answers.

For a pair of representative puzzles we may turn to the letters of the composer Hector Berlioz (1803–1869). These letters have kept appearing on the market as the publication of a new Complete Correspondence goes forward. It becomes the scholar's task to fit the new items among the hundreds already classified. Before this can be done, the deficiencies of place, date, or addressee's name must be supplied. Two forms that this operation can take may be briefly illustrated. The A.L.S. says, in French:

19 rue de Boursault,
Thursday June 23

DEAR SIR:

Here is the Table of Contents of the book about which I had the honor of speaking to you. If you will kindly look it over, you will have a rough idea of the subjects dealt with and the general tone of the work. Till next Monday.

Yours faithfully,
HECTOR BERLIOZ

Now the address with which the note starts is in Paris, and it is one at which Berlioz resided from July 1849 till April 1856. (This knowledge comes from a table that the researcher has prepared for himself from a survey of the letters extant.[19]) So the piece to be identified falls within those seven years. The next step is to the perpetual calendar, which gives Thursday, June 23, as falling in 1853. This seems to settle the matter, except that the only book Berlioz had in hand during those years was ready by May 1852 and was published the same December. We are forced to conclude that despite the "Thursday June 23" the note was written not in 1853, but in 1852. This is at once confirmed by the table of domiciles, which shows that in June 1853 Berlioz was in London, not Paris. We know from other instances that he frequently mistook the day of the week. Moreover, in June 1852 the twenty-third falls on a Wednesday; so that, assuming a mistake, his dating would be only one day off. Combining these likelihoods, and knowing also who accepted the book when presented, we conclude that the note was sent to Michel Lévy, a well-known publisher. An inquiry at the present offices of the firm showed that no records of the period were preserved. Internal evidence is therefore our only guide.

The subject of the note just examined was of small moment, but sometimes the identification and collation of an original will rectify a universally held opinion.[20] Witness our second example. In 1846, when Central Europe was seething with nationalistic passion, Berlioz was giving concerts in Hungary and Bohemia and performing there for the first time his rousing *Rákóczy March*. Soon after the premiere, a German periodical got hold of one of his letters to a young Czech musicologist, who was also a patriot, and printed a piece of it as if it were the whole, garbling it in such a way as to turn the message into something of a political document. As late as 1940, when a Hungarian scholar quoted it again in the New York *Musical Quarterly*, no one questioned the letter, and its editor commented on the politico-musical passion it displayed.

Ten years later, in tracking down Berlioz letters in private collec-

---

[19]For this table and examples of the dating techniques, see Jacques Barzun, *New Letters of Berlioz*, 2nd ed., New York, 1974, 304–305 and 273ff.

[20]For further reference to the technique, see Chapter 16, p. 386.

tions, one of the authors of this book was given an opportunity to copy a long letter dated one day before the published one. Suddenly, in the midst of it, familiar words appeared: they were part of the famous "political" letter, which the German paper had garbled and reduced to one paragraph out of eight. In the full text, all but half a dozen lines have to do with music, and these few lines show that the newspaper resorted to grave distortion, while also misdating the letter for reasons no longer ascertainable.[21]

Each such correction may be small in itself, but the cumulative effect over a series filling several volumes may be very great. Moreover, the editor of a famous artist's complete letters never knows when the rectification of a single date or name, unimportant from his point of view, may not resolve the difficulty of someone else who is searching for the verification of other uncertain data.

Disentanglement, or Undoing the Knots in Facts

Not every problem of textual verification is found in rare manuscript letters. Most researchers never use anything but printed sources. Yet these too are full of contradictions that have to be resolved, as are also the inferences from artifacts. Imagine, for instance, an observant student who has noticed that the words "In God We Trust" appear on some of our old coins but not on others, nor on old paper money. Imagine him further as writing a textbook on American history, for which he wants to verify his reasonable guess that the four words in question form the official, yet seemingly optional, motto of the United States.

His first step might be to find out how early in our history the slogan was used on our coins. Thumbing through *The Standard Catalogue of United States Coins*, he would learn that the phrase is not be found before 1864. It first appeared on the bronze two-cent pieces, and two years later on all gold and silver coins. The verifier would also observe that it disappeared from the five-cent piece in 1883 and did not return till 1938. What is more, it appeared on some of the gold coins struck in 1908 and not on others. Clearly, this

[21]Barzun, *New Letters of Berlioz*, 308.

"now-you-see-it, now-you-don't" suggests either fickleness or the probability that inscriptions on American money are not ruled by settled official policy.

Noticing that the picture of Secretary of the Treasury Salmon P. Chase adorns the greenbacks, or paper money, issued during the Civil War, when the motto was first used, the historian might conclude that Chase had a special interest in the design of our money. The obvious course would be to seek more light in a biography of Chase. The surmise about Chase would be wrong but the upshot would carry the researcher one step forward. He would find that although Chase took no interest in the numismatic art, he was a religious man. He put "In God We Trust" on the coins to satisfy a crusading clergyman who thought it imperative. Next, from the issuance of coins both with and without the motto in 1908, our scholar would correctly conclude that the choice lay within the discretion of the Secretary of the Treasury.

No sooner would he be confident that the motto had no official standing than he would discover in his research a newspaper story about the decision of Congress—ninety-two years after Chase's—to make the words official and inscribe them on all the currency, both metal and paper.[22]

Note by way of summary that this verifier had to consult a coin catalogue, one or more books about Chase, one or more about Theodore Roosevelt for the events of 1908, and a newspaper file before he could solve his puzzle.

Clarification, or Destroying Myths

The amount of verifying one does depends not only on one's own curiosity but also on the grasp of one's subject that one possesses at the start. The more one understands at the beginning, the more one finds to question and ascertain. It is expected, of course, that the

---

[22]Bill signed by President Eisenhower, July 30, 1956. The President offered no public comment on the occasion. Since then, a silver dollar memorializing Susan B. Anthony, the women's rights leader, has been coined, bearing the motto. Her admirers have objected that "she trusted no deity" and might have agreed with the Texas woman, head of an atheist group, who petitioned the Supreme Court to order the removal of the motto. The whole series of facts from 1864 on are indicators for the social and cultural historian.

FIGURE 12   *Fiction into Fact*

XVII

BOARD OF INLAND REVENUE *v.*
HADDOCK; REX *v.* HADDOCK

THE NEGOTIABLE COW

'WAS the cow crossed?'
  'No, your worship, it was an open cow.'
  These and similar passages provoked laughter at Bow
Street to-day when the Negotiable Cow case was concluded.
  *Sir Joshua Hoot, K.C. (appearing for the Public Prose-
cutor)*: Sir Basil, these summonses, by leave of the Court,
are being heard together, an unusual but convenient arrangement.
  The defendant, Mr. Albert Haddock, has for many
months, in spite of earnest endeavours on both sides, been
unable to establish harmonious relations between himself
and the Collector of Taxes. The Collector maintains that
Mr. Haddock should make over a large part of his earn-
ings to the Government. Mr. Haddock replies that the proportion demanded is excessive, in view of the inadequate
services or consideration which he himself has received
from that Government. After an exchange of endearing
letters, telephone calls, and even cheques, the sum demanded was reduced to fifty-seven pounds; and about this
sum the exchange of opinions continued.

 **PHYLLIS BATTELLE**
Write A Cow Check?

  Imagine writing a check on a tobacco
pouch, and telling the teller to stick that in
his pipe and cash it. Fun? Boy!
  Regulation J came to my attention a few
weeks ago when the New York Public Library received a $20,000 check drafted on a
specially-designed scarf from R. J. Rey-
nolds Industries, which underwrote a fashion show for the benefit of the library. The
idea for the scarf-check was to grab attention. It did. The First National City Bank in
New York promptly cashed it.
  Savvy people — especially when angry
— have benefitted from the regulation. A
Mr. and Mrs. Haldock, incensed at what
they considered an unjust tax levy, presented their tax collector with a check written on the side of their cow. The collector
said it was ridiculous, and took the case to
court, where the judge looked into the law
and ruled the bovine was negotiable. The
assessor returned to his office with the
cow's left hoofprint on the tax return.
  An Elmira, N. Y., woman literally took
the shirt off her husband's back and wrote a
check on it for a creditor. A Charlottesville,
Va., man paid his telephone bill with a
check written on a coconut.

In a book published in 1935 (its parts having appeared serially in *Punch*),
A. P. Herbert included one of his "Misleading Cases"—parodies of the law.
His regular hero, the plaintiff Albert Haddock, attempts to bedevil the
Revenue service by sending to it a check written on the side of a cow. Forty
years later, in an American syndicated column, the same "fact" is related as
having occurred in the United States. A couple reported as being a Mr. and
Mrs. Haldock, are credited with the use of the promissory cow. The change
of name and venue strongly suggests that the original idea was transmitted by
word of mouth through a great many storytellers. (A "crossed" check—see
dialogue above—is one marked with two parallel lines across the front; it can
then be cashed only by the payee.)

researcher into any subject will approach it with a well-developed
sense of time—whether the time be the few weeks or months of a
particular crisis or the centuries separating St. Augustine from St.
Thomas. Thus the narrator of the French Revolution or the First
World War proceeds by days in those fateful summer and autumn

months, whereas the historian of Rome must without stumbling move across a span of twenty generations.

But the investigator's original fund of knowledge must embrace even more than a well-populated chronology; it must include an understanding of how people in other eras lived and behaved, what they believed, and how they managed their institutions. This kind of mastery fills the mind with images and also with questions, which, when answered and discussed, make for what we term depth. Meanwhile the funded information suggests the means for conducting the research.

Consider the sort of inquiry that leads to the exploding of a great myth, which is to say one that is old, widespread, and regarded as "a well-known truth." The importance of verifying or disproving such myths is that new ideas are often based on them. Thus a reputable psychiatrist's study of the states of mind of dying patients drew from his clinical researches conclusions affecting our present culture. Unfortunately, he buttressed them with historical statements, one of which is a myth:

> When the first millennium after the birth of Christ approached its end, Occidental man was seized by the fear of and hope for the Lord's return. The end of the world was envisaged, which meant man's final end [sic] had arrived. With the approach of the second millennium, the conviction again has spread that the days of man are counted. . . .[23]

That this parallel is false in every respect will be clear if we retrace the path of the scholar who more than eighty years ago disposed of the legend about the end of the world coming in the year 1000.[24]

His first step was to discover when the tale originally came out in print. He found that this was in a 1690 edition of a late-fifteenth-century chronicle. Thus the first public record of the story is found about seven hundred years after the supposed date of doom. Seven hundred years is a long time—about twice the span since

[23]K. R. Eissler, *The Psychiatrist and the Dying Patient*, New York, 1955, 108.

[24]George L. Burr, "The Year 1000 and the Antecedents of the Crusades," *American Historical Review*, 6 (April 1901), 429–439.

Shakespeare's death, three and a half times since the Declaration of Independence. By the eighteenth century, a period when the Middle Ages were in disrepute and instances of their superstition were gladly seized on, the published tale of 1690 referring to an event seven centuries earlier was first widely circulated. Indeed, it became usual to ascribe the launching of the Crusades to the relief felt by the Christians when the end of the world did not come in A.D. 1000. This emotion was also said to account for the remarkable increase in church building. Although these several explanations were discredited by nineteenth-century historians, educated people have continued to believe the myth. The terror of the year 1000 has been the core of many a piece of moralizing. Said one confident writer of the 1880s about the people of A.D. 999:

> Some squandered their substance in riotous living, others bestowed it for the salvation of their souls on churches and convents, bewailing multitudes lay by day and by night about the altars, many looked with terror, yet most with secret hope, for the conflagration of the earth and the falling of the heavens.[25]

In the face of such vivid, though belated, reports, what could make a thoughtful scholar suspect the truth of the whole episode? The answer is his intimate knowledge of the Middle Ages.

George Burr knew, to begin with, that the end of the world had been foretold so often that only the ignorant in the year 1000 would seriously believe a new rumor. Moreover, long before that year, it had become orthodox belief and teaching that if the end of the world were really to come no one would know the time in advance.

Third, he knew that however impressive round numbers based on the decimal system are to us, they had no such hold on the imagination of medieval man. The numerals of that era were the Roman Is, Vs, Xs, Ls, Cs, Ds, and Ms. For the Middle Ages no magic property would attach to "The Year M." Rather, mystery and significance would have been connected with 3s, 7s, 12s and their multiples. For these were the sacred numbers of the Jews, and the Christians had repeatedly used them for prophecy.

---

[25]H. v. Sybel, *Geschichte des ersten Kreuzzugs*, 2nd and rev. ed., Leipzig, 1881, 150; quoted in Burr, *op. cit.*, 429.

Fourth, our scholar knew that the Christian calendar did not come into general use until after 1000. And even then there was no agreement on dating. Nor was this the only difficulty arising from the calendar. When did the year 1000 begin? At Christmas, at Annunciation, at Easter, on the first of March (as in Venice), at the vernal equinox (as in Russia), on the first of September (as in the Greek Empire), or on the first of January (as in Spain)? In such a state of things the world obviously could not end everywhere on schedule.

Fifth, our accomplished medievalist knew that bare numerical dates meant little or nothing to the ordinary medieval man. He guided his life by the feast and fast days of the Church, not, as we do, by engagement books in which not merely the days, months, and years are marked, but the hours and half-hours, A.M. and P.M. We carry watches and consult them every few minutes. Medieval time, differently divided, was of a different texture.[26]

In short, it is profoundly unhistorical to read back our habits and behavior into a past era, and the conclusion is plain: taking the lack of any contemporaneous evidence of panic together with the facts of daily life and thought in the Middle Ages, the scholar demolishes a legend whose potent effects would continue to mislead researchers in cognate fields if his work had not enlightened at least a part of the educated public.

The dissemination of historical knowledge tends to be slow in proportion as the error is dramatic and "fitting." Thus the late Henri Focillon, a scholar highly respected in France and well known as a lecturer in the United States, acknowledges in his last, unfinished work, *The Year One Thousand* (1969), that historians doubt the "terrors" of that year. But he finds it "convenient" to keep up the myth in his first chapter. He writes about "the approach of the fateful date. . . . But the year passes, the world is not destroyed, mankind breathes relief and sets out on a new road."[27]

Again, like the year 1000, the capture of Constantinople by the Turks in 1453 has struck the general imagination and provided a

---

[26]On this vast technological change, see David S. Landes, *Revolution in Time: Clocks and the Making of the Modern World*, Cambridge, Mass., 1983.

[27]The latest reiteration of the fiction, which now appears perdurable, is in a front-page review of Mario Varga Llosa's novel, *The War of the End of the World* (New York, 1984) in the *New York Times Book Review*, August 12, 1984.

convenient "cause" for Columbus's discovery of America: European traders could no longer go East; they sought a westward passage. As late as 1967, this notion was used to introduce the visitor to a superb exhibition of the Dutch in Manhattan at the Museum of the City of New York. Professor A. H. Lybyer, who conclusively disproved the connection between the Turks and westward voyages, had published his study exactly fifty-two years earlier.[28]

Identification, or Ascertaining Worth through Authorship

Sometimes a problem of verification is solved by reaching behind your desk and taking down the apt reference book that contains the fact you need.[29] Sometimes a day or two in the library is required. More often the task becomes for a time one's central occupation.

This is almost sure to be true when the problem is to trace the unnamed or disputed authorship of a large and important document. If there is no chance of examining and comparing handwritings, because the document exists only in print, the undertaking can be extremely difficult. Even with a manuscript original one may be foiled by the fact that it is the work of an amanuensis. One example of the reverse confusion is the recent discovery regarding Alexander Hamilton's most famous state paper, the classic Report on Manufactures of 1791. With his other two Reports, on Public Credit and on the Bank, it is known to have helped launch America on the road to industrialization. But did Hamilton himself write that influential document? An impertinent question to some people, it was a necessary and obvious one to Jacob E. Cooke, an authority on early American history. Some historians had long speculated on the Report's authorship, but two recent scholarly works had declared that Hamilton himself was indeed the author.

[28]"The Ottoman Turks and the Routes of Oriental Trade," *English Historical Review*, 120 (October 1915), 577–588.

[29]The researcher will soon discover that reference books frequently disagree. This does not always mean that all are wrong except one; what happens is that one book in giving, say, the date of a treaty will give the year of its signing, and another book the date of its ratification, months later. Similar disparities can and do occur about most events, private and public, so that the "right" date is frequently a conventional choice among several possibilities.

Cooke began by satisfying himself from printed sources that Tench Coxe, Assistant Secretary of the Treasury under Hamilton, had played an important role in the drafting of the report. Beyond that Cooke could not go. What was the evidence at large?

1. In January 1790 the House of Representatives called upon the Secretary of the Treasury—Hamilton—to prepare "a plan or plans" for the encouragement of manufacture.

2. Hamilton, not being expert in the subject, cast about for information, sending a circular of inquiry to organizations that were promoting the idea of manufacturing. Among these was a Philadelphia society whose spokesman, nationally known for his zeal on the subject, was Tench Coxe.

3. Coxe's response to the inquiry was a long paper on the country's needs, which concurred with Hamilton's own views.

4. Hamilton appointed Coxe Assistant Secretary of the Treasury in May 1790, and assigned him the task of preparing a report on manufacturing in the United States and how to improve and increase it.

5. Coxe quickly assembled his facts and composed the report "perhaps in a day or two." His data were at his fingertips.

6. A comparison between Coxe's draft—the only one he prepared—and the report Hamilton submitted to Congress in December 1791 shows a remarkable similarity of principles and proposals. The articles of manufacture Coxe deemed indispensable to America were essentially those Hamilton listed six months later.

An historian writing some years ago had concluded that Hamilton was sole author of the Report because the manuscript is mostly in his handwriting—good circumstantial evidence, but not infallible. In 1965, the *Hamilton Papers* project at Columbia University—of which Cooke was an editor—obtained access to a draft of the Coxe report and unknowingly accepted it as complete. It seemed to follow that Hamilton's Report was his own because it was significantly different from Coxe's draft.

But Cooke persisted, unsatisfied with the conclusion he had helped to draw. For he knew that Coxe was a doer and promoter—

twenty years an advocate of manufacturing—who would hardly have served Hamilton as mere researcher and passive amanuensis. Yet no proof could be had until the opening of the Coxe papers, which was delayed until 1973. The mass of manuscripts had become scrambled in the 175 years since Coxe's death; seven full pages and two partial pages of Coxe's work for Hamilton had become separated from the rest. Cooke recognized them among other, unrelated documents and was able to confirm his lingering suspicion. He could now declare with authority: "The famous report indubitably bore the imprint of Hamilton's own ideas and program. . . . Hamilton doubtless relied on whatever sources were at hand, but when the lineage of the Report on Manufactures is traced, the major threads are found to lead to Tench Coxe."[30]

Patience, a mature sense of how public affairs are conducted, and a willingness to alter a judgment he himself had once committed to print led to findings that compel us to modify, at least in some degree, the view of Hamilton as the intellectual planner of industrial America. For the researcher, the moral is not only "Don't give up till you are satisfied"; it is also "Don't be afraid to write that difficult sentence: I was mistaken."

Of all the problems of authorship in American history, that of finding out who wrote "The Diary of a Public Man" has been the most gigantic. Indeed, the odyssey on which it took the chief investigator is unparalleled. The document first appeared in 1879 in four installments published by the influential *North American Review*. Covering the winter of Secession, 1860–1861, the diary consists of entries for twenty-one days between December 28, 1860, and March 15, 1861. A fact of central importance to the user of the diary and, as we shall see, to the verifier, is that on twenty of these days the author was in Washington; on one, February 20, 1861, he was in New York City.

The value of the document may be gauged from the fact that it is the only source for a number of incidents about Lincoln's acts during

[30]*William and Mary Quarterly*, 3rd series, 32 (July 1975), 369–392. How such extensive research is incorporated unobstrusively in a life of the principal is seen in Jacob Ernest Cooke, *Alexander Hamilton*, New York, 1982, p. 98f.

the crisis of the Union. Among its more picturesque revelations is the account of Douglas's conduct at Lincoln's inauguration, which schoolchildren have learned ever since: "A miserable little rickety table had been provided for the President, on which he could hardly find room for his hat, and Senator Douglas, reaching forward, took it with a smile and held it during the delivery of the address. It was a trifling act, but a symbolic one, and not to be forgotten, and it attracted much attention all around me."

Who then was "me"? Professor Frank Maloy Anderson spent nearly thirty-five years trying to find the answer.[31] His undeviating pursuit of truth must surely count as the most tireless and single-minded of any in the history of verification. The fact that the question is still in dispute does not lessen the utility of his labors or their exemplary value for the researcher. Every attempt at verification advances knowledge, whether or not luck rewards the effort.

Anderson's earliest move—in 1913, a long generation after the "Diary" appeared—was to try to identify the document by external means. He wanted to find out how the *North American Review* had received it in the first place. The editor of the *Review*, he discovered, had refused to discuss the question at the time of publication and his papers had disappeared after his death. The publisher, D. Appleton and Company, had acted as printer and distributor only and therefore had no record of payments to the contributor. Mr. Anderson then shifted course, in several steps:

1. He tried to discover if persons mentioned in the "Diary" had been interviewed in 1879 by journalists attempting to identify the author.

2. He examined the files of fifty important newspapers and magazines to find out if they had discussed the likely authorship of the document when it first appeared.

3. He investigated the qualifications for authorship of a number of persons previously suggested.

[31] *The Mystery of "A Public Man": A Historical Detective Story*, Minneapolis, 1948.

When these efforts yielded nothing, Mr. Anderson tackled the question: What *kind* of person was the writer? A Senator? He found in the *Congressional Globe* the names of the Senators absent from their places on February 20, 1861, but none of them fulfilled the Diarist's description of himself as a man of "long experience in Washington." A member of the House of Representatives? He eliminated for various reasons each of the fifty-four Representatives who were absent on that day. It seemed highly suggestive that the Diarist nowhere refers to the proceedings of the House. What were his politics? Whig? Republican? Democrat? Was he a Southerner? A New Englander? The text provided no conclusive evidence that the man had been one of these things more than another.

Mr. Anderson now decided to list the characteristics of the man that he thought he could discern in the "Diary." The most important were:

1. He was a man of weight in Washington: the entries show that his advice and prestige were enlisted by important people who had to deal with Lincoln.

2. He was a tall man. (Lincoln, he reports, asked him if he had ever matched backs with Charles Sumner, who was a tall man.)[32]

3. He was an experienced writer, who knew the French language.

4. He was a sophisticated man of the world, amused that Lincoln had worn *black* gloves to the opera.

5. He had many well-placed friends, and he himself had long resided in Washington.

6. He was devoted to the cause of the Union, but knew the South well.

7. He had met Lincoln in 1848 and again in 1861, but the Diarist had no recollection of the earlier meeting. ("I can not place him even with the help of all the pictures I have seen of such an extraordinary looking mortal.")

[32] According to the New York *Herald* for December 28, 1871, Sumner was "six feet three inches high," though on Sumner's passport his height is indicated as six feet two. David Donald, *Charles Sumner and the Coming of the Civil War*, New York, 1960, 27.

8. He was interested in business conditions and especially in tariff, patent, and postal problems.

9. He frequently attended the sessions of the Senate.

10. He was an intimate of William H. Seward and Stephen A. Douglas.

11. He was familiar with New York City and on easy terms with its leading citizens.

12. He was in New York on February 20, 1861, and in Washington on twenty other days between December 28, 1860, and March 15, 1861.

Mr. Anderson's search was correspondingly detailed and thorough. A long list of possibilities was methodically reduced, one by one, until the name of Amos Kendall[33] emerged as the best candidate. Imagine the researcher's excitement as point after point of Kendall's life and personality met the requirements: he was tall; he had traveled extensively in the South; he had for fifteen years been involved in patent litigation, as a result of his association with S.F.B. Morse, chief inventor of the telegraph; he was a former postmaster-general. Would such a man have spent a great deal of time in the Senate galleries? Of course—the Senate in the Secession Winter had before it a bill to renew the Morse telegraph patent.

Every requirement Mr. Anderson had established for the Diarist, Amos Kendall met—all except one, which would now require the closest investigation. Was Kendall in New York on February 20, 1861? The evidence showed that Morse had left New York to visit Washington on February 19. It seems certain that he stayed with the Kendalls in the capital. Only the most urgent business, therefore, could have brought Amos Kendall to New York during Morse's visit.

Mr. Anderson studied the lists of hotel arrivals that were published in the New York newspapers, in vain. Next he learned that Kendall, whenever he came to New York, stayed at the Astor House. If only Mr. Anderson could put his hands on the hotel register! His heart must have skipped a beat when he heard that the brother of a

---

[33] Amos Kendall (1789–1869) is best known as an important member of Andrew Jackson's "Kitchen Cabinet."

woman working at the Morgan Library in New York had been the last manager of the old Astor. Maybe he knew where the registers were deposited. Alas, he did not.

Now Mr. Anderson recalled that as a boy in Minneapolis he had distributed a newspaper called the *Hotel Gazette*, which listed hotel arrivals, and he remembered hearing at the time that all big cities had such a paper. He set out to find the name of the one in New York. After much effort he discovered a reference to *The Transcript*. Now to find a file of it. There was one at Yale, but to his dismay it lacked the issues he needed. Back from New Haven, he went to the New-York Historical Society. The catalogue showed no *Transcript*, but Mr. Anderson, running his eye down the list of newspaper headings, noticed *The Daily Transcript*. The file proved to be complete for the desired period. With mixed doubt and delight, the researcher found that the issue for February 19, 1861, contained an entry for a "J. Kendall" at the Astor House. Was this a misprint for "A. Kendall"? Or was this Amos's nephew J. E. Kendall, or perhaps Amos's son John, who had recently moved to New York?

Whoever it was, Amos Kendall's presence in New York could not yet be established beyond a doubt. Mr. Anderson now turned to establishing his man's presence in Washington on the stated twenty days. The evidence conclusively proved that Kendall could *not* be the Diarist, for on at least two of the critical days he had certainly not been in Washington. No one, perhaps, can adequately describe Professor Anderson's feelings as he struck Kendall's name off the list.

Because no other figure had come so close as Kendall to matching the requirements, Mr. Anderson now tried another line of investigation. Was the document authentic? A number of points had already given the scholar pause:

1. Virtually all the persons mentioned in the document were dead by the time of its publication in 1879.

2. The dashes that replaced the names of other persons appeared to stand for fictitious characters, because few could be identified from the context.

3. The "Diary" was usually vague on points about which a diarist could be expected to be precise.

4. There was a suspiciously large number of quotable remarks ascribed to Lincoln.

5. A good many striking incidents were recorded for what is after all a brief span.

6. The Diarist's uncanny penetration in judging men and events was unusual for a contemporaneous reporter.

7. A good many important facts contained in the "Diary" could not be confirmed by any other source.

8. The polished style of the "Diary" contrasted with the expectable carelessness of diary-keepers.

Mr. Anderson's examination of the Diarist's account of his interviews with Lincoln now raised many questions about their truthfulness; and among the anecdotes, that of Douglas's holding Lincoln's hat seemed diagnostic. After exhausting research Mr. Anderson found only one contemporaneous account of this incident and in a dubious source—poor evidence indeed for such a striking fact, especially considering all that had been written by eyewitnesses about the inauguration. Mr. Anderson, moreover, showed convincingly that the Diarist's portraits of Douglas and Seward reflected the historical estimate of those men rather than the contemporary one of 1860–61.

Mr. Anderson decided that he could now entertain two hypotheses: (1) the "Diary" was a work of fiction; or (2) it was a combination of fiction and truth.

Mr. Anderson accepted the second alternative because he could not find a single instance of what is common in complete fabrications—the Diarist slipping up and referring to something provably false.

At long last, then, the original question, "Who was the Diarist?" had become "Who was the fabricator?" An inspiration came to him while he was engaged on a quite different project. He suddenly thought of a man who had been in Washington in the Secession Winter and who was a friend of Seward's. This was Samuel Ward, brother of Julia Ward Howe, who wrote "The Battle Hymn of the Republic."

Indefatigably again, Mr. Anderson went in pursuit of his quarry. For fifteen years he tracked down Ward's relatives and descendants to find the private letters from which he could learn enough about the man to confirm his new hypothesis. The facts of Ward's life fitted the image given in the "Diary." Known as "King of the Lobby," Ward was a familiar figure in Washington; he was in that city during the Secession Winter; his acquaintance was extensive; he was said to have kept a diary; he was a man of the world who unquestionably knew French; he was a strong Unionist; he was interested in business, especially in the tariff, coastwise trade, patents, and postal matters; he was a New Yorker, on close terms with his leading fellow citizens; he disliked Sumner and would have ridiculed him with pleasure as the Diarist obviously did; he was an admiring intimate of Seward's and an acquaintance of Douglas's.

At last Mr. Anderson was able to answer a number of his own critical questions. First, why the "Diary" stopped abruptly with the entry for March 15, 1861. This was obviously because Ward left Washington to accompany on a tour of the Confederate States the London journalist William H. Russell, who had landed in New York on March 16. Second, who the people were who appeared in the "Diary" by dashes or initials. They were Ward's close friends, and their remarks formed the fictitious parts of the document.

The search for the "Public Man" had apparently ended. As Mr. Anderson left the question, Sam Ward had spun his fiction around a core of genuine diary. Blessed with an uncanny memory and considerable literary gifts, Ward was the kind of man who would have delighted in perpetrating a hoax.[34] The editor of the *North American Review* was no doubt a party to the imposture, which would account for his silence. The "Diary" fooled many researchers because its foundation was genuine; thanks to its grounding in fact, no discrepan-

---

[34]The fashioning of a "contemporary" narrative by carefully piecing together the fruits of research is always possible, and when the author is accomplished its exposure may be as laborious as the manufacture. In the 1960s a book appeared in England, entitled *Flashman: From the Flashman Papers, 1839–42*, which purported to be the memoirs of Brigadier General Sir Harry Page Flashman, V.C., a celebrated Victorian soldier who fought in India and Afghanistan and had as many scrapes and affairs as honors and royal thanks. The ostensible editor of the work, George MacDonald Fraser, was highly praised by his reviewers, of whom ten out of thirty four (in the United States) were deceived into believing the memoirs authentic. An attentive reader could note certain phrasings and uses of words that did not belong to the period, but they were few, and it took a sharp eye to catch them. Semantics, too, is part of a verifier's resources.

cies can be shown. Yet for the historian—except the one who writes Sam Ward's biography—the document is worthless.[35]

Not all historians accept Mr. Anderson's findings.[36] Some advance objections to the verifier's reasoning from the text and propose other candidates for the honor of authorship. But almost every disputant agrees with the conclusion that the work itself is a hybrid of fact and fiction, which leaves its documentary value precisely what Professor Anderson showed it to be: nil. This result of his scholarship thus justifies the time, labor, and ingenuity it cost.

Few researchers will choose, or be confronted with, a problem of the magnitude of Mr. Anderson's, but occasions arise when the contents of an otherwise acceptable book raise doubts in the reader which, whether or not he is just then "researching," he feels he wants to settle. For example, many books of the seventeenth and eighteenth centuries are attributed falsely to famous authors. And there is the matter of sequels: four were written after the great success of Voltaire's *Candide*, none of them by Voltaire.[37] The practice of using pseudonyms only heightens the confusion, and it is not generated only by forgers and imitators. Voltaire himself is said to have published under 160 pseudonyms and Franklin under 57. In the early nineteenth century, one L.A.C. Bombet published a book called *The Lives of Haydn, Mozart, and Metastasio*; it had had some currency in France and was translated into English. Copies of it occasionally

---

[35]Lately Thomas (the pseudonym of Robert V. Steele), in his *Sam Ward: "King of the Lobby"* (Boston, 1965), calls "unwarranted" the attribution of the "Diary" to Ward. But Thomas includes it in his Bibliography as a valuable "source reference for the world of Washington in Sam Ward's time."

[36]See, for example, Evelyn Page, "The Diary and the Public Man," *New England Quarterly*, 22 (June 1949), 147–172; Roy N. Lokken, "Has the Mystery of 'A Public Man' Been Solved?" *Mississippi Valley Historical Review*, 40 (December 1953), 419–435; Anderson's reply and Lokken's rejoinder, *ibid.*, 42 (June 1955), 101–109; and Benjamin M. Price, "That Baffling Diary," *South Atlantic Quarterly*, 54 (January 1955), 56–64. Professor Jerome L. Sternstein, in the course of research on the Civil War era some years ago, found a manuscript letter dated 1909 from Edgar T. Welles, the son of Lincoln's Secretary of the Navy, in which Welles says that he has finally decided that the authorship of the "Diary" "belongs to Sam Ward." Thus, we have a contemporary's opinion that Ward was the man—a piece of testimony that Anderson had vainly sought.

[37]For a long while, one of these sequels was regularly reprinted as Part 2 of *Candide* in a popular series of classic texts, giving the reader the false notion that Voltaire had had second thoughts about his "unhappy ending."

appear in modern catalogues of second-hand books under that author's name. But you will not find Bombet in any French biographical dictionary; for he is in fact Henri Beyle, otherwise Stendhal, the great novelist of *The Red and the Black* and *The Charterhouse of Parma*. To top it all, his *Lives* are largely copied from Carpani and five other writers—a mosaic of plagiarisms, though done with verve and genius.

How does one find one's way through such mazes of deliberate or accidental misdirection? For an author as famous as Bernard Shaw, consult the critical bibliography that has undoubtedly been compiled about him. It turns out to be by Dan H. Laurence and it occupies two stout volumes.[38] For lesser and earlier writers, go to *The Bibliographical History of Anonyma and Pseudonyma* by Archer Taylor and Fredric J. Mosher, which lists many dictionaries and other reference works likely to afford help. Their discussion of the problems will by itself spur the imagination to find the path of discovery. For recent or contemporary writers, some dictionaries of authors such as the *International Authors and Writers Who's Who* will give lists of pseudonyms. But take care! These are not all accurate and must be cross-checked, either by consulting a list in a solider-looking work, or more simply by looking up the catalogue of the national library—British Library, Library of Congress, etc. Finally, the authenticity or genuineness of a text will prove relatively easy if there is a large, scholarly, so-called definitive biography of the (real) author, for these questions are bound to be taken up as part of the story of his life.

Going through a search of this kind incidentally suggests that for scholarly work (as against recreation) it is important to get hold of an author's best text. This usually, but not invariably, means the latest. The preface will tell you what the editor has done or not done, and the "apparatus"—footnotes and appendices—will show what kind of information has been gathered as a help to understanding. Judging the thing itself is the only guarantee, because even reputable publishers and "series" make mistakes. *Candide* is one example. The universally accepted text of James Joyce's *Ulysses* provides another—a desperate case. Not until 1984—upwards of forty years after the first publication during the author's lifetime—did someone discover

[38]Clarendon Press, Oxford, 1983.

that the transcriber of the manuscript had permitted himself omissions and transpositions amounting to some 5,000 misrepresentations of Joyce's work.

No historian can hope to unravel every mystery and contradiction or uncover every untruth, half-truth, or downright deception that lurks in the raw materials with which he must deal. But his unceasing demand for accuracy must make him put to the test all the materials he uses. There is no substitute for well-placed skepticism.

6

Handling Ideas

Fact and Idea: An Elusive Distinction

Daily speech encourages the belief that "a fact is a fact" and that it is useless to argue about it. And indeed it would be idle to dispute about pure fact. Yet we know that argument continues—in politics, science, the arts, family life, casual conversation, and the insides of books. A library is a sort of ammunition dump of unexploded arguments ready to burst forth the moment a live reader opens a book. Why should this be, if we assume that most books—aside from fiction—honestly attempt to deal with verified facts?

The answer is that facts seldom occur pure, free from interpretation or ideas. We all make the familiar distinction between "gathering facts" and "expressing ideas," but in reality most of the facts we gather come dripping with ideas. We may or may not be aware of these ideas as we move the facts about from the printed page to our minds, our notes, and our reports, but there they are, clinging together nevertheless. The only pure facts in any kind of reporting are those statements that express a conventional relation in conventional terms:

Thomas Jefferson was born on April 2, 1743.[1]
The Monroe Doctrine was promulgated on December 2, 1823.
President Garfield was shot by Charles J. Guiteau.

Through conventional phrasings like "born" and "was shot," conventional names like "Monroe Doctrine," and conventional terms for day, year, and length are expressed fixed relations of time, things, and persons.[2] These relations may be said to be strictly factual because each term is clear and distinct and remains so by tacit agreement. No one disputes the calendar, not even the Muslim, for whom the Christian year 1743 is the year 1156. Both calendars are conventions and their numbers are convertible.[3]

But if in the Garfield example we add to the phrase "shot by Charles J. Guiteau," the words "a disappointed office-seeker," we immediately pass from conventional fact into a different realm of discourse. True, it is a fact that Guiteau had sought a government post and had failed to get it. But putting these events into a phrase next to the statement of Garfield's assassination generates an idea. The effect is to say: "Guiteau's disappointment was the motive for the assassination." This is an inference, a hypothesis, an idea. No law of nature declares that all disgruntled officeholders shoot their President. A psychoanalyst might maintain that the cause alleged was not sufficient; that Garfield was shot because he had a beard that reminded the killer of his stepfather; that, in any case, all human acts result from more than one motive.[4]

[1] Or April 13 according to the New Style calendar, which came into effect in 1752. See Chapter 4, p. 91.

[2] Conventions may vary with time and place: among a remote tribe in Burma, a child at birth is considered to be sixty and its age decreases yearly. *So it is said.* We have not yet set out to verify.

[3] The Moslem year is computed from the Hejira, or Flight of Mohammed, in A.D. 622. Since it is a lunar year, it is shorter than ours, and this accounts for the fact that 622 plus 1156 equals more than 1743.

[4] The complexity of Guiteau's motives as they are now understood is examined by a medical historian, Charles E. Rosenberg, in *The Trial of the Assassin Guiteau: Psychiatry and the Law in the Gilded Age*, Chicago, 1968. See also the study "Symbolic Aspects of Presidential Assassination," by E. A. Weinstein and O. G. Lyerly *Psychiatry*, 32 (February 1969), 1–11, from which it appears that some of the assassins look upon the President as a substitute *mother*-figure. Another contribution to the subject is Annalise Pontius, "Threats to Assassinate the King-President While Propitiating Mother," *Journal of Analytical Psychology*, 19 (January 1974), 38–53.

Historians, it is true, do not dispute the simple idea of disappointment as the motive for Garfield's murder. This may be because no great issue hangs upon it. But historians go on to say that, owing to this motive, the shooting of the President swung public opinion in favor of Civil Service reform—a further idea for which there is good evidence, but which, once again, is not a mere fact of convention.

What then is an idea? In a large dictionary you may find upwards of forty definitions, which shows how indistinct the term is. Nor is this to be regretted, because ideas correspond to the substance of our inner life, which is also fluid, indefinite, and changeable, besides being (as we know) very powerful and (as we say) "very real." For our purposes as reporters of the past we may put it that an idea is *an image, inference, or suggestion that goes beyond the data namable in conventional terms.*

This definition is merely a convenient one to keep in mind at this stage of our work as researchers and reporters; it may not be applicable elsewhere. The statement of a fact gives the impression of ending with itself, whereas an idea leads us on. Once you have ascertained that the Monroe Doctrine was promulgated in a presidential message to Congress on December 2, 1823, what then? Any question that arises must be supplied from outside the fact: Was the doctrine really the work of one man or the joint product of Monroe, Canning, and Adams's efforts? Is the doctrine of 1823 precisely the same as the one referred to under the same name since? Did the United States have the right to make such a declaration? Did it have the power to enforce it? These questions are ideas. They suggest doubts and possibilities. We know in a rough way what they involve, but before they can be answered they have to be further narrowed down and studied in relation to "facts," as well as compared with other "ideas" in the minds of hundreds, living and dead. As a result, the authoritative work on the Monroe Doctrine by Dexter Perkins is in three volumes totaling over 1,300 pages.

It is obvious that History-as-Event is not made up of facts alone, but of facts merged in ideas. The Monroe Doctrine's influence on the course of hemisphere history has derived from its being a powerful idea. From time to time this idea has been reinforced and also modified by such facts as the following:

French power is supporting the Austrian Maximilian in Mexico.
The Special Task Force has landed on Grenada.
The Soviet Union subsidizes the Castro regime.

Fact and idea in ceaseless interplay constitute the stuff of experience; or rather, in the seamless stuff of experience that we ponder within ourselves or report to others, we learn to make a distinction between the agreed-upon element of fact and the variable element of idea. This does not mean that ideas are less certain. It does mean that the report-maker, in order to be accurate, goes to work differently on each. There is a technique to be learned for the handling of ideas.

With facts, as we saw in the last chapter, the reporter's effort is to be exact about the conventional terms—names, dates, titles, and other agreed-upon details. With ideas he must be no less exacting, though he cannot ever receive the same assurance of accuracy in return for his pains. Yet his main role is to manage those more difficult matters with deftness and judgment; he is of use to others only insofar as he reports ideas intelligibly and precisely, for the "bare facts" generally do not *interest*, in the sense of engaging attention. Even the chronicler and the statistician hazard comments and conclusions, and these are ideas.

But before we take up the means by which special care about ideas is to be exercised, we have to consider still another aspect of ideas in history.

Large Ideas as Facts of History

By defining ideas as accretions upon conventional fact, we separated into two parts what most people rightly treat as one unit of thought: "Jefferson was a great President." We now know how to analyze this into the conventional part: "Jefferson was a President"; and the debatable part: "his greatness." But this distinction does not cover "ideas" in the large, notable, historic sense—the idea of Evolution, the ideas in the Declaration of Independence, Nietzsche's ideas: these and a million more have the property of being facts as well: they *occurred*. Like any other event they have a place and a date. But their history is not easily reducible to conventional terms.

For example, how would you date the idea of Evolution? Some textbooks say, "By his publication of *The Origin of Species* in 1859, Darwin established the idea of Evolution in Western thought." But research shows that similar ideas had made a stir in Western thought for a whole century before 1859. The contradiction would seem to hinge on the meaning of "established"—except that *The Origin of Species* did not immediately persuade mankind, but set off a violent controversy that lasted twenty years. Faced with these complications, we may wonder what we mean by "a great idea" and its destiny.

Obviously, when we speak of ideas on this scale we are not talking about a *single* entity. Evolution is not one and the same idea from the beginning; nor was it after it came to be recognized and accepted with the passage of years. Darwin himself was not putting forward Evolution but what he believed to be a means (not *the* means) of evolution, namely Natural Selection, and on the precise role of this means he himself varied his estimate in the six editions of his book. Ideas, in short, are neither single things nor simple things. To illustrate this truth by another example, what are the so-called ideas of the Declaration of Independence? We know they were clear and governing ideas to Lincoln and presumably to his American contemporaries, but in his speeches he had to demonstrate their meaning and validity again and again. In his time and ours, those same ideas have been called "glittering generalities" (in blame, though without showing what is wrong with generalities or why they should not glitter). As for the theory of natural rights underlying the Declaration, it is almost everywhere disputed by people who in practice uphold the principles of the Declaration.

It is evident that the domain of ideas is full of unexpected turns, misleading appearances, pitfalls of every kind. And since ideas cling to every important fact, since ideas are what make the fact important and interesting, the reporters of events will fall into one trap after another if they are not adept at handling ideas. They must not only infer correct ideas from the evidence they have marshaled; they must also be critical about all the minds through which the facts have passed, not least their own. In other words, the management of ideas is the part of historical and other reporting in which the virtue of self-awareness must be acute, vigilant, and sustained. Perceptiveness about ideas is the duty of every moment, to exactly the same degree than in factual verification a sharp eye for dates, page numbers, and other minutiae is essential to success.

Technical Terms: All or None

The many different difficulties about ideas have one thing in common: they occur in the medium of words. Unlike figures or other fixed symbols, words possess connotations, overtones, and hence the power of suggesting more than they say. Their arrangement, too, automatically conveys qualities and degrees of emphasis which strike the reader's mind and affect meaning in very subtle ways. We saw above how the mere putting of two statements about President Garfield side by side irresistibly suggested an idea contained in neither of them. This happened because the reader brings something with him to every act of reading. He brings his own experience of life and a variable amount of knowledge gathered from previous reading. The result is that unless the vocabulary of a new piece of reading matter is visibly technical and strange to him, he will almost always think he understands it. This will take place even when what is said is badly put, repeatedly misleading, or adroitly tendentious. The whole power of propaganda lies in this human propensity to catch the drift, to make out a meaning, to believe what is in print, with no thought of resistance by analysis and criticism. This being so, whoever communicates the findings of research must from the start turn into a professional critic of words and wording.

Since History—findings about the past—is for everyone to read, and since it embraces every conceivable activity of man, it has no technical terms. You may say that "revolution," "hegemony," "detente" are technical terms. They are in fact borrowings from other subjects that history has occasion to discuss in its inclusive sweep. In a history of chemistry you would hear about oxygen and phlogiston; in a history of war, about howitzers and demilunes, and so on. To repeat, history has no technical terms of its own. But the difficulties we have been pointing out, and the reporter's determination to be accurate in more than details, cause the historian to attach such importance to words that he ends by inverting the generalization and says that for him *every ordinary word becomes a technical term.*

Compare three kinds of statements:

1. $(a + b)(a + b) = a^2 + 2ab + b^2$

2. Two molecules of common salt react with one of sulfuric acid to give one molecule of sodium sulfate plus two of hydrogen chloride.

3. "It is a just though trite observation that victorious Rome was itself subdued by the arts of Greece."

In 1, we have a statement in the most general terms used by man. The statement gives no particulars. For any a or b the relation expressed by the equal sign will hold; you can make a or b stand for anything you like, provided the ultimate things are units that are identical and hence can be added and multiplied.

In 2, particular substances enter into the same relation of equivalence, and a change in their form is described. This brings us closer to the tangible reality than No. 1 did. But the chemical statement is still general enough to permit any amounts of sodium chloride (salt) and sulfuric acid to be used, with identical results, provided the correct proportions are kept. The idea is broad and timeless so that, as everyone knows, it too can be expressed in formulas made up of unvarying symbols.

Number 3, which is a sentence taken at random from Gibbon, is also a broad generality and as exact as the other two. But in it none of the symbols is fixed. Each word is used with precision in a unique way, but the readers have to bring their own understanding and knowledge of particulars to fill out the "equation." In some later sentence, perhaps, the same words "observation," "victorious," "subdued," and "arts" would have to be filled with different meanings, and "Greece" and "Rome" themselves might not indicate the same realities.

All this may be hard to believe, though everybody goes through these shifting operations all day long. Consider: in Gibbon's statement the word "observation" means simply "a remark." It does not mean the same thing as it would in "The patient was kept under observation." Again, "victorious" in Gibbon does not refer to any particular war or battle but to the general domination of the Roman Empire over the Mediterranean world, time unspecified. As for "subdued," it has in this sentence no connection whatever with war.

The arts subdue a people only when that people—or some of them—develop a taste for art and go out of their way to acquire books, statues, and the like. We somehow knew that this is what "arts" meant in that context, but how different from a reference to "the arts by which Cleopatra captivated Mark Antony"—no statues there.

Lastly, "Greece" and "Rome" are also shifting terms, because at different times the names do not cover the same territory, power, form of government, or degree of civilization. Rome is first a city under kings, then a nation under a republic, then an empire under emperors, and so on. Each word in its present place has a special meaning; it fulfills for Gibbon the role of a technical word if, as happened here, it says just what he intended, no more and no less.

But could not Gibbon have used other words and kept the same idea? We tend to think that he could. Suppose he had said, "It is an old story that when the Roman conquerors had seized all the wealth and power of the ancient world into their hands, their henchmen began buying up Greek ornaments and works of art and sank into self-indulgent luxury." The "general idea," as we loosely say, remains the same—but does it really? The same three facts do rattle around somewhere in the bottom of each remark: (1) Rome conquered the ancient world. (2) Romans came to enjoy the products of Greek art. (3) This is well known. But the idea, the precise, particular, all-important idea is utterly different in Gibbon and in the rewording. In each we are told many things between the lines, and the things differ in the two versions. Let us compare:

Gibbon reminds us (a) that in his century educated people knew some ancient history; (b) that the cliché he is about to repeat is correct; (c) that Greece and Rome exemplify the connection between conquest and civilization, the conquerors being usually the "newer" people, who acquire a higher culture from contact with the "older" and defeated nation; (d) that Roman art was largely borrowed; (e) that Greece maintained her cultural supremacy after defeat; (f) that Gibbon regards the whole process as admirable and majestic.

As against this, the rewritten version thrusts on the reader the conviction that (a) the remark to follow is only another sordid fact from the past; (b) the Roman Empire was the handiwork of a collection of greedy gangsters; (c) the upper class in Rome were merely the hangers-on of the conquerors; (d) these fellow brigands were philistines who bought Greek *objets d'art* mostly for show; (e) the cultivation of the arts is softening to the moral fiber; and (f) the writer considers History a tale of violence, ignorance, and turpitude.

The Technique of Self-Criticism

We are not now concerned with who is right—Gibbon or the Pseudo-Gibbon. We are concerned with the profound difference of effect produced by different words purporting to relate the same facts. Now it is bad enough when a willful or unconscious bias distorts in the written report what the researcher has discovered. It is obviously far worse when verbal incompetence distorts without the writer's being guilty of bias. The unfortunate truth is that the reader is always more sensitive to the *expressed meaning* than the writer himself. It is not hard to see why: the writer has his *intended meaning* at the forefront of his mind, and it too often hides from him the sense of the actual words he writes down.

The remedy is simple but arduous: to scan every word, not once but many times, until you are assured that it is *the* word corresponding to what you know and want to say. Apply the rule that in reporting every word is a technical word. For example, you as a writer would feel ashamed to call a general a captain or to write that B. was "executed" when he was only convicted and imprisoned. These distinctions are so well established that to fail to observe them is a blunder that your readers and reviewers will note and you will not forgive yourself for. But less glaring mistakes are often far more important.[5] In handling ideas, once again, you must consider every defining word in exactly the same way as you do conventional technical terms. Here are illustrations to enforce the lesson and suggest the way to practice. The examples were not made up to be easily shown wrong, but are taken from students' work—advanced students and good ones at that. The first has to do with Shelley's marital difficulties with his first wife, Harriet, who ultimately drowned herself:

Had Shelley bided his time and talked over his problems, perhaps the couple might have found themselves incompatible and might have been

[5]See pp. 380–382.

legally and justly separated. Had Shelley acted in this way he would not be
the Shelley we know.

The trouble here begins with an unexpressed antihistorical idea,
which comes out in the last sentence and vitiates the language in
between. "Talked over his problems" is obviously a piece of modern
jargon. Vague enough now, it would have meant little or nothing in
the early nineteenth century. In the passage under review its only
effect is to suggest, falsely, that Shelley refused to talk to his wife
about their mismating. The very word "problem" is wrong here, for it
is a recent idea to regard all the accidents of life as "problems." The
opening should perhaps read: "Had Shelley been more patient and
let his wife understand his character more fully. . . ."

The next remark as it stands is nonsense: "The couple might
have found themselves incompatible. . . ." That is just what they did
find; they had no need to wait to make this discovery. What the writer
really meant appears in the sentence following: "They might have
been legally and justly separated." But they *were* separated! One
dimly gathers the notion hovering in the writer's mind: had the couple
proved their incompatibility before a court, they might have been
divorced and Harriet might not have committed suicide. This is, once
again, to flout historical probability and to misunderstand human
emotions. Divorce was not and is not granted for incompatibility in
England, nor is there any reason to suppose that Harriet would have
been made happier by a divorce. The suspicion that all these loose
remarks are contrary to fact and to good sense comes out in the
writer's last sentence declaring that if all these so-called ideas had
been carried out Shelley would "not be the Shelley we know." When
a writer of history reaches such a conclusion, it is time to cross out
and start again.

This example clearly shows two things: first, that a passage which
"anybody can understand" may very well contain not one iota of
sense; second, that the way to test one's writing for sense is to take
each word or phrase, shake out its contents, and look at them with
skepticism—almost with hostility: what in heaven's name *does* this
mean? If the answer is satisfactory, let the phrase stand provisionally.
How does it square with the next one? Use each to test the rest until
every part is acceptable. When you have done this, reconsider the

order of your words and sentences until you are sure that the ideas they evoke in the reader's mind are *your* ideas at their most exact.

Language being metaphorical to start with, this necessary and close scrutiny of words should include a testing of images, figures of speech, and set expressions. It will not only disclose mixed metaphors, which are often ridiculous, but more important it will show you where you are missing the idea altogether as a result of loose coupling between images. Take an example from a book review: "This set of documents emphasizes the legal aspect of the United Nations." Can anything "emphasize an aspect"? An aspect is what one looks at. Besides, is it the documents that emphasize, or is it the editor who chose some documents and not others? The reader is in doubt, as he would not be if the reviewer had said simply: "Most of these documents [or, "The most important of these documents"] have to do with the legal history of the United Nations."

One more example, to suggest that, even in an acceptable statement, refining the thought adds strength at the same time as it sharpens the critical faculty. "We must not," says an author, "neglect the place of the individual in history." Good, but not quite good enough, for on reflection the remark raises a doubt, owing to the inevitable ambiguity of the word "history." The author may mean: "In writing history we must not neglect to make a place for the individual," that is, we must not write only about forces and factors. Or he may mean: "We must not neglect the *role* of the individual in *making* history," which is an entirely different idea. A remark two paragraphs away from the sentence in question showed which was the right interpretation, but suppose the sentence were lifted out of that context and quoted. The author would be misrepresented and might have to defend or explain himself, which is to say, do at the last what he should have done at first.

Historians' Fallacies: How to Avoid Them

So much for words, which are both the cause of our trouble and the means to repair it. In the handling of ideas we must also be on the watch for fallacies that words mask or make attractive. There is no room in this book to discuss more than a few kinds of fallacy among those to which reporters of events are especially liable. Doing the exercises in an elementary textbook on logic might help detect the fundamental forms of bad reasoning, such as begging the question, *non sequitur*, denying the antecedent, and the like. But the researcher or writer seldom encounters or produces fallacies in their pure form. He or she is apt, rather, to generalize beyond the facts. Bad generalizations are often the result of careless language: the author says "all" or "every" or "never" when the evidence goes but a little way toward such a universal proposition. Modifiers must be brought into play: "almost," "nearly," "by and large," "in a manner of speaking," "hardly," and the ubiquitous "perhaps."

And yet the reporter must avoid giving the impression of perpetual timidity and indecision. He will infallibly do so if every sentence he writes hedges with "often" and "almost." The account must be as precise as close research and guarded statement can make it, but it must not lose vividness and impetus. An irritated reviewer was right to complain of a book in which "every sentence reads as if it would have to be defended in court."

When overextended generalization does not come from the careless use of universals, it comes from the failure to think of negative instances. If after searching into the lives of Keats, Chopin, and Musset you are tempted to write one of those dubious generalities couched in the singular such as: "The Romantic artist is tubercular and dies young," you must at once test it by negative instances. Wordsworth, Hugo, Landor, Goethe are there to prove you wrong with their eighty years or more apiece. Four cases are more than enough to ruin your description of a type that is largely imaginary. The corollary caution is to beware of what is new and striking in your research. It may be new only to you; and even if generally new, its effect must not overwhelm other impressions. Remember the old ancedote about the English traveler who saw three red-headed girls at the inn where he stopped and who wrote in his diary: "All the women in this country have red hair."

Only the quite inexperienced researcher will generalize from a single instance or from too few. The danger that besets the more practiced is rather the opposite, called the Reductive Fallacy. As its name suggests, it reduces diversity to one thing: All this is nothing but *That*. Beware of the phrase itself; "nothing but" can be used only when you are absolutely sure of your ground and when that ground is limited in scope. For example, to make an event as vast as the French Revolution (no single event, really, but a group of related events) result from a conspiracy is reductive in the extreme. So is ascribing war exclusively to "economics" or to the wirepulling of munitions makers. The study of history teaches the exact contrary of simple-minded reduction. Its most valuable lesson is that all so-called events, like all human motives, are complex. A true researcher shows the parts that make up the complexity, each part in its place and relation to the rest. Let the newspaper, which lacks time and room, enjoy the monopoly of reductionism.[6]

Between reduction and overexpansion lurks hidden repetition, or Tautology. It is a frequent error in histories, business reports, statistical analyses, and the like. Here is an example, again from student work: "English aggressiveness spurred the nation to stimulate commerce on the seas and win the supremacy of trade routes." Here a thing called English aggressiveness works upon the nation (England), and England works upon English commerce in a stimulating manner. The three things are in fact one, as the writer would have seen if he had stepped out of his abstractions and visualized something concrete—not commerce but a merchant, a shipowner. *He* is English aggressiveness, and he is the nation, and he is the trader who wins the trade routes. Perhaps the writer's mind was visited by a flitting idea of the English *government* acting independently of the trader, but this thought was unexpressed and it left three wordings of one thing acting on one another like separate powers.[7]

Another fallacy less easily discovered by the reader is Misplaced Literalism. It has many forms, and it is particularly insidious because the reporter must always *begin* by being literal. He must ascertain

---

[6]A distinguished newspaper editor writes: "No week passes without someone prominent in politics, industry, labor or civic affairs complaining to me, always in virtually identical terms: 'Whenever I read a story about something in which I really know what's going on, I'm astonished at how little of what's important gets into the papers—and how often even that little is wrong.'" A. H. Raskin, "What's Wrong with American Newspapers?" *New York Times Magazine*, June 11, 1967, 77.

[7]In a textbook fortunately long out of use, one found listed among the causes that brought one or another party to power: (1) the strength of the party; (2) the weakness of the opposition. This is a truly convenient way to double the number of reasons for the result of any election.

with all possible precision what his original text tells him. Lord Acton does *not* say, "Power corrupts and absolute power corrupts absolutely"; he says, "Power tends to corrupt and absolute power corrupts absolutely."[8] A slight but consequential difference, for it allows the possibility that a business executive or a public officeholder will not be corrupted by wielding power.

Having ascertained the author's very words, the reporter scans them for what they say, scans the neighboring words, the author's other works on the same subject, and gradually acquires familiarity with the natural movement of the man's thought. It is at this point that Literalism would be misplaced if it reentered. Its most obvious form would be to quote a remark such as Lord Acton's as if its being in print automatically gave it the same weight as every other by the same author. It may have more or less, depending on place and circumstance. Is the idea expressed the conclusion of a piece of reasoning in, say, an essay? Or is it a notion struck off in a letter to a friend? Or, conversely, is it an improvised retort to an opponent? It is the critic's duty to judge importance and value in the light of his wider knowledge. If he remains baldly literal and contents himself with quoting extracts, he invariably ends by showing his human subject to have been a mass of contradictions.

The Scholar and the Great Ideas

Important words, then, require interpretation, and most thinkers are likely to use certain words in peculiar senses. The scholar is in the best position to do this interpreting, because he is professionally interested in circumstances and origins. That these are bound to throw light on meanings and intentions is shown by the practice of the American courts in interpreting a statute: they go back to the debates in the legislature and the known opinions of the proponents. The student is likewise accustomed to analyzing documents and knowing where to turn for sources that will tell him what meanings words bore in earlier times and remote places.

[8]Letter to Bishop Creighton in Acton, *Historical Essays and Studies*, London, 1907, 504.

The various ideas clustering around predestination, for example—justification by faith, consubstantiation, theodicy, and so on—impelled people in the sixteenth century to kill others who disbelieved in their creed or defined it differently from themselves. Since these ideas no longer grip us, we can scarcely understand their meaning—let alone their importance—until it is resurrected for us, revivified, so that we begin to reconceive and feel the lost power. To put this differently, the *quality of belief* that goes into the ideas of an age or a thinker is as great a concern of the historian as the genuineness of the document that brings them to his notice. He cannot be merely literal and reportorial about ideas without losing his *raison d'être.* A simple summarizer or "rewrite man" fails to interest us and forfeits his claim to our confidence.

We rely on the historian particularly in the study of great ideas—religious beliefs or political and philosophical systems, about which we shall have more to say. Here it is enough to point out that a statement such as "Nietzsche believed in the idea of Eternal Recurrence" is by itself inadequate, even if Eternal Recurrence is explained as the doctrine that after an unspecified number of events have taken place in History, the world goes through the identical sequence again from the beginning, and so on in an infinite cycle. What we have to know at once is whether Nietzsche arrived at this notion by intuition or by reasoning, whether he adopted it as the completion or as the starting point of his system, how vivid or abstract were his imaginings about it, whether he spoke more of its scientific or of its moral consequences—all questions to which the answers may bring us to understand the *quality of his belief.*

It is for lack of such comments and interpretations that many textbooks and encyclopedia articles give such a starved and false image of the ideas that have moved great characters or inspired great movements. Students who memorize the tags to pass examinations literally do not know what they are talking about. What live meaning can they attach to the statement that Rousseau "wanted to go back to Nature?" It is a false statement anyway, but suppose it were true: Where *is* Nature and when did we leave it behind? What has it been doing all this time and how do we return to it? The so-called idea that such students think they have learned is but an empty form of words, which they fill with their own imperfect notions and gratuitously ascribe to a thinker.

This common situation defines for the writer what he must do whenever he raises the ghost of a great idea. He must avoid the ultimate fallacy of Vulgarity, that is to say, avoid falling into the cheap and easy ways of thought that are so fatally congenial to the uninformed. This temptation—Vulgarity being only a convenient name for it—was exemplified earlier in our warnings against the reductive fallacy: the historian should not help things lose their distinctive characters by saying they are "nothing but" something else. Similarly, the historian should not rival the gossip in assigning crude motives at sight. If Jonathan Swift satirized mankind in *Gulliver's Travels* it was not "because he wanted to be a bishop and had been thwarted in this ambition." At that rate he should have shot Queen Anne as Guiteau shot Garfield.

The historian, finally, must not assume an intellectual pose or mood that gives every event the same coloring. In recent times the tendency has been to affect cynicism—as in the example we made up for our Pseudo-Gibbon. In this way History is vulgarly debunked. Some cast the blame for this tendency on mankind's earlier mood of optimism and respect for authority. On the scale of exact ideas, automatic skepticism is as low as automatic belief. In sound reporting there is no need of bunking, debunking, or rebunking, because historiography lays down the rules for presenting all things *in their diversity*.

The English historian Collingwood (like the German Dilthey) arrived at the conviction that the writing of history was nothing more nor less than a rethinking of the past—recapturing in consciousness bygone events and thoughts. To these writers all history was the history of ideas in the sense that the researchers' findings without exception must once upon a time have occupied somebody's mind. Jefferson probably said or wrote down his birth date: April 2, 1743. If he did not, his parents did, or the parish clerk and recorder. In rediscovering or restating a "fact" we are rethinking a previous thought, someone's idea. Similarly with every event, from the "invasion" of Rome by Greek art to the "disappointment" of Guiteau and the shooting of Garfield: every item of fact or feeling or idea that we have any inkling of must have occurred as somebody's mental state— a perception, a hope or fear, a memory, or an imagining.

Whether this account is the final truth about the nature of historiography does not matter for the moment. It contains this much truth, that in dealing with everything beyond the bare conventional facts, the reporter must make himself and his works a mirror of the utmost smoothness and reflecting power. Every distortion due to wrong expression, fallacious thought, inadequate feeling, or irrelevant mood is a grievous error—an error far worse than the easily detected kind, such as a mistake in a name or date. We blush more for the latter, but we should in truth be more ashamed of distortion, and we should toil equally to avoid both.

7

Truth and Causation

The Evidences of Historical Truth

The previous chapter has perhaps left the reader wondering how much or how little of history can be trusted. If the only indisputable facts are those we have called conventional and if they are generally of little interest in themselves, then the veracity or truth-value of history seems slight indeed. The thoughtful reader's question to the historian, which we quoted in Chapter 3,[1] contrasts the shifting uncertainty of history with the mathematical rigor of science and concludes that truth is absent from history because it lacks the form—and the formulas—of science.

This conclusion is plausible but false. In order to see why it rests on a fallacy, one must take up several distinct problems. The first is, What kinds of evidence are available on which to base historical assertions?

These kinds can be variously described and grouped for convenience. One may divide them first into Verbal and Mute—the mute consisting of objects such as buildings, drawings, tools, fragments of pottery, any physical object bearing no words. A coin may belong to both kinds if it has an inscription on it. Verbal, or speaking, evidence need not, of course, be written: an oral tradition has validity under

[1]See p. 52.

certain circumstances and, with the growing use of tape recordings, oral testimony may once more regain its prehistoriographic prominence.[2] But as everyone knows, the great bulk of what is commonly handled and offered as historical evidence is in written form.

Written evidence again falls into several subgroups: manuscript and printed, private and public, intentional and unpremeditated. The last distinction has diagnostic importance for arriving at truth. Intentional pieces of written evidence are such things as affidavits, court testimony, secret or published memoirs. The author of any of these meant to record a sequence of events for future perusal. He presumably had an interest in furthering his view of the facts. But a receipt for the sale of a slave, jotted down in the second century on a bit of papyrus, is no premeditated piece of historical writing. Its sole intended use was commercial, and it is only as "unconscious evidence" that it becomes part of an historical narrative. The laws of states, ordinances of cities, charters of corporations, and the like are similarly unpremeditated evidence—as are the account books of a modern corporation or of a Florentine banker of the fifteenth century.

Yet, important as this difference is, the assumption that unconscious evidence is always sounder is by no means warranted; for with the widespread consciousness of history to which we drew attention earlier, there has been a general tendency to inject purposeful "historicity" into apparently unpremeditated documents. State papers nowadays frequently attempt to say more than is required by their ostensible purpose. They subtly or crudely address the world and posterity.[3] And even business documents, such as reports to stock-

---

[2]In Oral History centers such as the one at Columbia University, the remarks of important persons who might not write memoirs are recorded on tape. The written word is still so compelling, however, that these recordings are transcribed and the typescripts filed like books. Catalogues of the available materials are published periodically.

[3]Consider the publication *Polish Acts of Atrocity against the German Minority in Poland*, issued by the German Library of Information, New York, 1940, 259 pp. Its internal terminology and arrangement are those of an historical monograph, but its apparent record of fact is but disguised argument. More deceptive because more roundabout are the carefully "planted" documents left by public figures; for instance, the so-called posterity letters that Theodore Roosevelt wrote to various correspondents. For examples see Elting E. Morison, ed., *The Letters of Theodore Roosevelt*, 8 vols., Cambridge, Mass., 1951–1954.

holders, contain interpretations of purpose and behavior that amount to propaganda. In other words, we have become so accustomed to the idea of "the record" that we are continually tempted to tamper with it. When we mean to be candid, we are careful to specify that our words must be "off the record."

This enumeration of the several kinds of historical evidence is enough to suggest the many difficulties arising from the materials. Figure 13 shows how the namable kinds of evidence can be grouped for quick review. Obviously not all kinds of evidence are available for every historical report; and their classification is certainly not to be thought of as marking fixed boundaries. Where, for example, would you place a film clip of a student riot? or evidence of the collision of the *Andrea Doria* exhibited to landsmen by means of a film made by a deep-sea diver and a European actress? It is stretching terms to answer, as the table would imply, "Works of Art."

No matter how it is described, *no piece of evidence can be used for historiography in the state in which it is found.* It is necessarily subjected to the action of the researcher's mind. When that action is methodical and apt, what is being applied is known as the critical method. Faced with a piece of evidence, the critical mind of the searcher for truth asks the fundamental questions:

> Is this object or piece of writing genuine?
> Is its message trustworthy?
> How do I know?

This leads to an unfolding series of subordinate questions:

1. What does it state or imply?

2. Who is its author or maker?

3. What is the relation in time and space between the author and the information, overt or implied, that is conveyed by the object?

4. How does the statement compare with other statements on the same point?

5. What do we know independently about the author and his credibility?

FIGURE 13   *The Evidences of History**

RECORDS
(intentional transmitters of fact)

Written

1. Chronicles, annals, biographies, genealogies
2. Memoirs, diaries
3. Certain kinds of inscriptions

Oral

4. Ballads, anecdotes, tales, sagas
5. Recordings in various forms (tape, disc, etc.)

Works of Art

6. Portraits, historical paintings, scenic sculpture, coins, and medals
7. Certain kinds of films, videotape, etc.

RELICS
(unpremeditated transmitters of fact)

8. Human remains, letters, literature, public documents, business records, and certain kinds of inscriptions
9. Language, customs, and institutions
10. Tools and other artifacts

---

*Adapted from John Martin Vincent's *Historical Research*, New York, 1911.

The point of these questions is easily grasped:

1. It is essential to ascertain with more than ordinary care what the document states and what may be inferred from it. As in law, false conclusions are ruled out by the good judge.

2. If the document or the coin is not by the ostensible maker, it has no value as evidence. Gauging the truth of any statement is obviously assisted by a knowledge of who made it.[4]

[4]The truthfulness of the presentment may also have value as evidence to convict the forger, or as evidence of his skill—witness the Van Meegeren forgeries of Vermeer paintings.

3. The value of a piece of testimony usually increases in proportion to the nearness in time and space between the witness and the events about which he testifies.[5] An eyewitness has a good chance of knowing what happened; a reporter distant from the event by only a few years has a better chance than one separated by a century. (Recall the story of the year 1000 in Chapter 5.)

4. A single witness may be quite accurate, but two witnesses, if independent, increase the chances of eliminating human fallibility. If a dozen reports already exist, a thirteenth just discovered is compared point for point with the others in an effort to resolve puzzling allusions or contradictions, to strengthen or destroy an interpretation.

5. What can be learned about the author's life and character helps make up our judgment on several of the previous points. If we know his life we can answer the queries: Was he there? Had he the expertness to appreciate the facts? Was he biased by partisan interest? Did he habitually tell the truth? (Recall the clues to the "Public Man" who wrote a diary, Chapter 5.)

The principles contained in all these questions and assertions guide the researcher's mind at all times and develop in him the habit of criticism. Its operation becomes automatic, whether he is reading a president's inaugural or a rabid editorial in a tabloid. Every reader or writer of reports should train himself in this form of criticism. It is unlikely that the ordinary researcher will encounter problems requiring familiarity with the science of Diplomatics, which teaches the technique of testing and dating documents, chiefly medieval. This takes special study and much practice, as does the reading of Greek papyri or the assessment of archeological finds. If a point requiring such knowledge arises in your "book research," consult an expert, just as you would if you came across a suspicious document.[6] But on

---

[5]This rule was doubtless hovering in the mind of the student who wrote in a comparison of Herodotus and Thucydides that Thucydides "had the advantage of being alive at the time he was writing."

[6]Reading the Osborns' *Questioned Document Problems* and Weller's *Die falschen und fingierten Druckorte* (on pretended publishing places) is, however, an instructive and entertaining use of spare time. And persons interested will want to look up the latest methods of dating and testing by technical means—carbon 14 or other radiation, infrared and reflected light rays, or aspartic acid racemization.

ordinary printed matter no one can be critical and historical-minded for you. If you are so by nature, it can be guaranteed that this mental faculty will find much scope even when its exercise is limited to print.

Probability the Guide

The historical method ascertains the truth by means of common sense. When that sense is systematically applied, it becomes a stronger and sharper instrument than is usually found at work in daily life. It shows a closer attention to detail and a stouter hold on consecutiveness and order. The exercise of these capacities turns into a new power by which new intellectual possessions may be acquired. For the historian's common sense must be understood to mean more than common knowledge and the clichés of ordinary thought. Methodical common sense takes in both what is usually known by the well educated and any special information relevant to the historical question being studied; and to these bodies of fact and ideas it brings the habit of comparing and judging with detached deliberation.

This point about *informed* common sense is most obvious in the writing of biography. The narrator of a life must become familiar with all the subject's activities and concerns, some of which may be special; and the common sense of these matters is not simply the knowledge we have of them today, but also the state of knowledge in the subject's lifetime. A life of Caesar presupposes a knowledge of Roman roads and Roman weapons in the first century B.C., to which is added the awareness of incommensurables, such as Roman character, superstition, *gravitas*, etc.

All these distinctions need only be stated to be understood, and no one disputes them. What is often ill understood and easily misconstrued is the role of high common sense in matters that seem quite ordinary but are not so, matters that the plain man encounters daily in the newspaper and that the educated citizen will come across again in his casual reading of books. For example, ever since the Warren Commission Report on the assassination of President Kennedy, many persons have attacked its conclusions, some in very elaborate works based on the published testimony. In a critique of several of these books, John Sparrow, an English scholar who was also trained as a lawyer, makes the point that concerns us here. It has no bearing on one's opinion about the Warren Report; its bearing is on common notions of evidence that unfortunately are lacking in "low common sense." John Sparrow shows what the denouncers of the Report all expect before they will accord belief: they trust only consistent and congruent witnesses. Yet, as he reminds us,

> Every lawyer knows that a witness . . . while wrong on a number of points may yet be right on others, perhaps including the essential one. Every lawyer knows that honest and truthful witnesses may contradict themselves, particularly on questions concerning their own and others' motives and states of mind, without thereby forfeiting credibility. . . . Finally, every lawyer knows that in a big and complicated case there is always, at the end of it all, a residue of improbable, inexplicable fact. You do not invalidate a hypothesis by showing that the chances were against the occurrence of some of the events that it presupposes: many things that happen are actually improbable, but they happen.[7]

Such is the higher common sense at work upon evidence when it comes from ordinary testimony, that is, the declarations of persons, not experts, who are by chance witnesses of some important event or part of an event. Sparrow takes us even further along the road that historian and lawyer tread together when he says: "To make up its mind, if it can, what *must* have happened, in spite of incidental improbabilities—that is the task of a Commission of Inquiry."[8] The historian is in himself such a Commission, and when he has done his work it is no refutation of it to say that he has selected his facts to suit his case. Mr. Sparrow gives us the right view of that tiresome cliché: "What else should an investigator do? It is for the critics to show that they themselves have evaluated all the evidence, and can make a selection from it as reliable as [the other], and base upon that selection conclusions that compel acceptance. . . ."[9]

So much for the lawyer's wisdom, which an intelligent reader might have worked out for himself. There is a further step that the

[7]John Sparrow, *After the Assassination*, New York, 1968, 13–14.
[8]*Ibid.*, 14.
[9]*Ibid.*, 15.

historian must often take, that which brings him or her possession of technical knowledge strictly so-called. Here no amount of intelligence will serve: experience certified by experts is the only source of help. In the same attacks on the official view of the murder of President Kennedy, inferences are freely made from the bullet wounds as to the number of assassins and the places where they stood. The fact seems to be that rifle bullets do the most unexpected things, contrary to "common sense." Thus "if a high-velocity bullet is fired into soft clay it does not, as one might expect, pass through it. After tunneling in for a few inches it suddenly produces a cavity many times its own diameter, and quite frequently the bullet itself is smashed into fragments." The writer, long a medico-legal expert in Egypt and Scotland, goes on to give an account of the shooting of an official by a nervous sentry. The bullet passed through a car window and struck the victim on the chin, causing facial wounds of which he subsequently died. And when the car was examined,

not one but a number of bullet marks were found. There were two holes in the license holder and the wind-screen under it, each of which looked as if it had been caused by a separate bullet. The upper part of the left traffic-indicator had also been pierced, and there were several other marks apparently produced by the passage of projectiles. . . . On the back seat a portion of a .303 bullet was found, consisting of the aluminium tip and the cupro-nickel jacket. . . . It was thought that a number of shots had been fired. From the holes in the wind-screen alone, it seemed that two or three bullets must have struck the car. However, all the eye-witnesses spoke of only one shot being fired, and one cartridge case only was found on the scene; out of a clip of five bullets, the remaining four were still in the rifle. . . . Finally, a reconstruction of the affair . . . showed pretty conclusively that not more than one bullet had struck the car.[10]

It is in such cases that ordinary people are likely to display ignorant skepticism. They know better; they "use common sense": bullets fly in straight lines and make neat round holes.

[10]Sir Sydney Smith, *Mostly Murder*, London, 1959, 272–274.

Clio and the Doctors

At the same time, especially among readers, there is a counter-tendency to believe expert evidence if it is of a familiar kind—not the ballistics laboratory, but, say, the doctor. And today, when psychiatrists and physicians are more than ever oracles, those among them who make an avocation of diagnosing contemporary or historical persons are credited with knowledge about things well outside the consulting room. But the evidence is usually slight, and mixed, and sometimes the reasoning is circular.

For example, did the Romantic composer Robert Schumann's mental disorder come from syphilis? Recently examined, a sample of his hair showed traces of mercury, the substance used in his day to treat that disease. Yes, but (it is argued) his mental symptoms began in early youth, before sexual maturity. And at the very end of his life he produced well-conceived and well-crafted music. No, says another, the music is much inferior to his best, as it was bound to be in the third stage of syphilis. Ah, but remember: Schumann was a confirmed wearer of felt hats and these were commonly "blocked"—shaped and reshaped—with mercury. Let the jury decide a point of rather academic interest.

A case on which it is thought that greater issues hang is that of Woodrow Wilson, and it has accordingly been studied with greater insistence. Wilson's catastrophic stroke during the struggle over the ratification of the Treaty of Versailles in 1919 appears now to have been compelling in his effort to promote the League of Nations. Was his collapse a sudden medical "accident" or was it only the climax of a series of episodes long affecting his personality, outlook, and public performance? In particular, was his fierce struggle with Senator Lodge over the Treaty foreshadowed earlier in his stormy encounter with Dean West at Princeton over a university issue? These episodes have become part of presidential history and are taken as signs of a stubborn man's devotion to principle, his unwillingness to yield to expediency. If, on the contrary, they are interpreted as morbid symptoms of a recurrent affliction, the events appear in another light entirely.

In 1981, Edwin A. Weinstein, a distinguished neurologist, published the results of many years' search into Woodrow Wilson's medical history.[11] Weinstein concluded that Wilson had suffered a series of strokes during the productive years of his career, beginning in 1896, or possibly earlier. Partial loss of sight ten years later was the result of another stroke, and still other less serious ones occurred when Wilson was Governor of New Jersey and during his White House years. Weinstein holds that Wilson's characteristic response to each was a burst of public activity, an expression of his resolve that the body be forced to serve the spirit.

Nor does Weinstein stop there. He speculates also that Wilson grew up suffering from what is nowadays called dyslexia, an impaired ability to read; hence the ignorant father's hectoring about young Wilson's "laziness," and the boy's shame and guilt. Step by step, the President's exhausting attempt to make something "good" come out of the war into which he took the United States emerges as atonement for "guilt" about the loss of thousands of American lives.

These assertions and conjectures have been questioned, naturally. An ophthalmologist at Stanford University, Michael F. Marmor,[12] argues that what Wilson suffered from in early years was not strokes but "writer's cramp" or neuritis. The temporary blindness in 1906, which Weinstein diagnosed as a "major stroke," is held by Marmor to have been an "interocular hemorrhage." Repeated strokes must cause changes in personality, and "to find substantial changes in personality without a loss of cognitive power or the development of dementia would be unusual." Marmor is confident that there is little in Wilson's performance up to his breakdown in 1919 to suggest cognitive loss.

Which expert to believe? The historian who reads the record of Wilson's cordial and imaginative relations with Congress over his

---

[11]*Woodrow Wilson: A Medical and Psychological Biography*, Princeton. He had foreshadowed his findings in an article in the *Journal of American History*, 57 (September 1970), 324–351.

[12]"Wilson, Strokes, and Zebras," *New England Journal of Medicine*, 307 (August 26, 1982), 528–535. See also the follow-up, 308 (January 20, 1983), 163f. and Marmor's "The Eyes of Woodrow Wilson," *Ophthalmology*, 92 (March 1985), 454f.

legislative program in 1913 asks himself whether the same personality was at work in the struggle over the Treaty and the League in 1919. Wilson's irritability and stubbornness do seem excessive, quite apart from "principle" and the strains of conducting the First World War. Meanwhile, a close study by each of two independent German historians of Wilson's negotiations of the Treaty in Paris, against the master strategists Lloyd George and Clemenceau, shows Wilson as himself a master, flexible, resourceful, imaginative, and successful.[13]

The mystery of human personality remains. And in any case—which means in *every* case—explanations by means of a single cause, hidden, startling, "scientific," is to be distrusted, if not on the face of it disallowed. The concatenation of acts, motives, and results can only be understood and described by the intuitive skill of the historian as artist. He will see Wilson or any other figure not as victim, but as doer. If before his breakdown the President was ever handicapped by a defective circulatory system, his abilities and his determination were all the more remarkable.

A further caution is in order about what might be called taking a holiday from discipline. Even great scholars will repeat campus gossip that they would scorn to accept as evidence in one of their monographs. This very fact shows the importance of method: it is a safeguard, a means of protecting one's mind (and reputation) from oneself.

A classic case of ignoring the demand for evidence is an English work on Wordsworth which concluded that the poet married because he had found in himself and his sister the beginnings of an incestuous attachment: "Wordsworth's object in making straight for Sockburn [where his future wife lived] . . . is clear enough. . . . By the time they reached Sockburn William was undoubtedly fully aware of the nature of his feelings for Dorothy."[14]

---

[13]The principal one is Klaus Schwabe, *Deutsche Revolution und Wilson Frieden: die Amerikanische und deutsche Friedens-strategie zwischen Ideologie und Machtpolitik, 1918–19.* (Düsseldorf 1971). See also the *Journal of Modern History,* 45 (September 1973), 536 f.

[14]F. W. Bateson, *Wordsworth: A Re-interpretation,* London, 1954, 156. In a second edition (1956) the author modified his statement with evasive words but adhered to his thesis.

Neither in this passage nor elsewhere in the book is any evidence presented except that of the well-known close companionship of brother and sister and some ambiguous allusions in poems and letters. The new "truth" about the attachment rests solely on the author's repeated "it is clear enough," "undoubtedly," and the like. Upon this a scholarly critic wrote a definitive paragraph:

> If Mr. Bateson suggested that there was a morbid strain in her attachment to her brother, we would perhaps agree—with the proviso that she was probably in love with Coleridge. If Mr. Bateson fancied that she and her brother might have been consciously alarmed by mutual and illicit desires, he would be entitled to air his suspicion, wildly improbable as we might think it. To present their alarm not as a hypothesis but as an undoubted fact strikes me as inexcusable.[15]

Inexcusable it is, because the rule of "Give evidence" is not to be violated with impunity. No matter how possible or plausible the author's conjecture, it cannot be accepted as historical truth if he has only his hunch to support it. What would be more than adequate for village gossip does not begin to be enough for history.

The particular error we have been examining is worth a word more, because it enshrines a common slippage from one use of evidence to another: the writer on Wordsworth found his hypothesis consistent with the facts he had gathered, and from this consistency he deduced confirmation. He may be imagined as saying: "Since there is nothing against my view; since, on the contrary, certain facts can be made to support my view, therefore my view is proved." But proof demands *decisive evidence*; this means *evidence that confirms one view and excludes its rivals*. Mr. Bateson's facts will fit his view *and* his critic's *and* several other possible views as well. To say this is to say that they support none of them in such a way as to discriminate between truth and conjecture. In short, mere consistency is not enough, nor mere plausibility, for both can apply to a wide variety of hypotheses.

The commandment about furnishing evidence that is decisive leads us, therefore, to a second fundamental rule: in history, as in life

---

[15] Raymond Mortimer in the *Sunday Times* (London), October 17, 1954.

critically considered, *truth rests not on possibility nor on plausibility but on probability.*

Probability is used here in a strict sense. It means the balance of chances that, given such and such evidence, the event it records happened in a certain way; or, in other cases, that a supposed event did not in fact take place. This balance is not computable in figures as it is in mathematical probability; but it is no less attentively *weighed and judged.* Judgment is the historian's form of genius, and he himself is judged by the amount of it he can muster. The grounds on which he passes judgment are, again, the common grounds derived from life: general truths, personal and vicarious experience (which includes a knowledge of previous history), and any other kind of special or particular knowledge that proves relevant.

Here, for example, is an improbable set of facts which are nonetheless not to be doubted, the local records and testimony being evidence of the most solid kind. In Liverpool, over half a century ago, one of the great unsolved murders of all time took place, in a small and shabby back street never before brought by any event to the world's attention. Thirty-four small red-brick houses made up the whole of Wolverton Street, yet the frequency of sudden death along that double row exceeds plausibility and invites disbelief, though the facts are on record: within about a year, three persons had committed suicide and five other residents were widows of men who had just died in unusual circumstances.[16] Then came the killing of Julia Wallace, the inoffensive wife of an insurance-premium collector. Since it was only the strange puzzle of her murder that made the street an object of interest lasting to this day, we may note how far coincidence has to go before it draws attention to itself and upsets our conventional ideas of what is likely or unlikely.

At many points, then, the estimate of probability made by the student will coincide with that of an ordinary citizen; but there is this difference, that the scholar will not have reached it offhand; it will not be a correct snap judgment, but a correct *critical* judgment.

An historian would say, for example, that under the conditions prevailing in this country today it is not probable that a public official,

---

[16]Jonathan Goodman, *The Killing of Julia Wallace*, New York, 1976, 25.

such as the governor of a state, could be entirely misrepresented to posterity as regards appearance, actions, and character. Too many devices of publicity are continually playing on public figures; whereas the probability of successful misrepresentation was far greater in fifteenth-century England. This judgment is what has enabled a number of scholars to believe that Richard III was not the murderer of his nephews, not crooked-backed, not the villain depicted in Shakespeare's play. They cannot fully prove their contention, for conclusive evidence is lacking, but they win a hearing for it because it is not against probability that the Tudor kings could blacken Richard's character and sustain the "big lie."[17]

The point here is not the pros and cons of this particular question. The point is that the carefully assessed probabilities of a known situation govern every part of the historian's judgment. What applies to a large situation like Richard III's applies to each document or relic that is put in evidence, for each document or relic is in fact the center of a "situation." We defined that situation in asking our five questions. The answer to each always rests on a balance of probabilities.

This is true even when a scientific test is applied, say to the paper on which a suspected document is written or printed. The reasoning goes: This paper is made from esparto grass. The document is said to have been written in 1850. But in 1850 esparto paper was not made, it having been introduced by Thomas Routledge in 1857. Therefore the document is forged.[18] This seems conclusive, yet it is only highly probable. It is just possible that some other, unsung papermaker introduced grass into one batch before Routledge; or—to be more subtle—the tests applied may not be exact enough to differentiate between similar fibers that might have been in the paper at the earlier date.

---

[17]For the latest review of the evidence, see Paul Murray Kendall, *Richard III*, New York, 1956; and for a condensed account, V. B. Lamb, *The Betrayal of Richard III*, London, 1965. An entertaining piece of fiction on the subject is Josephine Tey's detective story *The Daughter of Time*, New York, 1952.

[18]See Richard D. Altick, "The Scholar and the Scientist," Chapter 7 of *The Scholar Adventurers*, New York, 1951; and Altick's *The Art of Literary Research*, 3rd ed., New York, 1982.

We have repeatedly referred in the last few pages to "the situation." Some puzzles may be resolved by seeking outside what seems the complete story, enlarging "the situation" and finding in its outskirts the resolving elements. What is more, recourse to this device will on occasion uncover a puzzle where all seemed straightforward, an open-and-shut affair resting on the solid base of a clear and genuine document. These words describe in effect Dr. Johnson's famous letter to Lord Chesterfield. The theme and style of the epistle are so splendid that even though it is an attack on Chesterfield, he himself relished it, and showed it to all his friends with evident admiration.

Now what the letter plainly says is that Chesterfield promised Johnson support in his enterprise of making a Dictionary of the English Language, failed to give that help, and now that the work is done is "encumbering" Johnson with public praise. So clear is the statement that one might well think it a complete account of what happened, especially since Chesterfield did not rebut the charge and the well-wishers of each man kept silent. On the surface it is a clear-cut case of lordly indifference followed by an officious gesture of approval.

Yet a few additional facts change the whole scene. Chesterfield, busy with high office and many claimants for his patronage, had indeed forgotten the relatively unknown Johnson and his project of a dictionary. But shortly before the appearance of the work, the publisher Dodsley approached Chesterfield for a statement about it that might help sales. Though old and ailing, Chesterfield did not refuse but wrote two "papers" of sincere praise in the weekly journal, *The World*, and these were widely reprinted.

Dodsley in his delight told Johnson, who nevertheless felt bound to write to Chesterfield as he did, not because of the long neglect—he would not complain of what is the common lot of authors until they "arrive"—but because of the misleading effect of Chesterfield's two articles. The original *Plan* of the Dictionary had announced to the public, correctly, that the project had won Chesterfield's patronage. Now Chesterfield praised the result. The obvious assumption would be that Johnson had enjoyed his lordship's help from first to last. Yet in the Preface to the great book that was about to appear, Johnson asserted, also correctly, that he had carried the burden unaided. Writing a protest to the noble lord was clearly required by so complicated a series of events. The need for it was confirmed by one reviewer's statement that Johnson had written a Preface (instead of reprinting the *Plan*) only that he might deny his debt to Chesterfield.

The happy postscript to the affair is that a message from the dying Chesterfield to Johnson earned the Doctor's entire forgiveness. After his *faux pas* and the letter of rebuke, Chesterfield behaved magnanimously to Johnson, as Johnson did in reverse, never letting any copy of his letter out of his hands, though many asked to have one. Compare now the facts with the general opinion of the facts.[19]

Facing the Doubtful in All Reports

The tale of misunderstanding just related would not do in an historical novel, but it is tenable in history, for History produced it. If we lend our minds to such a probability, even though noting it as low in the scale, how much more confident we feel when a set of events is public from the start and attested to by dozens of independent witnesses. In such instances we *know*. Let us recapitulate the two reasons why: (1) we have abundant documentary evidence, and (2) a critical examination of it discloses the high probability of its truth.

"But," says the skeptic, "you were not there. All you know is what others choose to tell you—in memoirs, newspapers, and your other vaunted evidences. How can you be sure? Most people are notoriously bad observers; some are deliberate or unconscious liars; there is no such thing as a perfect witness. And yet you naively trust any casual passerby, and on his say-so you proclaim: 'This is what happened.'"

Except for the words "naively trust," everything said above is true. But in its effort to discredit history it proves too much. The key sentences are "You were not there" and "There is no such thing as a

---

[19]James H. Sledd and Gwin J. Kolb, *Dr. Johnson's Dictionary*, Chicago, 1955, 85–104.

perfect witness." Granting the force of these two statements, what follows? It is that if any of us had been there, there would simply have been one more imperfect witness on the scene. We might be convinced that our vision, our recollection, our interpretation was *the* right one, but other witnesses would still feel no less certain about theirs.

To put it differently, every observer's knowledge of the event doubtless contains some exact and some erroneous knowledge, and these two parts, multipled by as many observers as may be, are all the knowledge there can be. Only a divine being would have perfect and complete knowledge of the event—"as it really happened." Outside our imperfect knowledge, the event has no independent existence; it is not hidden in some "repository of the real" where we can find it. This is important to grasp and remember; it makes one both humble and grateful about the known and knowable past.[20]

In trying to discredit this "second-hand" knowledge, the skeptic about historical truth unconsciously assumes that because he is alive and observant he knows the actuality of his own time, which future reporters will garble in their accounts. Or he compares the doubts honestly expressed about some event by historians themselves with an absolute record which he imagines as existing somewhere, like the standard yard in the government Bureau of Standards. He speaks of "the real past" as of a solid entity hidden from us like a mountain hidden by a mist. But this is a figment of his imagination. The only past there is is the past we have—a thing of opinions and reports.

Indeed, a famous American historian of the Civil War and Reconstruction, William A. Dunning, was convinced that in history what the contemporaries of an event believed it to be is truer—more genuinely "the past"—than anything discovered later that the con-

---

[20]The plethora of documents that the modern age generates is providing a fresh challenge to the historian. In response to the public's so-called right to know, Congress passed the Freedom of Information Acts of 1966 and 1974, which opened to diggers government records hitherto beyond reach. But these seemingly liberating laws have created an insuperable problem: in many cases the researcher, who must apply for the files he seeks, cannot be certain he has asked for everything of possible value and may therefore draw a one-sided conclusion. A useful manual is Robert Bouchard, *Guidebook to the Freedom of Information and Privacy Acts*, New York, 1980.

temporaries did not know. Their views had consequences, whereas ours about their times played no part in the web of thought and action.[21]

In any case, comparisons with an absolute knowledge or the substitution of a divine mind for the human ones that remember the past and write history are irrelevant to historiography. Far from disproving the truth of history, they lead to the conclusion that a capable researcher can know more about the past than did those contemporary with it, which is one reason why under the historian's hand the known past changes and grows.

A typical illustration will make this clear. The story of D-Day, June 6, 1944, still fascinates historians no less than the general public, one of the debatable questions being the heavy pounding that some Americans experienced upon their landing. Eisenhower explained it by writing: "In the Omaha sector an alert enemy division, the 352d, which prisoners stated had been in the area on maneuvers and defense exercises, accounted for some of the intense fighting in that locality."[22] Writing more casually, Winston Churchill offered a slightly different explanation: "By an unlucky chance the enemy defences in this sector had recently been taken over by a complete German division in full strength and on the alert."[23]

How does one decide between the word of the Supreme Commander four years after the event and of the Prime Minister of Britain, himself an accomplished historian, after the lapse of seven years? The researcher doubtless turns to the memoirs of the ground commander, General Omar Bradley, and finds confirmation of Eisenhower's statement, somewhat modified: "the 352d had been moved from St.-Lô to the assault beaches for a defense exercise."[24]

---

[21]"Truth in History," in the volume of that name, New York, 1937, 3–20. For example, as Admiral Rickover has persuasively shown, if the United States had believed in 1898 that the *Maine* in Havana harbor had blown up "by an internal explosion or that the ship was destroyed by causes unknown . . . war might have been avoided" (H. G. Rickover, *How the Battleship* Maine *Was Destroyed*, Washington, D.C., 1976, 104–105).

[22]Dwight D. Eisenhower, *Crusade in Europe*, New York, 1948, 253.

[23]Winston S. Churchill, *The Second World War: Triumph and Tragedy*, New York, 1953, 4. Similarly, on the Michelin map of the whole theater, issued in 1946 and reissued for the commemoration of 1984, the English translation does not match, on this key situation, the French explanatory text.

[24]Omar N. Bradley, *A Soldier's Story*, New York, 1951, 272.

Obviously, one cannot stop here. A determined American student probed further. He could aver that "up to June 4 Allied intelligence had still placed the 352nd around St.-Lô, more than twenty miles away" from Omaha Beach.[25] Now the leading English authority asserts that some time before D-Day, British intelligence "suggested that the 352nd Division had been moved forward to the area below the elbow of the American beaches, although the evidence . . . circulated proved too uncertain to disturb the American planners."[26] So the researcher concludes that despite what Eisenhower and Churchill wrote, Allied intelligence gathering, which had otherwise succeeded in divining the enemy order of battle, failed at one critical point. Autobiographical accounts, even when not self-serving, can mislead. The authors, though competent witnesses on the spot, did not know the reality before them. Later comers reconstruct it with the advantage of perspective and multiplicity of sources, but still without certitude. Speculating about historical possibilities has led able historians to write sustained accounts of what would have followed if—e.g., Napoleon had won at Waterloo. Such "counterfactual history" can be both entertaining and instructive.[27]

To sum up, we must be content with the vast amount of imperfect knowledge that critical history discusses and delivers to us. Since all human knowledge is imperfect, we should take from each discipline its characteristic truths and accept the imperfections inherent in the purpose that the discipline fulfills. If historical knowledge sometimes seems more imperfect than other kinds, this is but an appearance due to the vividness with which it reembodies and makes articulate what is gone. It arouses interests as passionate as those of the present, and it moves people because its literary embodiment

[25]Cornelius Ryan, *The Longest Day*, New York, 1959, 162. See also the maps accompanying the U.S. Army publication, *Omaha Beachhead*, Washington, 1945; reprinted, 1984.

[26]Max Hastings, *Operation Overlord: D-Day and the Battle for Normandy*, New York, 1984, 67.

[27]See David Herbert Donald, *Liberty and Union* (Boston, 1978), pp. 171 ff.; and the lively symposium *If: Or History Rewritten*, edited by Sir John Squire and numbering among its contributors Philip Guedalla, Hilaire Belloc, G. K. Chesterton, Hendrik W. Van Loon, and others (New York, 1931; reprinted, Port Washington, N.Y., Kennikat, 1964).

requires no initiation—"any number can play." Those who read and study history most closely do not disdain to give it credence: that too is an attested fact, whereas thoroughgoing skepticism is often a pose.[28] To the justly skeptical and comparing mind, history at its best is no more uncertain than the descriptive earth sciences whose assertions most people seem willing to take on faith.[29] Large parts of man's history are thoroughly well known and beyond dispute. True, the interpretations and the meanings attached to the parts are and will continue open to debate. But who has settled the interpretation or meaning of human life? Taken all in all, history is genuine knowledge, and we should be lost without it.

Subjective and Objective: The Right Usage

Our cumulative reasons for trusting history are now four: we have documents; they are critically tested; the rule governing judgment is Probability; and the notion of an absolute past, which we might know if only writers did not produce faulty copies, is a delusion. Within the history we possess we can, of course, distinguish good and bad witnesses, good and bad judges of events. An historian might conceivably decide, on the evidence of the individual's habitual inattention, that a cabinet member was a bad judge of what went on at meetings, and that the resulting diary or memoirs were of no use to history.

Such a conclusion could then tempt the devil's advocate to bring up the idea of the "subjective" and point out that since, on our own showing, all history rests on "subjective impressions," therefore all accounts are equally biased and worthless. History would then be like a distorting mirror—a real reflection but all askew.

[28]It has, we believe, never been noted that Voltaire, supposedly the professional doubter par excellence, did not doubt history and was on the contrary an indefatigable historian. In 1769 he published a long essay in rejoinder to Horace Walpole in which he rejected equally "an extreme skepticism and a ridiculous credulity." *Le Pyrrhonisme de l'histoire*, in *Oeuvres*, Kehl, 1785, 27: 9–10.

[29]The public is also docile about accepting radical revisions in the huge spans of time that geologists assign to the periods of prehistory including the age of man on earth.

This is another misunderstanding to clear up. The words "subjective" and "biased" are in the first place not synonyms. Reserving the treatment of bias to the next chapter, let us try here to halt the all-too-common misuse of "subjective." Originally a technical term in a special brand of philosophy, the word has come into the marketplace, where it disturbs not only discussions of history but also ordinary conversation. It is always a danger to borrow technical terms without observing their definitions or without redefining them. In loose speech "subjective" has come to mean "one person's opinion," usually odd or false; whereas "objective" is taken to mean "what everybody agrees on," or correct opinion. According to this, if one witness to a particular event was contradicted on a main point by six other people he would automatically be thought "subjective" and wrong. They would be thought "objective" and right. This common belief is quite mistaken.[30]

"Subjective" and "objective" properly apply not to persons and opinions but to sensations and judgments. Every person, that is, every living subject, is necessarily subjective in *all* his sensations. But some of his subjective sensations are *of* objects, others of himself, or "subject." Your toothache is said to be subjective because it occurs within you as a feeling subject. It is not an object in the world for all to see; it is yours alone. The tooth that the dentist extracts *is* an object and with its removal goes your subjective ache. While the pain lasted, both tooth and ache were real. Now only the tooth is real—hence the tendency to believe that an object is somehow "more real," that is, more lasting, more public, than a *purely* subjective impression. But objects themselves are known only by subjects—persons—so the distinction is not clear-cut, much less a test of reality.[31] If this reasoning strains the ordinary faculties, get rid of the whole matter by

[30]In colleges and universities the misusage has probably been encouraged by the term "objective examinations," which is a misnomer to describe multiple-choice questions. See Banesh Hoffmann's pioneering work, *The Tyranny of Testing*, New York, 1962.

[31]Another example for good measure: if you see spots before your eyes, they may be objective—a piece of material with polka dots—or subjective, a diseased condition of the body. Take quinine and you may hear a ringing in your ears—purely subjective, though real. But you have no difficulty ascertaining the absence of an objective bell that could account for the sensation.

dropping the jargon use of "objective" and "subjective" as synonyms for "true" and "false." To sum up, *an objective judgment is one made by testing in all ways possible one's subjective impressions, so as to arrive at a knowledge of objects*.

The researcher naturally strives for objective judgments. His "objects"—the events of history—are known to him indirectly through the testimony of witnesses, whose competence is in turn judged as we showed earlier. Comparison with other objects and other judgments is the researcher's endless task. In history-writing as in life, objective judgments are made every time a capable mind attends to the evidence before it. Such a mind may reach a wrong conclusion, an error may later be proved upon him, new evidence may modify his hitherto sound report, but the judgment when made was objective.

One more point about judgment: competence, and not majority opinion, is decisive; there have been collective hallucinations that deceived large majorities. Now translate this into a researcher's typical situation. From noted literary figures who knew Henry James we have many reports on the novelist's appearance, manners, and speech. Most of them refer to him as either stuttering or hemming and hawing. One and only one entranced listener, herself trained in speech, has written down, with the aid of tempo marks, a characteristic sentence as James spoke it. From this it clearly appears that James was not stammering or fumbling for words at all, but repeating himself in various emphatic ways as he went along, or—to quote his interpreter—"instinctively bringing out the perfect sentence the first time; repeating it [in bits] more deliberately to test every word the second time; accepting it as satisfactory the third time, and triumphantly sending it forth as produced by Henry James."[32] This extraordinary mode of speech needed an extraordinary witness to record it for posterity. Against her objective judgment and manifest competence, no amount of careless reporting can avail.

In relation to his documents the historian is of course in the position of "the single competent witness." It is he who is being

[32]Elizabeth Jordan, quoted in S. Nowell-Smith, *The Legend of the Master*, New York, 1948, 16.

objective as he reviews the evidence, not the thousands of heedless persons who reason ignorantly on inadequate information. In the Henry James instance it would be plausible but uncritical to argue that people who knew James well—H. G. Wells, Hugh Walpole, Ford Madox Ford, and a dozen others—would be better judges of his mannerisms than a comparative stranger meeting him casually at dinner. The opposite is true—provided, once again, that the stranger had competence and enough subjective interest in James to wish to make an objective judgment.

The researcher is accordingly quick to seize upon the single witness's account, which, though telling, has for one reason or another not become common knowledge. Facts like these throw light on well-known events from such unexpected corners that the mere recital gives a sense of the "thickness" of History. General Eisenhower furnished a particularly striking instance of this sudden illumination when he wrote of the nerve-wracking decision he had to make during the war about seizing Pantelleria, a small island off Sicily. He related the incident in *Crusade in Europe*;[33] the memory still haunted him years later: " . . . the decision was so difficult that had the predictions of the pessimists been carried out or been realized I certainly would have been relieved [of my command]. So you can never tell at the moment, is history going to say this was right or this was wrong."[34] The only thing that "history" in the popular sense has to say about this turning point and the emotion it aroused in one man is that very few have ever heard of it. Yet in the narrative of the great struggle, the leap across from Africa to Pantelleria was equivalent to Caesar's crossing of the Rubicon, about which everyone *has* heard, thanks to historians.

Knowledge of Fact and Knowledge of Causes

The vast consequences of such pivotal moves inevitably pose the problem of causation. Though we have steadily strengthened our defenses against the skeptic and shown how documentary evidence

[33]New York, 1948, 164 ff.
[34]*New York Times*, March 24, 1955.

and its handling successively raise our certitude about the past higher than any imaginable certitude about the present, this favorable comparison itself spurs the skeptic to a last effort: "Granted that you may know enough to tell a reliable story, full of significant detail, you really know nothing unless at every point you also know the causes."

The challenge takes one into deep waters. Whole books have been written about Causation. Their contents could not be reviewed in a few pages even if one omitted all the manifest errors in them. Only a sketch of the question at large can be given. The chief difficulty lies in what is meant by Cause. Neither philosophers nor scientists agree on what causation is or does. In the mid-eighteenth century, the philosopher David Hume showed that the conception of Cause as a compelling push that produces an effect is an illusion. Man has no immediate sense of the necessity that makes one billiard ball propel another after striking it; he has only an expectation of the event, an expectation bred in him by habitual experience. Ever since Hume, all that has been agreed upon is that where Cause is, there is Regularity.

Everyone nevertheless continues to believe in causes that compel. We say, "The manager's behavior caused X to resign," and we think we know what we mean. But as soon as we try to say precisely what we mean our confidence breaks down. A psychologist will show how inadequate is our grasp of the cause: the alleged cause was a mere pretext; the manager's offensive behavior was imaginary—a "projection" on the subordinate's part. Or again, the latter's behavior may have provoked the other's—hence the man himself was the cause of his own resignation. Or possibly his wife caused it, unknown to herself and to him.

These speculations are meant only to show that when we speak of causes in human affairs we are usually dealing with a variety of elements that stand at different degrees of distance from the observed event and that are not easily discerned or separated. Judge Hand called them incommensurables because they cannot be measured and sometimes cannot even be discerned.[35] If a man kills himself sixteen

---

[35]See above, p. 51.

days, five hours, and twenty-three minutes after receiving a piece of bad news, what is the cause of his suicide? In ordinary speech we say either "Things became too much for him," or "A man's vitality is lowest in the early morning," or "A man of John's tradition and character could not face bankruptcy." In other words we ascribe his death either to an unfathomable psychological state, or to a physiological fact, or to a recognizable idea born in response to a situation. We are not likely to ascribe it to the bullet and the gun, because that cause does not interest us: it interests only the Medical Examiner.

Generalizing from this we conclude that what history reveals to mankind about its past does not uncover *the* cause (one or more indispensable antecedents) of any event, large or small, but only the *conditions* (some of the prerequisites) attending its emergence. Not only can we not isolate the cause, but we cannot properly define of what sort it would be. When Pascal said that if Cleopatra's nose had been shorter this would have changed the face of the world (to say nothing of her own), he was pointing out that personality plays a role in History. He did not mean that Cleopatra's nose in all its beauty was *the* cause of Mark Antony's defeat at Actium: it was at best one of the antecedent conditions. In short, when we give an account of human events we fasten upon those points that seem to us suitable to connect believably with our present concerns and previous experience. If these connections are duly brought out we say we "understand."[36]

The thought occurs that we might come closer to a real cause, and obtain results akin to those of physical science, if we could only deal with well-defined kinds of events, such as, say, automobile accidents. We do in fact classify these and learn that mechanical failure caused so many percent, speeding so many, and intoxication so many. Can this possibility of classification and statistical measurements be extended throughout the realm of History so as to conquer and annex it to science?

The question is complex, and one part of it—the practical part—must await treatment till Chapter 10. The other parts belong to

---

[36]For a subtle and authoritative account of causation as it is conceived in physical science and as it must be conceived in the "historical" realm which includes all that is not science, see Henry Margenau, *Open Vistas*, New Haven, 1961, esp. 191–214.

philosophy and the logic of science.[37] Let it suffice here to say that although historical events are unique, many of them are enough alike to permit us to refer to them by the same name, and hence to discern regularities. History does and does not repeat; and science deals, though in a different way, with the same paradoxical situation: no two laboratory "events" are alike, though designed to be so.

There is another sense in which history is a part of the realm of science, and which should prevent us from thinking of the two as opposed or radically distinct from each other: the events of history occur in the same universe and follow the same material "laws" as the objects of science. Living beings are subject to gravitation and decay, statesmen in transit are no different from other moving bodies, and what is most important, men's minds work upon historical data with the same perceptions and logical rules as they do in science.

A difference remains, of course, which most observers feel intuitively even when they find it difficult to assess. History cannot, like physical science, pare down events and reproduce them at will in the simple forms and controlled conditions that we call experiment. Nor, as we saw above, can the historian sort out his materials into independent units that will stay put long enough for him to measure and relate them as constants and variables.[38] Even when we count automobile accidents we pursue our practical interest at the expense of strict causal analysis. The *immediate* error that caused the drunken driver's accident interests us no more than the remote cause that led him to drink.[39]

[37] A wonderfully lucid and conclusive treatment of these two related topics was given by James Fitzjames Stephen in "The Study of History," *Cornhill Magazine*, 4 (1861), 32.

[38] We can of course achieve this relation intuitively through historical *judgment*, as Garrett Mattingly, the great historian of early modern times, has pointed out: "Conscious that every human situation contains certain elements of uniformity and certain elements of uniqueness, we scrutinize each new one and compare it with everything we can find out about similar situations in the past, seeking to assign values to constants and to isolate the variables, to decide which factors are significant, what choices are actually present, and what the probable consequences are of choosing course A and rejecting B."

[39] For a trenchant discussion of the logic of historical analysis, see an article under that title by Ernest Nagel in *Scientific Monthly*, 74 (March 1952), 162–169.

On Cause and Measurement

Every attempt in historical writing to formalize causal description or make a show of exactitude by assigning one "paramount" cause and several "contributory" causes ends in self-stultification. Any such distinction implies a measurement that we cannot in fact make; it foolishly apes the chemical formula by which a compound requires several elements in stated proportions. For if, as Edward Lucas White once contended,[40] it took malaria-bearing mosquitoes and the spread of Christianity to undo the Roman Empire, the mosquitoes were as necessary as the Christians and neither is paramount to the other.[41]

The historical researcher is thus led to adopt a practical distinction about causality that has already commended itself to workers in physical science. They draw attention to the difference between causation that occurs in a long chain of events of various kinds and causation within a closed system. An example of the first is the forming of a cloud, the darkening of the sun to earth dwellers, the lowering of temperature, people putting on coats, a thunderstorm bursting, a person taking refuge under a tree and being struck by lightning and killed. This chain of "causes" is miscellaneous and each event in it unpredictable, not because it is not determined, but because it occurs outside any controllable limits. As against this, in the physics laboratory, an elastic body of known stresses and strains goes through a series of evolving states; at any moment a single definite distribution of measured stresses and strains follows that of the previous moment, which may therefore be regarded as its complete "cause," as "*the* cause."

The distinctive feature of the first kind of causality is that there is no restriction on the events that may be related. It is open to the

---

[40] In *Why Rome Fell*, New York, 1927.

[41] See a recent archeological hypothesis of the same simplicity: "Downfall of Indus Civilization Is Traced to Mud," *New York Times*, May 23, 1966. And, reverting to the Romans, recent advocates of the single, hidden cause have suggested gout, "the bacchanalian appetites of ancient Rome," or lead pots and pipes, or all three (*New York Times*, March 18, 1983).

observer's insight to select, not causes in sense number 2, but conditions that belong to the chain and have the merit of interesting him and his audience. It is for them to judge whether the resulting narrative is intelligible, consonant with the experience of the race, and useful in orienting the mind amid the welter of facts.

This view, which may be described as pragmatic,[42] is peculiarly suited to historiography because of the impossibility of separating human activities into independent portions and units. Suppose—contrary to our view, but as some people do believe—that through the study of history, a case were made out for thinking that *the* cause of war was trade, or sexual aggressiveness, or diplomacy. Clearly, this result would be untestable as long as it was impossible to uproot the singled-out component of our nature and our civilization and thus abolish war. Indeed, war would probably break out over the issue of abolition, for war is also "caused" by ideas.

It is enough to state the supposition to see its absurdity. As a noted theorist said many years ago:

> Nothing could be more artificial than the scientific separation of man's religious, aesthetic, economic, political, intellectual and bellicose properties. These may be studied, each by itself, with advantage, but specialization would lead to the most absurd results if there were not someone to study the process as a whole; and that someone is the historian.[43]

On the view we have called pragmatic, and which attends not to causes but to variously relevant conditions, certain of the old puzzles and objections fall away. The objection that historians select their facts to suit themselves is seen to be no objection but a helpful necessity. They are meant to think and to choose, and they are judged by the intelligence and honesty with which they do both. Again, the objection that history cannot be true because it has to be rewritten every thirty years appears as a sign of the usefulness of history: it not only should respond to the demands made upon it but it *can*

---

[42]"Pragmatic" is here used in its technical, Jamesian sense; it does not mean "convenient" or "practical," but "tested by consequences rather than antecedents"— the pragmatic test. See Mommsen's comparable usage, derived from the ancient historian Polybius, in the epigraph to this book.

[43]James Harvey Robinson, *The New History*, New York, 1913, 66.

respond.[44] The successive revisions of the past do not cancel each other out, they are additive: we know more and more about the past through history, as we know more and more about nature through physical science, eliminating untenable views as we go. Finally, the need to choose among conditions in order to delineate events points to the truth that history, like all narrative, must present a pattern to the mind, must have form. Without a form, the accumulation of names and events is unintelligible and useless. It is the organization of the past that makes the past valuable, just as it is the organization of phenomena in scientific formulas that makes the study of nature valuable.

The ultimate question for the historian therefore is: What pattern?

[44]But see below, Revisionism, pp. 238–247.

8

Pattern, Bias,
and the Great Systems

The Reason of Historical Periods and Labels

When six historians were invited by a leading monthly journal to
select by way of Bicentennial tribute the most formative events in
United States history, they suggested a total of 356 events; they
agreed unanimously on five.[1]

Few historians would be surprised by this fact, and most would
gladly have explained to the publisher that although the answers
might be of some interest, the inquiry was based on a misappre-
hension. For to try to determine for oneself or for others *the* formative moments in history, whether 15 or 100, is an intellectual impossibility. To understand why this is so calls for an understanding of the
related subjects of Pattern, Period, Bias, and System.

The last chapter concluded with the assertion that the writing of
history requires a pattern, the reason being that the human mind
cannot fix its attention on anything that does not present or suggest
form. The mind tends to impose a form if one is not supplied. Throw
down a dozen paper clips on a table and look at them for a few

---

[1] *Life Special Report: 100 Events that Shaped America*, New York, 1975.

seconds: they are scattered at random, yet you will find yourself "seeing" a triangle of three in one corner, a sort of cross in the middle, and a little rosette at the left. The constellations in the sky are the product of this inevitable penchant for grouping-in-order-to-grasp.

Similarly in story and in history. We expect them to offer us incidents in clusters that follow "rationally" upon one another. We may keep reading straight ahead uncritically, but on looking back we like to feel that the whole somehow possesses dramatic form. This does not necessarily mean emotional excitement; it means an acceptable progression from a clear beginning to an intelligible end. This is why Macaulay, proposing to give a vast panorama of the events that filled the "momentous" years from 1685 to 1701, was so concerned with his arrangement. When his *History* was done he kept scrutinizing the form and comparing it with that of his favorite, Thucydides: "I admire him more than ever. He is the great historian. The others one may hope to match: him never . . . [but] . . . his arrangement is bad. . . . How much better is my order than that of Thucydides."[2]

Some few historians have at times repudiated this interest in "order" and declared that for history to be scientifically true the facts should arrange themselves. This is a misconception of both history and science. In the study of nature the facts do not arrange themselves either. A formula, or little form, implies the selection of certain phenomena that observation, followed by experiment, have related, first to a scale of measurement and then to other facts in fixed or variable connections. The choice of facts and of relations is dictated by human interest as well as by nature. It is curiosity that moves the inquirer to ascertain the relation between the behavior of a gas and the phenomena of heat and pressure. The facts, moreover, are seen through ideas (for example, the idea of a molecule) that are not immediately visible and ready to be noted down. They are searched for with a purpose in mind. The facts and connections once ascertained, a mind has to frame a hypothesis to arrive at what is properly called *theory*: a total view of related events.

---

[2]G. O. Trevelyan, *Life and Letters of Lord Macaulay* (first published 1876), diary entries for November 25 and December 4, 1848.

Historians work under the same necessity of giving shape to the events that they have found and verified. Only, the historian has no scale with which to measure the facts, and few symbols other than words with which to express their relations. His purpose being to portray intelligibly, he must "relate" in the ordinary sense of *recount* lifelike sequences. He presents human affairs as in a story, describing conditions and complications, and reaching climaxes and conclusions to aid understanding.

He can of course measure time, and chronology supplies a natural order among his facts. But, as we shall see, chronology is long and its contents are a mixed bag. For both these reasons it too needs a pattern before it can be thought and felt.[3] This leads the historian to carve out manageable periods: reigns, centuries, eras. He also finds ready-made certain other patterns or "constellations" created by the laity, contemporary or not, out of *their* need to group things: these groupings go by names such as Gothic and Baroque, Renaissance and Romantic. These the historian must accept as having meaning, even if the meaning has to be explained at length, and even if it remains less clear-cut than that of molecule; for the historical labels refer to the thoughts and acts of once living beings, who were precisely *not* molecules.

Groups and their names usually arise in the course of intellectual or artistic debate. Thus the name "Hudson River School," now used in scholarly writing to describe a notable group of American painters, was first used by a critic in scorn of certain artists and their works. It was not an exact label, as one might guess, for the men attacked did not invariably paint the Hudson River or live on its banks. But the name is now indispensable, in the first place because it is an historical datum; and in the second, because it links fact and idea in the true manner of history. The ideas consist of certain pictorial principles and poetic intentions; the facts make up the biography of certain men, their dates, works, careers.

To object to labels or periods and say that "historians invent them, hence they are false" is a cliché that is itself false to the way

[3]For the relation of the chronological and topical treatments, see Chapter 11, pp. 274 ff.

things happen, besides amounting to a failure of imagination. Without divisions of time, groupings of men, aggregates of ideas, the historian would be reduced to unreadable, unrememberable chronicling. The value of the historic term "Hudson River School" is that it denotes a number of great painters who share some important characteristics. It is of course not enough to learn the tag; learning history means learning its details. One ends up knowing that the Hudson River painters were not merely local and aquatic, but America's first and many-sided national school. Superficially misleading, the tag "Hudson River" is nonetheless the proper History-encrusted symbol of events, expressing a combination of facts in a pattern.

The Conditions of Pattern-Making

Having accepted historic groupings as given, we still remain critical of patterns at large and we ask: What elements of thought and observation go into the making of any "constellation" that unites the loose particles of fact? Not all periods, patterns, and labels are equally apt and useful; but we may for the moment leave in abeyance the question of value and merit. The first element in an historical pattern is obviously a comparison of some sort, natural or artificial. We decide that X is more like Y than like M. The difference between the natural and the arbitrary groupings of this kind is always difficult to state. As in the example of the scattered paper clips, we can argue that once scattered some of them naturally *are* in the form of a cross, or again that we *choose to see them as a cross*. Trying to settle the debate would lead us back to the philosophy of perception, which is too large a subject to be summarized here. The researcher will profit more from another distinction between random (or historic) grouping and systematic grouping (or classification).

The first kind is given to the researcher ready-made, as in the Hudson River School. The hostile critic who made this pattern to impress the readers of the New York *Tribune* with his disapproval did not conduct a thorough survey of contemporary American painters and select a certain number on the basis of features verifiably present.

He was simply hurling an epithet at random—and it stuck.[4] We may assume that it did so because it corresponded to some vague kinship that needed to be named; but as we saw, in order to extract the value of this naming we have to go back to the facts themselves and make them modify the oversimple idea that the bare term raises in our minds.

A systematic grouping, on the other hand, is usually the work of a researcher who stands farther away from the living reality than the contemporary critic, and who wishes to study a genuine set or class of facts. Thus when the late Crane Brinton prepared his book *The Jacobins*, he did not take merely the first half dozen whose names he happened to know, or content himself with the membership of the Paris group; he systematically sampled the membership of that historic party by examining the records of chosen Jacobin Clubs all over France. Such a study resembles what we know as sociology, but its principle is fundamental to all descriptive disciplines: generalization depends on adequate enumeration. If you want to make an assertion about the views of a board of directors, you must look up in the minutes the votes and opinions of all the members. In other words, your classification must cover the ground. Definition determines the limits of the class, even though you are still grouping together people who differ in appearance and opinion from one another.

The next condition of pattern-making grows out of this human diversity, which makes it either impossible or fruitless to report on human affairs in cut-and-dried fashion. In looking for "the views of the board of directors," it would not be enough to give a tabulation of their votes on various issues. To conceive the situation of the company accurately, we must know the words, the personalities, the intrigues, the emotions represented. And since the historian cannot and should not "tell all," he must select. We thus arrive at our first

---

[4]Compare the various origins of "Quakers," "Muckrakers," "Sea Beggars," "Diggers," "Fauves," "Cubists," "Rosicrucians," "The Bloomsbury Group," "Girond-ists," "Jacobins," "Jacobites," "Whigs," "Tories," "Spartacists," "Huguenots," "Know-Nothings," "Suffragettes," "Irreconcilables," "Existentialists," "Beatniks," "Hawks and Doves," "Supply-siders," "New Leftists." A useful work on this age-old social and political practice is G. E. Shankle, *American Nicknames and Their Significance*, New York, 1955.

rule of pattern-making: *To be successful and right, a selection must face two ways: it must fairly correspond to the mass of evidence, and it must offer a graspable design to the beholder.*

The researcher never sees the facts fully displayed before him like someone selecting jewelry laid out on a counter. The researcher has begun with but little knowledge of the subject and has gradually acquired a mass of information beyond the capacity of both the mind's eye and the memory. When he selects, therefore, he is to be compared not to the customer with the synoptic view, but to the traveler exploring new country. The explorer forms his opinions as he progresses, and they change with increasing knowledge. Yet they are always conditioned by two things: the observer's temperament, including his preconceptions, and the motive or purpose of his search.

The Sources of Bias and Its Correctives

The researcher, it is clear, looks for his facts even more actively than the traveler. He must piece together the "scenery" of the past from fragments that lie scattered in many places. This means that the researcher soon develops a guiding idea to propel him along his route, a hypothesis ahead of the facts, which steadily reminds him of what to look for. "Ideas," says one critic,

are themes of historical research—though not of all historical research. The clearer we are about the theme of our own research, the clearer we become about our own bias. And the clearer we are about our own bias, the more honest and efficient we are likely to be in our own research. Many of the rules laid down about the correct methods of historical research are in fact disguised declarations of the purposes of the research itself.[5]

To which might be added: in research as in life one is far more likely to find what one looks for than what one neglects.

Since guiding ideas affect both search and selection, let us call the researcher's temperament (that is, the whole tendency of his

[5]Arnaldo Momigliano, "A Hundred Years After Ranke," *Diogenes*, 6 (Summer 1954), 57–58.

mind) and his present intentions and hypotheses, his total *interest*. We may then say without implying any blame that his interest will determine his discoveries, his selection, his pattern-making, and his exposition. This is unavoidable in all products of the mind. Mathematicians themselves recognize in the work of their colleagues the individuality that produces solutions of certain kinds or arrives at them in certain ways. In research and writing there are of course many kinds and qualities of "interest," ranging from the downright dishonest to that which in Thucydides elicited Macaulay's breathless admiration. Apart from degrees of talent, the dividing line between the good and bad kinds of interest is usually drawn through the point where interest begins to spoil the product altogether. It is then called Bias.

Bias is an uncontrolled form of interest.[6] It is easily detected, but its presence does not tell us all we need to know about an historical report. Gibbon, for example, was biased in favor of pagan Rome and against Christianity, so much so that he devoted two long chapters to an ironic castigation of the early Church. As a result, one does not go to Gibbon for a sympathetic understanding of primitive Christianity. But the remainder of his history—the larger part—stands firm. And that valuable part, as far as we can tell, could not have been produced apart from the rest. The work as a whole would never have been undertaken and carried through without Gibbon's animus, his bias.

Again, Macaulay is sometimes dismissed with the phrase "the Whig historian." The description is not wrong, but the implication usually is. Macaulay's sympathies were with the Whigs in the Revolution of 1688 and with their descendants, the Liberals of his own day. Yet his *History* also stands. What he wrote is neither a party pamphlet, nor a whitewashing, nor anything less than a great history. One of his later opponents in politics, Lord Acton, who was deeply

---

[6]That bias can be controlled, indeed suppressed, by a trained mind which is also self-aware is vividly shown by a remark in a contemporary history: "[Professor] Nock," says Morton Smith in his work of discovery and interpretation, *The Secret Gospel*, "was a tower of strength in this. His philological knowledge was vast, his judgment impeccable, and his objectivity such that, in spite of his prejudice against Clementine authorship, he often pointed out evidence that went to confirm it" (New York, 1973, 27).

repelled by Macaulay's faults, nevertheless called him "one of the greatest of all writers and masters."[7]

Because "bias" is used pejoratively, it is assumed that some workers are biased, others not. This is to think in black and white. Gaetano Salvemini put the situation better when he told his students: "Impartiality is a dream and honesty a duty. We cannot be impartial, but we can be intellectually honest." The student of history responds to the need for pattern and wants a strong motive to propel research; hence he cannot be neutral. Without interest on his part, his work will lack interest too.

In assessing bias, the researcher must bring to bear a certain sophistication of mind. As a thoughtful scholar he recognizes the double condition of the search for truth—it must in the end produce a form and at any point it answers some implied or expressed interest. And as a critical judge tracing the way in which the historian's interest has contributed to the form, he asks:

1. Was the writer fastidious or crude in selecting and marshaling his facts? That is, was he hard upon his own hypotheses, fair-minded to his opponents, committed to the truth first and foremost?

2. Was he self-aware enough to recognize—perhaps to acknowledge—the assumptions connected with his interest?

3. Does the work as a whole exhibit the indispensable scholarly virtues, however noticeable the bias?

In answering these questions, the researcher will of course try to be as fair as he would like all his witnesses to be. For whoever judges another's interest is also moved by an interest of his own—an interest that is often heightened by the fact that many others share it unquestioningly. At any one time, politics all over the globe is powered by

[7]James W. Thompson, *A History of Historical Writing*, New York, 1942, 2: 300. On one occasion Acton told the Trinity College Society at Cambridge: "'I was once with two eminent men, the late Bishop of Oxford [William Stubbs] and the present Bishop of London [Mandell Creighton]. On another occasion I was with two far more eminent men, the two most learned men in the world. I need hardly tell you their names—they were Mommsen and Harnack. On each occasion the question arose: who was the greatest historian the world had ever produced. On each occasion the name first mentioned and on each occasion the name finally agreed upon, was that of Macaulay.'"

thoughts of the past mixed with hopes for the future—and this not just unconsciously, but overtly in the form of arguments, appeals, and recriminations. The present conflict in Northern Ireland, for example, is both an outcome of long historical memories and a subject of historical controversy in other places. An English newspaper says: "Ulster: what can we do? No peace until historic facts are faced." Shortly before, the American ambassador felt called upon to state that "many Americans, particularly Irish-Americans, misunderstand the background of the Northern Ireland question, and think the British Army is there to suppress the Ulstermen rather than to protect the (Roman Catholic) minority."[8]

Whatever they may understand of the complex situation, Americans write to the papers and argue with it and with each other in historical terms. One man challenges the Prime Minister about Irish terrorism in London: the members of the IRA are killers, not patriots, said the Prime Minister. The writer points out that decades earlier the future President of the Irish Republic was denounced by the English government as a murderer. And so were the American patriots of 1776, adds this vehement expounder of history.[9] The next day, another writer argues that the IRA and the Irish people are distinct groups and that Protestant Ulster would die rather than be incorporated into Eire, as was shown in 1922 when the present border was drawn.

And soon that piece of history is attacked by yet another debater, who urges the "need" for the IRA. He looks down "the dark corridors of Irish history" and sees the action of the British government as "recruiting calls for Irish revolutionary organizations."[10] That the rights and wrongs of the question, if they depend on historical truths as is claimed, cannot be settled in the few paragraphs of a letter does not prevent "history" from being confidently used. The probability that a critical inquiry would show an appalling equality of misdeeds on both sides of the conflict does not deter the combatants, on paper or in actuality. For Northern Ireland, the religious wars of the sixteenth and seventeenth centuries are not yet over.

[8]*New York Times*, January 3, 1976.
[9]*Ibid.*, December 29, 1975.
[10]*Ibid.*, January 16, 1976.

In these conditions the effort of self-awareness required to over-come bias is, for most people, superhuman. But the critical scholar approaching a piece of testimony must gauge whether fact or bias is its principal message. Measuring self-awareness most often means being alive to implications; for there is no law requiring a writer to say in so many words: "These are my assumptions, how do you like them?" The writer may be content with statements of principle that he or she hopes you will accept as true, or at least as working hypotheses. For example, when Macaulay remarks that

> During more than a hundred years . . . every [English] man has felt entire confidence that the state would protect him in the possession of what had been earned by his diligence and hoarded by his self-denial. Under the benignant influence of peace and liberty, science has flourished and has been applied to practical purposes on a scale never before known. The conse-quence is that a change to which the history of the old world furnishes no parallel has taken place in our country,[11]

we easily infer that the writer favors peace, liberty, property, applied science, and the Industrial Revolution. He is also a Little Englander, patriotic but not imperialistic, an advocate of laissez-faire and of the moral traits that go with that philosophy: self-reliance, rationalism, and a respect for worldly achievements.

The value of knowing all this as one reads an account of the past is that it affords a basis for judging the writer's own judgments. The reader proceeds by a sort of triangulation: here I stand; there, to left or right, stands Macaulay; and beyond are the events that he reports. Knowing his position in relation to mine, I can work out a perspective upon events as I could not if I saw them exclusively through his eyes—or mine.

Practicing this triangulation is not the same as dismissing an author after having "doped out" that he is a Whig, a Catholic, a Dutchman, a Muslim, an alcoholic, or a divorced man. Dismissal or systematic discounting of what a person says because of his or her nationality, religion, or personal history is only the crude and dull form of the delicate assessment here called for. One might as well

---

[11] *History of England from the Accession of James Second*, New York, 1899, 1:261.

spare oneself the effort of reading at all if one is going to make the text a mere peg for a gloating distrust. The aim should be rather to obtain a large return in knowledge, some of it held under caution until two, three, or four other accounts have modified or strengthened its solid parts.

In short, reader's suspiciousness is no answer to the question of writer's bias. On the contrary, sympathy is prerequisite to understanding, for history presents people once alive and their active emotions, which can be understood in no other way. Woodrow Wilson, an accomplished historian, went even further:

> The historian needs something more than sympathy, for sympathy may be condescending, pitying, contemptuous. . . . Sympathy there must be . . . but it must be the sympathy of the man who stands in the midst and sees like one within, not like one without, like a native, not like an alien. He must not sit like a judge exercising extraterritorial jurisdiction.[12]

Here, surely, is our old friend Imagination under another name. The fact that it is a dangerous quality does not mean that it can be dispensed with. Imagination that suggests what facts we want and where they may be found also tells us what they mean. An Australian historian, Sir Keith Hancock, has told how in writing his first book on the Risorgimento in Tuscany he identified himself with each party, one after the other: "I was zealous in turn for the House of Austria, the House of Savoy, the Papacy, the Mazzinian People, and half a dozen brands of liberalism or democracy."[13] An imaginative sympathy with all the participants sets up in the researcher's mind that internal debate which re-creates the actuality, and out of this comes right judgment. Juxtaposing his successive enthusiasms, the faithful student formed a total view that none of the actors themselves had had, and his intellect apportioned to each element its due. In his own words, "Getting inside the situation is the opening movement, getting outside it is the concluding one."[14]

The impossibility and undesirability of eliminating interest and

---

[12] "The Variety and Unity of History," *Congress of Arts and Science, Universal Exposition, St. Louis, 1904*, Howard J. Rogers, ed., Boston, 1906, 2:17.

[13] *Country and Calling*, London, 1954, 220.

[14] *Ibid.*, 221.

the effort to detect and allow for bias reconcile us to the lack of unanimity in historical writing. The reason for all variations and contradictions is of course perspective. A large subject is like a mountain, which no beholder ever sees entire: if he climbs it he discovers only selected aspects; if he stands off, he sees but an outline and from one side only; if he flies over it, he flattens it out. No two minds see things precisely alike and no two eras possess exactly the same interest in human affairs, the same collective "mind." What interests an age has to do with recent events or present predicaments. After a world war, international relations and earlier great wars have intrinsic interest. After a great depression, it is economic systems and policies that engage public attention. A large-scale revolution tending left or right brings out works about revolutions as far back as Cromwell and the republics of antiquity.

Yet the cliché that history must be rewritten every generation should run somewhat differently: the past cannot help being reconceived by every generation, but the earlier reports upon it are in the main as good and true as they ever were. Anyone who would know the full history of any period will do well to read its successive treatments, just as the ordinary researcher who would know the truth of a single incident seeks out all its witnesses. The rewriting of history, rightly considered, does not substitute; it subtracts a little and adds more.

A further advantage of trying to harmonize the views of different periods into a larger but still coherent pattern is that in so doing one learns a great deal about the mind of each period. Pierre Bayle, the critical historian previously cited, put this with some exaggeration: "I almost never read historians with a view to learning what occurred, but only in order to know what is said in each nation about what occurred."[15] A modern researcher into Bayle's own century expressed the nub of this more exactly when she said:

> The major changes in historical interpretation do not, as the layman often imagines, arise from the discovery of new evidence—the chest full of unsuspected documents . . . what is most likely to happen is that the historian will find what he is looking for, namely, the documents which will explain

---

[15] "Critique générale de *l'Histoire du Calvinisme* de M. Maimbourg," *Oeuvres Diverses*, The Hague, 1727, 2:10.

and illustrate his own point of view. But what *is* he looking for? Surely he is looking for the truth—for what really happened. It is his job as a scholar to form as exact an idea of past events as he can from the surviving evidence. But the instrument with which he looks at the past is modern. It was made, and shaped, and it operates, in the present. It is his own mind. And however much he bends his thoughts toward the past, his own way of thinking, his outlook, his opinions are the products of the time in which he lives. So that all written history . . . [is] a compound of past and present.[16]

Revisionism with a Big R

These shifts of outlook, then, are a constant in human experience itself. But within the last quarter century, something like a fresh motive has been added to this expectable restlessness. It is called Revisionism and it springs from the conviction that all earlier views of men and events are wrong, vitiated by prejudice and falsified by lack of modern methods. The prejudice is supposed to come from the very customs and principles of Western civilization. The missing methods are supposed to be supplied by science, defined as depth psychology and quantitative sociology. The influence of Marxism is visible in the attitude that a new age of the world has begun and that nothing deemed true before can be true now. The change is thus not one of perspective or interest but, as it were, of reality itself. Revisionism aims at a total overturn, as when Christianity conquered the Roman Empire.

It is noticeable, moreover, that Revisionism owes part of its animus to the temper of the modern arts, which have accustomed the public to the idea that any work deserving attention must affront existing ideas and turn them upside down. Only the offbeat, startling, "revolutionary" has merit; the rest is dull imitation. The model is doubtless science, which steadily overturns and defies common sense.

In revisionist history and biography heroes and villains are apt to change places while causes and results contradict, not just some detail or tendency, but also the received and hitherto probable explanations. Thus, as will be noted in the next chapter, scholars have tried to show that slaveholding in the South was not as harsh as abolitionists

---

[16]C. V. Wedgwood, "The Present in the Past," *Listener*, 53 (February 10, 1955), 235.

said it was, that the railroad had little or no influence in developing the continent, and that the country's power of assimilation—the "melting pot" that made Irish, Sicilians, Finns, Jews, Hungarians, Germans, Swedes, Greeks, and other Europeans into Americans—was a fiction.

Now that a woman of Italian descent has been nominated for the vice presidency who seemed well matched in speech, attitudes, and manners with her running mate of Norwegian descent, the pre-revisionist notion of cultural melting and recasting appears to have been prematurely overthrown. Similarly, a return to the sources that describe the advent and effects of the railroad as it advanced westward reminds us forcibly that it was not an ineffectual toy for the sole amusement of tourists and cows in the field.

As regards the new methods, their application has given results ranging from the useful to the absurd. The useful results, as will be shown in greater detail in Chapter 10, have not been histories but sociological studies of past times and situations. An historian could well make use of them in the course of his or her narrative, to depict conditions of life and states of fact or of mind. But it remains to be seen which of those innumerable studies by historians not trained in sociology or statistical method are reliable enough for the social historian with a keen sense of evidence.

The Philosophy and the Laws of History

We shall see in the next chapter how patterns, traditions, biases, and cultural and other controlling assumptions have affected the work of European and American historians in modern times. The circumstances of Europe and of the New World having been different, the views of the past have also differed without on that account playing false to the zeal for truth, much less nullifying the results of copious research.

But before glancing at these important effects of interest or bias, we must look briefly at a special kind of interest that continues to furnish a motive to certain historians—the interest in discovering "the laws" of history. This interest goes by various names—it purports to give the "philosophy of history," or it establishes an historical "system," or it lays down "the law of historical evolution," as in Marx's "materialist conception of history."

The most recent of these systems, Arnold Toynbee's *A Study of History*,[17] is the most inductive, at least in the beginning, but it too winds up with a recurrent pattern, in which regularity is disclosed amid the "apparent" disorder of events. Wars or tyrants or revolutions or decadence follow in ordered succession on one another or upon some stated condition. One might say that just as Bias is the extreme of Interest, so System is the extreme of Pattern.

What validates any pattern, as we saw, is that it permits *a* meaning to be attached to a group of otherwise dumb, disconnected facts. What prompts the systematic historian is the desire to find *the* meaning of *all* the facts—the meaning of History and thus of man's destiny on earth. He starts from the assumption that nothing in the chaos of human events known for the last 10,000 years can be pointless. His faith is strong that somewhere and at some time the good and evil, the successes and failures, the pluses and minuses must produce a kind of total that, when read off, will have universal significance. History to him is not what it seems to us: a vast network of incomplete stories, upon which patterns slightly clearer than life's confusion are imposed for convenience only; rather it is *one* story, with a beginning, a middle, and an end.

When an absolute system is believed to be discoverable, the believer offers a demonstration: he shows that despite surface differences, there is unity underneath. He is then forced to explain how the governing agency "underneath" produces the welter above, and he is thus brought to the view that some one powerful force, acting by necessity, has woven the great web of History. Systematic historians, in short, are committed to the doctrine of the Single Cause.

In Christendom from St. Augustine in the fifth century to Bossuet in the seventeenth, the Single Cause is God, and His law is reflected in Christian ethics. In the *New Science* of Vico, published in the early eighteenth century, the universal law is the cyclical development of the human mind through the divine, heroic, and purely human stages. The division of history into three stages is a pattern

---

[17]12 vols., London, 1934–1961. An abridgment in two volumes was made by D. C. Somervell, New York and London, 1947, 1957.

congenial to many systematists, and so is the analogy of the birth, maturity, and decline of nations, which had already been suggested by the ancient historian Polybius. A century after Vico, Saint-Simon was but the first of a group of philosophers who saw in history the maturing of mankind. He traced this evolution from childhood (Egyptian civilization) through youth (the Greek and Roman world) to maturity (the medieval and modern world).

Soon after the death of Saint-Simon and the first theorizings of his part disciple Comte[18] appeared Hegel's *Philosophy of History* (1831), which justly deserves its commanding place among modern systems. Hegel's powerful mind saw the chief defect of previous systems and tried to remedy it. That defect lay in the fact that History does not ever tend all one way. As a philosopher Hegel wanted to reduce the chaos to simple principles, but he was enough of an historian to recognize the helter-skelter of life. History is a perpetual, incoherent struggle, a mess. Yet systems interpret it to mean "fundamentally" one thing; the mess becomes a pageant.

To do this, the Christian systematists had had to say that history was a moral tale: when right triumphed it was Providence rewarding the good; when disaster befell it was again Providence punishing the wicked; when seeming injustice prevailed it was a trial of the worthy that would be made up to them hereafter. But until Hegel the philosophers of history who kept on the earthly plane had no means of fitting conflict into their systems. He solved the difficulty by pointing to the "dialectical process" at work in history.

Dialectic means dialoguelike, and Hegel applies this image to the bloody frays of History because conflicts to him are always conflicts of ideas. The Reformation is the struggle of the idea of a universal church with the idea of religious individualism. The men who fight one another in armies, or the men who fight one another in books, are alike manifestations, embodiments of an idea. The new idea is the antithesis of the old (or "thesis"), and fierce passions pit one against the other. But no antithesis triumphs completely and no old thesis survives completely. What happens at length is a mingling, sealed in blood, known as the synthesis. It contains elements of both

---

[18]For the relation of Comte's Positivism to the doctrine of biological evolution, see Chapter 10, pp. 256f.

thesis and antithesis while differing from either. In History, Hegel rightly observed, no individual or group ever accomplishes what it aims at. The product of their effort, which is History, is therefore the realization of something other than their desires. It is, says Hegel, the realization of Spirit (*Geist*), which is free, unpredicted and unpredictable, but also invisible until men reveal it through their combined and conflicting acts. The Spirit or Idea of a period is shown when the period is over; or to put it differently, mankind makes its History partly consciously, partly unconsciously, and in so doing it develops the potentialities of Universal Reason or *Geist*.

This takes care of the visible chaos in History and it makes the single cause (*Geist*) indefinite enough to allow human passions a role in "realizing" (that is, making real) the unseen Spirit. To bring down this high abstraction to the plane of historical experience, Hegel makes room for what he calls the World-Historical character—the great leader who, like Alexander, Caesar, Luther, or Napoleon, seems superhuman in his ability to move the masses toward a new goal. In Hegel's scheme, such men are explained as being so exactly in tune with mankind's brooding will, and with the step that Spirit is about to take, that one individual's natural endowments are magnified to the size we behold.

Despite its rigidity, Hegel's system thus leaves scope for men at large and for great men in particular. After him, the great-man theory of history could be defended against the fatalists. They held that the course of History was absolutely determined, either because men had no free will or because mass movements were the real "forces" in History, and these were so mighty that any man's thought or effort had the weight of a feather in comparison. Carlyle disputed the fatalists in theory and by example. He wrote an unforgettable history of the French Revolution, which showed individuals making History; and he rehabilitated Cromwell and attempted a glorification of Frederick the Great, all the while deploring the absence of such great men in contemporary England:

> This . . . is an age that as it were denies the existence of great men, denies the desirableness of great men. Show our critics a great man, a Luther for example, they begin to what they call "account" for him . . . and bring him out to be a little kind of man! He was the "creature of the Time," they

say; the Time called him forth, the Time did everything, he nothing—but what we [sic] the little critic could have done too! This seems to me but melancholy work. The Time call forth? Alas, we have known Times *call* loudly enough for their great man; but not find him when they called! He was not there . . . the Time, *calling* its loudest, had to go down to confusion and wreck because he would not come when called.[19]

The great-man theory need not, of course, imply that great men do all the work; it implies that their presence and their individual characters make a tangible difference. And not only do great men have this power, but so do men of small or middling stature when occupying the seat of authority. It can further be shown that such a view is not incompatible with a systematic determinism derived from the assumptions of physical science.[20]

The continuing argument whether people or "forces" are the ultimate cause of events is itself affected by changing circumstances and what they inspire in the minds of the living. The impact of the factory system, the doubling of the population, and the increase in material production and human misery worked upon the minds of Friedrich Engels and Karl Marx in such a way that they combined the system of Hegel and the social and economic criticism of Saint-Simon and others with their sense of present realities into a new theory of History which, they were confident, solved the great riddle of "what makes History go."

According to Marx, Hegel was standing on his head when he supposed that the war in society was one of ideas. He should have recognized that the war is for bread, hence that the fundamental cause of historical events is economic. In great changes, men have neither free will nor clear consciousness of the outcome. They are determined to the performance of their social roles by the existing form of the means of production. Their relation to these means defines the class they belong to, and the struggle between classes for the possession of economic strength is the motive power of History.

Everything else in society—laws, customs, morality, religion, art—is a "superstructure" without force or meaning except as ener-

[19]Thomas Carlyle, *On Heroes, Hero-Worship, and the Heroic in History* (1840), Everyman edition, 249f.

[20]See Sidney Hook's classic work, *The Hero in History,* New York, 1943.

gized by the real cause and force below. In turning Marxist, the Hegelian dialectic stirs mankind through the class war, itself generated automatically by economic fact. Marx elaborated his system while the ideas of biological evolution were gaining ground, and his materialism parallels Charles Darwin's without being influenced by any biological considerations. Nor is Marx's system neutral, but optimistic and progressive, its prophecy serving as a premium to adherents.

It was left to another systematic historian, Count Arthur de Gobineau, to rewrite Western history as a prophecy of doom, on the biological-cultural principle that race is the prime mover and that its "law" is downward motion.[21] According to Gobineau each of the three major races—white, yellow, and black—enjoys special inherited characteristics. When any two meet and mix, their differences of custom and outlook stimulate invention, and a new civilization is born. Overdo the mixture and decadence follows.

Though race theories sprouted by the dozen during the second half of the nineteenth century and were applied in Germany and elsewhere during the twentieth, Gobineau's system was meant neither to destroy nor to humiliate nations but to enlighten them about their inevitable fate. Disillusioned about Europe after the revolutions of 1848, Gobineau thought he could see his contemporaries falling into decadence. Only a strong infusion of vigorous "white blood" could restore the balance that was first disturbed by many centuries of hybridization along the Mediterranean shores and finally upset by Europe's colonizing the world and further mingling the races.

Since Gobineau, all but a few systematists have like him been prophets of doom. The best known of them, Oswald Spengler, entitled his book *The Decline of the West*. Not many years earlier, in 1911, Sir Flinders Petrie, an Egyptologist of note, who was more historian than philosopher and therefore did not produce the slogans that appeal to a wide public, brought out his *Revolutions of Civilization*, in which he likened the symptoms of decay in our most advanced institutions to similar signs of decline in the ancient world. Spengler's

---

[21] On the antecedents of the gloomy historians, see K. F. Helleiner, "An Essay on the Rise of Historical Pessimism in the Nineteenth Century," *Canadian Journal of Economics and Political Science*, 8 (November 1942), 514–536.

FIGURE 14A   *Famous Philosophies of History: Cyclical Progression*

PLATO (388–368 B.C.)

1. Egyptian (?) fable of periodic destruction by fire
2. Tale of the lost Atlantis

LUCRETIUS (c. 55 B.C.)

Atoms form worlds and revert to atoms

VICO (A.D. 1725)

Progress of nations through divine, heroic, human stages and return to primitive

VOLTAIRE (1750)

Irregular recurrences of high civilizations: four ages in 2,000 years

MALTHUS (1798)

The perpetual action of want, war, and disease keeps mankind from ever "perfecting" itself as hoped by the *philosophes*

GOBINEAU (1853–1855)

Race mixture brings about and then destroys civilizations

NIETZSCHE (1885–1889)

Necessity working through all things without interference from (nonexistent) spirit brings about the return of all events in exact sequence forever

FLINDERS PETRIE (1911)

Civilizations rise and die from the effects of size and complexity

SPENGLER (1918–1922)

Forms (morphology) determine cultural growth and breed decay, causing the death of the societies based upon them

TOYNBEE (1934–1955)

The organic response of civilizations to inner or outer challenges propels them until the spirit (psychological and religious) leaves them

---

Among the "cyclical historians" one can distinguish those who posit a periodic destruction followed by rebuilding; those who believe in an "organic" law of rise and fall; and those who infer "eternal recurrence" from laws of material necessity. As to this recurrence, Shakespeare wrote a striking quatrain in Sonnet 59:

> If there be nothing new, but that which is
> Hath been before, how are our brains beguiled
> Which, laboring for invention, bear amiss
> The second burden of a former child.

FIGURE 14B   *Famous Philosophies of History: Linear Progression*

The BIBLE (c. 8th century B.C.; 2nd century of our era)
1. Partial destruction but hope of messiah
2. End of the world and day of judgment

VIRGIL (c. 20 B.C.)
Golden age not in past but in future

ST. AUGUSTINE (A.D. 413–426)
Human history a part of eternal destiny of man; hence greatness and fall of Rome intelligible as moral and religious lesson

BOSSUET (1681)
The progress of revelation from the Jews to the Romans and to Western Europe demonstrates the presence of God in history

CONDORCET (1793)
The progress already made by reason through eight stages opens the prospect of a world that will be ruled entirely by knowledge, reason, and brotherly love

SAINT-SIMON (1825)
Three stages of intellectual development usher in harmony and Christian technocracy

COMTE (1830–1842)
Three stages of intellectual development usher in positivist thought, with the triumph of science and a rationalist religion of humanity

HEGEL (1820–1830)
A dialectical interplay moves all history, whose three stages of freedom usher in the freedom of all under a strong but just state

SPENCER (1850)
Natural forces move all things from the simple and alike to the complex and unlike, which in human affairs means moral and mechanical progress

BUCKLE (1857)
Intellect working under freedom achieves increasing order and power

MARX (1848–1867)
The dialectical movement is rooted in matter taking the form of economic production. Successive class struggles usher in freedom and justice under anarchy

DARWIN (1871)
Natural struggle and sexual selection produce higher societies that recognize civil and moral law

work, written during the First World War, came out in 1918, and fifteen years later Toynbee began publishing his long survey of twenty-one civilizations. Vico, Nietzsche, Petrie, Spengler, and Toynbee are all "cyclical historians" in the sense that they believe human groups are fated to rise, flourish, and fall. But Spengler is the most rigid and abstract among them, more rigid and abstract than Hegel himself, as a sample will show:

Because the key to the master pattern of culture is the idea of space, a deep identity unites the awakening of the soul, its birth into clear existence in the name of a culture, with the sudden realization of distance and time, the birth of its outer world through the symbol of extension; and thenceforth this symbol is and remains the prime symbol of that life, imparting to it its specific style and the historical form in which it progressively actualizes its inward possibilities.[22]

We see here the extreme of abstraction in the use of "historical" patterns. Instead of trying to master the rich confusion of facts, our systematist empties out all but a handful of them and coordinates pure patterns. This does not mean that Spengler must be denied the title of historian; it means that in his pursuit of laws and forms he could not stay close to his data. He is often illuminating, usually at the point where some well-known event first suggests to him an inference or a relation; but when he reaches the goal of his peculiar undertaking, he has left the student of history baffled that so much intelligence should fail to see how the facts overthrow the scaffolding of generalizations.

Of what use, then, are these systems? Apart from the pleasure given by the display of human ingenuity, systems have served, historically, two useful purposes. The great systems, at least, have afforded a thorough review of large periods and have led to a breaking up and recasting of old patterns of understanding. In so doing, the philosophers of history have drawn attention to the importance of neglected classes of facts. Vico's revision of ancient history influenced legal and linguistic studies and in the nineteenth century helped establish the idea of social evolution. Hegel's dialectic reinforced the

---

[22] *The Decline of the West*, New York, 1926 (authorized English translation of *Der Untergang des Abendlandes*), 1:174.

vision that regimes and nations are small things compared to the sweep of civilization, and that the unfathomable agitation of human beings conceals the potency of new ideas and great movements. Marx led historians to study economic conditions in as much detail as political and military. Gobineau dwelt on the significance of culture and custom and the anthropological method. Petrie showed what phenomena were common to advanced civilizations—feminism, for example, and the urban life of the "mass man"—and helped destroy the faith in unending progress. Spengler gave sharper contour to the meaning of certain historical terms, such as "classic" and "Faustian," and drew seductive projections of certain ages, such as that of Louis XIV. And Toynbee, besides strengthening the notion of a civilization as an historical unit, has shown that the breakdown of civilizations comes not alone from external attacks but also from inner failures of nerve and brain.[23]

No philosopher has demonstrated "the laws" of history, and every one—Toynbee as much as Spengler, though differently—has violated the elementary canon of historiography by neglecting contrary evidence. They have forced facts into arbitrary classifications; given credence to the Single Cause; called into play the reductive fallacy—"this is nothing but—"; lost, in short, the imagination of the real, because of an overmastering desire for the one principle that will explain the career of mankind.

To explain it by such means would of course be to explain it away. The final formula would reduce the story to its outline, the edifice to its blueprint; and with this reduction would go the implication that story and edifice will henceforth duplicate endlessly, with minor alterations not worth notice. Systems, the researcher will conclude, are of incidental use; not what they assert but only what they suggest can be converted to the legitimate uses of reporting on the past.

[23] In a closely argued thesis on the same vast subjects, William H. McNeill takes issue with the Spengler-Toynbee view that cultures "fall" as the result of internal defects or failures. He offers the counterproposition that the cultures of mankind have always been interrelated and that changes in their relative strengths are owing to periodic cultural "explosions" or "disturbances" that upset the established cultural balance in the world (*The Rise of the West: A History of the Human Community*, Chicago, 1963).

9

Historians in Europe and America

Likeness in Difference

It is a commonplace that the events comprised under the head of American History are the continuation of those known as European History, an extension into the New World of the ancient European civilization. But if we use a small letter for history and mean historiography—the writing of History—we observe that the continuity in the facts is not matched by a corresponding likeness in the styles and forms of historical narrative.

The differences between American and European historians are numerous, though not necessarily fundamental. Rather, they mark, through emotional tendencies and habits of mind, the obvious differences in the social and cultural circumstances of the old and the new continents. History, as we saw in the last chapter, is written under the sway of interest, as well as of bias and system. This means that it is written with an eye on one's contemporaries and one's past. And almost from the beginning the American scene diverged from the European—hence the differences in historiography that we are about to discuss. They do not put the two sets of historians in antithesis each to each. Both groups continue to belong to the same civilization, to imitate and borrow from one another, and to present deviations from strict contrast. But lines of separation can be traced if one will admit exceptions and take comments as simply suggestive.

The utility of lending one's mind to this differentiation is most apparent in the reading of sources: the researcher should be aware of subtle signals, if only to avoid misinterpreting what Europe addresses to us in the way of historical narrative, whether professional or propagandistic. Moreover, European customs of library research are also worth glancing at by way of warning against possible disappointments.

The first striking feature of European history is that it is national in a different sense from the American. With us the meaning of "national" is primarily geographic; it is contrasted with "local," "state," or "regional." In Europe "national" calls up not so much *nation* as *nationality*—a unique set of political and cultural facts that stand against a corresponding set in every other country. This feature of European historical thought is an outgrowth of the conditions that tended to isolate social groups during the Middle Ages and to promote differences among languages, cultures, and political states. When the Western peoples began to approach unity, about the year 1500, the unifying force was the monarchy. Histories were written about the rising dynasties and their deeds. Soon the type of history known as "battle-and-king" history became the established genre. Kings appointed "historiographers" whose writings were national in the sense that they glorified the ruling house. This was true despite the intermarriages between dynasties and despite the sovereign claims and campaigns that reached beyond the national frontiers.

At a later time, and notably after the French Revolution, the liberal or democratic states inherited the mantle of kings and became the object of self-worship. Nationalism became more intense, a common European faith divided into many sects, equally aggressive and especially potent in the writing of history. Exceptions to these generalities are themselves signs of Europe's deep sense of national selfhood. Whenever the nation is not the organizing principle of European history, that principle is found in partisanship, and the party is represented as incarnating the "true nation." For example, the Reformation cut across national lines and scrambled frontiers, but the histories referring to the struggle take sides. They are Catholic or Calvinist or Lutheran or Socinian. In like manner, liberals and reactionaries, royalists and republicans, believers and freethinkers, racialists and socialists, form large "sects" that rewrite the national history from their point of view.

In the cosmopolitan eighteenth century, while the monarchical and diplomatic histories continued to appear, Voltaire made a great effort to enlarge what was then called "universal history." It did not embrace the universe, but it went beyond the single nation to what was deemed the whole of the civilized world, usually Christendom. Voltaire's *Essay on the Customs and Manners of Nations* was a sketch of a new type of history, cultural in substance and global in character; it freely roamed beyond the boundaries of Europe. But Voltaire was a pioneer with few imitators. His readers were used to the more familiar arrangement by nations, whose role was still concentrated in a king. Thus his *Age of Louis XIV*, though cosmopolitan in outlook, also appealed to patriotic pride and continued to make attractive the idea of a single power's predominance in Europe. That idea may have died in the wars of our century, but we have not as yet the makings of a truly European (that is, Continental) history, except perhaps in economic or populist terms.[1]

In Voltaire's day the cosmopolitan outlook held national egotism in check; a philosopher like Hume could say, with faulty historical feeling, that anyone who wanted to know the character of the French and the English had only to consult the history of the Greeks and the Romans. Yet when Hume himself undertook history-writing, tradition prevailed and he produced a strongly royalist history of England that remained "standard" for three quarters of a century.

However cosmopolitan, the feeling of nationhood favored the militant ideas that prepared the French Revolution of 1789. With kings dethroned after decades of ideological warfare, national spirit grew, and hence required the writing of new histories in which the people was the hero. This meant reaching back for national beginnings to late Roman times. The uniqueness of each nation was shown

[1]See Chapter 11, pp. 263ff.

at every point by an endless contrast with the neighboring nations, the "hereditary enemy" or the "nefarious foreign influence."

The materials for this expanding historiography were abundant and accessible. Already in the eighteenth century the members of certain monastic orders had begun to make great collections of medieval documents with a view to showing the civilizing role of the Church. These efforts, notably those of the French Benedictines at St. Maur, were scholarship of the finest sort, a model of technique and industry. In the next century the search for documents spread from the cloister to the public place and began to serve not one but all the conceivable interests of that "evolutionary" age. As was said in Chapter 3, since the nineteenth century, history explains everything and argues or proves everything.

The first large-scale collections of national documents were begun in the 1820s at the instigation of the national governments. Every European state vied with the rest in building up and publishing what we now take for granted as national archives. England began to bring out its "Rolls Series" and "Calendars of State Papers." Germany undertook a vast issue of *Monumenta Germaniae Historica*. The French *Société d'Histoire de France*, animated by the young politician and historian Guizot, brought out dozens of volumes of hitherto hidden sources. Old châteaux were ransacked, government bureaus became research centers, and private papers emerged from cellars and attics to be classified and published with zealous care. Universities everywhere started or multiplied courses in history, with the national interest strongly in mind. This often took the form of demonstrating the antiquity and continuity of the national culture. English literature, which had formerly been thought to begin with Chaucer in the fourteenth century, now began with *Beowulf* in the eighth. Angles, Saxons, Danes, and Jutes became the historic fathers of modern England. By the same reasoning the British parliament was believed to descend from the Anglo-Saxon witenagemot. Anglo-Saxonism was born, with important racialist consequences, of which the "Celtic" reaction and renaissance was one.[2]

---

[2]Another was the form and purpose of the Rhodes Scholarships established at Oxford in 1904: they were to prepare young Germans and Americans to take part with Englishmen in governing the world.

This nation-and-party interest manifested itself all over Europe in startling parallels and combinations. For example, Hegel's lectures on the *Philosophy of History*, which had been delivered in the late 1820s at the newly founded University of Berlin, propounded the view that all of history could be divided into three stages: the Oriental, in which one man, the despot, was free; the Classical (Greek and Roman), in which some were free; and the Germanic (Late Medieval and Modern), in which all were free. Hegel saw the developing state as the guarantor of this universal freedom, and since he called the modern period Germanic, he has been taken for an apostle of Prussian domination. This is a misunderstanding of his revolutionary and liberal intentions—intentions that made him suspect to the Prussian government and incurred censorship for his last writings.

About the same time Guizot, whom no one can accuse of having supported Prussian hegemony, was using much the same language to explain the *History of Civilization in Europe* (1828–1832). Guizot saw three shaping influences: the Roman Empire and its rigid hierarchical tendency; Christianity and its moral influence; and the Germanic ideas brought into the Roman Empire by the barbarians. It was they who had injected the idea of freedom into the legal and moral system built up by the other two institutions. When the scholarly Leopold von Ranke published his *History of the Latin and Teutonic Nations* (1824), or when the journalist Armand Carrel published a hasty account of the Glorious English Revolution of 1688 just before Paris rose up against the Bourbons in 1830, the recurrent "interests" of European historians were being shown and exploited. No American reader of European history can afford to be unaware of these permanent concerns, which begin as motives for research and often end as bias, "revisionism," or philosophic system.

Since this book cannot retrace in detail the work of the European historians in the great age of history-writing that followed the French Revolution, it may be convenient to indicate here the broad tendencies of their thought.

1. There is first the purely *national*, which ranges all the way from the cultural nationalism of a writer like Michelet to the state imposition of crudely patriotic textbooks such as the one that used to make the boys and girls of the former French Equatorial Africa

speak of "our ancestors the Gauls." Moreover, the old idea of conquering all Europe lives on, even when it is only an organizing principle for the mass of facts. In recent times the large cooperative histories of Europe produced in France have continued to cut up that history into periods of national predominance—Spain's, France's, England's, and so on.

As a subclass under the national "form" must be listed all the histories written on behalf of would-be nations seeking independence from foreign oppressors—Italy and Germany before unification, the Balkan and Baltic states in endless profusion and confusion. We have witnessed in our day a new wave of this national "irredentism" in many parts of the globe, notably in Africa and Asia—a product of many forces, among which must be counted a partisan knowledge of history. As literacy spreads in those regions, national histories get written.[3] These are another legacy of Western culture as potent as machinery.

2. A second series of alignments follows the issues bequeathed to the nineteenth century by the French Revolution. The numerous parties are reducible to two pairs of contending groups, the one political, the other religious. The egalitarian liberals combat all forms of aristocratic or monarchical rule; or in political jargon, they constitute the Left, battling the Right. Often allied with the liberals are the anticlerical secular forces that fight the established church, Catholic or other. In England these parties bear slightly different names: Whig or Liberal versus Tory or Conservative, and Dissenters or Nonconformists versus the Church of England. In general, the Left is freethinking, republican, and egalitarian; the Right is clerical, monarchical, and in favor of the class system.

3. Since political ideas cross frontiers and split nations, European historians have often felt a need to substitute for the national unit a new homogeneous bloc of peoples supposedly sharing some great idea. The notion of the Protestant North and the Catholic South has been tried. It is a poor fit, but it is lent passing plausibility by the doctrine mentioned earlier, of Roman domination

---

[3]To take one example, when Zimbabwe was known as Rhodesia, children there learned that their history began with Livingstone's discovery of the region in 1855. Now new history texts teach that the black people have an older history, with kingdoms rising and falling and national heroes in the form of spirit mediums influential in shaping events (*New York Times*, October 17, 1982).

breached by Germanic freedom. The marked Anglo-Saxon bias of English historians before 1914 was not limited to so-called Anglo-Saxon countries. Throughout the Continent one can find "Romanists" and "Germanists," with a few "Celticists" thrown in for good measure.

4. The fourth and last dividing idea whose influence may be detected in certain European historians dates from the middle of the last century and generates two familiar types of history-writing. One is the racialist interpretation of history; the other is the Marxist. Both are materialist in principle, but the one finds the "single cause" of history in biological fact; the other in economic. The first is particularly "reductive" in histories of the arts and thought generally; the second is particularly subversive in histories of social life and in the interpretation of great political events such as the French Revolution or America's entry into the First World War.

European Innovations

From 1870 on, in France and Germany, the effort was made to reach in historiography a "scientific" precision that critical scholarship could not in any way attain—no amount of "stylistics," for example, could prove that a series of medieval charters came from such and such a person or place: it could only suggest a probability. Such enterprises in minuteness led to the shrinking of fields of study. A few years' span, a small territory were felt to be the only manageable projects. In England, where the same attitude came to prevail, work of this sort was known ironically as "biennial history."

One or two great synthesizers still appeared. Henri Pirenne (1862–1935), after many studies in medieval history, social and economic, produced a "definitive" *History of Belgium*. In France, Camille Jullian (1859–1933) wrote a comprehensive *History of Gaul*. In Germany, the great producer in this period was Karl Lamprecht (1856–1915), whose *History of Germany* long evoked admiration and amazement. But after them the large works are collective—*The Cambridge Modern History*, planned by Lord Acton, and the two French series edited by Lavisse and Rambaud and by Halpern and

Sagnac. It is easy to understand that detailed researches and the power of synthesis are not easily reconciled: it is a question of energy and time not being available twice over. What may be harder to understand is that the division of labor has not brought about collaboration—the minute researchers bringing their bricks, the architectonic scholars making the edifice. One reason is that in order to master a subject the historian must work in it himself, for many years, until he has gained the "feel" of the time and its actors.

Despairing of the possibility that large-scale narrative history could be enduring work, European historians influenced by the resurgence of sociology after 1895 were drawn into the orbit of the new "social scientists," or spent much of their time in controversy over method. More will be said on this still-lively issue in the next chapter. One offshoot of the desire for "science" in the history was the movement led by Henri Berr, which was to give an account of the "Evolution of Mankind": no more events, but social panoramas. The effort was only partly successful in fulfilling its resolve to ignore events, and it struck difficulties in making clear, without mentioning events, the characteristics of periods and countries on a comparative basis. But out of it came the next wave of modernization in French historiography, which sought to "psychologize" cultures, regions, ages, and classes. Chronology plays no role and topics are the main substance, again handled by contrast and comparison.

This was very much what Lamprecht's *History of Germany* had professed to do, on a somewhat more traditional basis of chronology and economic interpretation. But it was his younger colleagues Max Weber, Friedrich Meinecke, and Werner Sombart who swung German historiography into the full tide of "characterological" research. In various ways they sought types, constants, "forms"; and though they were not responsible for Spengler's conclusions, they prepared the ground for the success of his "cultural forms," which like their "ideal types" bear a family resemblance to the entities launched by Hegel in his *Philosophy of History*.[4]

---

[4]One might add the name of Benedetto Croce (1866–1952) to the number of modern "Hegelian" historians, though he began as a Marxist before writing his *History of Italy*.

The influence of Karl Marx (a one-time Hegelian too) was also at work in the historiography of the period before the First World War, and not merely in Jean Jaurès's *Socialist History*. Many studies offered a dialectical or class interpretation of events, notably of the French Revolution; others professed to uncover the economic bases of thought and culture. The journal founded in France by Lucien Febvre and Marc Bloch, helped to form the so-called *Annales* group, this title of the magazine carrying the qualifier "of social and economic history." A deep preoccupation with life in an industrial mass civilization, that is, with "the modern predicament," is visible in these anti-literary studies.

Peculiarities and Research Problems

So much for the fundamental features of recent European history-writing. Certain characteristics of its traditional materials also deserve notice. European History is plentifully supplied with great figures, and of these a large number are villains. Baldly stated, this generality seems either obvious or unimportant, or both; but a moment's thought will show that its truth helps explain the form and tone of its classic historiography and confirms the antagonisms found within it. Great figures are more frequent in European History than in American, because the European cultural tradition is mainly a feudal, monarchical, and aristocratic tradition. As such it has provided a well-lit stage for individual action, putting a premium on boldness, violence, and risk, which often end in tragedy. A democratic society, and even more one that is also a *business* society, seldom provides such a stage for heroes; the leader is, or tries to look as if he were, part of a team. Being highly organized, moreover, trade and industry give less opportunity for the public display of strength, talent, or ruthlessness. A "respectable" democratic nation would not let King Edward VIII marry a divorced woman, whereas his predecessor Henry VIII married six wives, divorced two, and variously disposed of all but the last.

Many European villains may thus be said to have been encouraged by political and social conditions, including small populations, the acceptance of economic scarcity, and the precariousness of human life. But there are also in European history villains-by-definition, that is, figures that are permanently villains to one party and heroes to another. Cromwell, for example, who after his death was execrated by all but a few Englishmen until his rehabilitation in the 1840s, is no hero to the Irish, nor to the influential body of English Jacobites and Catholics. Similarly, Luther cannot be expected to be a hero to the Papacy and its millions of faithful. Bismarck is suspect to German liberals and a villain to French patriots; Karl Marx is the great prophet or the great enemy to opposing groups in Italy, Germany, France, Belgium, Holland, and Sweden, while in the Soviet Union he is the master philosopher.

In keeping with partisanship and prophecy, European historians tend to make their writings the vehicle of something more than mere opinions. They propound theses and formulate schemes. These are favored by their upbringing and that of their audience. Both writer and reader have until recently been products of a highly selective school system. Within each nation, education is remarkably uniform, so that the writer can expect from his readers a common preparation as well as a certain skill in following, detecting, and resisting ideology. The members of the history-reading public not only have an intellectual position of their own, but they want one from the writer. No doubt he must be a "good" German or Austrian or Italian, but he must also belong to an identifiable party or school of thought.

As against this, American history appears baldly unintellectual. It is full of views, to be sure, but these follow no long traditions to which names could be given. Rather, the public love of Americana is scenic or regional, narrowly geographical or antiquarian. The nearest thing to a great divide has been the antagonism of North and South, but this was never ideological. Next in intensity is the feeling of rivalry existing between East and West, the crowded Atlantic coast and the great open spaces. But this is on the whole a tolerant feeling, which has cost no academic historian his post and no popular one his laurels. Lately, Marxist and other Revisionist ideologies have begun to make inroads, but they are not yet widely received.

In Europe, the "positions" are much more closely guarded and the encounters do draw blood. The state being (at least on the

Continent) dispenser of favors and director of the educational system, the opportunity to write and teach history depends sooner or later on alliance with a recognized party. Throughout the nineteenth century the Continental universities were political arenas for both students and teachers—as they are today in virtually all parts of the world. Ostracism, dismissals, and retaliation in print were common events reflected in historical writings. One has only to study the successive French histories of the French Revolution to unfold the story of a two-hundred-years' war. In most of these same party-ridden countries, however, freedom of research is achieved by the operation of give-and-take. Academic historians are government employees, but their tenure is generally assured by the balance of opposite forces: when a "rightist" historian retires from a faculty, he must be replaced by one of his kind lest the equilibrium be disrupted.[5]

This autonomy has permitted historiography since about 1860 to branch out into specialties at the will of the individual. The choice is perhaps less influenced by fashion than it is in America. Diplomatic, military, intellectual, and institutional history have continued to be pursued in Europe, though they are now less popular than the new genres: social, economic, and psychological. The work of the demographers and "opinion researchers" once received greater attention in European historical circles than here, where these and other numerical techniques have been carrying on extensive operations.[6]

Finally, one must point out that the materials of European history are less highly organized mechanically than those of American history. The libraries abroad are rich and great and induplicable, but their catalogues, shelving systems, delivery methods, hours of access. modes of lighting, and stores of human helpfulness are generally inferior to ours. There are fewer microfilms and fewer machines to read them by, no interlibrary loans, no "union lists" of newspapers, and no possibility, at this late date, of the standardization that so

---

[5]Times of trouble, of course, bring on the old bloodshed and proscriptions: witness the fate of such historians as Salvemini under Mussolini, Bernard Faÿ and Marc Bloch under opposing regimes in France, and the mass exodus of European scholars under Hitler and Stalin.

[6]See Chapter 10, pp. 236–266.

greatly facilitates research. The United States enjoys the accidental advantage of having started late and the credit of having made the most of it.

Although every researcher who has been abroad will remember notable exceptions, the tendency of European intellectuals is to be somewhat more suspicious, jealous, and reticent than their American counterparts. They see no reason to help a competitor in the race for honors, and they scent competition in almost every undertaking that is likely to succeed. Even in tight little England, for all its fair play and friendliness, one must not expect the American open-door policy. Europeans generally cherish privacy more than do Americans, and family feeling has a touch of the dynastic. Hence they will not so readily put their papers at the disposal of strangers. Anything like the opening of the Ford and Rockefeller archives so soon after the death of the head of the family is very rare, if not unexampled. But this same closeness works in reverse once the researcher has been "properly introduced." Then he enjoys an unrestricted monopoly: he is trusted, with an unquestioning faith in his honor and discretion.[7]

All this is but to say in different words that European intellectual society is more individualistic than ours in tone and temper; and this in turn reminds us of its origins, which are based on class and privilege, with but a recent addition of industrial democracy to modify those powerful forces.

American Opposites and Counterparts

The United States, reared on a different political tradition, has written its history in a different mood and with different aims. The circumstances of America's settlement were apparent in our historiography from the beginning—the physical distance from Europe, the experimental, exploratory outlook, the uniqueness in modern times

---

[7]Regarding access to the official records of the countries of Europe—and of the rest of the world—the rules vary widely and one should try to learn them in advance of one's research trip. A good source of information is the mimeographed publication "Public Availability of Diplomatic Archives" of the Historical Office of the U.S. Department of State (an updated version is expected in 1985).

of settling a vast continent under one national state. The influence of these facts has continued to play upon American writing and has marked it off from Europe's. It may be for the same reasons that until recently our history has been of interest chiefly to ourselves. Already in the seventeenth century, the Puritan divine Cotton Mather recognized this when he wrote: "If a war between us and a handful of Indians do appear no more than a Batrachomyomachie [a war between frogs and mice] to the world abroad, yet unto us at home it hath been considerable enough to make a history."[8]

Many of the early colonial histories were little more than chronicles; for instance, John Smith's *A True Relation*, which was a brief account of the settlement of Virginia; or *Mourt's Relation* by William Bradford and Edward Winslow, which was a description of the Plymouth Plantation. The first self-consciously and artistically prepared history in America was William Bradford's *History of Plimoth Plantation*, which this distinguished colonial governor wrote between 1630 and 1650. We can infer something about early tastes in American history when we learn that Bradford's work, although used by scholars in manuscript form for over two centuries, was not published in full until 1856. Before the Revolution, Americans, when they had time to read history, read Europe's. In addition to church histories, they read Gibbon, Voltaire, Rollin, Hume, and Robertson. Of the secular historians Voltaire enjoyed wide popularity and exercised marked influence on readers and writers in America.[9] He was an intellectual force well before the Americans began to awaken to a sense of nationhood. European events and cosmopolitan ideas conspired to enlarge the Americans' historical panorama; they could "universalize" history by transcending state or sectional boundaries; so that in the New World "universal" history paradoxically became national history, thus giving rise to a new meaning of nation: far from

---

[8] *Magnalia Christi Americana*, Hartford, 1853, 2:581.

[9] Michael Kraus, *The Writing of American History*, Norman, Okla., 1968, 61. According to Joseph Towne Wheeler, if we except Le Sage's novel *Gil Blas*, Voltaire's historical works were the most-read foreign books in pre-Revolutionary Maryland ("Books Owned by Marylanders, 1700–1776," *Maryland Historical Magazine*, 35 [December 1940], 350). But see also Bernard Faÿ, *The Revolutionary Spirit in France and America* (New York, 1927, 40), in which it appears that Montesquieu was the foreign writer most often reprinted in colonial newspapers.

being unitary, self-centered, and defensive, the national outlook in the United States was inclusive, variegated, federal.

Besides, owing to the diversity of the immigration, the national origins were many rather than one. "The past" was not altogether plain, not being a common past. As a result, American historians had in a sense to manufacture a unified American heritage, and before the thrilling events of the Revolutionary period they lacked the raw materials. One of the first and most learned exploiters of the nascent attitudes was Jared Sparks, whose biographies of the Founding Fathers created some indelible portraits that the passage of time has not significantly altered.[10] He was soon followed by George Bancroft, the most famous American historian of his time, whose ten-volume *History of the United States* (1834–1874) was acclaimed as the best ever written from the democratic viewpoint. Bancroft, it was said, "voted for Jackson on every page"; he celebrated at every turn the unique merits of his country's achievement. His fellow Americans, he said in his conclusion, were "more sincerely religious, better educated, of serener minds and of purer morals than the men of any former republic."[11] Here nationalism of the European brand is perhaps perceptible, yet it includes without distinction all the European nationalities represented on this continent. Fighting alien principles rather than hostile neighbors, American nationalism lacks the clannish and apprehensive tone of its European counterparts.

A further feature of American historiography that tends to dwarf its issues is the great size of the canvas, the scale deliberately adopted

---

[10]Portraits in the metaphorical sense are reinforced by visual repetition—Napoleon with his hat or Mona Lisa with her smile. These facilitate communication to be sure, but they also encourage thought clichés. These have been especially strong in American popular culture. How many people, for example, ever think of George Washington as a young man or of Abraham Lincoln as a beardless man laughing? Coins and postage stamps and books and advertising have frozen these men's characters into one likeness each, respectively the solemn father of his country and its sad-eyed savior, even though there exist upwards of seventy likenesses of Washington, from youth onwards, and hundreds of Lincoln's, most of them photographs. (See Stefan Lorant, *Lincoln: A Picture Story of His Life*, New York, 1957; and Gabor Boritt, Harold Holzer, and Mark E. Neely, Jr., *The Lincoln Image*, New York, 1984.)

[11]In 1879 the Senate voted Bancroft the privileges of the Senate floor—the only unelected citizen to whom this honor has ever been accorded. When he died in 1891 the flag was flown at half-mast in Washington and in all cities through which his remains passed on the way to their resting place in Massachusetts. His funeral was attended by the President, the Vice President, and the Chief Justice.

by the historians. They deal with successive presidential administrations as if they were of equal importance. One shudders to think of the size of our school histories two centuries hence, when the list of presidents approaches in number the present size of the list of popes. To the layman, the two great popes Gregory—the one of the chant and the other of the calendar—have merged into a single misty figure although they lived a thousand years apart; and ten others are unremembered. Will the two Roosevelts similarly merge into one with comparable convenience?

After Bancroft, the writing of American history came under the influence of the German style of scholarship that took root in the new American graduate schools of the 1880s. The great works now came out of the history seminar. Historians learned method from the followers of Ranke and, somewhat distorting the meaning of his maxim, sought to write of the past "as it really happened"; they conceived of themselves as writing "scientific history." They analyzed sources, criticized authorities, compared parallel documents, and when they had finished, they were ready to maintain that they knew what had happened in the past. Inescapably, they worked on stubborn preconceptions that, though hidden from themselves and their readers, we can now readily discern. In an age of faith in political methods, for example, they accepted without question the dictum that "History is past politics,"[12] and thus neglected or made subservient all other elements in the record.

A by-product of the "scientific" method was that historians came more and more to write for one another rather than for the large public. Like other masters of a special field and its literature, the historian became a "professional." He rarely aimed at broad cultural attainments like some of his European counterparts, but rather took pride in his devotion to a narrow segment of History. He was working to produce a treatment of it that should be definitive. Although he had isolated himself from contact with the American people about whom he wrote, he did not escape the straitjacket of contemporary culture. He was a product of the age like his predecessors, though less popular and influential.

[12]Edward A. Freeman, *The Methods of Historical Study*, London, 1886, 44.

Even so, the faith that here all immigrants could make a new start in life, could indeed remake themselves, continued to shape our image of ourselves. Historians no longer agreed with Bancroft that the history of the United States was the history of the wonder-working hand of God, but they held such other notions as: the special nature of American genius (McMaster) or the equalizing influence of the American frontier (Turner) or the compelling character of the physical setting (Webb). With a few important exceptions our history has been written largely without reference to domestic events on the other side of the Atlantic. We have studied Jacksonian democracy, for example, without relating it to the contemporaneous reform movements that culminated in revolutions in Belgium and France and in the Reform Bill of 1832 in England. Despite all that has been written about the Civil War, it is never studied as an aspect of national unification that had its counterparts in Germany and Italy in the same decade. Similarly, the so-called Progressive Era is yet to be examined in the context of similar changes occurring elsewhere in the world.

The perennially astonishing success of the United States in political and business innovation has also left its mark on our history-writing. The successful artist or scientist or philosopher among us has usually had to wait before becoming the subject of a biography. Far more attractive have been the figures who "got elected" or "made a million."[13] Until recently it has been hard to avoid the conclusion that our national self-conceit has depended on our ability to measure success quantitatively. At the same time, the writing of American history continues to draw inspiration from rural notions of the good life. Jefferson, the spokesman for agriculture, still receives more affection than Hamilton, the spokesman for industry. Urban political machines, like Tammany Hall, are denounced for their corruptness, but rarely praised for providing moderately effective "Americaniza-

[13]Herbert Heaton once suggested that the Industrial Revolution could be usefully reconsidered—and perhaps better understood—if written from the point of view of those who failed. The records of the New York Court of Bankruptcy, which have been preserved since the beginning of the republic, have yet to be exploited by historians. Richard B. Morris has elaborated this idea in a number of articles. See, for example, *American Historical Review*, 42 (January 1937), 268.

tion" and antipoverty programs. The "farmer's revolt" of the late nineteenth century continues to absorb an inordinate amount of scholarly time and energy; but its adverse and unfair attitude to the railroads has been steadily overlooked.[14]

The development of technology and the economic growth of the United States are clearly intertwined. Yet, with the exception of John Kouwenhoven, historians of the United States have been slow to deal with changing technology as a force in American life. The airline routes and broadcast networks, which have reshaped American culture, including the hope of universal literacy, have yet to be studied and interpreted.

What is also important to the researcher (and striking to the foreign student) is that no European nation affords its historians such abundant written records as does the United States. The effect of this stockpile of raw data upon our historiography is incalculable. Almost everything the American historian chooses to deal with is capable of lavish documentation. In the rare instances when the necessary proofs are missing we know precisely when they were destroyed: in the Chicago fire or the Battle of Atlanta or the San Francisco earthquake. With our love of record-keeping—doubtless a mark of our business society—the origin of almost everything is known or easily discoverable. We may dispute about the source of the nickname "Hoosier" or the word "okay," but there are at least rival etymologies to choose from; and no matter how small our home town, we know exactly when it was founded and how it got its name, who its first mayor was, and what his business and his pedigree were.[15]

A side effect of this specificity is that encyclopedic fullness of detail has tended to take up all the historian's energies. Rather than advance broad syntheses, the careful researcher prefers to establish masses of related facts. None seems too small to deserve notice, even in general works. The editors of the first supplements to the *Dictio-*

---

[14]See Albro Martin, *Enterprise Denied*, New York, 1971.

[15]The zeal with which the federal government protects its historical records is nowhere better illustrated than in its relentless efforts to recover possession of certain documents pertaining to the Lewis and Clark expedition. See Calvin Tompkins, "Annals of Law: The Lewis and Clark Case," *New Yorker*, 42 (October 29, 1966), 105–148.

nary of American Biography asked contributors to provide, among other things, the cause of death and place of burial of their subjects— apparently a serious omission from previous volumes. It is theoretically possible to locate every will ever filed for probate in every county in the United States. We can instantaneously find out how many articles on Andrew Jackson were published in the magazines of the 1890s and lay our hands on all of them. The service records of every soldier and sailor are available—many of them stored in the same drawers that they occupied when they were current.

American historiography, thriving on abundance, has acquired a degree of particularization, a minute tangibleness found nowhere else. No mystery of origins permits us to build national myths, no stories of Romulus and Remus suckled by a she-wolf lend poetry to our beginnings. We sing a ballad about Casey Jones, but we know when and why he died and a photograph shows us how he looked. His heroism is part of the files of the Interstate Commerce Commission. In other words, the American past is entirely in the age of History. Our few folk heroes—Davy Crockett or Johnny Appleseed—turn out to have been distressingly real persons about whom fairly full records are extant, ready to be studied, and (if necessary) measured in cubic feet. Ambrose Bierce had to die abroad for the event to remain enigmatic. No major figure like Shakespeare, whose life will forever be partly mysterious, remains to haunt us.

This plethora of written materials has been a tremendous burden. Of all researchers, the American historian can never feel safe from the charge of incompleteness: unpublished records and private letters threaten him on every side. These in turn have inspired the writing of "histories" of every conceivable subject from municipal sewage disposal and the making of sod houses on the Great Plains to George Washington's experiments in breeding donkeys and the versatile forms of the corkscrew. Indiscriminate interest in every part of our lives encourages the writing of books on subjects rarely treated in European history.

Still, the ceaseless proliferation of sources is a matter of concern to all researchers. It seems as if every piece of paper with writing on it is now saved and stored; and not originals only but the photocopies so readily made also. The National Archives continually outstrip available space.[16] A presidential library is founded after every administration. Governors get their papers published at the taxpayer's expense, "for the sense of history downrange," as a recent governor of New York put it. There are historical societies around every corner and the passion for oral history has become endemic, so that artifacts and magnetic tapes confront the searcher as well as tons of paper. Being an historian of America is not work for the indolent or the impatient.

The Harvest of Facts

Documentary abundance and the short span of American history have favored even-temperedness. Unlike Europe's, the history of the United States has been remarkably ordered and placid. This is not to say that violence has not been an ingredient of our political life, but that we have recognized as one of the controlling ideals of American history the bridling of passion and the art of compromise. So far, at any rate, no deep ideological divisions have scored our history, leaving in their wake "schools" of historians to keep up the fight from generation to generation. We have had no investiture struggle, no wars of religion, no political exiles and massacres, no recurrent revolutions. We have produced no Pretenders, no Robespierres, no Lenins and Hitlers, no saints and devils to divide the nation. The New Deal, which temporarily divided us, might have formed an exception, but it was soon absorbed and condoned by the Republicans; so that only the Civil War remains as an exception to our historical unity. Yet the very interest still taken in it by the whole nation shows our predominant feeling: Americans find it almost unbelievable that such a catastrophe could have happened to *us*. Nor do we cherish the old feud: both Lincoln and Lee rank as heroes throughout the nation.

The histories that nineteenth-century Americans read were by and large written by New Englanders, and New England had greater economic need of a well-knit nation than any other section. Uncle Sam himself came to look like a New Englander, his rolled-up sleeves suggesting his habits of hard work just as his facial expression sug-

---

[16]See H. G. Jones, *The Records of a Nation*, New York, 1969; and Herman J. Viola, *The National Archives of the United States*, New York, 1984.

gests his Calvinist origins. The word "Yankee," which was once used to refer only to the settlers of Connecticut, was enlarged to include all New Englanders; gradually it was made to mean any Northerner, and today it is used everywhere (the South excepted) to refer to every American. The writing of American history, which owes so much to the New England historians, continues even in the present to suggest a misleading idea of the homogeneity of the United States.

It may well be that the tendency to extrapolate from sectional history is in itself a characteristic of American historiography. We naturally think of groups rather than individuals, of collective action rather than single-handed accomplishment. Once the New England outlook had been writ large as "American," it was not challenged until near the end of the nineteenth century, when Frederick Jackson Turner advanced his theory of the frontier. It asserted that a steadily westward-moving line of settlements had left an indelible impress on the American nation, and especially on the growth of American democratic institutions. Turner was wresting the nation's history-writing from New England and resettling it in his native region, the upper Mississippi Valley. From the history of that section he was now building an image for the entire country.

In similar fashion, American historians, almost to the present day, have tended to study the unique and then to make the findings representative of social groups. From the lives of unusual women like Susan B. Anthony or Elizabeth Cady Stanton we have been prone to derive our view of how the nineteenth-century woman lived in America. From a few literate and articulate frontiersmen we have drawn our pictures of frontier life. This is a natural temptation. What is paradoxical is that we have fallen into these errors because of the strong persuasive power of the written record. This does not mean that our original studies of uncommon subjects have not been reliable history; it only means that a generous "democratizing" of the uncommon is as likely to distort as bad research. We study Buchanan's weakness as Chief Executive and dogmatize about the requirements for successful Presidents; we examine Woodrow Wilson's mistakes as a peacemaker and apply the "lesson" to terminating the Second World War.

Space and self-help having conspired to bring about in American life hitherto an uncommon freedom from ideological passion, this indifference has forced historiography to cultivate artificial enmities. The Federalists, for example, have been set so starkly against the anti-Federalists that it shocks our dramatic sense to have Burr rather than, say, Jefferson fight a duel with Hamilton. The Signers of the Declaration of Independence are contrasted with the Framers of the Constitution, as if they were two different breeds of men. In fact, the Declaration Signers who survived to 1787 were ardent supporters of the Constitution and almost to a man became Federalists. In the same search for lines of demarcation historians have made much of the struggles over the tariff, of the debate between "sound money" men and the silver party, of the conflict between the New Freedom and the New Nationalism.

Continued Quest and Questioning

In recent years generalizations in the writing of American history have been notably lacking, and this, despite the promise held out by devotees of quantifying of "more solid research" on large bodies of data. The argument has run that through quantification the historian is able to write more representative history and better explanations of the past, especially as it relates to the anonymous mass of people. Now, after some thirty years of effort, the promise remains unfulfilled.

Meanwhile, the older consensus as to what constitutes the stuff of American history has broken up. The subject once consisted of the actions of political, social, religious, and military leaders and their organized and unorganized followers, all white, English-speaking, and Protestant—that is, after the colonial period, when French, Dutch, Spanish, and Indians manifestly played a role. Now, history is regarded as multiracial and widely varied owing to every kind of material and moral affiliation. The result has been a confused—even chaotic—view of the past, for the turbulent feelings and physical violence of the twentieth century have burdened the historian with the duty to help people find a "usable past." Exacerbating the difficulty is the aforementioned Niagara of documentation on all aspects of all lives and events. The availability of this torrent of paper gives the impression that the details of history render all generalizations futile: wrong or misleading or politically inspired.

In short, presentmindedness has segmented the national history. The "studies"—say of women, or Indians, or businesses—do not fit together as the parts of a comprehensive narration and explanation should. Rather, they emerge helter-skelter, remain unconnected, appear perhaps unconnectable. Moreover, the insistent reminders of the shortsightedness of earlier generations with respect to race relations, hard-core poverty, and abuse of the environment keep alive the desire for self-flagellation and self-hatred. A corrective to earlier self-congratulatory history was no doubt needed, but surely the correction, once made, ought not to become a permanent theme; its reiteration negates the very goal of writing a history in keeping with an enlarged and perfected view of the past.

True, the political use of history is a well-rooted tradition, though with this difference that it formerly aimed at synthesis. But even if modern politicized history is altering and confusing the American mind through textbooks and popularizations, such love of history as remains active among the people is directed elsewhere; it attaches itself to the epic or tragic moments of the past made memorable by the conspicuous acts of namable figures—witness the best-selling books of Louis L'Amour and Gore Vidal. In such recitals and their academic sources, some reputations are raised or lowered from time to time. Ulysses S. Grant, for instance, gets somewhat higher marks these days because his policies made it possible for freedmen of the former Confederacy to vote; Harry Truman, on the other hand, has suffered a slight lowering of esteem, because he is thought responsible for the temper of the Cold War; and Eisenhower's stock is rising for having insisted on staying out of Vietnam. The whirligig of time brings in his revenges as in former days, and one may expect that when the pleasures of unmasking and denigration and basing theories on the improbable have worn off, the historian's instinct for creating order out of chaos will once again satisfy itself by large and sober surveys of this nation's odyssey.

Cliometrics, the Measure

In recent decades a new direction has been given to historiographic energies by a new kind of research whose popularity here and abroad reflects obvious changes in Western culture and its technology. Calling itself cliometrics and sharing its scientific confidence with the older econometrics and sociometrics, it proceeds on the assumption that through the use of mathematical statistics and computers new and profitable truths can be learned about the past. Presumably, cliometrics can make an end of the complaint against the "artificial" theses just mentioned and the lure of generalizing from too little evidence. Alfred H. Conrad and John R. Meyer are said to be the intellectual fathers of this elaborate technique, having published two seminal essays on the subject in 1957, at the beginning of their academic careers. The dream of knowing fully and indisputably what happened in the past is an ancient one, and modern electronic equipment has given it new impetus and fresh hope.[17]

The work of "quantifying" documentary materials is suffused with a desire to form novel interpretations: readers have come to expect that cliometrics will produce on well-known topics "shocking" conclusions. Some of these have been: that the presidential election of 1884 did not turn on Rum, Romanism, and Rebellion, as students used to be told, but on a shift in the traditional voting pattern of one upstate New York county; that the unsettled economic conditions in the Age of Jackson, once ascribed to unbridled land speculation, are now attributable to events in Mexico and Great Britain; that the Civil War, formerly regarded as the great push that transformed America into an industrial nation, was in fact a powerful retardant; that the British Navigation Acts in no wise hobbled the economic growth of the American colonies and therefore cannot justly be regarded as a cause of the Revolution. The examples multiply and suggest that hitherto history has been blind.

A book widely regarded as a landmark in the use of the new method is R. W. Fogel and S. L. Engerman's *Time on the Cross*,[18] a

---

[17]See pp. 103–106 and 260–267.
[18]Boston, 1974.

study of the economics of American slavery, which deals at the same time with such other matters as the sex mores, the diet, and the family structure of the black bondsmen. Based on a vast array of sources and employing a "data collection team," the study consists of a "primary volume" of 286 pages and a supplement ("Evidence and Methods") of 267 pages given over to the mathematical formulae and schemata. The preparation required "thousands of man-and-computer hours" and the report is proffered as "the most complete body of information ever assembled on the operation of the slave system." Its intellectual burden or message challenges almost every assumption made hitherto by historians of slavery:

1. Slavery, profitable to slaveholders, was becoming more so as 1860 approached.

2. Slave agriculture was 35 percent more efficient than family farming in the North, for slaves had made the Protestant "work ethic" their own.

3. Slaves were rarely whipped, enjoyed especially good treatment, including a satisfactory diet, and fared materially better than white farm hands.

4. Slaves were not sexually promiscuous, as both abolitionists and proslavery spokesmen had once suggested; they were, in fact, as prudish as good Victorians and managed against great odds to maintain stable families.

Time on the Cross has been severely, but for the most part respectfully, criticized. The very title suggests the authors' conviction that the slaves as a body held to their personal dignity and self-respect despite an unalterable fate. Whatever comfort racist-minded readers might take in the conclusions, such comfort was not the intention of the authors. The criticism has borne on a wide range of issues, from particular to general and historical to mathematical. The most trenchant has been set forth by Herbert G. Gutman and Richard Sutch.[19] They find distortions of evidence and other misuses so grave and

[19]Herbert G. Gutman, *Slavery and the Numbers Game: A Critique of Time on the Cross*, Urbana, Ill. 1975; and Richard Sutch, "The Treatment Received by American Slaves: A Critical Review of the Evidence Presented in *Time on the Cross*," in *Explorations in Economic History*, 12 (October 1975), 335–438.

extensive that Fogel and Engerman's major conclusions must be not only questioned but rejected where they are not reversed. In the view of these critics, many of the old conclusions about black slavery in America must be restored.

Substance apart, the method itself is examined by these same reviewers. They conclude that although *Time on the Cross* fails, cliometrics as such is not the cause. Even so, the new methods "can only supplement, but never supplant the conventional tools of the historian. Statistics are useful. They can add precision and dimension to our interpretation of the past. They can deepen our understanding of history. But they *cannot* stand alone as history."[20] The historian, the fully informed interpreter and his time-tested ways, thus comes out of the cliometric assault relatively whole. The traditional methods are still indispensable—and not archaic—still capable of adding to the well-known means of research any new ones that technology provides.

Some Notable Rewritings

In most computer studies of historical situations the assumption tends to be that up to now we have been ill-informed or misinformed about the facts under review. That review is to lead to a revision. This is legitimate. Like careers after Napoleon's dictum, revisions are always "open to talent." An early classic in the modern revisionist movement was Percy A. Scholes's *Puritans and Music* (1934), which removed the universal impression that the Puritans were a joyless and antiartistic lot. And an authoritative reviewer of the revisionist work *Self and Society in Ming Thought*[21] points out how it alters the character of the period it treats: "Clichés of Chinese history fall by the dozen." Clearly, as in the theories of science, in the constitution of a country, or the decisions of its supreme court, a change of opinion is a permanent possibility; though it would surprise some who distrust history to learn how much stands firm in the work of the great historians even under repeated waves of revisionism. Indeed, later

---

[20] Sutch, *op. cit.*, 429.
[21] W. T. DeBary and others, New York, 1970.

students often find that the earlier accounts are essentially truer than the modish alteration of views. There is often need of a revision of revisionism.[22]

Nor is this dialectic always about the same large or small issues. Many points of interest and moment can be overlooked for a long time. Take as an instance the common notion that for 200 years after the English settled in America their diet and their cookery were limited and monotonous—salt pork and dried beans all winter, fresh corn and beans in summer. All the textbooks and leading social historians have repeated in much the same words this plausible generality. But it is no longer repeatable since 1976, when two articles by Waverly Root demonstrated, on the evidence of cookbooks and contemporary testimony from natives, immigrants, and visitors to America, that the diet of the early Americans was varied, abundant, and cheap, and their cooking often elaborate and even refined. The "plausibility" disappeared, too, when one's attention was drawn to the plentiful supply of fish, game, and widely diversified farm produce mentioned in the sources. And as often happens, the findings on one point led to a new estimate of wider social matters.[23]

The American colonies are only three centuries in the past and the sources readily at hand. What about much older matters, which must surely have been thoroughly worked over? Well, the killing of William Rufus, son of William the Conqueror and King of England after him, took place in August 1100, yet until a few years ago there was still something to be done about the how and the why of that well-documented but variously interpreted death. That missing thing was the investigation of the site, the New Forest, a partly wooded area north of Southampton Water. No one had thought of examining the spot of the accident—or murder. But—who knows? Studying the site might change the reputation of the central figure from that of a bad king and point to a particular murderer.

---

[22]For example, the late Garrett Mattingly, an authority on Renaissance politics, found that his contemporaries' revisionist accounts of certain important situations were wrong and the original estimates of Burckhardt, Motley, and Michelet were right. ("Some Revisions of the Political History of the Renaissance," in Tensley Hilton, ed. *The Renaissance*, Madison, Wis., 1961, 3–23.)

[23]"The Early American Larder" and "Early American Cookery," *Gourmet*, 36 (January and February 1976), 16ff., 18ff.

The scholar who carried out this piece of detective work had no illusion that traces of the event would be left after nearly 900 years.[24] But he wanted to "see for himself," so as to understand the indications in the contemporary sources and carry away a picture of the conditions in which the king was killed. This the placid history of the New Forest, set apart by William the Conqueror as a royal domain, might permit. What followed is a good example of the truth that an historian must possess a wide-ranging curiosity and an experiencing mind: William Rufus was shot by an arrow while hunting at dusk. The unquestioned fact raised questions that could only be answered by a knowledge of the topography of the clearing and its cartography in recent centuries; by acquaintance with the arts of venery and archery, and with the habits of deer and wind and weather in the Forest; all this in addition to the more traditional subjects of inquiry: who was there, why, and what were their characters, antecedents, and interests at the moment.

The report of this undertaking fills only a small volume, but the results are extensive and so rich in detail that they cannot be further summarized—to say nothing of spoiling a good detective story by giving away the solution. But it may be said without harm that not just one but two kings and one nobleman come out with altered reputations, and that the arrogant nineteenth-century historian, Edward A. Freeman, whose work on William Rufus was first discredited by an earlier critic, appears conclusively as no historian at all, but a prejudiced man pushing a thesis in the teeth of the evidence.[25]

Force and Function of Presentmindedness

In all human affairs the burden of proof is on the advocate of the fresh hypothesis, which must not only be sustained from within, but also be shown as consonant with all surrounding knowledge. That

[24]Duncan Grinnell-Milne, *The Killing of William Rufus: An Investigation in the New Forest*, Newton Abbot, 1968.

[25]This "revision" has further importance as a material point in the rehabilitation of James Anthony Froude, the historian of England, whom Freeman pursued with malicious hatred and succeeded in belittling on the strength of his own false reputation for faultlessness. (See W. H. Dunn, *James Anthony Froude*, 2 vols., New York, 1961.)

knowledge of course includes the contents of the contemporary mind as it is moulded by current events. In the writing of American history in recent years, the most powerful such influence has come from the social changes felt and witnessed since the mid-1950s. The cold and hot wars and their vicissitudes have played a role second only to the gradual alteration of many established ideas. The old conviction of being a uniquely formed nation, the old respect for the flag and the uniform, the old cheerful self-confidence were seriously undermined and the darker side of national life was brought into full view; incidents of past violence, accounts of political oppression in the land of freedom, fresh evidence of the neglect of minorities, and explicit hostility toward business and technology became engrossing subjects of research.

This new concern had many different results inside and outside historiography. One was the self-hatred already mentioned. Another was expressed in the word "politicizing," which meant that in the eyes of some the ideal of "objective," "value-free" scholarship inherited from the 1880s came to be deemed immoral. And somehow this view was held not incompatible with the faith that the new statistical and mechanical methods of research were more scientific than the old.[26]

In any case, History was called on to provide the neglected or injured groups in the nation with a sense of their importance by teaching them (and their once-indifferent neighbors) the role they had played in the past. Hence the many college offerings designated as "Studies" with a qualifying adjective. The model seems to have been the "American Studies," which had a great vogue after the Second World War. Now the studies bore the names of those whom "America" had overlooked: Blacks, Women, Indians ("Native Americans"), Mexican-Americans. There seemed no reason why the list should not be extended to the French, Spanish, Scandinavian, and other minorities, on the same principle and with good effect upon the general knowledge of history in the land of pluralism.

A difficulty which at first limited the value and appeal of such studies was the lack of scholarly materials on the great many different

---

[26]For example, students of anthropology at the University of Arizona sift through bags of garbage each week to find out how Americans really live.

subjects that belong to the systematic survey of any minority group's past life.[27] But this is being overcome as the interest persists. A greater obstacle lies in the definition—or rather lack of definition—in any subject matter that is both topical and not "organized," even haphazardly, by history itself. This difficulty has long been experienced by those who have tried to write a History of Latin America. The geographical portions of it being in many respects unrelated, there is no binding thread, no "common fate." The History of Women or Black History is similarly hampered by discontinuities of many kinds; the patterns are faint and the relevant disciplines interfere with each other: women and the law, women and music, women and pioneer life, women and the professions, and so on require attention, but in what overarching scheme? Where are the beginning, middle, and end? Whenever lack of inner unity is present it works against "pattern" and tends to baffle memory.

In spite of obstacles, presentmindedness in European and American historical writing continues to ramify. The world conflict of 1939–1945 awakened in the West a renewed surge of interest in Eastern civilizations. Continuing relations—including wars—have both deepened knowledge and increased curiosity; to such a degree that it has become something of a fashion to charge Western historians with self-centered complacency, not to say rooted provincialism.

The truth happens to be different. From the Crusades and Marco Polo to Dr. Livingstone and Lafcadio Hearn, it is the West which during the last thousand years has explored, studied, described, and learned from the East—not the other way around. Western scholarship on all Asiatic and African lands and civilizations has long been extensive, in high repute, and as widely disseminated as any other of comparable difficulty. The complaint that "all we learn in school" is American and European history, not Chinese or Indian, Japanese or African, is rather wrong-headed on both counts. We scarcely learn "home" history any more; certainly not that of the ancient and medieval West. And even if that history were still well and widely

---

[27]See, however, the three volumes of essays and documents, *The Negro in American History*, Chicago, 1969. The comparable work on the first Americans is Wilcomb E. Washburn, comp., *The American Indian and the United States: A Documentary History*, 4 vols., New York, 1973.

taught, it would seem reasonable to begin with the familiar and nearby (as is done for geography) before stretching the imagination and the memory with names and accounts of distant places and alien institutions. These are best learned about and appreciated after acquaintance with the texture of human history in one's own culture. It requires a strong effort of imagination to understand what life may have been like in one's hometown 100 or 300 years ago. If provincialism is to be removed—as it can be—by historical studies, the student enlightened about his own past has the best chance of going on with profit to read about the East.

In spite of new attractions and methods, in spite also of political ferment, it is likely that in the immediate future American national history will continue to be perforated along the dotted lines of our presidential administrations. In Europe, the state itself is the repository of national prestige, and premiers are only passing figures in its history. In America, the presidency is the center of honor and attention and its temporary occupant must be very dull or delinquent to be denied a permanent place in our pantheon. True, every president is vilified by the opposition press and party, but he is nearly always glorified in our history-writing when his service is over. This is a comforting thought, of course, but it flatters our good nature rather than our good judgment—unless there is in this leniency the unconscious wisdom of a people that wants to thrive without the unending struggles of Europe over ideas and their standardbearers.

No less than in Europe, then, the history written in America reflects the culture that produces it. Our historians have chosen subjects that, like our party system and our social life, leave small room for intellectual debate. For good or ill, American historiography has generated but few strong theses. The works of Turner, Charles A. Beard, Vernon L. Parrington, Walter Prescott Webb, and Richard Hofstadter are the chief exceptions that come to mind. Perhaps the avidity with which they were seized upon by their contemporaries testifies to a great hunger which it is a mistake to leave unsatisfied. But the subjects that historians choose are a cause as well as an offshoot of the culture in which they work. In any case, it is as impossible for the historian as for anybody else to decide: "I will now have a great idea." Even modest Ph.D. candidates who think of themselves as digging a small unregarded well of truth find out that background, inclination, and training make them do with their materials what broader assumptions than their own have determined. A lifetime of effort is not too great a price for the courageous and intelligent to pay if they mean to change a single facet of the national consciousness.

10

Relic-Hunting, Anti-History, and Social Science

The Cult of the Fragmentary

Though the word *history* is continually on people's lips and greets their eyes everywhere—in the newspaper, in business, in government documents, in hospital records, and in academic affairs—it is doubtful whether these uses of the word imply any clear idea of what a genuine history is like. Yet to read the papers one would think that modern man felt a passionate interest in the subject. Anniversaries are celebrated every day: the twenty-fifth of NASA, the fiftieth of the National Archives and of the German-American newspaper *Aufbau*; the sixtieth in Hollywood of Metro-Goldwyn Mayer; and at Disneyland of Donald Duck.

All the while, the anniversaries of national figures such as Washington and Lincoln are shifted around to one date or another in the neighborhood of the right one for the sake of a longer weekend. But never mind: we make up for it in other ways. For instance, at Gettysburg every February 12, Union and Confederate soldiers in uniform stroll along the streets preparatory to parading and cavorting

249

on the battlefield. Elsewhere, people reenact Washington's crossing of the Delaware or get into costume to perform "a Colonial house-raising." There is nothing wrong with these pastimes, but they must not be mistaken for an interest in history. They rank with the old-fashioned fancy dress ball with masks on and the school pageant or "Greek games."

True, respect for history is undiminished and the award of a Special Congressional Gold medal to Louis L'Amour for his well-researched historical novels surely expressed a popular feeling.[1] But fiction is not history and the respect for actual history perhaps explains why the public stays at a *respectful* distance from it. Ideas about history, the historical, and the historic are confused.

For example, innumerable landmarks commissions save what they call historic houses. In New Jersey alone, 2,000 "historic sites" were added to the National Register in 1984. This grand sweep included "one thematic group," which probably means a collection of buildings similar in style. Meanwhile in New York, part of the upper East side has been declared a landmark and the inhabitants of a portion beyond now clamor to be taken in, though most of that region is undistinguished or ugly. These details show that landmarks are but old houses, not historic. Thus the interest is not *historical* but something else. It is part nostalgia, part disaffection from modern shoe-box architecture and resistance to heedless real estate development. These are worthy motives but have little to do with history.

In the same mood, a good many persons laboriously probe their genealogy, "search for their roots" as the current phrase has it.[2] So strong is the desire for ancestry that unscrupulous firms prey upon eager gullibility by promising information for high fees and giving little or nothing to the purpose. Here again is pseudo history, though a legitimate concern with one's past.[3] How shall we characterize these

---

[1] September 24, 1983.

[2] Those who are so inclined can begin their work by examining Timothy Field Beard, with Denise Demong, *How to Find Your Family Roots*, New York, 1977; and Val D. Greenwood, *The Researcher's Guide to American Genealogy*, Baltimore, 1973.

[3] The pleasure of having namable ancestors brought together in London in 1984 some of the 1,700 descendants of Nell Gwynn, the orange girl who became the mistress of Charles II.

feelings? We get a clue when we hear that the local association that wants inclusion of its quarter among the landmarks is also raising funds "to secure an historian for Historic District Research." *Antiquarian* is the proper word here, and it describes several other types of activity that are almost as ubiquitous as saving old houses, namely saving papers, artifacts, and relics. Something has been said earlier (see pp. 234–235) about the accumulation due to the preservation of archives, public and private, which include the presidential libraries, the publishing of governors' papers, the bequests and purchases lodged in university and city libraries. When the government released the contents of thousands of safe-deposit boxes garnered from the bank failures of the Great Depression, a huge mass of papers was left after some 5,000 valid claims had been satisfied. At that point the historical societies put in a bid for the remainder. All this zest for hoarding no doubt reflects the awareness that historians rely on records, but the saving and housing and sorting is neither reading history nor writing it: it feeds rather the collector's instinct, which emerges again in a fast multiplying institution—the local or the specialist museum.[4]

Every community has to have one; it is of interest to tourists and as such more important than a post office. Many willing hands are ready to help fill it with rescued and restored artifacts. If it is not the devotees of "industrial archeology," who collect old tools and urge the preservation of disused forges and bridges, it may be delvers and divers into lakes and oceans who look for jetsam and wrecks. On the seas, this search is a worldwide phenomenon, sometimes due to hope of treasure, but much more often spurred by the desire for relics. When the anchor of the armored ship *Monitor* was heaved up, it was hailed as "a piece of the Civil War." Ships associated with John Paul Jones, Napoleon, and Henry VIII have recently been raised. In Virginia, three amateurs are trying to recover an unusual old canal boat—"no other like it," said the State Underwater Archeologist,

[4]When a once-useful building proves obsolete, make it a museum! For example, the movie studios at Astoria in New York City have defied revival; the foundation that saved the crumbling structure plans to house in it film memorabilia. As one of the promoters aptly put it: "To create a museum, you must see things that are not really there" (*New York Times*, July 16, 1984).

whose predestined name is Broadwater. Elsewhere, there has been protest against free-flipping divers because they harm "historic ship-wrecks," remove objects, and disturb the sand and silt from which invaluable knowledge could be inferred by aquatic antiquarians.

Part of this concern must be attributed to the influence of the French historical doctrines of the *Annales* group already mentioned. The modern desire is to find out how "the people" lived and worked, and for this purpose to prefer material evidence over written sources; it is more "democratic" and "scientific." The appeal of archeology to certain minds has always been this intellectual game of inferring large conclusions from small clues—broken pots in midden heaps—and now that a new branch of study calls itself ethnoarcheology, the field is wide open for making the most of every scrap of man-shaped matter.

Yet when one considers the plentiful difficulties encountered by the historian who deals with direct, human evidence, it seems rash to base conclusions on inferences from silt and sand. At any rate, great caution seems advisable: one should remember that astrophysicists, who have the advantage of elaborate devices, precise measurements, and a close-knit guild checking all results, found a good many of their cast-iron inferences falsified when instrument-laden vehicles actually "went and looked" at the places and the planets about which those accepted inferences had been drawn. At best, then, the study of relics can add details—possibly curious or vivid—to the history of our recent past, which is already so fully documented by conscious, literate beings. There is moreover something—shall we say—defeat-ist about treating our own civilization as if the most interesting and valuable record of it consisted of its refuse in bits and pieces.

For all the gathering and collecting and delving clearly corre-sponds to an interest in curious items which is greater than an interest in synthesis and broad understanding. Just because the pleasure of the hunt is paramount, it does not seem likely that modern antiquar-ian discoveries will inspire the writing of great histories as the discov-ery of coins and steles inspired Mommsen to write his history of Rome. Likewise, the specialized archives such as those of broadcast-ing or of the printed word must by their excessive completeness (not a tautology but a fair description) lead at most to the production of various monographs—specialization within specialization.[5]

In some quarters, it is true, there is some unease about the relation to history of these collectibles. When the Smithsonian Institution opened its large public-display building twenty years ago, it was called the Museum of History and Technology. In 1980 the name was changed to National Museum of American History because the contents ranged from George Washington's tent to a steam locomotive and from the dresses of presidential wives to 14 million postage stamps. But still the Regents are not satisfied and they are looking for a name that shall be "more fully descriptive." They evidently sense that these objects are and are not "American History," but cannot exactly resolve the contradiction. And this is one reason why the building had better do without a descriptive name and simply be the National Museum, on a par with the National Gallery and the National Archives.

The cause of such uncertainties, as we have suggested, is that the public no longer has an adequate conception of what history is. It takes some of the elements of history for the thing itself; it believes that satisfying one's curiosity about this or that piece of the past is knowledge of history, when it is only the beginning of possible knowledge. With this misconception the public thinks that the many works now offered as history deserve that name. On this point confusion is forgivable: for it is the historians themselves who have abandoned their art for another, while keeping the old name.

What History Is: A Reminder

History proper is more than its elements; it is more than information about objects, customs, and situations: it is a chronological narrative of actions by persons with motives, these actions and motives cluster-

[5]The International Association of Sound Archives (for "audiohistory") has set standards for re-recording old products of phonography: for Clio's sake some of the new records must faithfully reproduce what the listener heard in Edison's day or at any specified time of origin, not the improved sound now retrievable from the old record.

ing in what is called events. To understand the motives and their outcome certainly requires knowledge about artifacts, habits, and institutions, but unless a synthesis is made of these elements with each other and with the element of time, the reader is not supplied with a history. The sense of the past may be awakened by a description of this or that object, site, incident, or person, but it remains skewed and incomplete until developed by the reading of a genuine history. Where are modern histories to be found?

If nowadays one turns to the catalogues of scholarly publishers, the books one finds in them under the rubric of History are for the most part studies of elements or situations. For example: *Murdering Mothers: Infanticide in England and New England, 1558–1803; American Collegiate Populations; A Prison of Expectations: The Family in Victorian Culture; Old Age in the New Land: The American Experience since 1790; Poverty and Welfare in Habsburg Spain; Crime in Seventeenth-Century England.* And in history journals one finds articles of similar type, such as: "Infant Birthright and Nutrition in Industrializing Montreal."[6]

All these subjects are "of historical interest" and some are important, but their treatment does not make them into histories. For one thing, most of them do not fully answer to their titles; they rely on a sample. The study of poverty and welfare in Spain is subtitled: "The example of Toledo." *Crime in Seventeenth-Century England* deals only with one county, Essex. The study of the Victorian family "prison" relies on the lives of five Victorian novelists. Even if one accepts these samplings as statistically valid—truly representative cases—one sees that the subjects under inquiry in these works are sociological. The purpose is to learn about a state of affairs: it is retrospective sociology. The result may be of use to a future historian, but as given it is not yet history. At this point it will aid understanding if we retrace briefly the sequence through which history gave birth to the modes of study called social sciences, studies which now increasingly usurp their progenitor's name.

---

[6]*American Historical Review*, 89 (April 1984), 324f.

Clio's Offspring, the Ologies

The earliest historians in the West, Herodotus and Thucydides, were quite aware that the simplest recital of events had manifold implications. From the start, history contained ancillary subject matter: Herodotus held the Athenians spellbound with his *historiai* (researches) by relating how the Egyptians and other peoples lived and worshiped and carried on agriculture. He was a sociologist, anthropologist, demographer, and even psychologist—as when he reported the experiment by which Psammetichus tried to find out which language an untaught child would speak (Book 2, 2). Thucydides possessed a different sort of curiosity. He wondered what principles of action—in politics, diplomacy, and war—could be discerned in the history of the long Peloponnesian struggle. He was the father of political science without departing from his main role of historian.

There is nothing surprising in the fact that history, when deliberately written, should suggest general truths in the same way as the individual's private experience suggests rules of thumb for workaday guidance. Similarities in any course of events are bound to put the idea of norm and regularity into reflective minds. It is from this simple beginning that the social sciences spring, and from it too that we can understand their present attitude toward history.

For a long time history remained the hospitable container of the diversified interest that men take in other men, past or distant, as well as in the possible "nature" of man universally considered. Since an aspect of this second concern is man's political life, the earliest quarrying of history for specialized materials was directed at a science of politics. Aristotle collected and compared constitutions, and other ancient writers with the same purpose illustrated their ideas from history. After the collapse of Rome, to account for so great a fall, nothing less than a cosmic, theological interpretation seemed adequate. St. Augustine gave the outline of it in *The City of God* and Orosius the details in *Seven Books against the Pagans*.

Explanation by divine will was a double setback, for history and for political science, and its effects lasted nearly a millennium. The painstaking and often picturesque chronicles and "lives" produced in the Middle Ages were necessarily limited by the theological outlook. To the writers, it was not *a* view of the universe; it was its reality. Historical inquiry as such, the desire to know what happened as a matter of fact, was logically subordinated to the search for moral and religious meaning.

Only with the profound transformation of Christendom in early modern times did the older human curiosity return in strength. And with the resulting cultivation of secular history came the renewed search in it for principles of human action. Machiavelli, Bodin, Vico, Montesquieu, Voltaire, Herder are some of the men who sought in the substance of history the outlines of a permanent, secular truth. The "explanation" of history might be physical (geography, climate) in Bodin and Montesquieu, biological (cultural) in Vico, Voltaire, and Herder. This desire for general conclusions grew as history acquired polemical importance in the eighteenth century and became in the nineteenth virtually the dominant form of thought: evolution was but history writ large over the physical and biological world.

This preoccupation with the origin and development of nearly everything led in turn to a vast enterprise of unearthing sources, and from the 1830s onward these began to be studied—ransacked might be the better word—for evidence in support of new kinds of studies, the nascent social sciences. It is no discredit to the ologies that among the first were phrenology, physical anthropology, and historical philology and ethnology—all of them tending to establish the existence of races with distinct traits that might prove to be the "factors" in nationality. The political arguments about Celts, Gallo-Romans, and (the supposedly superior) Germans date from that time. In many variations they "explained" all of European history.[7]

Soon, under the influence of Positivism, it was felt that closer methods must be used to ascertain the character of groups and individuals. Comte, the creator of the Positive Philosophy, coined the word sociology to designate the science of man in society;[8] and somewhat later Buckle embarked on the national "characterology"

[7]See above pp. 221ff.

[8]Comte's sociology was in fact a typology. He did not allow for the intervention of psychology between sociology and its biological base and was in this regard a direct forerunner of Emile Durkheim.

that informs his sizable, though unfinished *Introduction to the History of Civilization in England* (1857–1861). He had been struck and inspired by the work of such statisticians as Dufau and Quetelet, which showed striking regularities in social behavior: the number of suicides, letters misaddressed, verdicts of acquittal, and other human actions seemed ruled by "laws" as strict as gravitation. If such laws existed, they must account for all the phenomena that history disjointedly records.

But as always, the "ological" purpose was not simply to chalk up these numbers and percentages and laws. It meant also to relate them to institutions and doctrines, nationalities and "races," so as to control and modify the course of events. Men's interest in Man is even more interventionist than his interest in the physical world. In imitation of science, the experimental method was by 1850 well launched in psychology and anthropology, the comparative method in philology, and the so-called scientific in historiography. The instigator of this rigor in history was not Karl Marx, as is often believed, but Leopold von Ranke. After him, the familiar demands of scrupulous verification, thorough sifting of evidence, total review of "the literature," and minute exactitude in reporting became moral absolutes. It was not yet clear that the analogy between "scientific" history and the sciences of man was ill-drawn and that these last should never find a counterpart or fear a competitor in history.

This awareness came with the "revolution" that took place in the ologies during the 1880s and 1890s. It was the time when a vast collective effort—the work of great minds and industrious disciples—reshaped all the sciences, social and physical. The former, redefined and redirected, took on something like their present form. The names of Durkheim, Tarde, LeBon in sociology; of Charcot, William James, and Freud in psychology; of Franz Boas, J. G. Frazer, and Francis Galton in the several branches of anthropology are attached to the fruitful innovations of that creative period.

Progress and popularization were so rapid that the manifest difference between these new studies and even the most painstaking history became apparent to every educated person. The chief novelty in history was the adoption of the so-called economic interpretation, under the influence of Marx's writings. That influence had been long delayed by the difficulty and the tendentiousness of these writings, and when it took effect upon historians, it was as part of a more general response to the problems of an industrialized mass civilization. There was a desire for social history, for economic history, and for the newest "new history," which gave up political and diplomatic acts and motives in favor of great "forces," including movements of ideas.

Persistent Goals and Motives

But still no part of this new history was science. The radical difference mentioned above remained—to the "new historians" a clear deficiency, and one that might be repaired. When the great German academic, Karl Lamprecht, came to the United States in 1904, to foregather with representatives of all the arts and sciences at the Congress in St. Louis that was celebrating the centenary of the Louisiana Purchase, he challenged his fellow scholars:

History is primarily a psycho-sociological science. . . . The new progressive and therefore aggressive point of view . . . is the socio-psychological, which may be termed modern. . . . The rise of sociology and anthropology during the last decades . . . has meant a fresh start in the writing of cultural history and in the development of method. . . . It is only the beginning of an intensive psycho-sociological method.[9]

The observer of today can see that the intention of those who want to reform and improve history has not changed. All that is new is the assertion that the reform has succeeded and the improvement taken place. At the turn of the century, the long debate called in Germany the *Methodenstreit*, or struggle over method, did at any rate envisage the continued writing of history. The one step taken toward "science" was the general condemnation of "literary" history, which in practice meant little more than that well-written works were sus-

---

[9]"Historical Development and Present Character of History," *Congress of Arts and Science*, Howard J. Rogers, ed., Boston, 1906, 2:ii.

pect. Dullness, or at least hard reading, was the mark of the scholar-scientist.

But what of the "progressive and aggressive psycho-sociological method"? The great difficulty, then as now, was to choose which among the rival schools of sociology, anthropology, and psychology was best suited to fertilize history. Unlike the natural sciences, the social have so far shown little agreement or unified advance, nor is it clear in what way the method of these *inductive* and diagnostic studies should be grafted on the simple *documentary* scholarship of the historian. The meaning of "documentary" has been made plain throughout our earlier chapters: it is not limited to words on paper; it embraces any relic and any conclusion of the sciences, including measurements and statistics, provided these fit into the description of events in chronological succession. In other words, the elements of "social science" that were originally part of history can be reintegrated as needed.

It is a different matter when the historian is summoned to abandon the recital of events, enriched or not by analysis and generalization, and devote himself exclusively to the study of situations, institutions, and individual or group character, using for the purpose quantitative surveys or depth psychology. Clearly the application of such a theory and its method must change the nature of the product. This statement is not an opinion but a description. By counting instances or interpreting psychological symptoms related to a given topic, the student is establishing the sociology or the psychology of that topic; his tables and graphs or diagnoses may possibly serve in the future writing of history, but in the original reports they do not constitute "a history of" anything. The counting of selected social facts may permit some inductive generality, say, about "violence" before a revolution; the psychoanalysis of acts or decisions may warrant the application of a technical label to an individual or collective mood, say, "obsessional" or "anxiety-ridden." But the place and significance of such findings in an intelligible account of some portion of the past remains to be assigned by somebody else. And that somebody can only be the historian, since all the other researchers are busy producing sociological and psychological studies.

The paradox here is particularly striking, for it is evident that psycho- and quanto-historians must rely more or less on the work of past historians and biographers for the data to be recycled by the new methods. The new methodists do indeed turn up new sources—parish registers or unpublished correspondence—but their search is necessarily guided by a previous knowledge of history-as-events and their results have point only in relation to those events: if the revolutions of 1848 were unknown or unimportant or unconnected with other events, there would be no interest in learning how much violence came beforehand. The desired extinction of narrative history at the hands of the newcomers would therefore seem to entail their own ultimate suicide.

Problems Not Periods: One Reason Why

To stress this paradox is not to disqualify the attempts at fresh understanding. It is evident that dissatisfaction with plain history has gone on for a long enough time to earn respectful attention; the loss of confidence must signify something. Toward the end of his life, Lord Acton, who designed the *Cambridge Modern History* as a narrative in twelve volumes, was recommending "Study a problem, not a period."[10] He did not quite mean the sort of problem favored by the new disciplines, but his maxim records his early sense of the helplessness engendered by the contemplation of any period and its crushing documentation.

Across the Channel, the new generation of historians were restless in the face of the ordinary tasks and wanted to break new ground. The upshot was the socioeconomic typology of Lucien Febvre and Marc Bloch, which later turned into the so-called *psychologie historique* of George Rude, Ignace Meyerson, Robert Mandrou, Fernand Braudel, and others, whose works depict regions, or compare widely separate events, or trace topics (e.g., "the crowd") through long periods. The bearing of this movement may be gathered from the fact

---

[10]Quoted in G. R. Elton, *The Practice of History*, New York, 1967, 127. Yet Acton planned the *Cambridge Modern History* for the layman and explicitly to "overcome" the advances into arcanery made by specialists.

that the chair Robert Mandrou holds at the Sorbonne is designated not simply as one of history but as of the *Histoire sociale des menta-lités modernes.* Meanwhile an older practitioner, Georges Lefebvre, taught as a fundamental lesson that "no one can be an historian who does not know how to count." We shall look more closely in a moment at some consequences of the dictum.

With such deep and widespread roots, the contemporary American zeal for psychology and quantification must be seen as a more diffuse cultural phenomenon than it seems on the surface—not merely an intellectual step suggested by the availability of methods, but an emotion and state of mind possibly shared by all thinking people. But the loss of interest in history that tells *how* and the yearning for studies that answer *why* extends beyond the professional circle. The general disquiet in Western civilization strengthens the belief that answers may be found by ingenious research. Social problems (a term that goes not much farther back than 1900) press upon the mind with enormous force, because of their number and extent and because of the moral attitude that views all difficulties as creating obligations. And the word "problem" implies that solutions can be found.

If this is so, then mere narrative history is bound to appear too detached to be "helpful," whereas various conceivable types of analytic "study" would supply clues if not answers to the Why. The generous motive behind the "new disciplines" is unmistakable, and their appeal is as much to moral impulse as to the inventive mind. It may be by a related movement of sensibility that history's half-sister, the novel, has also abandoned narrative and description. Readers formerly content with the spectacle of life now want to know why the depicted characters behave as they do; and in the "new novel" characters themselves have given place to situations and states, mostly psychological, in which time itself is abolished. Everywhere, persons and events are disappearing.

To step outside the present for a moment and view it from a distant perspective suggests a further explanation: great history writing, like great art, requires for its production a public that shares a common mood and a solid set of assumptions, not a variable temper and shifting set of anxieties such as we suffer from. The present time, seeking from history solutions to pressing problems and, being convinced that history cannot give them, does not want history at all. There is logic in the instinctive pinning of hopes to sociology and psychology. The illogic is to suppose that quanto-history and psycho-history offer a compound different from sociology and psychology and really correspond to the names they bear.

But what does the name matter if the research has brought out some truth about the past? The answer is that works of the mind that differ in important ways deserve distinctive names. A lyric poem and an epic are kept separate by names that indicate the features of each. From an epic we expect large scope and a story; likewise with a history. A recital of social or moral conditions in a town or a county, or even the pursuit of a single narrow theme through many years, does not constitute a story, a history. For the essence of story or history is palpable continuity and a rich contexture, an unbroken chain of actions and manifold results. That is why it is possible to write the history of the American people but not a history of red-headed people in America: in the second case no continuity could be found and the context would be incoherent as well.

In retrospective sociology, however, changed habits or circumstances can be described in successive chapters without the obligation to establish a chain by means of important figures and linked events. Any figures or events that are named are merely illustrative; they are not the agents in a tight-knit drama.

How and why did history-writing shift from its narrative tradition and become something else? The answer takes us back to the cultural pressure of science, which has been mentioned earlier as gathering strength since the middle of the nineteenth century. The model of scientific certainty, was affecting all intellectual endeavors and many historians thought that by greater "rigor," history too could become a science. That meant examining *all* original sources of every kind. Since the century's passion for history kept unearthing more and more of these, the urge to be encyclopedic meant reducing the scope of each history: "a couple of years in the history of the eleventh century" was all that a famous English historian thought could be done in a lifetime. Clearly, monographs of this type would not attract even the highly educated reader, only the specialist.

Simultaneously (as we have seen) the revamped social sciences—anthropology, psychology, and sociology—were making the same claim to being wholly scientific and were capturing public attention by their often startling reports. These were more lively than the monograph on two years in the eleventh century. It was then that the idea occurred to revitalize history with borrowings from the social sciences. After all, people in the past lived in societies, had their distinctive "culture" and "psychology." Like Lord Acton, historians everywhere turned to "problems." In the United States, James Harvey Robinson sought a new history in the onward march of great ideas; in France, François Simiand also proposed the abandonment of chronology and narrative: ignore facts and events that are unique and concentrate on those that repeat, so as to draw general conclusions, like social science.

These ideas fermented in the minds of the younger generation, the appeal of a "new history" being reinforced by the conviction which is still ours that the study of troubles in the past could lead to useful social action in the present. The social sciences, too, by dealing with widespread conditions, seemed more democratic than history, which concentrates on visible doers with names, titles, and powers. The true source of motion was felt to lie with the great anonymous forces embodied in the people.

The Annales *Group Yesterday and Today*

That generation of historians was kept from carrying out its intentions until after the war of 1914–1918, both by the cataclysm of the war itself and by the momentum of the older form of history entrenched in the universities. But by 1920, Henri Berr could confidently utter the slogan "No more event-based history!" Nine years later, a group of disciples founded the now-famous journal known by its short title, the *Annales*. By the vigor and brilliance of its contributors, it has launched a "school" that has influenced students of history everywhere; its doctrine has replaced what we are calling retrospective sociology the former chronological, narrative history. In a word, the *Annales* group created the present-day orthodoxy.

Its natural offshoots have been quantitative history, inspired by the belief derived from Marx that economics is the ultimate power in historical change; and psycho-history, inspired by the belief derived from Freud that the unconscious is the hidden spring of all human action. In both systems the individual disappears: in the first he is merged in the mass molded by the forces of production and exchange; in the second, he is reduced to a type moved by some generalized psychic force. That is how we get "the" slave owner and "his" psycho-history.

There are signs today of disquiet and of mounting objections to these "new disciplines" which have promised to satisfy historical curiosity in a superior way. The leading representative of the *Annales* school, Fernand Braudel, was greeted with acclaim on the appearance of his large work on the Mediterranean world, but there was also some skepticism and a shrewd guess at the cause for the acclaim: "We are becoming a numerate society: almost instinctively there seems now to be a greater degree of truth in evidence expressed numerically, . . . no matter how shaky the statistical evidence. . . ." In *The Mediterranean*, the author

> spends pages calculating the average income in ducats of the agricultural worker. The evidence is slender, uncertain, disparate. The margins of error, Braudel admits, are so very great that the calculations are almost meaningless. And the upshot is that . . . workers lived on the margin of subsistence, which of course we knew from scores of literary sources.[11]

Since then, a more direct attack has been made on Braudel's subsequent *Civilization and Capitalism, Fifteenth to Eighteenth Century:*

> The mistakes and distortions which abound in all Braudel's work are not so much incidental as inherent in his method, in his very approach to historical studies. For he will identify his long- and medium-term patterns and cycles irrespective of events and policies, of political and military power . . .: a systematic disregard of statesmen and the impact of alliances, treaties, and blockades. Occasionally, he stumbles awkwardly against the fatal contradictions in his own method. . . . Braudel, for all his qualities, has an unhistorical mind.[12]

When found in honest researchers, the flaws in the *Annales* method are as it were pointed out by the author himself. For instance, in the two-volume *France: 1848–1945* by the Oxford scholar Theodore Zeldin, the author modestly offers his findings as estab-

[11] J. H. Plumb in *Encounter*, April 1973, 64.
[12] *Times Literary Supplement*, January 21, 1983, 63.

lishing "the permanent features of French society, to counterbalance the study of events, developments, movements, and fashions. . . ."[13] The subject headings show how this is attempted: "Politics," "Ambition," "Intellect," "Marriage and Morals," "Anxiety," etc.—all of them sociological topics. What the chapters contain is items drawn from statistical reports, newspapers, letters, contemporary fiction, political and social commentary, court trials, and the like. These fragments of fact or opinion are loosely linked within ad hoc categories. Six occupations, for instance, represent the bourgeoisie, one of the occupations being "the rich." But again and again the author is at pains to warn us of his failure to deliver the thing promised: "How these occupations interacted and how they related to the rest of the country is a complex affair," beyond recovery. "Nothing is more difficult to define than the bourgeois . . . it must be accepted that the notion is necessarily vague." As for "the ambitions of ordinary men, they are difficult to write about, because seldom recorded."[14]

Lacking chronology or any other kind of consecutiveness, the retailing of facts and opinions leaves no clear impression and defies remembering. The confusion indeed arouses awkward questions: Is it likely that between 1848 and 1945 the status of doctors remained unchanged? Is it allowable to put side by side as evidence a quotation from an obscure marriage manual of 1806, a critique of 1883, and a poll of French youth in 1947? And, to return to "method," what is it worth if the user himself repeatedly confesses his bafflement, as in: "The answers during the period were varied." "The history of the emotional reactions between married couples [sic] is even more difficult to trace." Whether there is "more premarital sex in France than a hundred years ago, it is impossible to say."[15] Where then are the "permanent features"?

Quanto- and Psycho-History Are Typologies

In so-called quantitative history, the investigator is usually unable to study the facts directly; he is compelled to take "indicators." He will

13 Oxford, 1973, 1:2–3.
14 *Ibid.*, 13, 22, 87.
15 *Ibid.*, 287, 291, 306.

take the records of matriculation at Oxford and Cambridge to assess the education of the English upper classes in the sixteenth century. Or again, he merges a variety of events under a large rubric—Violence—over a series of years. In the sampling, everything on the police blotter, from drunken brawls to murders, counts as a violent act. Motives, events, and consequences are obliterated. A recent study of twenty-one democracies elicited a judicious remark applicable to most attempts at quantifying history; the few exceptions are the obvious ones of studies of inanimate and numerable things, e.g., tons of coal, barrels of oil. When it comes to democracies,

the method . . . is likely to lead only to the discovery of interesting statistical correlations. . . . But these . . . tell us comparatively little about the forces at work sustaining or undermining particular systems. For that, an entirely different type of inquiry would be needed, one which attempted to grasp the nature of each political system through understanding its history. . . .[16]

Acknowledging at last these deep deficiencies, a symposium of French scholars at the University of Montpellier recently showed a strong urge to "return to chronology" and restore events and human beings to their place in history. The Minister for Education concurred.[17]

How Not to Honor "The People"

As for psycho-history, still popular in the United States, it is the scarcity of evidence about past states of mind and the ambiguity of the subject's actions as reported that must always throw grave doubts on the "diagnosis." If we knew only of Dr. Johnson's oddities and obsessions, we might possibly infer the character of his religious anxiety, but we would never guess the remarkable balance and penetration of his judging mind. Psychiatry itself has within the last decade much lowered its pretentions with regard to the living, from whom "evidence" is at least readily obtainable. Psycho-historians

[16] *Times Literary Supplement*, June 8, 1984, 631.
[17] *Le Figaro*, January 23, 1984.

should ponder these new doubts, as well as question the validity of making up types—the slave owner, the pioneer woman, the business tycoon. It is no proof of democratic feeling, no compliment to "the people," to reduce the varieties of humankind to stock characters fit only for melodrama or the penny novelette.[18]

It is in fact the supreme merit of genuine history to show us diversity. By narrating events, naming names, and assessing motives, purposes, and results, history teaches us what life beyond our immediate experience is like. The lesson of history is not at all like the moral of a fable, nor is it a direct practical guide, like a usable precedent in law or business; it is the lesson of how things go and *may* go. From reading histories that are true narratives, the citizen—and even more, the researcher—acquires a vicarious experience that blends with his lived experience to broaden his imagination and sharpen his judgment.

Unlike science and social science, history is narrative and synthetic, not static and analytic. The distinguished diplomat Abba Eban has insisted on this point apropos of a new analytic discipline in *his* profession:

I don't really think it can compare with the vivid, living spectacle of history. And if . . . one had to sacrifice something, I would prefer to sacrifice the somewhat abstract jargon of these analyses rather than . . . the direct contemplation of predicaments in which nations have found themselves, out of which they have emerged. . . . I still believe that history—by which I mean the narration of situations [and] predicaments— . . . is a much more fruitful background than the algebraic formulas. . . . I don't think they can be a substitute for the deeply human content of historical study.[19]

The Ambit and Permanence of History

To repeat and also to conclude, it is foolish to say that names do not matter and that history is whatever an historian does. The empirical look and feel of his own kind of work which nobody else will supply,

---

[18]See "Denigrating the Rule of Reason: The 'New History' Goes Bottom Up" by the distinguished historian Gertrude Himmelfarb (*Harper's*, 268 [April 1984], 84–90).

[19]*Seminar Reports*, Columbia University, 2, (January 27, 1975), 3.

justifies him in stressing the character of his unique contribution. So far, no convincing argument has been advanced why he is bound to give up the recital of events and the portraying of participants in favor of the analysis of problems, the comparison of social forms, and the description of institutional or individual essences. The demand that he abdicate is all the more out of place that its declared motive is the wish to solve pressing problems in contemporary society—a worthy goal: let those who can, do so. The historian knows his work well enough to recognize that he cannot compete on that ground. His effectiveness is quite other. The reading of history, as Burckhardt put it with finality, makes one "not more clever for the next time, but wiser forever."

And if one wanted to be invidious, one might ask what practical present-day use has in fact been made of the supposedly revealing, enlightening studies of classes, institutions, conditions, and movements. That history—narrative, literary history—no longer commands unclouded public attention as it did in the last century is understandable, for the reasons we cited and doubtless others. The fact should cause no dismay. Taste and opinion go in loops, if not in cycles, and must be served in their way. But after all deductions are made, there is still an important class of readers to be considered, for whom the writing of history must continue—and in its proper form, for they will accept no substitues.[20] What is offered today performs a different function, or tries to. The lover of history is entitled to receive and enjoy a piece of work which uses the terms of common discourse and which puts before him, at no remove from his everyday mind, a spectacle to be attended simply by reading.

As for the maker of such works, he remains hospitable to every bringer of usable information, regardless of kind, for he is still able to say, in the impetuous words of the eighteenth-century American, William Douglass: "As an Historian, everything is my province."

---

[20]It is worth noting that most of the great historians continue in print: Gibbon, Hume, Macaulay, Motley, Parkman, Prescott, Mommsen, Henry Adams, Lecky, Michelet, Burckhardt, Machiavelli, Croce, Carlyle, Herder, Guizot. Others are to be had in abridgments—Robertson, Treitschke, and others—edited by well-known scholars. And of course the ancient ones in full: Herodotus, Thucydides, Tacitus, Livy, Sallust, and the rest.

PART III

Writing

11

Organizing: Paragraph, Chapter, and Part

The Function of Form and of Forms

Everything that we have said in this book about historical reporting has urged or implied the importance of Form. In discussing "literary" history on p. 258, we were discussing an aspect of Form. Without Form in every sense, the facts of the past, like the jumbled visions of a sleeper in a dream, elude us. The attentive researcher soon discovers that facts and ideas in disorder cannot be conveyed to another's mind without loss and are hardly likely to carry meaning very long even for the possessor. This is because the mind is so constituted that it demands some degree of regularity and symmetry. A shop window in which the objects for sale had been thrown helter-skelter would not only give no pleasure to the passer-by, but would make it hard for him to notice anything in particular.

In one sense, of course, any grouping has form of some kind, but when we speak of Form with approval we mean attractive and suitable form. In works of the mind we notice the presence or absence of these qualities, whether or not we analyze their character and effect. In writing, the role of Form is continuous, for in the act of *im*pressing something on the mind, Form also *ex*presses. For example, in the

271

sentence you have just read, the formal contrast of the ideas "impress" and "express" is driven in, as well as brought out, by the echoing similarity of the two words and by the further device of italicizing their first syllables. The same thing could be said without the same effect: but would it be the same thing? True, when one discusses what a piece of writing is trying to say one often distinguishes its "contents" from its "form," but this separation is unreal; it is a feat of abstraction. Actually, we know the contents only through the form, though we may guess at what the contents would have been had the form been more clear-cut. It is the duty of the researcher to make sure that the contents he is in fact delivering are precisely those he intended. Form and intention should fit like skin on flesh.

In written matter, the most frequent and visible failure of form is that which comes from wrong emphasis. Why take pains to distribute emphasis in the right places? Because the mind cannot give equal attention to every part; it must be guided to those parts—of a sentence or a book—that it should attend to for a correct understanding. On the printed page, a "little form" such as italics is a signpost directing the mind to look this way or that. A footnote is likewise a form, whose makeup and uses we shall describe farther on. The larger forms we are about to discuss have less definable ways of producing emphasis than italics or footnotes, but length, beginnings, interruptions, and internal arrangements are also pointers.

We shall also be concerned about right emphasis when we look at the form of sentences, in Chapter 13. Right now, the principle will be exemplified through the larger forms of the *part, chapter,* and *paragraph*, which are the main masses that impress the reader while expressing the truth. All direct the mind, and so does the shape of any passage taken at random, even though its form goes by no special name. If the form fits, it aids understanding, and hence is an aid to memory. Consider the difficulty of following and retaining the congeries of disjointed ideas in this extract from what is a most scholarly and valuable work.

The most important document for seventeenth-century balladry is the Percy MS. Of this, and of the editing which its contents appear to have undergone, something has already been said. It contains no less than forty-six ballads, often unfortunately left in fragments by Humphrey Pitt's housemaids, and of these no less than nineteen are not found elsewhere. Several types are represented. There is a second text of *Adam Bell*. There are eight ballads of Robin Hood, but of these only one is unique, the tale of *Guy of Gisborne*, which has already been traced as existing in some form as far back as 1475. That of *Friar Tuck* may also be of early origin. There are six ballads including four unique ones, the themes of which are taken from medieval romance. There are fourteen, five of them unique, which can only be described as imaginative. But a main interest of the collector appears to have been in historical ballads, of which there are no less than seventeen, eight unique ones and nine others. Perhaps some of these would be better described as pseudo-historical, or at the most quasi-historical. Of *Sir Aldingar* enough has perhaps been said. The personages of *Hugh Spencer* and *Sir John Butler* existed, but the incidents described in the ballads lack verification. Of the strictly historical ballads *Durham Field, Chevy Chase, Musselburgh Field*, and *Sir Andrew Barton* describe battles on land and sea between English and Scottish, and are written from an English standpoint. *The Rose of England*, which celebrates the coming of Henry VII and the battle of Bosworth, is on a purely English theme. So is *Thomas Cromwell*. And although the themes of *Earl Bothwell* and *King James and Brown* are Scottish, the tone is still English. The Scots are 'false' and 'cruel', and 'false Scotland' is contrasted with 'merry England'. The subject of *Captain Car*, on the other hand, is an internal Aberdeenshire feud, with which England was not concerned. Three other historical ballads, *The Rising in the North, Northumberland Betrayed by Douglas*, and *The Earl of Westmoreland*, are of special interest. They deal with the fortunes of Thomas Percy, Earl of Northumberland, and Charles Neville, Earl of Westmoreland, who led a Catholic rebellion against Queen Elizabeth in 1569 and on its failure took refuge in Scotland. Here the sympathies of the ballad-writer are wholly with the rebels. The hero of a fourth ballad, *Jock o' the Side*, took part in the adventures of the fugitive earls, but the ballad itself only deals with a Border raid. The tune of it was known in England as early as 1592. I think the inference must be that the historical interest of the compiler of the Percy MS. lay in England rather than in Scotland, but in England of the northern Border, rather than in southern England. And in so far as earlier versions of his ballads can be traced, these come from English sources.[1]

The trouble with this passage, plainly, is that the facts have not been organized. The separate bits of information are all there, but the full meaning is not, because grouping, subordination, and logical

---

[1] Edmund K. Chambers, *English Literature at the Close of the Middle Ages*, Oxford, 1945, 162–163.

links are missing. Ordinarily, the reader has not the time, and most often has not the knowledge, to put everything in its place and restore the intended meaning for himself. The passage just quoted has a form, but it is a bad form; what the learned author has served up is his notes raw. If the word "form" by itself has become a term of praise, it is partly because the world recognizes what labor goes into achieving it. It takes effort to put everything where it belongs, to make one thing follow upon another, to leave nothing essential out. Form is always the result of a struggle.

A book reviewer's complaint adds to this maxim another piece of useful advice: "Within the various chapters, he tends to leave out those vital little phrases and sentences that relate the parts to the whole, that remind us what his point is, where he's going and where he's been.[2] And since it is inspiring to see a workman at grips with his material, the student should read in the letters and diaries of Macaulay what an amount of thinking and worrying, of doing and undoing, went into composing the *History of England*.[3] When the first part was out Macaulay reread his work and then the eighth book of Thucydides,

which, I am sorry to say, I found much better than mine. . . . On the whole he is the first of historians. What is good in him is better than anything that can be found elsewhere. But his dry parts are dreadfully dry; and his arrangement is bad. Mere chronological order is not the order for a complicated narrative.[4]

A year later, still fretting about arrangement, Macaulay notes:

To make the narrative flow along as it ought, every part naturally springing from that which precedes; to carry the reader backward and forward across St. George's Channel without distracting his attention, is not easy. Yet it may be done. I believe that this art of transitions is as important, or nearly so, to history, as the art of narration.[5]

---

[2]*New York Times*, February 25, 1980.

[3]In any edition of G. O. Trevelyan's *Life and Letters of Macaulay* the principal passages will be found under these dates: December 18, 1838; November 5, 1841, through July 1843; December 19, 1845; and July 17, 1848 ff.

[4]Trevelyan, *op. cit.*, Diary, November 29–December 4, 1848.

[5]*Ibid.*, April 15, 1850.

Nearly four years after this, when one might have assumed that long practice had brought facility, Macaulay is still fighting against the same odds as any other writer:

> Chapter XIV will require a good deal of work. I toiled on it some hours, and now and then felt dispirited. But we must be resolute and work doggedly, as Johnson said. . . . Arrangement and transition are arts which I value much, but which I do not flatter myself that I have attained.[6]

And to conclude, a month later: "I worked hard at altering the arrangement of the first three chapters of the third volume. What labour it is to make a tolerable book, and how little readers know how much trouble the ordering of the parts has cost the writer!"[7]

"The ordering of the parts"—that is the first problem, once the writer has acquired a body of material and is designing the finished work. Chronology, Macaulay tells us, is not the answer; its order will only produce chronicles, which are notoriously unreadable.

Now there is only one other kind of order, the *topical*. This is the order dictated by subject instead of time. And subjects, as we saw in Chapter 2, are characterized by unity. They are intelligible units suitable for description. Why hesitate, then? The reporter of historical events who wants to be read will adopt the topical order. Yes, but not without modification. The pure topical order, exhausting one topic and jumping to the next, will deprive a story of all coherence. A history is a recital of events that took place in Time, and this must never be forgotten. You will kill interest as surely by leaving out the time sequence as by breaking up the natural clusters of ideas. Nothing replaces the strong effect of beholding one mass of facts *after* another, as we can verify by recalling those movies of which we happened to see the second half first.

The two fundamental forms of organization may be contrasted by imagining a biography built on the one and then on the other plan:

CHRONOLOGICAL ORDER

X is born, goes to school, breaks his leg, learns to smoke, is expelled from college, studies law, meets Jane Smith, finds a five-dollar bill, is called a liar,

---

[6]*Ibid.*, Diary, January 1, 1854.
[7]*Ibid.*, February 6, 1854.

gets into towering rage, marries Susan Black, is elected mayor, goes fishing, is thought a radical, plays the stock market, suffers from asthma, sues opponent for slander, reads in bed, loses senatorial race, employs body-guard, is accused of treason, goes to Mayo Clinic, dies. Will probated, widow remarries, memoirs published.

The fault of a strict chronological order is that it mixes events great and small without due subordination, and that it combines incidents that occur only once with permanent truths about habits and tastes, character and belief: it is a parody of life. The mind asks for something better than this jumble and says: "One thing at a time," meaning that it wants one subject, one idea gone into thoroughly, even if the parts of it were separated by many years. Yet the purely topical treatment will not do either:

TOPICAL ORDER
1. Character: in boyhood, youth, maturity, old age
2. Hobbies: in boyhood, youth, maturity, old age
3. Health: in boyhood, youth, maturity, old age
4. Income: in boyhood, youth, maturity, old age
5. Friends: in boyhood, youth, maturity, old age

Such a run up and down a man's lifespan would be tedious in the extreme, and while entailing an enormous amount of repetition, would not leave a clear portrait. The only way therefore is *to combine, in all but the briefest narratives, the topical and the chronological arrangements.* "Combining" defines the task and suggests its difficulty.

The Steps in Organizing

In the combined form, the chronology moves forward while embracing each topic and giving an occasional backward or forward glance as needed. Each small section of the work deals with a topic or one of its natural subdivisions at some length, and *completely as far as that subject goes.*

The full bearing of this last sentence is important to grasp. Suppose, to continue our biographical example, that X's character is referred to in twenty places but is extensively discussed in three, these places corresponding to youth, maturity, and old age. In each place, enough must be said to engage the reader's interest and to settle whatever questions X's character raises. Nothing is more annoying than to find a few facts in one spot, a judgment in another, then more details about the earlier events because a fresh incident brings them up, and elsewhere again a dispute with another writer about the previous judgment. Such scattering leaves a confused and often a contradictory impression, coupled with the surmise that the writer himself has not cleared his own mind and said his say.

A biographer who was also a poet, the late L.A.G. Strong, has given a vivid analogy for what has just been discussed. He described a famous vaudeville entertainer named the Great Wieland, whose act

consisted in spinning plates on a long trestle table. Starting with three or four, he would soon have a dozen spinning, and be obliged to run from one end of the table to the other, in order to give a reviving twist of the fingers to one that was on the point of collapse. . . . The number of plates grew and grew, and the audience would cry out with excitement. . . . I saw him several times, and he never let a single plate wobble to a stop.

Everyone who attempts to write an account of a complex period or undertaking sooner or later finds himself in the Great Wieland's position, though not always equipped with the same skill. The story has so many aspects, all of which have to be kept alive in the reader's mind. Concentrate on one and the others will fall. Keep to a strict chronological sequence, and you will fail to trace the growth of individual elements. Attend to the elements, and you will have to dodge about in time, running like Wieland from one century back into the one before to keep an interest alive.[8]

Quite evidently the combination of Topic and Time calls for the art of Transition. The forms of transition—words, sentences, paragraphs, sections—take the reader by the elbow, so to speak, and make him face in the right direction for the next topic. Transitions, in short, are devices of emphasis. They belong to Form and to forms, whether they are small words like "hence," "but," "accordingly," "nevertheless," or long passages that sum up and forecast, in one pivoting movement of thought.

Macaulay's problem—every writer's problem—can now be seen in its fullness: to be effective a mass of words must have Form. That form must satisfy the conflicting demands of Unity (one thing at a

[8] *The Rolling Road*, London, 1956, 82.

time) and Chronology (a series of things one after the other), while also holding the reader's interest through Coherence (smooth passing from one thing to another). Any good arrangement will meet these demands. To find the right arrangement there is no magic formula. The necessity to do so recurs with every piece of writing; it can only be solved by hard and intelligent work upon the given sets of facts.

Let us therefore put ourselves back to that earlier stage where the researcher confronts the mass of notes he has taken. Its form, we hope, is not that of complete but of modified chaos. Thanks to system, the cards or slips or notebook entries are indexed so as to produce (we will suppose) six broad categories. To vary the example, we shall drop biography and imagine a piece of business history:

1. The founding of the company
2. First success and next twenty years
3. The big lawsuit
4. Reorganization
5. Takeover and expansion
6. Research and charitable enterprises
7. Prospects

Now for a simple test: are these matters equal in importance? If so, in the finished book their treatment should be of approximately equal length. How long would the longest of these parts be, at a guess? The stack of classified notes will give us some idea. Supposing numbers 4 and 5 run to about fifty pages each, we see at once that the two largest of our six divisions must be thought of as parts and not chapters. A fifty-page chapter, though not impossible, is ordinarily too long. But our concern is now with chapters; we want to settle on some headings to cover subdivisions of equal and moderate length— say twenty to twenty-five double-spaced typewritten pages—6,000 to 7,500 words. Hence numbers 4 and 5, which are parts, amount to four or five chapters.

A chapter is not a set form like the fourteen-line sonnet, but it has some of the properties of a set form: it has unity and completeness, and for convenience it may be assumed to have the length just stated. The function of a chapter is to dispose of one good-sized topic comfortably and give the reader as much as can be taken in at one sitting. Hence it is also the right length for an essay. Moreover, if this approximate wordage is adopted for one chapter, it will generally be possible to make the others roughly equal. Chapters of fifteen or of forty pages would probably be harder to keep even; one could not count on their being all as short or as long. Of course, one can—sometimes must—vary the length from chapter to chapter, but there is a marked advantage to having similar units to juggle with in the search for the right arrangement: the longer the chapters, the fewer the breaking-off points in the work, and hence the fewer rearrangements that are possible. If the chapters are too brief, too many breaks occur and coherence gives way to choppiness.

With the goal of equal and rounded-off units in mind, the researcher turns back to his notes and finds, on matching them with his six divisions, that whereas numbers 1 and 2 ("The founding of the company" and "First success and next twenty years") each propose a single topic falling neatly into a pair of chapters, the next two ("The big lawsuit" and "Reorganization") are badly entangled. The company's reorganization was proposed before the lawsuit, and this in fact brought on the case. Besides, the reorganization was the start of the next set of events ("Takeover and Expansion"). In short, the middle of the projected work is one big snarl.

The only solution is for the researcher to start with one distinct subject that could be separated from the rest and see what this leaves. If it destroys all possibility of making a realignment that will fit chronology and topical unity, he has probably taken out too large a piece as his first morsel. He must try again—in his mind, of course—or with just a piece of scratch paper to jot down each successive chunk of material, until the pieces form "natural" clusters; he discovers these whenever things hang together more than they hang with neighboring matters. Going over one's notes slowly and watching for clues will help, but remember there is no substitute for imagination—"How would it be if—?" To make the trial and error progress, one makes successive tables of contents, that is, chapter headings that will have the same weight—not minding the wording—and recasting them till the series sounds convincing. One may wind up with something like this:

1. Founding the company
2. Success and the first twenty years

3. Cracking at the seams
4. The big lawsuit
5. Reorganization: New management and new projects
6. The year of the takeover
7. The conglomerate empire
8. Research and charitable enterprises
9. Present doldrums and hopes for the future

With nine units, the writer's previous estimate of 230 to 250 pages divides into chapters of about 25, as desired.

Now take a look at the foreseeable character of each chapter from the point of view of narrative: 1 and 2 have forward motion from the inevitable "background" through the early struggles to the end of twenty years full of persons and incidents. Then comes a more static chapter, "Cracking at the seams," which is largely descriptive and which resolves itself into a new drama, "The big lawsuit."

After this there is description again, to make clear the reorganization; then the account moves ahead once again through the scrimmage of the takeover and the details of the subsidiaries added one by one to make up the conglomerate. Next comes a picture of the firm at its high point; then perhaps a backtracking to the very beginning: old Mr. Bingham had always wanted to add a research unit but not until . . . , etc. The same for the outlays to education and the like. The story of these two side-enterprises keeps the reader moving back and forth from beginning to end and affords an unconscious review of the ground he has covered since page 1. To leave him there would be inconclusive. Hence a short chapter to tie all the loose ends together and close on the idea of prospects and forward motion. To test the scheme, the writer must make sure that the several chapters add up to the story as a whole, with nothing left out and no overlapping of subjects, though with as many cross references as are necessary for internal clarity.

Composing: By Instinct or by Outline?

Having reached this point you are not at the end of your troubles, but you have something like a structure. It remains to allot your notes to each chapter, after which you begin with one chapter and try to construct *it*. The same considerations of chronology, topical unity, coherence, and transition apply throughout: the part, the chapter, and the paragraph should have comparable Form. But there is this difference: as you get nearer to the paragraph, you cannot (and should not try to) forecast your structure completely. A series of paragraphs each built to one pattern like the pieces of a prefabricated house would be intolerable. Nor should a chapter be assembled according to a blueprint. These cautions raise the question of outlines.

Writers divide fairly evenly into those who find outlines useful or indispensable, and those to whom they are a nuisance. By all means use them if they do not cost you too much in time and spontaneity. But do not force yourself if making them up does not come easily, or if once drawn up the outline drags you back. Certainly the best order for the parts of a paper is the order that comes out of one's sense of the subject and seems dictated by it. To a writer who develops that sense from the mere growth of the data under his hand, the outline is bound to seem stiff and suspiciously logical. When the time comes to fill it out, the material runs away and the outline loses control over the writer's thoughts. Conscience then inspires vain efforts to patch up the outline while groping for new transitions where the writing got off the prearranged track.

For such a writer the better procedure is to use the outline not as a guide beforehand but as a verifier afterward. We may picture the sequence of events something like this: you have set aside all but one batch of organized notes. A run through them (yes, once again) suggests that they fall quite evidently into three subgroups—perhaps four or five, but three is normal because every subject and subsubject has a beginning (exposition), a middle (complication), and an end (resolution or conclusion). At any rate you now have a small number of smaller piles of notes.[9] You take the first pile in order, shuffle its contents until a rough sequence is established not so much in the cards as in your mind. You put them to one side and start writing. Some people need to look at their notes while composing;

---

[9]If the notes are not on cards or detached slips, the sorting is done by a further, more exact marginal indexing. This suits people who prefer not to handle or look at their notes while writing, but who arrange them mentally and simply refresh their memory now and again by consulting the notebook.

FIGURE 15A   *One Way to Use Cards for Notes*

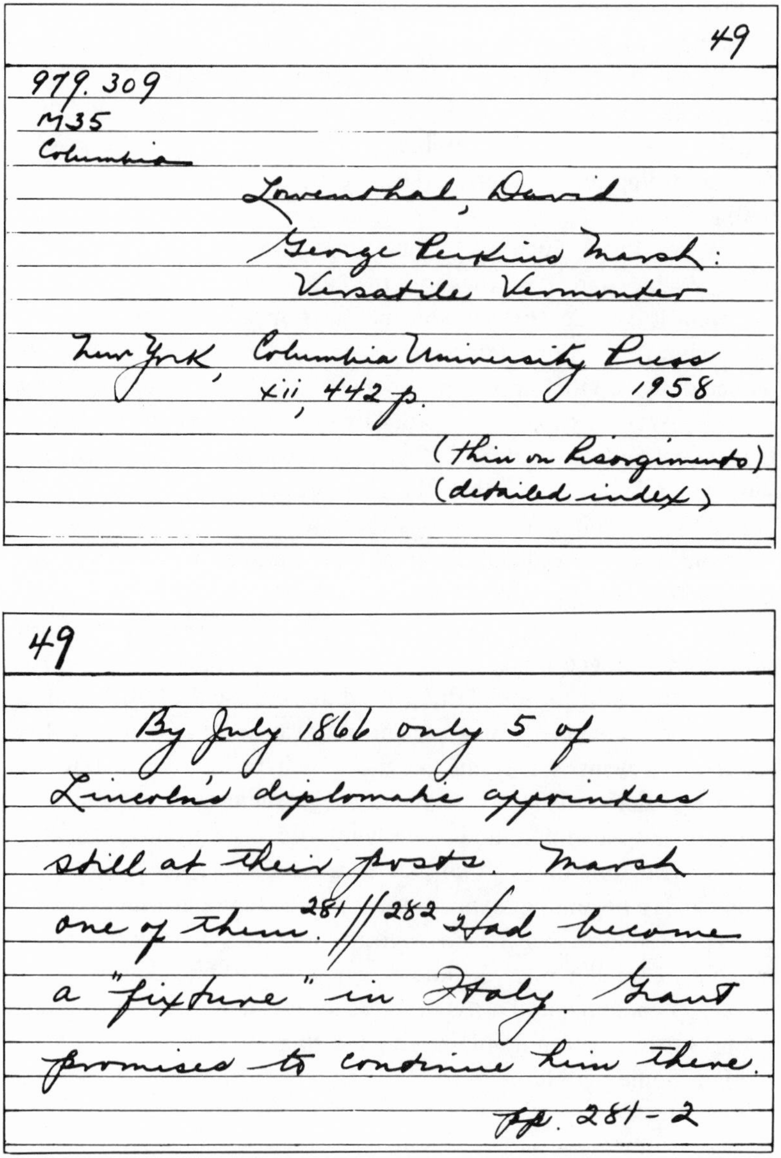

49

979.309
M35
Columbia

Lowenthal, David

George Perkins Marsh:
Versatile Vermonter

New York, Columbia University Press
xii, 442 p.   1958

(thin on Risorgimento)
(detailed index)

49

By July 1866 only 5 of
Lincoln's diplomatic appointees
still at their posts. Marsh
one of them. 281 // 282 Had become
a "fixture" in Italy. Grant
promised to continue him there.

pp. 281-2

FIGURE   15B   *Incorporating the Note into the Outline*

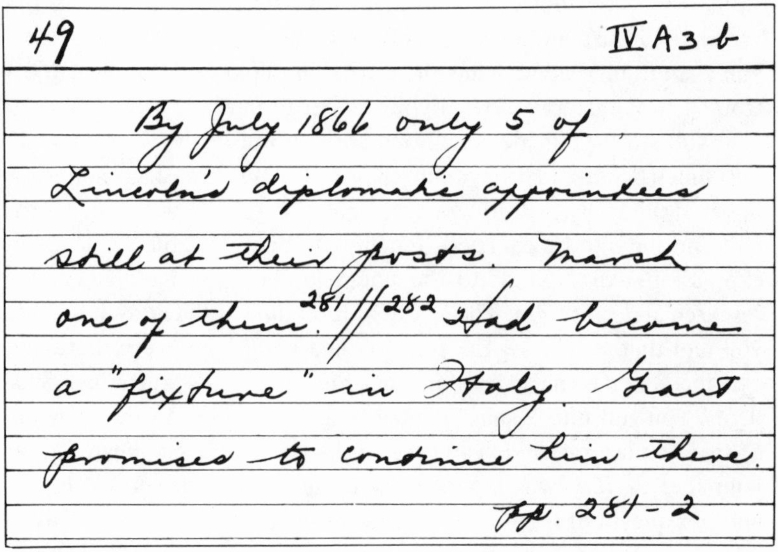

The researcher who uses an outline has assigned numbers and letters in the usual way to each head and subhead of the outline. When ready to write any one portion of his work, he goes through the cards, sorting and marking them with the letters and numbers that show where they belong. In this case, the note has been assigned to section IV A3b of the outline and has been so marked in the upper right-hand corner.

The systematic researcher uses two cards, one for the book and one for the note or extract. The book card contains the full bibliographical citation as well as the call number and the library where the book was found, plus any time-saving comments as to its features and value. The researcher gives each book card a serial number which saves the trouble of repeating the full citation on each note card. The book cards are kept in numerical order until rearranged for making up the bibliography.

The note card contains information suitably abstracted (see Chapter 2, pp. 28f.), and is keyed to the book card by the number in the upper left-hand corner. The page number or numbers from which the note was made are written in any convenient spot.

others prefer to gaze on the subject with the inner eye of memory and imagination. In either case the mind must take part in the work. Composing does not consist in merely blowing up each note to full grammatical size and tacking it on to the next; it consists—at least if you want to be read with any pleasure—in thinking about the subject from *A* to *Z* just as you want your reader to think.

You start; your ideas pull one another out of the wordless dark into the articulate light—you are writing ahead. Your facts and ideas dovetail naturally, with only occasional effort, even when the words halt and have to be changed. Incomplete or rough, the sequence of expressions corresponds to the understanding you have gained by research and reflection. The frequent rereading of the notes has made you feel that you know the story by heart, that you were there and can recount it. The *story* flows despite your pen's stuttering. Suddenly, you run into a snag. It may be of two kinds. In the first, the course you are on obviously leads to the spot you see ahead, but at your feet there yawns a gap. How to get over? The answer lies in another question: Is it a fact that is wanting to connect the parts? If so it must be obtained—later. Or is it an idea, a transition? If so, mark the spot by some conventional sign in the margin, an *X* or a wavy line, pick up the thread wherever you can, and keep going forward.

The lack of certain facts is important to discover at this stage, and the way of composing here recommended offers the advantage that by going mentally from next to next you discover the flaws as you would if you were a reader. If you merely sew your notes together as they occur in the bundles of your first mechanical classification, you will probably conceal the gaps, and the reader will discover them as we did in reading the passage on English ballads quoted above. If what you lack is a deft transition, do not rack your brains. When you come to revise your first draft the right idea may pop into your head, or else you will quickly see what small rearrangements will bring the gaping edges together.

The lack of proper order, connection, or *composition* in the strict sense, is most glaring in the narration of physical events, where our daily experience supplies an immediate test. To remember and adapt the test to the recital of abstractions, examine this short fragment of fiction:

There was an office facing them, at the rear of the hall, and a man and woman were regarding them from a box window which opened above a ledge on which lay a register book. They were middle-aged folk: the man, a fleshy, round-faced, somewhat pompous-looking individual, who might at some time have been a butler; the woman, a tall, spare-figured, thin-featured, sharp-eyed person, who examined the newcomers with an enquiring gaze.[10]

In reading fast one may not notice the double flaw in this description. Yet it is evident, if one attempts to visualize what happens (as any reader of a report is entitled to do), that in line 2 a man and a woman are looking at the newcomers as they enter. Immediately before and after, the newcomers survey the box window, ledge, register—all quite uninteresting compared with the two picturesque characters gazing at them—making the reader shift unnecessarily from one set of observers to another. And at the end, when we are still hearing about the woman of the pair, there she is "examin[ing] the newcomers with an enquiring gaze" as she was already doing four lines above. Either the first reference to the newcomers' being gazed at is premature—if they were advancing from a certain distance—or it should be omitted from the end, since we knew it before and cannot take it as the new fact it pretends to be.

The second kind of snag in writing comes when you discover that you have steered around in a circle. The natural linking of ideas, instead of propelling you forward, has brought you back to a point earlier in your story. It is in this predicament that a scratch outline, made on the spot, can serve as straightener. Cast your eye back to your beginning, jotting down as you go the main and secondary ideas, using the same key word for each idea that belongs to one subject. It is necessary here to reduce each sentence to its simplest thought in order to classify it; otherwise you will not clear up the mess. Assigning symbols for ideas, then, you soon find where you got off the track by seeing where, let us say, ideas E, F, G, and H were followed by F again. This may have led you unconsciously to avoid a second G and H. You leaped ahead to K, but felt disquieted and, after a sentence or two, stopped to take stock.

The solution is scissors and paste. Cut out the intruding ideas but

[10]J. S. Fletcher, *The Middle Temple Murder*, New York, 1919, 36.

keep any good passage that you have written, though it is out of place (K), and set it aside. Cut back to the good original section (E F G H), see if there is anything valuable in the second reference to F, inserting it near the first if desirable; and throw away all the other false twistings and turnings. Write fresh matter to sew together any wounds created by this surgery and keep looking ahead until the place for K comes into sight. Remember that for these remedial purposes all subjects have not one but a dozen handles to grasp them by. Depending on which you seize and which you present to be seized, each in its turn, you produce logical flow or jerkiness.

Visualize a subject (S) with branches radiating from it, all of them relevant circumstances that you will have to mention. By taking

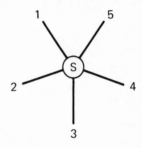

them in order you build up the unity of S. But there is along each branch a point where you get so far from the little round core that you cannot get back: the dotted line marks how far you can go without getting stranded. Always bear in mind that S, when completed, must

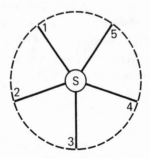

throw out a link to another topic, T. If you go beyond the end of S_5 you will never come within reach of T_1. On the other hand, a little ingenuity will tell you ahead of time that by keeping in sight the core of S and making the last of your journeys S_5 you can easily seize hold of T_1.

This obvious device will work between chapters as well as between sections of a chapter. There is always some topic that can come at the end of the chapter to relate it to the next, and there is also one that fits this arrangement by being the right beginning for the chapter following. This interlocking of ideas makes a tight book, yet it is not invariably necessary to fashion this kind of chain. Sometimes a new chapter will hark back to a much earlier topic in order to make clear the forthcoming facts, and this backward jump often provides variety in what would otherwise be a forced march at a relentless pace.

But no matter what is to be done at a given spot, it is indispensable to give the reader a clue. He will follow with docility for many paragraphs if the road is straight or gently winding. But if you want him to turn a corner you must firmly guide him: "We now turn back to those years when . . ."; or "From that day when he met his future wife"; or "Casting our minds ahead of the point we have reached"; or "Before we can understand the issue at stake, we must recall (or examine or describe)"; and so on. It is amazing what a reader will gladly absorb if he is occasionally told why, and given a hint of where the facts will take him.

There are, then, many exceptions to the rule of always going forward and they are inherent in topical treatment. We had a striking example of such an exception in the table of contents made up for the company history. In Chapter 8 of that hypothetical work the reader is to be brought back to the beginning twice. When this happens, the trip from the starting point forward should be speeded up in such a way that the necessary repetition is made to seem new. Otherwise the reader has the sinking feeling of going over the same ground needlessly.

The most frequent cause of interference with forward motion and straight chronological order occurs, oddly enough, at the very start of the book or paper. The reason for this is that a subject always has two possible beginnings: the natural one, which research has discovered, and the conventional one, which is whatever the reader is assumed to know. This pair of beginnings must somehow be reduced to one by compromise between them or postponement of the less enticing. This process may be decisive. A writer whose work calls for sustained attention through many pages wants to grip his readers from the outset—"from the word 'Go'" is here appropriate—and interest him so completely that he will be compelled to continue reading. The first chapter of any book, the first page of any essay, the first paragraph of any review are therefore supreme tests of the art of composition. Where they break into the subject, what goes into them, how they insert themselves into the reader's stream of thought and stock of knowledge, and what they promise of future interest, are so many delicate questions asking for precise answers.

Films use the flashback as one kind of answer, one that is as old as Homer's *Iliad*. In scholarship the device, when well handled, is fully justified. For instance in Lionel Trilling's *Matthew Arnold*, the logical beginning is Chapter 2, entitled "His Father and His England." But the effective beginning is the first chapter, mysteriously entitled "A," which opens with this beguiling sentence: "The secretary of old Lord Lansdowne, the liberal peer, was a singularly handsome young man, whose manners were Olympian and whose waistcoats were remarkable." After this one certainly wants to know more, which is not a feeling that arises of itself at the sight of any ordinary block of print.

Altering the normal order can also be used to accommodate distant antecedents or surrounding conditions before one opens the subject proper. Either mode poses the problem of making a smooth transition when the main topic is resumed. Thus Macaulay's *History* begins with a statement of his purpose, which is to write the story of England from the accession of James II to recent times. For this he must give "the background," and we hear about Celtic Britain, the Norman Conquest, the Papacy, and a quantity of other familiar landmarks, followed by some of the main themes of the work, presented in their earliest historical forms, the whole moving forward in seven-league boots.

Chapter 2 is chronologically more unified and static: it surveys the political and religious history of the seventeenth century and ends with the death of Charles II. Chapter 3, famous as "Macaulay's Third Chapter," is panoramic. It is a wonderful bird's-eye view of social and cultural England in 1685. We are by then on the spot and almost at the time of the true opening. Chapter 4 catches up the end left dangling in 2 by *depicting* the death of Charles II, and with the words "That morning . . ." we are finally at the starting point announced some two hundred pages back.[11]

A good beginning is good not only for the reader but also for the writer. It is like a running start, or rather, like propulsion from a rifled barrel: it keeps one going in a straight line. Yet it often happens that the perfect beginning cannot be found by mere thought. You choose what you think good and start writing, but the thought wanders, the facts do not fall in naturally. In this situation, keep on for a time until a direction becomes clear. When you have finished six or eight pages, reread, and you will generally find that somewhere on page 2 or 3 is the true place to start. What went before was akin to the dog's walking round and round to beat down the grass before settling down.

The Short Piece and the Paragraph

We have been talking about books. The reader may object that he is not ready to compose on the large scale. Can he possibly shrink all this advice to the dimensions of a short paper and—equally useful—

[11]Macaulay worried about a proper beginning for a long time. "The great difficulty of a work of this kind," he wrote ten years before its publication, "is the beginning. How is it to be joined on to the preceding events? Where am I to commence it? I cannot plunge, slap dash, into the middle of events and characters. I cannot, on the other hand, write a history of the whole reign of James the Second as a preface to the history of William the Third. If I did, a history of Charles the Second would still be necessary as a preface to that of the reign of James the Second. I sympathise with the poor man who began the war of Troy *'gemino ab ovo'* [starting with the egg from which Helen—the cause of the war—was born]. But, after much consideration, I think I can manage, by the help of an introductory chapter or two, to glide imperceptibly into the full current of my narrative" (Diary in Trevelyan, *op. cit.*, December 18, 1838).

to the dimensions of a paragraph? The answer is Yes as regards the short piece. The more practiced he becomes in the composition of papers ranging from the three-page book review to the thirty-page report, the better he will be able to handle the chapter (which is the "working part" of the book), and the finer will his eye become in tracing the plan of the book itself.

The longish report (forty to fifty pages) should be considered as a miniature book rather than an enlarged chapter. It has "chapters" and possibly "parts" of its own, though the chapters may be as short as five pages. For any of these subdivisions it is helpful to have headings, though they are not indispensable. What is essential is that the sections be separated, by numerals or by blank spaces. An unbroken stretch of many pages is hard to read, even in a novel, and very hard to compose, except for the virtuoso writer. The competent writer needs guidelines just as the reader needs breathing space.

As a sample of what such guidelines may be for writers in any of the shorter forms, here is a set of suggestions about the form of the book review. We will assume that it is written for a learned or literary periodical, where the space allotted will usually not exceed 1,500 words—say the *American Historical Review* or *The New Criterion*.

The beginning, we know, is important. The first of your twelve paragraphs should present an idea of interest to the readers who will leaf through the magazine. If your first words are "This book . . ." they will not be able to distinguish your review from twenty others, and they will be entitled to conclude that you have not expended much thought on enlisting their attention. The opening statement takes the readers from where they presumably stand in point of knowledge and brings them to the book under review. The briefest possible description of its aim, scope, and place in the world therefore follows the baited opening sentence and completes the first paragraph.

The second classifies the book: what thesis, tendency, bias does it uphold, suggest, evince? Paragraphs 3 to 5 go into the author's main contentions and discuss them. Do not repeat anything you said in the classificatory paragraph, but rather give detailed evidence of the grounds for your classification.

Paragraphs 6 and 7 may deal with additional or contrary points to be found in other authors or in your own research; but so far, these only amend or qualify what is acceptable in the new book. In 8 and 9 you deliver your chief objections and summarize shortcomings. If you have found errors, mention only the important ones—do not waste space on typographical or minor slips.

From errors you modulate into the broad field: how is our conception of it changed by the book? What further work is needed to clear up doubtful points? Where have gaps been left that must be filled? You have now used up paragraphs 10 and 11 and you have one more in which to strike a balance of merits and faults, ending with some words about the author—*not* yourself or the subject.

For with book reviewing goes a moral obligation: you hold the author's fate in your hands as far as one group of readers is concerned. Author and work should, through you, be given the floor, have the last word. What you say in the review will, rightly or wrongly, be taken seriously. You are in honor bound to be scrupulously fair. Never use the author's admissions against him, saying, "Mr. X entirely neglects the foreign implications," when it was he who warned you of this in the preface. Do not expect him to have written the book *you* have in mind, but the one *he* had. Recognize the amount of work that has gone into the product and be magnanimous: you may be severe on serious faults of interpretation and inference; but unless they are continual, forget the trifling errors in his text just as you concentrate on them in yours. Book reviewers are not infallible.

More than in the long work, essay, or article, it is in the paragraph that the writer's yearning for freedom can be indulged—up to a point. There is no formula for beginning or ending paragraphs that will not produce a dull, mechanical sound. The topic sentence, as its name indicates, comes early and announces the topic. But especially in reporting events, the topic sentence does not always live up to its promise of unifying the paragraph. It may and indeed will often be used, from habit, by good writers; but turning out such a sentence automatically, every time, is a mistake. Ask yourself, rather, what intertwined subjects the dozen lines of print will contain; what is the little core *S* and what are the branches it sends out as you employ your facts and use your ideas to make them join. In the paragraph as elsewhere this is a matter of linkage. The fault in the paragraph quoted at the beginning of this chapter is not the lack of a topic sentence: it has one; the fault is that the ensuing facts and ideas are not firmly linked but loosely associated.

Linking can be systematically practiced until it becomes habitual. In general—but only in general—the good writer makes the last thought in sentence A suggest the first thought in sentence B. At its most rigid this would give us the pattern: "Mr. Adams has written a book. The book is a history of the Jefferson and Madison administrations. Those administrations cover the years 1801–1817. Those years were notable for . . . ," and so on. Perfect coherence but grisly reading. The coherence to aim at is that of a normally constituted mind, which likes variety in continuity. If on looking over your first draft you find that your mind as reader is not satisfied with your mind as writer, change the writing and make a mental note of the sort of jumpiness that ails you in composing. No writer attains adequate coherence throughout a first draft. Everyone *must* revise, which means displace, add missing links, remove repetitions—in short, tinker. As we tinker, presumably we improve and polish.

These various operations will in time become second nature, but at first the tendency when reading over one's prose is to find it perfectly lucid and forceful, not to say sublime. This is because the mind that has framed it keeps on supplying its deficiencies from special knowledge and the memory of what was meant. You must therefore lay aside your manuscript for several days and return to it as if it were written by someone else. And since this may not provoke sufficient self-criticism, you must examine each statement for its accuracy of form as well as relevancy of contents. Verifying fact has already been dealt with. The correct use of little forms will occupy us in the last chapter of this book, it being the last virtue required of our work before it is sent on its journey to printer and public.

12

Plain Words: The War on Jargon and Clichés

Keep Conscious and Weigh Your Words

To the general public "revise" is a noble word and "tinker" is a trivial one, but to the writer the difference between them is only the difference between the details of the hard work and the effect it achieves. The successful revision of a book in manuscript is made up of an appalling number of small, local alterations. Rewriting is nothing but able tinkering. Consequently it is impossible to convey to a nonwriter an abstract idea of where the alterations should come or how to make them. Only an apprenticeship under a vigilant critic will gradually teach a would-be writer how to find and correct all the blunders and obscurities that bespangle every first draft.

The image of tailoring that the word "alterations" suggests is an apt one to bear in mind. A first draft is clumsy, heavy, stiff—you must shorten something here, lengthen it there, move a button or a link forward or back, smooth out a wrinkle, make the garment fit. Only, in writing, the words are not solely the garment of the thought, they are its body as well; so that the pulling and adjusting of words has to go on until the thought you hoped to present and the thought on paper coincide and displace the wrong thought or no-thought that accidentally got written down. This operation suggests what we can do to start our custom-tailoring: we must learn to see what does not fit. The rest depends on the apprentice's alertness and ingenuity.

Whoever wants to write and be read must develop a new habit of attending to words—not just to important words and on occasions of formal writng, but to all words at all times. A student of painting does not think it outside his duty to attend at all times to shape and color, or a musician to sounds and rhythms. The writer must have for words the eye of a jewel expert, who knows the worth of his gems at a glance. The writer must recognize words and be able to juggle their multiple meanings with ease. When words form sentences, he must be as alive as a lover or a diplomat to the shades they convey. Psychologists who have tried to ascertain the mental traits of competent writers have concluded from their studies that the effective writer is one who is alive to the overtones of the words he uses—that is, who is conscious of his audience and of the aim of the particular communication.

Any good writer could have told the experimenters as much. What their statement does is to define good writing and find its cause in the definition. But their conclusion is worth dwelling on because it restates with all the authority of "experiment" two fundamental points: the writer is *aware*, and whatever he writes has *a peculiar purpose*. It is out of these two necessities that the doctrine grew up of the *mot juste*, or "inevitable word" for a given spot. There is nothing frivolous or flossy about the demand for proper words in proper places; the only trouble with it is that the inevitable in this regard is something most of us are able to avoid with the greatest of ease. Take an example:

"Although this book differs from Harrisse's on Columbus, it is also important."

At least three words in this sentence are improper and darken understanding: "although," "differs," and "also." Taken together, "although" and "also" imply that a book which "differs" from a certain other book is unimportant. And "differs" by itself is an absurdity, since every work differs from every other. The writer may have meant something like this: "Although this book does not follow Harrisse's views on disputed points, it is not negligible," or "its interpretation is valuable." But more likely still, he had no such formulated idea. All he wanted to say was "Here is a book; it opposes Harrisse's views on Columbus; I think it important."

double negation

It is of course neither unusual nor criminal to write a first draft full of non-sense such as we have just quoted, or to begin with jerky, simpleminded remarks such as those that we substituted for the non-sense. The important thing is that in the second draft the writer—*you*—should have moved away from both these faults and produced a tenable statement. You discover what you really think by hacking away at your first spontaneous utterance. How to give your idea its definitive form is the subject of the next chapter. In this one we are concerned with the first step, which is to find out whether your original utterance is *un*tenable. This discovery comes from a close, unremitting scrutiny of words.

The State of the Language Today

The carrier of meaning, language, has latterly deteriorated at such a pace that public opinion has begun to take repeated note of the fact and some critics have gone so far as to speak of "degeneration." More than ever, the researcher who wants to report faithfully and to be understood accurately must attend to vocabulary and grammar. The pitfalls and temptations in his path multiply, for two very different reasons. One is the increasing deformation of accepted meanings; the other is the insidious influence on the mind of what we hear and read. The use of words is a social act so closely tied to communal feelings and purposes that vocables take on the coloring of the environment as they leap to our minds and come out of our lips. That is how a blunder or a smart innovation spreads and destroys. Thus *gender* has ousted *sex* with lightning speed and left *both* words indefinite, while robbing the language of a needed grammatical term.

The writing researcher will keep his mind clear and make his task easier if he will classify the types of trouble to which the modern vernacular perpetually invites. With these types at the forefront of his

FIGURE 16   *Danger: Watch Your Step*

---

1. *Jargon*: operant conditioning / macrodimensional / truismatic / access controller (for doorman) / unauthorized premature partial disclosure (for leak) / deconglomeratize / exercise facility (for gym) / investigative reporter (for reporter) / major thrust (for main point) / decision-making (for deciding) / general resource center (for library).

2. *Vogue Words*: parameter / paradigm / avid / sensitive / volatile / abrasive / profile / gap (credibility, gender, etc.) / empathy / breakthrough / creative / metaphor / strategy / ironically / hopefully / mundane.

3. *Neologisms*: acerb(ic) / acid(ic) / gift (as verb) / wellness / parenting / mentoring / fruitworthy / all words compounded with -thon, -tron, -matic, -mation and other scraps of pseudo Greek or Latin, e.g., "audioanimatronic Mickey Mouse" (at Disneyland).

4. *Misused or Misplaced Technicalities*: quantum (jump, leap) / catalyst / icecap / -itis (for addiction or obsession) / and all needless verbs in -ize (prioritize, finalize, folderize, laymanize).

5. *Failure to Make Distinctions*: fiscal and financial / assure and ensure / euphuism and euphemism / flout and flaunt / perspicacious and perspicuous / comity and community / sensuous and sensual / comprise and compose / revisit and review (or revise) / podium and lectern.

6. *Malaprops*: cohort (for companion) / peer (for fellow-) / meld (for combine) / torturous (for tortuous) / testament (for testimony or evidence) / critical (for ill) / personal (for private) / gender (for sex) / embattled (for besieged or beset) / legendary (for famous or excellent).

7. *Twisted Idioms*: hard put (lacking *to it*) / suffice to say (lacking *it*) / by the boards (omit *s*) / one on one (for one to one, in conferring, etc.) / and nor, but nor (omit and, but) / as of now, as of yet (omit *as of*) / have no bones (make no bones) / by a hare's breath (hair's breadth).

8. *Wrong Prepositions*: a writer with distinction (of) / acquiesce to (in) / worthy for (of) / identical to (with) / compliance in (with) / link to (with) / this dates to (dates *back* to; or is dated, without *to*). In addition: hundreds of other usages that can only be learned by reading good prose.

9. *Misdirected Verbs*: this door is alarmed / the company must divest (lacks *itself of*) / boggle the mind (the mind boggles, i.e.,

halts, resists) / it rankled him (omit *him*); this translates to ten dollars (is equivalent; or the translation is) / she was convinced to buy (persuaded to buy).

10. *Faulty Constructions*: based on fresh information, they . . . (basing themselves) / if I knew, I wouldn't have (if I had known) / it is not true, as the report says (ambiguous: does report say it is true or not true?) / with better luck they may have survived (might) / I didn't see him yet (haven't) / the officer insisted that she remained (remain) / it's got to be a risk (must be) / and all German-style constructions, e.g., "to-the-floor-draped stools."

---

thought he can recognize and weed out of his prose the particular specimens. The main types are (1) Jargon, (2) Vogue words, (3) Neologisms, (4) Misused or misplaced technicalities, (5) Failure to make distinctions, (6) Malaprops, (7) Twisted idioms, (8) Wrong prepositions, (9) Misdirected verbs, (10) Faulty constructions.

Each of these is briefly illustrated in Figure 16. In addition, the clear and considerate writer abstains from making up his own abbreviations and uses acronyms and initialese as little as possible. Puzzling the reader even for a second is discourtesy and contrary to the very purpose of writing.

In view of these dangers and difficulties, the dictionary becomes the chief reference work on the researcher's shelf—or rather on his desk—to be used *more often* than is necessary, so as to make sure that the words he knows "perfectly well" are not in fact words that he knows *im*perfectly.[1] The chances are good, for example, that four out of five readers of this book did not appreciate, before reading p. 112 n. the distinction between *genuine* and *authentic*. And in some contexts at least, they probably use with false or blurred meanings such words as *connive, drastic, cohort, disinterested, deprecate, mini-*

---

[1] For writers, regardless of specialization, the desk dictionaries that the authors of this book recommend are the *American Heritage Dictionary of the English Language*, rev. ed.; and *Webster's New World Dictionary*, college ed. The latter is not to be confused in size or linguistic philosophy with the large *Webster's Third International*, which proffers a questionable view of language and usage. For a good critique (among many others), see Robert P. Hudson, "Medical Writing and *Webster's Third*," *Annals of Internal Medicine*, 71 (August 1969), 435–438.

mize, supposititious, perspective, evince, and *decimate.* They probably neglect the useful difference between such pairs as *specific* and *particular, nomenclature* and *terminology, growth* and *development, component* and *constituent, mixture* and *compound, autonomy* and *independence, constant* and *continual*—in short, they find synonyms on every hand, whereas a glorious tradition has it that English can show but a single pair of exact synonyms, namely, "gorse" and "furze." Let this pleasant thought move you to reach for the dictionary again and again and learn there something to your advantage, which eventually means your reader's.

Be Strict about Signposts

Unfortunately, some of the most important words you cannot, in a sense, look up. The small guiding and linking words that recur on every page are plain without definition. But do you sufficiently query their use in your prose? An "although," an "also," a "but," a "because" can overthrow your meaning while your attention flags. It might be supposed that anyone who writes English at all would know how to use "a" and "the" and avoid confusing them. But the analysis of ordinary words is so out of favor that the misuse of the definite and indefinite articles is continual. In a recent book appeared the sentence: "She then married the relative of the theatre manager." One might make a guessing game out of such statements: "How many relatives did the theatre manager have?" Again, in 1984 one read reports of "an ailing Mr. Andropov." How many heads of state with that name did the Soviet Union have? Surely it was *the* ailing Mr. Andropov, who shortly died and was replaced. A moment's thought shows that nobody would write: "an ailing Mr. Andropov was so weak he could take no nourishment."

Other lazy writers misuse "but," making it serve as an elegant variation of "and," or as a universal joint with no distinct meaning: "The company overextended its operations in hopes of stimulating its liquid position, but the disastrous end product was not hard to foresee." Why "but"? "But" marks an opposition, and in this sequence of ideas there is none. The word serves here merely to connect the last idea with each of the two dissimilar ones that precede. The first idea, which ends with "operations," requires "and" to tie it to the third, since there is no opposition between overextension and bad consequences; there *is* opposition between the high hopes and the bad results that followed—and hence the misleading "but." The sentence wobbles at the joints and must be recast, the signal for alteration being given by the loose coupling.

The same, or worse, must be said of the myriad "howevers" that dot the printed page, usually at the head of the sentence. With some writers this mannerism says no more than that they are taking breath: ". . . escalation of the war. . . . Aahh—however, . . . much criticism was expressed at the time. . . . Aahh—however, . . . the enemy was winning. Aahh—however, . . ." The overuse of "however" is so flagrant that it deserves a place next to the tiresome "in terms of" about which something will be said in a moment. The hostile scrutiny recommended for *a, the, and, but, however* is to be applied to all other linking and organizing words. They are signals that guide the thought along its proper path and they must be kept accurate and strict. On this ground the doublings—*and/or, as to whether, if and when, unless and until*—are disallowed. They are needless, which is enough to condemn them, and they also betray the writer's ignorance or indecision. If you understand the meaning of *or*, you never want to write *and/or*; if you know how to use *whether*, you spare your readers the clumsiness of *as to whether*; if you grasp the force of *if*, you perceive that it includes *when*.

Picture All Images

When we pass from link words to nouns and verbs, the need is for concreteness and lucidity. You test your words by asking: Can this be touched or seen? If you write long strings of abstract nouns and use "have" or "are" and the passive voice instead of strong active verbs, your thought will be as hard to make out as an old faded photograph. Try reading this at a normal speed and then ask yourself what it says:

> Whatever may be the considerations that have caused the President to delay giving to the people a clearer concept than they possess of the enemy's

atomic threat and our ability to deal with it, surely an overriding reason why he should do this soon has now been supplied. That is the spate of conflicting and bewildering statements about the situation that recently have come from members of his own Administration and of Congress who may be presumed to have varying measures of inside information.

Not only are these sentences long and lacking in euphony, but they lack concrete nouns and active verbs. The result is a general haze.

The tendency of a culture like ours, which is tinged with technology, is to seek out or invent the word that will sound most general, so as to "cover" with sciencelike authority all possible instances. That is how "contact" became a verb, how "mass media" replaced "popular press and broadcasting," how "communication(s)" turned into an academic subject. Excuses have been found for this substituting of tentlike notions for the names of particular things, but scientific portentousness is an evil just the same. Notice how "goals" have vanished under the tyranny of "objectives," how "use" is yielding to "utilization," how "visit" has come to seem poor and inadequate when we have the lovely "visitation" to play with. All unnecessary abstraction sounds affected in print.

Some writers, who justly fear overabstraction, try to avoid it by figurative language and the use of bright, "efficient" words that happen to be in vogue. In one of the sentences quoted above, there occurred the phrase "stimulate its liquid position," and this was followed by the sentence: "The disastrous end product was not hard to foresee." These expressions are muddled and obscure through careless imagery and dull jargon. The two often go together and their appearance in prose is always a symptom of verbal dry rot.

To the alert mind, all words convey an image—the representation more or less vivid of an act or a situation. When we say "Do you grasp my meaning?" the listener half pictures a hand seizing something. When the answer is "No, I don't get you," the image is less vivid, yet it is clearly in the same plane: both remarks depict the taking hold of an object. In hasty speaking or writing one easily passes from image to image, saying perhaps: "It is difficult to grasp a meaning that is couched in florid language." The three images of "seizing," "lying on a bed," and "adorned as with flowers" do not develop a single coherent image, and though the result is intelligible enough it is neither sharp nor strong.

Two words badly mated are often enough to produce incoherence, which, when noticed, may destroy meaning. What, in our example, is "a liquid position"? Liquidity is a state of matter; position marks the place of a body in space: there is no coherence between them. The writer evidently combined the idea of being in a *good* position with the idea that it is good to have assets that are *liquid* (that is, fluid, taking any desired form, like water). From this came "What is his position?—oh, it's liquid." But try the double image in different words: "How does he stand?—he stands liquid."

To this analysis, which may seem like quibbling but is not, one might object that "liquid position" is by now an accepted phrase of which everyone knows the meaning. The phrase, in other words, is a piece of jargon, possibly indispensable to businessmen. We shall take up this question in a moment. It is in any case a dubious image, made still more muddled by the preceding verb "stimulate." How does one "stimulate a liquid position"? A stimulus is a push, a jab, a "shot in the arm." In fact, one suspects that the writer's first thought was "give a shot in the arm to our liquid position," but the silliness of that vision somehow broke through to his mind's eye and led him to substitute the less vivid "stimulate" for "shot in the arm." In short, like the rest of us, the author was thinking in a series of loosely connected images, and made some slight effort to trim and adjust them. Only, he did not go far enough. He was afraid of "mixed metaphor," which has become a bugbear (though the fault almost always draws attention to itself) but he did not detect incoherent imagery, which so often passes unnoticed by both writer and reader. What then is the harm? The harm is that it *conceals all or part of the meaning.*

Consider the whole passage we have been examining; it is painfully general and indefinite: what did the company *do* when they "overextended operations"? How did they think this was going to help them? What *was* the disastrous result? Let us come down to earth and suppose some facts: the company opened ten new branch stores, hoping that the money would roll in and add to their cash on hand. But half the stores failed and the firm sank deeper into debt. If this is what happened, why not say so? We then see something and pass judgment upon it. The images raised go together; they put us in the very presence of the overextension, the hope, the stimulus, the liquid position, and the "end product."

The merit of this rewording is not fanciful but practical. Given a chance to *see* all these things in clear words, a vigilant stockholder could have *fore*seen and said, "It can't be done. The installation of the new stores will eat up our profits for six months and the company needs cash in less than three. I move a vote of No Confidence in the Board of Directors." Somebody, one hopes, did ask and get answers on the concrete matters before the fatal policy was carried out. Of course, the modern indifference to verbiage being what it is, the likelihood is that some group of sleepy and trusting directors approved a hasty scheme expressed in generalities as incoherent as the one that occupies us. For images, if they are familiar enough and put together plausibly enough, will lull the half-attentive into accepting any amount of nonsense.

Analyze, as a game with serious uses, the following sentences taken at random from the inexhaustible supply in one's daily reading matter:

On the offensive side, the Air Force foresees a lethally vital future for its intercontinental strategic missiles.

But it was another [court] case that plummeted Carpenter to the pinnacle of the Wisconsin bar.

While on the money side of our business a point worth noting is the trend which continues to develop in commercial banking with respect to deposit growth.

And from student work:

The workers were pressed into back-to-back houses like sardines in a rabbit-warren.

Such were the innovative solutions which could foreground a shifting of boundaries between the problems.

The habitual maker of such visual monsters may from time to time catch himself at it and remove them. But most of the time he or she will continue to frame sentences made up of expressions like "integrate the major material," "a context that lends perspective," "a background that ushers in the realization of," or "drafted with a loophole which is now in the hands of the secretary." The authors of these improbabilities were in a state of waking sleep, like the reporter who in describing the setting of an outdoor game wrote "The birds filled the tree-tops with their morning song, making the air moist, cool, and pleasant."[2]

Decide Which Images Are Alive

The test of the images that occur to us and are put on paper is twofold: are they alive and are they compatible? Since most words have the power to raise images, it would be impossible to write if some of these images were not neutralized by a kind of remoteness, a deadness. For example, when a commercial firm is said to "open a branch" the image is dead and therefore acceptable. If our literal vision were aroused, the phrase would be absurd. "To stimulate conversation" is also a dead image, the two ideas of a push given and a man speaking produce no clash of images. But as we saw above, "stimulate" (or "rebuilding") and "liquid position" do clash. On coming together the two expressions spring into life again and make us smile by their incongruity.

The cure for clashing images may follow several courses: (1) Drop one of the live images. Say: "improve the liquid position"; nobody now remembers the image that lies dead in the word "improve." (2) Cut out all imagery and "translate" into the concrete particulars that stood behind them, as we did above in supposing the facts of the case. (3) Use abstract general terms instead of concrete particulars, taking care to remain sharp and clear, for example, "The company took on more responsibilities in hopes of recovering strength, but this proved unavailing almost from the start."[3]

---

[2]Quoted in William James, *Principles of Psychology*, New York, 1890, 1:263.

[3]Note that the "but" is here justified by the absence in the first clause of any hint that the company had overreached itself.

Jargon: Its Origin and Poisonous Effects

The foregoing examples show that the two straight roads to meaning are, on the one hand, simple particulars and, on the other, careful generality. The road of imagery, the third, is the winding and dangerous one. Nowadays everything a writer sees and hears tempts him to take it. Advertising pelts us with images to make commonplace objects alluring; business and professional men think to enliven their work by refreshing its vocabulary with new images, and statesmen and journalists try to influence our minds with slogans and catchwords based on images. All this is an indirect tribute to poetry, of course; meantime, the residue left in the writer's mind is jargon.

In the original meaning of the term, there is nothing wrong with jargon. All it means is the special tongue of a trade or art—what we now call technical terms—those of music or carpentry or sailing. Such terms are indispensable, there being usually no others to mean the same things; hence they must be accepted regardless of form or logic. When you discover that to a sailor the "mainsheet" is not a sail but a rope, there is nothing you can do about it. You learn the jargon and try to use it correctly.

But there is another kind of language called jargon, this time with a derogatory meaning, and which ought really to be called *pseudo-jargon*. This second kind is that which has gradually invaded business, the professions, government, and ordinary speech, until it now prevails over plain speaking.[4] It is made up of terms and expressions that purport to be special and indispensable even though they are not technical words. They are pretentious imitations of technicality. Two things prove their bastard origin: they are not definite and fixed in meaning and they can readily be dispensed with. They arise suddenly in some advertising, political, or academic circle, and they catch on, for no apparent reason but novelty and modishness.

In the sentence containing "liquid position," that piece of

[4]The Watergate investigations by Congress and the courts made plain to everybody, through oral testimony and subpoenaed documents, that supposedly competent officials relied on a kind of language in which it is virtually impossible to convey clear meaning. Sometimes this pseudo-speech was resorted to in order to evade responsibility or deceive opponents. But most often its habitual use in transacting official business meant, besides a steady failure of communication and the absence of an accurate record, the gradual crippling of the user's mind for sharp and consecutive thought.

pseudo-jargon was accompanied by another: "end product." This latter term is preferred by all jargon lovers over the simple "product." Now it is conceivable that in some industries it may avoid confusion to distinguish between by-products and end products. But in ordinary speech no such need exists. "End product," "end result" are tiresome tautologies. The first was particularly uncalled-for above, where the meaning is actually "consequence." But perhaps we should be grateful that we do not as yet hear of the "end consequence," "end outcome," and "end upshot."

Other examples of pseudo-jargon are *area* for subject; *concept* for notion, idea, conception; *contact* (verb) for get in touch with, get hold of, meet; *context* and *frame of reference* for connection, relation, bearing; *evaluate* for assess, judge, gauge; *focus on* for deal with, treat, discuss; *motivation* for motive, reason, pretext; *objective* for goal, aim, purpose, intention.

Certain adjectives, such as *basic* and *major*, are also dinned into our ears with a jargonlike "objective" as its "motivation." We are to sense something scientifically absolute about *basic*, something ultra-basic and supermajor; its jargonish tone and feeling will pervade a whole passage.

The writer who wants to present his ideas clearly and with force by eschewing jargon and sticking to plain words should first read Gowers's *Plain Words: Their ABC*, then extend his awareness of meanings and pitfalls by continual recourse to *Modern American Usage* and *Simple & Direct*.[5]

Some of the words and expressions discountenanced in those books or in these pages may pass out of use as quickly as they came in. That is not the point. The point is that at all times words and phrases are being launched that have the look and tone of jargon. Their long or short life on everybody's tongue has nothing to do with the permanent truth that no matter how mouth filling and thought saving for committee meetings, such words are fatal to good writing. One must therefore acquire a sensitiveness (the jargon user would say "an allergy") to new ones as they are made. Here is a specimen

[5]Sir Ernest Gowers, *Plain Words: Their ABC*, Baltimore, 1963; Wilson Follett, *Modern American Usage*, New York, 1966; Jacques Barzun, *Simple & Direct*, 2nd ed., New York, 1985.

from academic writing, followed by the reasons why its growth should be cut short: "He footnotes this idea to Dr. Johnson." What is wrong with the new jargon-use of the verb "to footnote" with an indirect object?

In the first place, the combination is, to the best of our knowledge, unheard of. This is not by itself a sufficient argument to disallow it, but it is enough to give us pause. An author should remember that writing is a social act, which imposes the duty of self-restraint. We try to spell alike and ought to keep to common meanings and usages for the same reason—common understanding, communication. In the second place, this new usage has the characteristic tone of jargon, the air of the showoff drawing attention to himself: "See what I can do? I can footnote an idea to a man." In the third place—and this is the conclusive objection—the new usage renders doubtful and ambiguous whatever meaning was intended. We gather roughly that X made Dr. Johnson responsible for a certain idea.

Or did he? "Make responsible for" is sharp and clear, so that we could accept or deny this imputed responsibility. But what did occur? What are the facts? The reader is understandably impatient. Think of the many possibilities and the many words to impart them that were available to the jargoneer. He could say: "In a footnote, *X assigns to, ascribes to, attributes to, credits with, blames for, makes responsible for, foists upon, fathers upon, palms off on, charges with, accuses of, discovers in* . . . Dr. Johnson . . . the idea in question." A slight rearrangement of name and noun would accommodate all these verbs, each of which carries a distinct meaning. The word chosen would not merely link Idea and Dr. Johnson, but would express the quality of the linkage as well as the opinion of the reporter. Instead of which, we have the vagueness and staleness of jargon surrounding the trivial fact that something took place in a footnote.

How to Live without Jargon and Clichés

In the light of these objections the "effective writer"—to go back to the psychologists' phrase—will make a further resolve. He will train himself not only to be aware of jargon and of the words that jargon displaces, but also to resist in his own mind the laziness implicit in all tricks of speech, all ready-made expressions that sound smart (or once did), all hackneyed tags and quotations, all seeming short cuts—for example the tacking on of "-wise" to some other word as a quick way to get nothing said: "The two nations got together trade-wise" (started to trade? increased their trade? signed a trade agreement?). He will avoid the same trick with "-conscious" and "-minded"—for example, "community-conscious" and "air-minded"—and will not pile up nouns without connectives as in "child sex education" and "population theory evidence." The lesson here is: to be heard and heeded you must do more than lay your ideas side by side like an infant babbling, you must *articulate* them.

Finally, and to the same end of saying what *you* mean, do not substitute semi-synonyms for the words that say something outright; avoid, for example, the widely prevalent use of "feel" for "think"— "Whitehead feels that Nature is a continuum." He does no such thing: he thinks, believes, argues, maintains, assumes, supposes, posits, postulates, imagines, demonstrates, proves; which of these is it? The same flabbiness occurs in "Karl Marx had the benefit of Engels's thinking" (i.e., Engels's thought, views, opinions, knowledge, advice, etc.). There is no such thing as a man's "thinking" apart from the indefinite activity. Reflect on it and you will see that this usage is *not* a parallel to "I enjoyed the violinist's *playing*," which is a sensible remark, but rather to "I am going to write the story of Napoleon's living."

Jargon, clichés, and tricks of speech, as you can see, are not simply sets of words or faults of writing, but forms of escape. They denote a failure of courage, an emotional weakness, a shuffling refusal to be pinned down to a declaration. The cowardice comes out on paper like fingerprints at the site of the crime.

To remember the mood and the menace of jargon, remember its typical product, the all-purpose connective *in terms of*. A book review once commended a book as "the best in terms of the Church of England." The enigma here is to find what "in terms of" signifies. Is it: the best book *about* the Church; the best *in the opinion of* the Church; or the best *for believers in* the Church? It is no small matter to take one interpretation rather than another. And the point is worth laboring because everyone meets such sentences every day without stopping to wonder what they really mean: "The general thinks in terms of army corps; the housewife plans her day in terms of dirty dishes; the child dreams in terms of electric trains." The trouble with the little phrase is that it fails to tell us how the action of the verb is related to its object. We want to know what *the terms* are.[6] We have to guess that perhaps the general thinks *on no less a scale* than that of army corps. The housekeeper plans her day *so as to allow time* for washing dishes. The child dreams that he *has been given* the promised train. But these "translations" are pure surmise. The meanings might just as easily be: "The general thinks that *he wants at least one* army corps"; "The housewife makes her day *revolve around* dishwashing"; "The child's dream *depicts his playing with trains*."

And this does not exhaust the possibilities. What the guessing game shows is that the capable writer begins by being a searching reader, a questioner of texts, who uses his imagination to squeeze all the meaning out of what has been well said and to solve the riddles in what has been only half said. In this role the alert writer is identical with the trained researcher. Reading and writing are correlative acts of the mind; both engage the full resources of one's knowledge and attention upon the medium of words.

Omnibus Words, Dressing Gowns, and Circumlocutions

It would be a mistake to think that because they prevail, jargon and cliché are the only enemies of proper words. There are at least three other kinds of words that are equally harmful to the twin virtues of vocabulary as such, the virtues of *felicity* and *force*. All three kinds resemble jargon and cliché in being loose, empty, thought-saving kinds of words, but they differ in that they are perfectly good words, which *need* not be used loosely and mindlessly. They are damaging only when out of place.

Words of the first category are especially dear to the writer of histories and reports, because they seem to correspond to what he

---

[6]The original use of the phrase in the physical sciences is logical and justified: there are terms. For example, one can measure force *in terms of* the acceleration imparted to a resistant mass, because the terms in which we express the acceleration— say, centimeters per second—are the terms in which we express the force.

deals with: such words as *trend, factor, forces, situation, movement, condition, elements, circumstances.* As all-too-commonly used, they are blank cartridges—they merely make a noise. The way to restore their force is to use them for distinct purposes and *invariably* where they belong. A *trend* denotes a clear or measurable collective tendency. It expresses motion. There is a trend toward early marriage or building smaller houses. Don't say: "These new self-service elevators are a regular trend." Similarly, a factor is something that *makes*. Hence the absurdity of: "The gap was a factor he could not bridge."

Whenever possible, use the name of the thing rather than conceal it behind a loftier word. "The maritime elements were disaffected"—No! Come out with it: "The sailors were rebellious." If you are beset by the modern desire to have words completely "cover" the facts as "maritime elements" purports to do, find a truly descriptive phrase such as: "the sailors and their families"; or "their well-wishers"; or "those dependent on them"; or better still, "the fishing villages" or "the seaboard population." As mentioned before, keep your eye on what your reader could go out and see or touch, and write accordingly. Then you have him.

In this same first category of "omnibus" words are certain adjectives that writers of textbooks have made depressingly habitual. These books contain nothing but *bitter* attacks, *crushing* defeats, *shrewd* diplomats, and *ruthless* ambition. All such standard epithets deserve a rest. Attacks can be angry, vehement, violent, reckless, impetuous, sinister, unforgivable, and perhaps half a hundred other things. Let us have each a little different. They certainly were so in reality, and they would be more easily remembered when free of the label that makes them all alike.

The parroting habit also leads writers to clutter up their prose with a second kind of empty words. Gowers has happily named them "adverbial dressing gowns." He has in mind such pairs as *seriously* consider, *fully* recognize, *wholly* unjustifiable, *thoroughly* mistaken. He calls them dressing gowns because the writer is shying away from the naked word they wrap around. Try stripping the main word and see how your utterance gains in strength. To say "His act was unjustifiable" is far stronger than "His act was wholly unjustifiable." With the adverb you are straining to prove; you are frothing a little at the mouth; in the former you have judged, there is nothing to add.

The third category of encumbrances is the familiar one of long words and circumlocutions. No rule can be given about the length of words it is desirable to use. The length of the same word varies with the context (the literal use of *context* here is not jargon). For example, in the first sentence of this paragraph "circumlocution" seemed the shortest way to say what was meant. Elsewhere it might not be—as in "Refrain from circumlocution" for "Don't beat around the bush." The misfortune is that many people who in speaking would not ask anyone to "refrain" from anything feel it their duty to elevate their tone when they write letters, reports, reviews, and books. Oddly enough, the long dressy word comes first to their minds, perhaps from an association of ideas between the authority they desire for their writing and the tone of official pronouncements.

If that is what happens to you, translate back into the vernacular, either at once or in your second draft. Remember that the vernacular does not mean "slang" and need not imply colloquialism. The vernacular is the language of good speakers who are not choosing their words but producing them easily and, on the whole, correctly. You cannot write as people speak, but you can write as people would be willing to speak if they were handed a part to read aloud. This is not the only way to write, but it is the best way to practice "translation" from jargon, clichés, empty words, and highfalutin.

When once you have the habit of translation in this sense you can adapt your diction to the occasion, for you will have at least mastered the instrument of vocabulary. In the classic musical *Guys and Dolls*, the dialogue is an artful mixture of slang, jargon, and highbrow bookishness. The effect is comic, yet one meets people who missed the virtuosity of it and who vaguely complain that the talk sounds "uneven," which shows that catching the drift is not the same as understanding words.

Idioms and Unwritten Laws

This last distinction is all-important for the would-be writer. He must not only recognize what is wrong with this or that word in his first draft; he must be able to summon up half a dozen in its place and choose among them. To his desk dictionary he may want to add a thesaurus—Roget's or another. But he will spend long hours turning over pages if he has to rely on these books for inspiration instead of verification. His need is to be prompt and fertile in suggestion whenever he writes. The quality and speed of notetaking, as we saw in Chapter 2, also depend on one's verbal resources. There is thus every inducement to make words as such a subject of continual study. In this self-discipline, eye and ear, mind and memory, must equally participate. The eye notes spelling, aided by the ear, which also records idiom. The mind looks for distinctions between apparent synonyms, which the memory stores up and delivers again, with connotations.

Idiom is frequently "cast-iron," to use one of H. W. Fowler's terms. You *must* say "He acquiesced *in* the proposal," not *to*. If you slip here, it is probably because of "he agreed to," but note at the same time that "agree to" has a different meaning from "agree with," just like "compare to" and "compare with." A writer who compares himself to Shakespeare will be thought conceited, but if he compares himself with Shakespeare, he can emerge a modest, indeed, a chastened man. Idiom follows neither logic nor illogic; it simply is, and has to be learned. That is the price paid for being born to a rich and sinewy language.[7]

Connotations or overtones are still harder to learn, though many are second nature to most adults. Just as they know that one *rides* a horse and *drives* a car, so they know that one *celebrates* a wedding and *conducts* a funeral; one *reciprocates* a favor and *retaliates* an injury—not the other way round. Such usages may be regarded as halfway between idiom and right diction. A writer should not confuse "hard work" with "hard labor," "mitigate" with "militate," "fortuitous" with "fortunate." Whoever wants to command language must first master its traditions. But the subtler though no less strong customs of other words are often overlooked, with a resulting diminution of force. "Drastic," for instance, which has become so

---

[7]Submitting to the fixity of idiom, good writers seldom tamper with common phrases that, superficially considered, seem to allow change. Write "past his prime," not "past his distinguished prime." Leave to the advertiser the privilege of saying "at its tastiest best"; and if you must qualify, do it outside the phrase, e.g., *not* "he put a reluctant stop," but "he reluctantly put a stop"—which also has the advantage of better logic.

popular, implies an act that affects both the doer and the victim, though perhaps unequally. The shopkeeper who announces "Drastic cut in prices" is correct—the drastic act hurts him while wreaking havoc among the price tags. To use "drastic" as a mere synonym for "violent" or "thoroughgoing" is to waste a good overtone, which after a while will cease resounding and be lost for good. People will then ask, "How do you express the idea of injuring yourself so as to injure your enemy more?"

The present answers to such questions are nowhere written down in full. The facts about idiom and connotations are not easily found except in good writing—writing that is "effective" because it is "sensitive to overtones and the peculiar purpose" of the moment. Hence, let us say it again, whoever writes must read—preferably pencil in hand. There is nothing childish in the practice of observing new words and turns of phrase; if the *Reader's Digest* can offer the great public an occasional page for vocabulary building, there is no affectation in doing the same for one's own convenience.

If in addition one has the opportunity of reading the manuscripts of other writers, the effort helps in the correcting of one's own. Printed matter is like the words one has just set down—they both have a paralyzing effect on the critical instinct—whereas somebody else's manuscript prose looks wonderfully improvable.

By way of conclusion, scrutinize a pair of sentences from essays by advanced students and apply the principles laid down in this chapter. The first defines the German Customs Union that preceded the Empire:

1. "A basically geographical concept permeated with political overtones dependent on arbitrary historical and political boundaries of the included states."

A critical reader's comments would run: *basically* is both jargon and an adverbial dressing gown. *Concept* (as we saw) is jargon for *idea* or *conception*. "Permeated *with*" is wrong; the idiom requires *by*. Moreover, the image is absurd: overtones cannot permeate a concept, and a geographical one at that. The rest is inoffensive but clumsy and vague.

2. "Memoirs must be studied for falsifications and for the author's own point of view, as well as sources, whether documentary or in the nature of narrative without official certification."

Comments: Memoirs are not *studied* for falsification; they are examined or scanned. "Falsifications" is the wrong word, anyway—try "errors" or "falsehoods." The sentence limps badly, but that fault belongs to our next chapter. "Sources . . . in the nature of narrative" are nothing more than narratives. "Official certification" is jargon here for *official* by itself, which should go before "documents" in the rewritten: "as well as sources in the form of official documents or plain narratives."

The ease with which even trained eyes can overlook error and nonsense should make every writer at once endlessly cautious and forever modest. At least half a dozen competent readers—colleagues, editors, and the author himself—must have gone over the preface of a valuable work on economics, which closes with these words: "Obviously, none of the people named above has the least responsibility for whatever may be found in this book. I alone am to blame."

What is the matter here—no jargon, no misfit among images, no false idioms? Nothing that is said is wrong, but something is left unsaid that turns the remark into a kind of joke. The intention was to tell the reader that for whatever *errors* he might find, he must blame the author, not the author's friends. As the words stand, the author "blames himself" for the entire contents of the book. The mistake is more amusing than grievous, and certainly not hard to forgive. If it is to be remembered at all, it should be for unwittingly revealing the spirit in which every writer must write and rewrite: "I alone am to blame."

13

Clear Sentences:
Right Emphasis
and Rhythm

Live Sentences for Lively Thoughts

As everybody knows, meaning does not come from single words, but from words put together in groups—phrases, clauses, sentences. A mysterious bond links these groups of words with our ideas, and this relation leads in turn to the miracle by which ideas pass from one mind to another. The reason for weighing words with care is to make sure that these units of speech correspond truly to one's inner vision; the reason for building sentences with care is to make sure that all the portions of our thought hang together correctly for truth and conveniently for understanding.

Everyone's mind, however eager it may be for information, offers a certain resistance to the reception of somebody else's ideas. Before one can take in another's intent, the shape, connection, and tendency of one's own ideas have to yield to those same features in the other person's. Accordingly, the writer must somehow induce in that other the willingness to receive the foreign matter. He does so with the aid of a great many devices which, when regularly used, are called the qualities of his speech or writing.

These qualities go by such names as: Clarity, Order, Logic, Ease,

315

Unity, Coherence, Rhythm, Force, Simplicity, Naturalness, Grace, Wit, and Movement. But these are not distinct things; they overlap and can reinforce or obscure one another, being but aspects of the single power called Style. Neither style nor any of its qualities can be aimed at separately. Nor are the pleasing characteristics of a writer's style laid on some preexisting surface the way sheathing and plaster are laid on the rough boards of a half-finished house. Rather, they are the by-product of an intense effort to make words work. By "making them work" we mean here reaching the mind of another and affecting it in such a way as to reproduce there *our* state of mind.

Since you cannot aim directly at style, clarity, precision, and all the rest, what can you do? You can remove the many natural obstacles to understanding, while preserving as much as you can of your spontaneous utterance. All attempts at imitating a recognized style, whether Biblical, Lincolnesque, or "stark" for modernity, defeat themselves. You cannot be someone other than yourself. The qualities we have listed, and others you can name, should therefore be regarded as so many tests that you apply in the course of revision by self-questioning. You do not, while writing, say to yourself: "Now I am going to be clear, logical, coherent." You write a sentence and ask, as you go over it: "Can anyone else follow? Perhaps not. Then what is the matter? I see: this does not match that. And here—is this in any way absurd?" Clarity is there when others can follow; coherence when thoughts hang together; logic when their sequence is valid. You achieve these results by changing, cutting, transposing. You may ask: "Is there no way to write so as to avoid all this patching after-the-fact?" There is—and learning how is the subject of this chapter. But note at the outset that any helpful hints will only reduce the amount of rewriting to be done, never remove its necessity.

It is an interesting proof of what has just been said that no satisfactory definition of a sentence has ever been given: there is no specification to which you can build. Yet every educated person recognizes a sentence when he sees one. The mystery of its connection with a train of thought is the point of departure for our effort to make the sentence and the total thought coincide. To say this is to say that notions of correctness or proffers of approved models for sentences will be useless, and even paralyzing, unless they are taken with imagination. Whatever image you may have in mind when you see or hear the word "sentence," that image should not be of something rigid, static, and absolute; a sentence is above all functional, dynamic, and relative. A sentence, perfectly good when taken by itself, may be all wrong when it follows or precedes another. For the thought has to keep moving and its track must be smooth. If you need a structural image of The Sentence, think of it as an organism possessing a skeleton, muscles, and skin.

Like a skeleton, a sentence is a piece of construction. Traditional grammar in fact speaks of related words as forming "a construction," and calls it awkward or harmonious, allowable or contrary to usage. But do not let the idea of a construction suggest a table or a house; to be sure, a sentence has to stand on its feet, but we liken it to a skeleton because a sentence, like the thought it carries, has to move. Motion is perhaps the fundamental quality of good writing. Motion is what makes writing correspond to thought, which is also a movement from one idea or vision to the next. A reader who knows nothing about the principles of writing may be incapable of describing what is wrong as he makes heavy weather through a book. But he feels very keenly whether his mind advances or sticks, goes straight or in circles, marches steadily forward or jerks two steps ahead and three back.

In order to move, the parts of the sentence skeleton must be properly jointed, articulated; the muscles and connective tissue must be strong and inserted at the right places; the burden of ideas must not be too great for the structure. And to cover all this machinery and make it pleasing, the surface must be smooth and reasonably varied in appearance. Translating this into writers' terms, we say: clauses and phrases must fall into the right pattern of syntax, and the words must be chosen so that the tone and rhythm of the whole are appropriate. A telegraphic message may be exact and well knit, but it lacks grace and sounds unnatural. It moves but does not flow. One cannot imagine reading three hundred pages in telegraphic style. The words omitted in that style and which are restored in ordinary prose are no decoration or added charm; they are simply the rounded contour of the thought, reduced in the telegram to the bare bones.

The return of this image of the skeleton tells us that we have come full circle in our attempt to define at one and the same time what a sentence is and what it does. You may as a result be a little wiser about the virtues to aim at in writing. But you probably think, with reason, that what you need even more than a definition is direct advice, and for this we must look at examples. Yet, we repeat: if you want the examples to be serviceable beyond their immediate instruction, you should study them with the force of our definitions behind them.

Five-Legged Sheep and Other Monsters

Let us begin with the schoolbook example: "The wind blew across the desert where the corpse lay and whistled." The sentence moves indeed, and the *information* it contains is not hard to find; but before we quite grasp it we laugh. And this alters the *meaning*, which was not intended to be jocular in the last three words. How to fix it? Our first impulse is to insert a comma after "lay." But reading the result gives an odd impression, as if "and whistled" was a dangling afterthought. Try it aloud and you will hear that a comma pause after "lay" makes "and whistled" sound not simply silly but a trifle puzzling. The only way the sentence sounds rhythmically satisfying is without the pause, and then the meaning is absurd.

The reason is that the meaning and the construction are at odds; bad rhythm gives the flaw away, the trouble being that the limb "and whistled" is attached to the wrong part of the body. The joke comes from the close link between the corpse and the whistling. We derive from this error our first rule of sentence-making: *bring as close together as possible the parts that occur together in the world or go together in your mind.*

Now try to apply the rule to our sentence: "The wind blew across the desert and whistled where the corpse lay." No longer comic, but wrong again, because the new close-linking suggests that the whistling took place only near the corpse. In framing a sentence the need to link and connect implies the need to unlink and detach. Try again: "The wind blew and whistled across the desert where the corpse lay." At last we have the limbs correctly distributed—no front leg is hitched on to the hindquarters. Our sentence passes the test as far as avoiding absurdity and false suggestion goes.

But say it aloud once more and you will notice that it still sounds odd. It leaves the voice up in the air, and with the voice, the meaning, because the emphases are off beat. In an ordinary declarative sentence, the two spots of emphasis are the beginning and the end. Hence the two most important elements in the thought must occupy those spots. In our example the main elements obviously are: the whistling wind and the corpse. Whether the corpse lay or stood or leaned is a detail. The last idea sounding in our mind's ear must be "the corpse." Can this be managed? Let us see. "The wind blew and whistled across the desert where lay the corpse." A trifle better, but far from perfect. Why? Because modern English shies away from inversions. Idiomatic turns make a language what it is; to defy idiom is to lose force. In short, to sound natural we must stick to "where the corpse lay."

By this time we are sick and tired of wrestling with these twelve words and we conclude that they cannot be juggled into a proper shape. We are ready to scrap the sentence and go at the idea by a different route, when a fresh form occurs to us. "The corpse lay in the desert, across which the wind blew and whistled." This is the best yet. The form is right and if the whole subject were only a little less dramatic we could let it stand. But there is a stiffness about "across which" that suits a description of scenery rather than of lonely death. This impression simply means that we have been made aware of Tone while trying to secure Right Emphasis, Right Linking, and Right Rhythm. These features of the sentence, we repeat, are not separable. On the contrary, a sentence is to be regarded as a compromise among their various demands.

If the Tone of "across which" is unsuitable, what *can* we do with the wretched corpse on our hands? Having twisted and turned it about, all that occurs is to abandon our second construction and try a third: "The corpse lay in the desert, and over it the wind blew and whistled."[1] This is still disappointing: a compound sentence is too weak for this gruesome vision; it separates what eye and ear bring together to the mind. We have dismembered and reconstructed without success. What next?

---

[1] The inveterate verifier is curious about the fact and he asks, *Does* the wind whistle when it blows across an unobstructed waste?

The true solution lies in the so-called periodic sentence, whose form heightens suspense and generally favors rhythm: "Across the desert where the corpse lay, the wind blew and whistled." A peculiarity of the periodic sentence is that its suspensive opening phrase does not monopolize the emphasis we associate with beginnings. The second portion is still emphatic because the forepart rushes down toward it, so to speak, in an effort to complete its own meaning by finding a main subject and verb.

From our experience with a single bad sentence, we can now confirm our first rule of thumb and add to it others for similar use in framing and straightening sentences:

1. Right linking is the prime requisite. Begin by seeing to it that things related are not divided, and that things remote are not falsely joined.

2. Right emphasis comes next. It is what gives momentum to the thought, what makes the sentence move. It starts from a point of superior interest, travels through a valley of detail, and reaches a second point of high interest, which ends the journey by completing or advancing our understanding of the first.

3. When our emphases are right, the rhythm is likely to be right also, for our speaking habits naturally follow our habits of wording and of thought.[2]

4. At any point in the structure, the phrasing must be in keeping with the tenor of the whole. This is a matter partly of diction and partly of construction. The two together produce Tone.

To these four propositions there is an important negative corollary: Although a comma that is missing from a sound sentence should be put in, a defective sentence cannot be cured by a comma. When you are tempted to waste time in this effort, just remember "and whistled."

---

[2]This does not mean that in speaking we usually place our words right for emphasis but that we sound them right, and hence the rhythm is natural. One says: "They *are* good—in *my* opinion." To convey the same meaning in print, one must write: "They are, in my opinion, good." Still judging the written word, explain the rather different meanings of: "In my opinion, they are good" and "They, in my opinion, are good."

With these truths in mind, we can refine a little on the art of construction, though with no hope of exhausting the subject of improved sentence-building. We go back to the difficult art of linking. The desire to bring kindred things together often tempts the unwary to use phrases that can be read in two or more ways. When that happens, the reader is sent on the wrong track; he must then back up and make a fresh start, or perhaps remain in doubt about the right fusion of ideas. Suppose one reads:

> If there is lost motion in the rods and boxes in a boiler of steam generating capacity and a valve distributing power properly when the lever is hooked down, it develops into a pound that is annoying and detrimental to the machinery.

The reader's trouble begins at "steam generating capacity." Should this be "steam-generating," a hyphenated adjective modifying "capacity"? Or should it be "a boiler of steam, generating [power at] capacity"? Below, a similar hesitation arises at "valve distributing power." Doubt is settled by our knowledge that valves distribute power and not the other way round ("valve-distributing power" is nonsense.) But we have had to stop and figure this out. The second phrase exactly parallels the first—"steam-generating capacity"—and our retentive ear entices us to give their parallel forms a parallel meaning. Next we are stopped for a further instant at whatever "it" is that "develops into a pound." After talk of steam power, the word "pound" is ambiguous. We see at once that it is not a pound of pressure that is meant but a pound*ing*. Still, we have been jerked to a halt a third time. Finally, another, somewhat different, parallel between the two adjectives in the last part of the sentence tells us that this pounding is "annoying . . . to the machinery."

On the whole, this sentence intended for the instruction of engineers can tell us more about writing than about machinery. And here is what it tells us: parallelism is so important a device in writing that its use must be kept pure. Do not give parallel forms to disparate ideas, and always carry out the parallels you start with. Do not ever suppose that variation is more elegant. Note the accumulation of horrors in the paragraph overleaf.

When it came right down to it, he was no more able to spell out a conceptual pattern than, in the last analysis, he felt he could muster up the imagination to face such explosive problems of ethics as his sadly unhappy life had left him no room to size up with detachment.

At the words "he was no more able to," the writer has made a contract with the reader. Those words forecast a "than," to be followed by a second action parallel to the first. The contract here is broken. The "than" duly comes, but its proper adjunct is forgotten while the writer pursues his wandering thought down winding channels. Jargon and rank images ("spell out a pattern," "explosive problems," "room to size up") are mixed with clichés ("in the last analysis"), tautologies ("sadly unhappy"), and the redundancies that spoil the parallel—"he [felt he] could," and the words following "imagination." The cure is to give up the "no more than" construction and make two sentences, one about the conceptual patterns—whatever they may be—and one about the ethical problems of a sadly unhappy life without room.

An observation made in passing when we examined the sentence from the engineer's manual furnishes a second rule of good construction: *the antecedents of pronouns must always be unmistakable.* In the welter of rods, boxes, and valves no one can tell what "it" is that "develops into a pound." It cannot be the engine, which is not even mentioned. The motion, no doubt, develops into a pound, but the only motion mentioned is four lines above and it is *lost* motion. Technically, it is a kind of motion, but in syntax it does not exist. In any event, no fewer than six nouns in the singular precede "it," and two would be enough to create confusion. By rights, the last in order should be the true antecedent, but that happens to be "lever," which makes nonsense. The "it" is an orphaned relative with no references to show when questioned.

Modern Prose: Its Virtues and Vices

After so much wallowing in uncertainty we are eager for a good sentence. Here is one embodying a double parallel and making of it a dramatic image: "Too blind to avert danger, too cowardly to withstand it, the most ancient government of Europe made not an instant's resistance: the peasants of Underwald died upon their mountains, the holders of Venice clung to their lives."[3]

The modern reader who appreciates this sentence may say that in spite of its clarity, richness, and rhythmical excellence, it is alien to our modes of thought and hence beyond our power to imitate. We no longer enjoy these complex and balanced forms; they seem to us artificial. We prefer to write simply, as we speak—or so we like to believe. If the engineer's sentence above, and the biographer's right after, are fair samples of serious prose in our century, we are forced to admit that the elements of complexity are still with us, though unorganized. We are not so simple and straightforward as we pretend, and the truth is that we could not follow the advice of "write as we speak" even if we wanted to.

What prevents the written word from reproducing speech is that, in speaking, the voice, stress, facial expression, and gesture contribute a quantity of meaning that fills out the insufficiency of colloquial phrasing. Read the transcript of court testimony and you will see how difficult it is to understand. You have to guess how every remark was spoken, inflected, made clear by something other than words. In good writing the writer has to supply these elements which give point and direction to utterance. Hence the use of those transitional and qualifying words that are almost entirely absent from conversation.

And it is this necessity, of course, that leads to the other extreme. The writer may think as he would speak; but half-conscious of a lack, he fills out his spontaneous sentence with many words—to stop the gaps, to bottle up his meaning, which always threatens to fizz away. Up to a point the effort succeeds. But superfluous words destroy explicitness. The fault of beginners and inattentive writers is that their sentences say the same thing twice over. Here is a sample from a government office memorandum: "I believe we all function best in a positive, supportive work environment where we are each

---

[3]Marguerite, Lady Blessington, in her *Conversations of Lord Byron* (Philadelphia, 1836, 96), reports that Byron exclaimed about this passage from Hallam's *Middle Ages*: "This is the way to write history if it is wished to impress it on the memory."

able to develop mutual respect for co-workers and work at a job that gives us a sense of self-fulfillment in the "work" category of our human activities."

Part of the difficulty with this sentence is that it is not stripped down to its analyzable meaning; for example, "positive and supportive environment" is jargon and remains vague until we make out that the *where* clause is in fact what the writer means by positive and supportive. Then the idea of mutual respect is foolishly attached to *each*, as if one person could develop anything *mutual* all alone. Finally, the definition of the desirable environment suffers from an afterthought, the relation of our feelings to the job in itself (no part of the coworkers' behavior), and this is topped by a tautology: where does self-fulfillment from a job belong except in the "work category"? Every phrase suggests a writer who did not sort out his ideas, ignored overlappings and demarcations of fact—in short, wrote down his thoughts just as they tumbled into his consciousness. The excess is not simply dropped by the reader. It stops his mind long enough to make him wonder whether he is missing some special point or nuance. Since in fact he is not, the effort has been wasted. Multiply this kind of fault through successive paragraphs and the reader bogs down.

From this we infer the generality that, all else being equal, *the ease with which thought can be gathered from words is in inverse ratio to their combined length.*

We did not say "to their number," for the length of the words themselves may be part of the impediment; it is a fact that each syllable the eye and the mind must take in causes a kind of friction, as in physical work. But we also said "all else being equal," which means that occasions are frequent in which long words and long sentences are preferable. But a simple thought buried in a sentence stuffed with long words inevitably produces the effect commonly called "a mouthful." Like the mouth, the mind cannot cope with it. The moral is, any sentence that grows on and on in a string of words ending in "-ity" or "-tion," hooked together with of's, to's, and which's must be whittled down to size with a hatchet.

Consider this statement, which purports to *make clearer* one of Shakespeare's plays:

The creation of character, indeed, is not to be regarded as the unique, or even principal, end of Shakespeare's dramatic creations, in which plot and motive, themselves handled with greater flexibility and insight, tend increasingly to find their proper context in a more ample artistic unity which embraces and illuminates them; but in the delineation of personality beyond the limits of convention his language first attained some sense of its full possibilities.

No mind, including the author's, can take in at one scoop the message of this clumsy compound. Therefore the critic had no excuse for offering it to the public, even if his mind does work on the rocket principle, shooting out fresh phrases at intervals as he proceeds where we cannot follow. He should make a first stop after "creations" and a second after "unity." Rereading this, the author would see that the portion beginning with "but" is so flabbily contrasted with what went before that he should ask himself what, in fact, he did have in mind.

Nor is sprawling his only sin against sense. He gives us an anthology of faults: (1) Awkward repetition: "creation" in line 1, "creations" in line 2. (2) Tautology: "themselves" in line 3, and the whole phrase beginning "find their proper context . . ." down to "embraces" ("context," "unity," and "embraces" say the same thing three times). (3) Illogic: how are we to interpret the comparison in "greater" and "more ample"? Than what? "Increasingly" suggests "as time went on," but we must guess this. (4) Pronouns adrift: "their" in line 4 and "them" in line 5 have two possible antecedents—"dramatic creations" on the one hand, and "plot and motive" on the other. (5) The vagueness of perpetual abstraction: what does it *mean* "to handle plot and motive with greater flexibility and insight"? "to find a proper context"? "to be embraced and illuminated by a more ample artistic unity"? "to delineate personality beyond the limits of convention"? And how in the name of heaven does a writer's *language* "attain some sense of *its* full possibilities"?

We see in this example what it means to be ponderous without being scholarly. The worst faults of "serious writing" are here conveniently grouped, the "noun plague" dominating them all. Not one plausible agent performs a recognizable act denoted by a strong verb. All is passive and diffuse and jargon-ridden.

As an antidote, let us turn to another writer on Shakespeare:

> Structurally, Tate has made few serious alterations. The most important is Bolingbroke's winning of the rabble. This is amusingly done and probably acted well enough. More serious is the "elevation" of Richard's character, a feat on which Tate plumes himself in the Preface. As a matter of fact, it spoils the play.[4]

Despite its choppiness, which might become tedious, and a lack of charm, which would preclude subtle thoughts, this passage at least answers the reader's prayer for simple and straightforward prose. What makes it such is the presence of what was absent in the former passage: plausible agents, recognizable acts, strong verbs. Of these last, there are still too few. A more searching writer would, for instance, have preferred: "Tate has altered but few structural parts. . . ." Then the logic could be stricter: if "the most important" alteration is the one about Bolingbroke, how can the one about Richard be "more serious"? And to a good ear—pronouns and parallels again!—the sentence "This is amusingly done and probably acted well enough" sounds disjointed. The shift in voice calls for a second subject: "and *it* probably acted . . ."; for the passive "is done" will not go in harness with the active verb "acted."

Carpentry or Cabinetmaking?

All we have been saying is an extension of our original proposition that "good writing is an intense effort to make words work." The complaints and suggestions about the passages we have examined boil down to the demand that each word—noun, verb, adverb, or any other kind—should contribute something to the sense, and this with economy. If one word can do the work of two, use one. If you absolutely need a phrase, make it short. If the thought is complex and the sentence has to contain several clauses, see to it that each clause expends its energy where none will be wasted, that is, close to the idea it enlarges or qualifies.

[4]Hazelton Spencer, *Shakespeare Improved*, Cambridge, Mass., 1927, 262.

A good rule to follow in order to achieve coherence with the least trouble is to stick to your subject, voice, or construction. Do not start with one idea or form and change it in mid-career. The writer above switched from a passive verb to an active and lost momentum. Another will write: "The topic one selects should be clear and precise and when one comes to look for the materials on it, it will be found that the subject itself serves as a guide to their selection." This is no doubt a faithful transcript of the way the thought arose in one mind, but its form is ill adapted to its penetrating another. In a second draft the writer should cling to the grammatical subject and see where it leads him: "The topic selected should be clear and precise—*so that* IT will guide the researcher—*when* HE comes to look for *his* materials." Twenty-three words in place of thirty-five, and a *continuous motion* instead of three hitches—from "the topic" to "when one comes" to an indefinite "it" and back to "the subject" again.

Only remain faithful to your subject and construction, making everything follow the one and fit into the other, and you will be surprised at the ease, speed, and clarity that you attain. All the thick connective tissue—or clanking chains, rather ("as regards," "as far as . . . is concerned," "in relation to," and the like)—will automatically fall away; associated ideas will be next to next; and your thought will be accessible to the reader who, by definition, is always on the run.[5]

For models of this kind of writing, study the advertising cards in any public vehicle. The ideas conveyed may be stupid, commonplace, or untrue; the words themselves may be flossy or jargonlike, but the construction is usually impeccable. One reason is that advertisers know they have only thirty seconds to make an impression. Another and a clinching reason is that they employ first-rate writing talents. When these are exerted in publicizing welfare agencies or, occasionally, political appeals, they produce classic utterances. What could be better than:

"Eighteen million Californians need a fighting Senator with experience, ideas, and a heart."

Note how the attention is arrested, without fuss, by the opening

---

[5]Go back to Chapter 2 and follow once again the rewriting of sentences from the report on the Cutter vaccine (pp. 33–36).

phrase, which addresses every voter in the state, and how adroitly the emphases are managed: having started with our interesting selves we wind up with an appeal to the feelings. But "ideas" are not wholly forgotten, though "experience," as the chief political virtue, comes first in the series. Notice also the function of the single adjective "fighting." It is a strong word, but here it is more than that. Without it, the sentence might be a bare statement of need, suggesting no candidate to fill it. But with the epithet, it is clear that the declaration aims at someone, and behold! his picture is underneath it.

You may say that the ease, lucidity, and force of this bid for votes comes from the inherent simplicity of the idea. Not so. It is always easy to write a muddy sentence, and it would be surprising if the one we have been admiring had been struck off impromptu. The normal tendency is to join chunks of wordage each to each as they come and then tap them here and there with a hammer till they more or less resemble a structure.

Here are examples of two phases of composition—if indeed the first fragment can claim the name. The writer is a high-school teacher of English whose examination paper suggests how illiterate are some of those who "educate" our young:

Hemingway works is the beginning of all modern American Literature. He doesn't write too much conversation in his books. Just enough to make the idea go across and his descriptions are brief with many adverbs.

Compare a hammered-down affair that is brisker and more literate but not much more satisfactory:

Thousands of years ago men first learned the secret of conducting water through crude pipes. ["Crude" is out of place here, since the secret sought was how to conduct water through pipes—which turned out to be crude.] Long before the birth of Christ, the Chinese transported water through bamboo. [Christ is brought in for vividness, but the effect fails by making one wonder what His birth contributed to plumbing.] . . . and there is much evidence of the fine water supply systems of the Romans. [By this point, the writer has given up, lost his grip on vividness, fact, and rhythm.]

The unpalatable truth is that since a really well-made sentence is not born, like the live body we compared it to, it can only be the result of much planing and fitting, of close measuring for balance, and of hidden jointing for solidity and smoothness—it is cabinetmaker's work, plus the living force that gives movement and stirs the inert frame into an animated whole.

The joiner's task calls for words that will bind the ideas together from end to end. And yet, in a second draft it is often desirable to omit some of the cross references. Where the reader's mind will take the jump alone, it is a waste to prod him. For example,

> What course of procedure does this suggest? In spite of all the study on the broad topic of productivity, the sum total of knowledge useful to management is small. Government and economic research agencies should be encouraged to expand studies of productivity.

This passage is clear and rapid because in the first sentence "this" refers adequately to the preceding paragraph and because in the second sentence the subject (productivity) is named again in a passing manner that allows our attention to dwell on the aspect of it that matters, namely, the *study* of productivity. The writer then omits a further reference after "the sum total of knowledge"—we know very well it is not knowledge at large, but knowledge about productivity. At the last gasp, however, the writer's art broke down: he repeated "studies of productivity" at an emphatic place, almost as if this were a new topic he was introducing. He might have said instead: "Government, etc., should be encouraged to enlarge this sum by extending [not 'expanding'] their studies."

When a writer falls back repeatedly on clumsy reference by means of "such information," "the above-mentioned," and insensitive repetitions of the subject in identical words, the paragraphs read like a lawyer's brief and must be worked out rather than simply read.

Now there is one place in any article or book where this sort of failure is fatal to the circulation of the work. That place is the beginning. To catch your reader, the hook must be baited with palatable stuff. A good writer will therefore toil over his opening sentence.

Let his model be the one that opens Jane Austen's *Pride and Prejudice*: "It is a truth universally acknowledged that a single man in possession of a good fortune must be in want of a wife." This far from truthful proposition is an ideal opening, because it foretells in the smallest compass what we are about to be concerned with—marriage and money; and how we are to be concerned with them—in the spirit of irony.

Conclusions, too, are important, being the last words ringing in the reader's ear. They may be as difficult as beginnings if you have said a great deal and want to recall it in one, final, pregnant sentence. Here is a good example dealing with England's defeat of the Great Armada: "This triumph of sea power insured the survival of the Reformation in England and to a lesser extent in Germany, and helped maintain Holland's independence from Spain."

The Sound of the Sense

These two examples of opening and closing are models only to the extent that they combine a number of the qualities every reader longs for in the prose he reads—clarity, balance, movement, force, and ease. Jane Austen's, it need hardly be pointed out, has grace and wit besides.

But the models further resemble each other in that they disclose a characteristic tone: we hear a voice and it is pleasing. Tone cannot be defined except negatively, when it is bad. Anyone can tell when a writer is talking down—that is the condescending tone. But there is also the pompous, the chattering, the precious, the chummy, the toplofty, the cynical and sneering, the vulgar out of the corner of the mouth: the varieties of bad tones are infinite, for they correspond to the many possible mixtures of human emotions.

The curious thing is that a good writer will occasionally fall into a tone that he himself would reprove, yet will never notice the lapse. Either he is seduced by "language," as in preciosity or pedantry; or else he is betrayed by his feelings about the subject, as in cynicism or arrogance. These are reasons, not excuses. The reader is quick to notice what rings false and to resent it. A writer may have to be on guard against his most congenial adult attitudes. Until spoiled by sophistication, children who write are free of these. In consequence, a writer such as the nine-year-old author of *The Young Visiters* has

perfect tone. Pick up the book anywhere and no matter how difficult
the subject, the tone suits:

> The Abbey was indeed thronged next day when Ethel and Bernard
> cantered up in a very fine carrage drawn by two prancing steeds who foamed
> a good deal. In the porch stood several clean altar boys who conducted the
> lucky pair up the aile while the organ pealed a merry blast. The mighty
> edifice was packed and seated in the front row was the Earl of Clincham
> looking very brisk as he was going to give Ethel away at the correct moment.
> Beside him sat Mr. Salteena all in black and looking bitterly sad and he
> ground his teeth as Ethel came marching up.[6]

What admirable control of rhythm and tone! The difficulty of
exercising control has inspired a rule of thumb: If you are especially
fond of a passage, strike it out. But this advice evidently goes too far,
since "fondness" can express a sound judgment about a sentence well
worked over. No. The only clue to bad tone is reading one's writing
after an interval and responding to the text like an unprepared
reader. Phrases will then begin to sound hollow, and they will be
judged falsehoods or padding or irrelevance.

But many writers entertain something more than a negative
ambition. They aim at a virtue beyond propriety of tone, and it is in
this effort that some will overreach themselves and produce what is
ironically stigmatized as "fine writing." The irony does not mean that
writing cannot or should not be fine. Masterpieces of prose are there
to prove that the quality is both desirable and achievable, and nobody
would maintain that it comes to a writer without effort. The objection
is to the striving after a fineness that is affected or commonplace—
fancy phrases.

If it were needed at this late date to prove that true fineness is at
once the result of work and of a born writer's personality, a decisive
example would be the famous ending of Lincoln's First Inaugural, for
which his Secretary of State, William H. Seward, had proposed a first
draft, as follows:

> I close. We are not, we must not be, aliens or enemies, but fellow
> countrymen and brethren. Although passion has strained our bonds of affec-

---

[6]By Daisy Ashford, New York, 1919, 99.

tion too hardly, they must not, I am sure they will not, be broken. The mystic chords which proceeding from so many battlefields and so many patriot graves, pass through all the hearts and hearths in this broad continent of ours, will yet again harmonize in their ancient music when breathed upon by the guardian angel of the nation.[7]

Lincoln worked it over four times and produced the well-known words:

I am loath to close. We are not enemies, but friends. We must not be enemies. Though passion may have strained, it must not break our bonds of affection. The mystic chords of memory, stretching from every battlefield, and patriot grave, to every living heart and hearthstone, all over this broad land, will yet swell the chorus of the Union, when again touched, as surely they will be, by the better angels of our nature.[8]

Lincoln did not, in one sense, change a single idea of Seward's. But in another sense he changed them all. By a greater simplicity of vision, a truer feeling for the meaning of words, and a superior sensitivity to rhythm, he produced his own incomparable music, where Seward had merely lined up some appropriate propositions. Seward is (as we say) adequate, but he lacks the complete adequacy that thinks of everything and sets it in its proper place. Just compare Seward's "guardian angel," who is a cliché of the political platform and not a force, with Lincoln's "better angels of our nature," who stand here for conscience and generous impulse in each *living heart*. There was a chance of averting bloodshed by appealing to those forces, whereas Seward's plea was a dead letter before the ink was dry.

To sum up, the search for complete adequacy is, first and last, the only general rule for good writing. Try to find out what you mean—what you would go to the stake for—and put it down without frills or apologetic gestures. Exhaust the means of literary expression, and you will produce sentences that parse and move and carry

---

[7] *The Collected Works of Abraham Lincoln*, ed. Roy P. Basler, 9 vols., New Brunswick, N.J., 1953–1955, 4:261, n. 99.

[8] *Ibid.*, 271.

the ring of your voice. Keep your eye constantly on your subject—that portion occupying your field of vision at the moment—and you will achieve, in addition to ease and lucidity, force. Contrary to common belief, this trinity of virtues does not mean that sentences must bark, or be cast in the same mold, or remain drearily declarative. Nor does keeping the subject ever in view mean that the writer's own personality vanishes. It mingles, rather, with every phrase he sets down, yet without interposing a thick mist of ego between the reader and the page.

Examine, by way of conclusion and summary of our suggestions, the following paragraph, taken from an English scholar's introduction to a volume of letters. Notice how much information is amassed and conveyed without being thrust at the reader; and respond also to the quiet working of a style in which no word is wasted and through which the native impulses of an urbane mind are revealed:

Saint Evremond admits that the company of his friends and their conversation were more important to him than his writings, which occupied his time only when there was nothing better to do. Like his contemporaries at the courts of Louis XIV and Charles II, he regarded literature as one of the necessary accomplishments of a person of quality, not as a means of earning money or reputation. And though posterity remembers him as a man of letters, he himself claimed to be remembered as a soldier first and afterwards as a courtier. For the fate of his compositions after they had left his pen he cared as little as tradition says he cared about his personal appearance in his old age. He wrote, as it has been said of another, for his own and for his friends' delight, and for the delight also, though he could not have foreseen it, of the pirate printers. They, of course, turned his carelessness to good account, and flourished on the proceeds of innumerable and horribly garbled impressions of his essays, exposed for sale on the bookstalls of London, Paris, and Amsterdam. Hitherto he has given no delight to the bibliographer, and I confess that I have profited little from an examination of a very large number of those unauthorized publications. At the same time my acquaintance with them, and with the one authentic edition of his collected works, has not altered my belief that a selection of his writings, even in translation, is worth reading, and therefore worth reprinting.[9]

[9]John Hayward, ed., *The Letters of Saint Evremond*, London, 1930, xiii.

FIGURE 17   *Questions to Ask in Writing and Revising*

I   a. Has my paper (chapter) a single informing theme, with its proper developments, or is it merely a series of loosely connected ideas and images?

   b. Does my beginning begin and does my conclusion conclude? (A beginning should not go back to the Flood, and a conclusion is not the same thing as a summing up.)

   c. Is each of my paragraphs a division with a purpose; that is, does it organize a number of sentences into a treatment of one idea and its modifications?

   d. Is each sentence contrived to stand on its own feet or is it thrown off balance by the load of qualifiers or the drag of afterthoughts?

   e. Have I made proper use of transitional words and phrases to keep all my connections clear? For example, *nevertheless, moreover, even, still, of course* (in its use of minimizing the idea before), *to be sure, admittedly.* (The transitional word or phrase is usually better in the course of the sentence than at the beginning.)

II a. What is the *tone* of my piece? Is it too stiff and too formal, trying for the effect of authority? Is it perhaps too relaxed, too familiar, too facetious? Or is it, as it should be, simple, direct?

   b. Are there any passages that I especially prize? If so, am I sure that, in my creative enthusiasm, I am not delighted with something "fancy"?

   c. Have I been conscious of the reader and have I consulted his convenience? Or have I, on the contrary, been easy only on myself and used a "private" language?

   d. Could I, if called upon to do so, explain the exact meaning and function of every word I have used? For example, *subjective, objective, realistic, impact, value, metaphor.*

   e. Are my images aids to the reader or merely ways for me to escape the difficulty of clear thought?

III a. Is it perfectly clear to which noun or noun-clause my pronouns refer? (The *slightest* ambiguity is fatal.)

   b. Have I tried to give an air of judicious reserve by repeating the words *somewhat, rather, perhaps,* and have I used for this purpose the illiterate "to an extent"? Or, conversely, have I overdone the emphatic with *very, invariably, tremendous, extraordinary,* and the like?

c. Have I arbitrarily broken or altered the idiomatic links between certain words, particularly between verbs and their allied prepositions, committing such solecisms as: *disagree . . . to, equally . . . as, prefer . . . than?*

d. Have I imported from science and disciplines in which I am interested a vocabulary out of place in civilized writing? What jargon and vogue words have slipped out by force of habit? Examples of jargon are: *integrate, area, parameter, frame of reference, methodology, in terms of, level, approach.*

e. Have I preferred the familiar word to the far-fetched? the concrete to the abstract? the single to the circumlocution? the short to the long?

14

The Arts of Quoting and Translating

Three Recurrent Tasks

Whether a researcher writes well or badly, he finds himself repeatedly quoting and citing. This is true regardless of his subject. And unless that subject is purely local, he also finds himself using sources in a foreign language, which perforce require translation.

Quoting other writers and citing the places where their words are to be found are by now such common practices that it is pardonable to look upon the habit as natural, not to say instinctive. It is of course nothing of the kind, but a very sophisticated act, peculiar to a civilization that uses printed books, believes in evidence, and makes a point of assigning credit or blame in a detailed, verifiable way.[1]

Accordingly, the conventions of quoting and citing should be mastered by anyone whose work makes him a steady user of these devices. Citing is in fact so stylized and yet so adaptable to varying needs that we shall devote to it most of the next chapter. The present one will deal with the two forms of quoting—in the original and in translation. They are capable of more skillful handling than is some-

---

[1]The vagaries of quoters and misquoters are studied and illustrated by Paul F. Boller, Jr., in his *Quotemanship: The Use and Abuse of Quotations for Polemical and Other Purposes*, Dallas, 1967.

times suspected, and a study of the technique will contribute to ease
and efficiency if not to art.

The Philosophy of Quoting

The habit of quoting in nearly every kind of printed and spoken
matter and the rules for doing it are quite recent developments in
Western culture. Formerly, the practice was limited to scholars, and
was taken as a sign of the unoriginal, timid, pedantic mind. Although
Montaigne's *Essays* and Burton's *Anatomy of Melancholy* were
admired for their abundance of quaint quotations, most writers preferred to appropriate the knowledge of others and to give it out again
in their own words. Emerson, by no means an unscholarly man,
expressed a common feeling when he said: "I hate quotations. Tell
me what you know." And another scholarly New Englander, of our
century, John Jay Chapman, pointed out that what the great quoters
seize upon, they alter as they repeat it.[2]

The views of these two American writers should be kept in mind,
not as a bar to quotation or as a license to quote inaccurately,[3] but as a
reminder that *your* paper, *your* essay, *your* book should be primarily
your work and *your* words. What was said in Chapter 2 about taking
notes through assimilation and rewording holds good on the larger
scale of the finished work. If you have not made other people's
knowledge your own by mixing it with your thoughts and your labor
of recomposition, you are not a writer but a compiler; you have not
written a report but done a scissors-and-paste job.

And the chief defect of such an evasion of responsibility is that
the piece will probably be tedious to read and lacking in force and
light. Many writers of master's essays and doctoral dissertations think
that what is expected of them is a string of passages from other
authors, tied together with: "on this point he said: . . ." and "in reply,

[2]*Lucian, Plato, and Greek Morals*, Boston, 1931, 3–4.

[3]But as H. W. Fowler says in his *Modern English Usage* under "Misquotation":
"The misquoting of phrases that have survived on their own merits out of little-read
authors . . . is a very venial offence; and indeed it is almost a pedantry to use the true
form instead of so established a wrong one; it would be absurd to demand that no one
should ever use a trite quotation without testing its verbal accuracy."

he stated: . . ." These are varied with: "Six months later, Thomson declared: . . ." and "Jennings thereupon differed as follows: . . ." The effect is of an unbearable monotony. Every page looks like a bad club sandwich—thin layers of dry bread barely enclosing large chunks of some heavy solid.

Unfit for handling, the sandwich falls apart, and the reason is easy to see: unless your words and your thoughts predominate in your work, you lose control of your "story." The six or eight people whom you quote in any given section had different purposes from yours when they wrote, and you cannot make a forward-moving whole out of their disjointed fragments. This fact of experience gives rise to the first principle of the art of quoting: *Quotations are illustrations, not proofs.* The proof of what you say is the whole body of facts and ideas to which you refer, that is, to which you *point.* From time to time you give a *sample* of this evidence to clinch your argument or to avail yourself of a characteristic or felicitous utterance. But it is not the length, depth, or weight of your quotations that convinces your reader.[4]

Two rules of thumb follow from the principle just enunciated: (1) Quotations must be kept short, and (2) they must as far as possible be merged into the text. The form of quoting that we have just used in introducing these two rules—stopping dead, a colon, and a new sentence—is convenient in books of instruction; it is awkward in writing that describes, argues, or narrates. Far better is the form that we use in the next line and that incorporates into your sentence "that portion of the author's original words which [you] could not have put more concisely" without losing accuracy.

Longer quotations than this cannot, of course, be inserted entire into your own sentence, but your words can lead to the brink of the other author's remarks and, *with or without an ushering verb, can make the two speakers produce one effect,* like singers in a duet. Consider a passage from the biography of a famous English trial lawyer, in which the author wants to make use of an important letter:

[4]An apparent exception to this rule occurs when you try to prove a point by reproducing documents. The exception is only apparent, because documents that are longer than a couple of pages should be relegated to an appendix and only discussed or quoted from in the text.

He was bitterly disappointed when his old friend Clavell Salter was given the first vacancy. "I am told that S. is to be recommended," he wrote to Lord Edmund Talbot, "Well, he is a splendid chap and a great friend of mine of thirty years standing. I think he will tell you he owes much to me in the early days . . ." The letter is that of a bitterly disappointed man, and ends with a prophecy about his future, which came almost exactly true. "Well, I am fifty-nine; if my health lasts, I suppose I can enjoy another ten years hard work at the Bar." Within a few months of ten years after the date of the letter he died, almost in harness. Shortly after this disappointment he was approached as to the writing of his memoirs and he discussed the project and even wrote a few pages. "What will you call the book?" he was asked. "Better call it *The Story of a Failure*," he said sadly, and laid aside his pen.[5]

If instead of this running narrative and commentary, the biographer had used the lazy way of heralding each quoted remark with "he said" or one of its variants, we should have halted and started and halted and started at least four times. Notice that the method of Merged Quotation here recommended has the advantage of preventing the kind of repetition that *Punch* once picked up from the London *Times*:

Land at Freshwater, Isle of Wight, is being prepared as a rocket-motor testing site, the Ministry of Supply said yesterday. "This land is being prepared for the ground testing of rocket motors," a Ministry official explained.
"Clear now?" asked *Punch*.

Whole books have been composed on the system of repetition, especially in graduate schools. When the candidate has collected his material, he "writes it up" by the simple process of (1) announcing what the quotation implies, (2) giving the quotation, and (3) rehashing what has just been said. To the reader this is death in triplicate. To the author, who has to pay for the typing and possibly the printing, it is a great waste. Knowing how to quote might have reduced the bulk of paper and wordage by more than a third; for what we have called the merged quotation is usually docked of head and tail—only the body of it plays its part in *your* presentation.

A final caveat: a researcher must quote only what he has himself read (or heard), and he must weigh carefully his choice of source

[5]Edward Marjoribanks, *The Life of Sir Edward Marshall Hall*, London, 1929, 377.

when variant texts present themselves. It is a shortcut but rarely an advantage to use another writer's quotation as one's own; the risks are not worth the time saved. Experienced editors of learned journals estimate that as many as fifteen percent of all footnotes contain errors of one kind or another in the average article even of careful scholars. And the texts of quotations are probably no more accurate.

The Mechanics of Quotation

Certain forms must, as we said, always be observed in quoting. The modern quotatiousness that has made everybody aware of whose words are which, and that comes out in the announcer's ". . . and I quote . . ." (or the careless speaker's "quote . . . unquote") has made us all slaves to a common reporting system.[6] But its mechanics have a spiritual meaning: the system became universal because people saw the value of respecting a man's *ipsissima verba*, because they acquired some notion of the influence of context upon meaning, and finally because the recognition of rights in literary property made "crediting" necessary.

The most important conventions that rule the quoting of words in print have been exemplified in the last three pages, as well as earlier in this book. We can now set them down in a row, with a few suggestions:

1. A quotation is introduced and closed by double quotation marks. A quotation within a quotation carries single quotation marks, and a third internal quotation, if required, brings double ones again.

2. The omission of a word, phrase, or sentence is shown by three dots. If that omission comes at the end of a sentence, the fourth dot that you will observe in some quoted material stands for the period at the end of the original sentence.

3. If intelligibility requires the addition of a word or short phrase (seldom more), the added words should be enclosed in square

---

[6]There is no necessity for either of these verbal devices; they are affectation based on the formality of the written word. Moreover, "unquote" is nonsense probably born of confusion with "end quote." See Follett, *Modern American Usage*, "quote, unquote," 270–271.

brackets.[7] These words will generally be possessive adjectives—for example, [her], [your]—or the definite article [the], or a pair of words expanding a pronoun, such as an "it" in a quotation that would be unintelligible without an antecedent. One replaces this "it" with: [the document], or some such unmistakable substitute. One may also supply a word where ambiguity might result from the lack of a context: see the word [court] in the quotation on p. 302.

4. The spelling, capitalization, and punctuation of the quoted passage must be faithfully reproduced unless (a) you modernize these features when quoting ancient texts, in which case you state your principles at some convenient point; or (b) you correct an obvious typographical or other error, in which case a footnote is required to draw attention to the change. If you wish to draw attention to an error without correcting it, put [sic] after it in square brackets.

5. An extension of the foregoing rule accounts for the familiar tag at the end of a quotation: [My italics.] It is perhaps a shade less obtrusive to use the phrase "Italics added"; in any case, a writer should not make a practice of sprinkling italics over other people's prose. If you choose your quotation with forethought and *set it with care* within your own remarks, it will generally not need the italicizing of words to make its point. If on rereading you think the force of the quotation somehow does not make itself felt, try cutting down the quoted words to those that actually contain the point. Then you will not have to underline them in order to make them stand out.

6. The quoting of titles and the like in the text is more properly called "citing" and this sometimes presents small problems. But note at the outset the second invariable rule of modern scholarship:[8] all book titles are printed in italics (words underlined in typescript), and all essay titles are enclosed within double quotation marks.[9]

Apart from this convention, a question sometimes arises as to the wording of the title to be cited. Readers feel a certain awkwardness in reading: "This he achieved in his *When Knighthood Was in*

[7]In legal scholarship, brackets are put around any capital letter that is supplied by the quoter when he changes the grammatical role of a word. This is rarely necessary in history- or report-writing.

[8]For the first, see Chapter 2, p. 27.

[9]Some periodicals devoted to book reviewing dislike the appearance of frequent italics in their pages and require book titles to be named within quotation marks. This practice does not lessen the importance of the rule or the unanimity with which it is observed in the world of research.

Flower." The remedy for this is simple: omit the "his," which adds
nothing to the meaning. If once in a while the possessive adds a
nuance, insert a cushion word or phrase, for example, "in his popular
tale," or "in his next novel," or more flatly: "in his book, *When*, etc."

The penchant for merging is a by-product of the desire to write
good sentences. This is so strong in good writers that they cut off the
A and *The* of a title that they cite in running text: "Motley's *Rise of
the Dutch Republic.*" This practice is sensible and long established,
but if you follow it, take care that you do not subtly alter the author's
intention. He may have been scrupulously exact in putting *A* in front
of his subject to show that his conclusions are tentative; for instance:
AN *Economic Interpretation of the Constitution* by Charles A. Beard.
Conversely, an acknowledged master may at the end of his life bring
out THE *Theory of the Cell*, that is, the complete and fully organized
view of the subject, which fears no rivals for none exist.

Except for these significant uses, the grammatical role of the
definite and indefinite articles can be taken by other words: Samuel
Smiles's *Life of George Stephenson, Railway Engineer.* We lose nothing by the omission, but watch again: we fall into gibberish if having
properly elided a redundant article in one place we begin to use the
decapitated title as if it were complete; do *not* write: "He then
published *Life of George Stephenson*, etc."; any more than you would
write: "Motley worked nine years on *Rise of the Dutch Republic.*"
The use of "a" and "the" in all contexts is a delicate measure of a
writer's sensitivity to what he is talking about.

7. There should be firmer rules than actually exist about the
right to quote. Legal doctrine is on this point indefinite, for all it says
is that "fair use" is allowed. "Fair use" covers most scholarly and
critical quoting, but it sets no clear limits to the amount that may be
quoted without special permission. Hence the demand of most publishers that the author of a manuscript ask permission of the copyright
holders for each of his quotations. But do you ask for six words?
Obviously not. Some publishers allow passages of 250 to 500 words to
be quoted without permission having to be asked. This latitude is
sometimes stated on the copyright page: look there for the exact
wordage granted free.

All American university presses allow one another's authors a
thousand words on the "no permission needed" principle. For the
rest, you must write and ask the publisher, giving the length, opening

and closing words, and page references of the passage you want to quote, and also the name of your own publisher. Allow plenty of time before your publication date, for you may have to write to the author or to a third party—the owner of the copyright—to whom the publisher will refer you. Most British authors will express surprise at your wanting a written permission for what they do every day without let or hindrance. In this country it is otherwise, and one must be particularly careful about quoting words from popular songs as well as poetry.

"Credit" should naturally be given for every quotation, but there is no need to be overcome by gratitude: you are keeping an author's thought and fame alive when you quote and name him, and for this he is in your debt. Some publishers will specify for your acknowledgment a formula of their own, occasionally quite long and in a style reminiscent of funerary inscriptions. They insist that its use is compulsory, but open a current book and you will see that thanks are given in a lump to all copyright owners on an acknowledgment page, or that each is named briefly at the point where his material is used.

In citing and crediting authors, you must, as in all other phases of research and writing, use judgment. Many obvious quotations need no author's name. For instance, if you are so unadventurous that you find yourself quoting "To be or not to be," leave the author in decent obscurity. If you quote for a purely decorative purpose an anecdote that is going the rounds and that you found in your local newspaper, or a trifling news item from the same source, no reference is needed to the place and date (see the extract from *Punch* above). Remember, in other words, that quoting is for illustration and that citing is for possible verification. What is illustrative but unimportant (and in any case not likely to have been garbled or forged) will not need to be verified. It would therefore be pedantry to refer the reader to its source. Like Emerson, he wants you to tell him what you know.

Difficulties and Dangers of Translation

When what you want to tell your reader is the opinion of a foreign authority, your wish to quote carries with it the duty to translate. We will assume that you can read the language you intend to quote from.

But this is the least of the prerequisites, even though the opinion is widespread that anyone who knows two languages can translate from the one into the other. Nothing could be further from the truth.[10] The result of this fallacious belief is that readers and critics are forever complaining of the unreadable matter palmed off on them as translations, and that the principles of the art of translating are unsuspected or ignored by those most in need of them—authors, publishers, journalists, researchers, and students generally.

In a world whose inhabitants are more and more involved with one another across the frontiers of politics and language, it is obvious that translation is a daily necessity. Yet good translators being scarce, the world's work is hampered or spoiled by mistranslation. This leads on occasion to grave misunderstanding and does nothing to allay any preexisting friction. The problem at its simplest often occurs between the two branches of what we still think of as one language, namely English and American. According to Churchill, the word "table," in "tabling a motion," plunged an important war council into a "long and even acrimonious discussion," because the Americans took "table" to mean indefinite postponement, whereas the English understood it to mean "put down for subsequent discussion."[11] Again, the familiar words of science and technology, many of which are international, sometimes mislead through unexpected overlappings or false similarities, as when the French *éther* is made to stand for both "ether" and "ester."

Such misunderstandings define the first duty of the translator: he must thoroughly understand the meaning of the words in his origi-

---

[10]An extreme yet frequent example is that of the person who, because he reads and understands a foreign language, thinks he can write it. Some years ago, an Italian publisher of scholarly books sent to his American patrons a magnificently printed and illustrated folder announcing a new edition of a medieval text. The description in "English" was all in this style:

Indispensable and basic to those who deal Dante's problems of Midiaeval Mysticism, *The Book of the Figures*, consisting in two volumes cloth bound and with superior cut gilt, reproduces the Reggian Codex and the other one, analogous, of Oxford, with very rich colour tables, which offer to the studious Enquirers a limpid Historical Document. . . . This new Edition will gain new consensus, especially out of Italy.

The fact that we can make out the drift of these remarks does not make them a translation of the original thought.

[11]See G. V. Carey, *American into English: A Handbook for Translators*, London, 1953, 1 and 87; and Norman W. Schur, *British Self-Taught*, New York, 1973.

nal—not their general purport, but their precise meaning. The researcher in his guise of translator must once again be a critical reader of words, a haggler over shades of meaning. The shorter the passage to be translated the more important is this hairline exactitude, for the occasional errors in a long work tend to be corrected by the context, whereas a single quotation eight lines long affords the reader no such corrective.

Let us suppose that the scholar, reporter, or technician has learned in one or more foreign tongues all the words in his special vocabulary; he is still far from fully equipped. For "what the original means" is not the same thing as "knowing the meaning of every word." It is words together that create meaning and give a statement its peculiar tone and clear implications. Take a phrase that recurs in political declarations coming from France. A quite simple statement by a minister in office will begin with: "*Je sais bien que. . . .*" Now throughout the English and American press this will be translated as either "I know well that . . ." or "I well know that. . . ." Neither sounds quite right, for English or American speakers do not commonly say those words. What they *do* say that is vaguely connected with the original French is the somewhat accusing: "You know very well that [you leaked the story]." In the first person singular the same expression conveys a different shade: "I know very well [what I did]"; which implies: "and it isn't what you think." But none of these phrases corresponds to the French. What then are those Frenchmen babbling about when they say "*Je sais bien que . . .*"? What is the force of *bien*, and how do we translate it? *Bien* has nothing to do with the literal "well" and it must be translated: "of course." What the original says is what we say when we begin with a concessive "Of course, I know [that this has already been tried, *but . . .*]."

Dictionaries and False Friends

The second rule of translation is that to ascertain the meaning of words as we are bidden by the first rule, we must go beyond the immediate dictionary meaning of the word to the significance of its role in the sentence. As an expert lexicographer puts it about *bien* in a handbook for translators, "it is only exceptionally that it should be translated 'well,'"[12] and he gives half a column of examples and equivalents.

What is true of all these troublesome little words in every language—*doch* in German, *più* in Italian, *más* in Spanish—is true in a different way of the connotations of abstract and important words. You cannot be sure that when you have the denotation firmly in mind you also have the right connotation. Worse, you will find that words coming from the same root have had different histories in two or more languages and have diverged completely. A dais in English is a platform; in French it is a canopy. A person described as *constipado* in Spanish merely has a cold. A *Friseur* in Germany will not curl or frizz your hair but will cut it.

A subtle and vexatious example of the same shifting of sense in diplomacy came to light at the League of Nations after the First World War. The French *contrôle* was frequently translated "control" until it appeared that in French the word means "supervise, pass upon, *have a voice in the control of*," while in English it means "govern completely." Thus a French conductor who punches your ticket is a *contrôleur*; this is etymologically correct, since the root of the word is *contre-rôle*, a counter-roll or, as we now say, a checklist.[13]

To enforce the lesson by sticking to French, one may cite a few of the commonest words that have become traps for the heedless in the translation of legal and diplomatic documents, and most frequently in newspaper accounts: *admettre* does not always mean "admit," as in "*Le gouvernement ne peut pas admettre que . . .*" where the meaning is a softened "allow," "tolerate"—"The government will not grant that. . . ." Again, goods that are described as *en provenance des États-Unis* do not necessarily "originate" in the United States; they are merely being shipped from there. Once an Anglo-French committee was stumped by the description of a proposed course of action as *fastidieux*. It soon appeared that "fastidious" was nowhere near the

---

[12] J. G. Anderson, *Le Mot Juste: An Anglo-French Lexicon*, London, 1932, 44. A revised edition was brought out by L. C. Harmer in 1938.

[13] The French meaning occurs in English in the single phrase "control experiment," which is a check upon other work, with no idea of "control" in the ordinary sense.

meaning, which indeed could not be guessed by inspection, since it turns out to be "wearisome," "dull and fatiguing." Finally, there are tricky words such as *ressentir*, which as a verb means simply "feel" or "experience," with no notion of animus as in our "resent," but which as the noun *ressentiment* does carry the notion of anger or rancor, even more strongly than does "resentment." Such are the pitfalls of language.[14]

It follows that every translator needs all the help he or she can get from (1) dictionaries, (2) special lexicons and manuals for translators, (3) extensive reading in as many languages as possible, (4) a studious pursuit of etymology and word connections, and (5) the advice of educated native speakers of the language from which he is likely to translate.

Except for traveling light, a pocket dictionary is worthless. If you are going to translate correctly you need the best foreign-English dictionary in the particular language *and* a reliable all-foreign dictionary in that language. The best bilingual dictionaries of the modern tongues are those that (1) give long lists of equivalents whenever possible, (2) supplement these with examples of use in sentences, and (3) have been revised by scholars within the last quarter-century.

In addition to dictionaries you should try to own or to consult the special works referred to under 2 two paragraphs above, which attempt to explain the differences that lurk under similarity, the so-called "false friends" that suggest a meaning belied by the fact. Such books do not exist for all languages, but a few can be found, though they are not to be thought free from imperfections.[15] A steady reader in a foreign language will make up his own small-scale lexicon as he notices the endless oddities of foreigners' speech and his own.

[14]The consequences of missing the nuances or supplying gratuitous ones in the translating of diplomatic documents are patent. But the problem rarely comes to public attention as it did when the United States, through Ambassador Edwin O. Reischauer, formally persuaded the Japanese government to change its official translation of the word "containment," the well-known description of American policy toward world communism during the Cold War. The Japanese had long been using the word *fujikome*, which Reischauer, an outstanding student of the Japanese language, regarded as having a connotation of aggressiveness, calling up, as it does, the picture of a bulldozer at work. The Japanese Ministry of Foreign Affairs finally changed the translation to *sekitome*, a milder word meaning simply "to check" or "to dam" (*New York Times*, May 29, 1966).

[15]See the list in the section "For Further Reading" on p. 431.

Literalism and Paraphrase

The successful reader in foreign languages will also be interested in everything he encounters that bears on translation. There is, for example, a lively little book by the late Monsignor Ronald Knox that deals with the difficulties and controversies he ran into when translating the Bible.[16] Now the Bible may be all Greek and Hebrew to you, but in these essays by Knox you come upon illuminating remarks that are applicable to translating to or from any language. For example:

> Among the many good things Mr. Belloc has done . . . is a little brochure . . . on Translation. The great principle he there lays down is that the business of a translator is not to ask "How shall I make this foreigner talk English?" but "What would an Englishman have said to express this?" For instance, he says, if you are faced with the French sentence, *"Il y avait dans cet homme je ne sais quoi de suffisance,"* you do not want to write "There was in this man I know not what of self-sufficiency"; you want to write, "There was a touch of complacency about him. . . ."
> Anybody who has really tackled the business of translation, at least where the classical languages are concerned, will tell you that the bother is not finding the equivalent for this or that word, it is finding how to turn the sentence. . . .
> The translator, let me suggest in passing, must never be frightened of the word "paraphrase"; it is a bogey of the half-educated. As I have already tried to point out, it is almost impossible to translate a *sentence* without paraphrasing; it is a paraphrase when you translate "Comment vous portez-vous?" by "How are you?"[17]

This last caution is worth expanding a little in order to banish once for all the fear that many writers and researchers have of being wrong when they depart from the word-by-word contents of their original. The term "paraphrase" frightens them because they know that a paraphrase from English verse to English prose entails a loss of meaning; you cannot paraphrase the soliloquies in *Hamlet* and say: "This is the equivalent of Shakespeare's meaning." It can only be a rough approximation. But in translating from a foreign language, what is loosely called paraphrasing is the only wording that deserves to be called a translation, no other being possible. To reinforce the

[16] *On Englishing the Bible*, London, 1949.
[17] *Ibid.*, 4 and 12.

Belloc example above, take the French expression: *"C'est une autre paire de manches."* The *only* possible translation of those words is: "That's a horse of another color." Plainly, none of the significant words has received its normal equivalent. The French says nothing about horses or their color; it talks of a pair of sleeves. But the horse is no "paraphrase" of the sleeves; it is their correct equivalent. To put into English each word separately would be to write nonsense.[18] Take it as an absolute rule that translation occurs not between words but between meanings. Father Knox gives the example of *en effet*, which he finds everybody translating "in effect" when the meaning is not in the least "in effect" but "sure enough"—no paraphrase, but an exact rendering of the force of the two French words.

What all these warning examples boil down to is this: *Accurate translating requires, in addition to a transfer of the full contents, a transfer of the full intention that goes with them.* This is of the utmost importance whenever a rhetorical device occurs in the original, such as irony, which conveys the opposite of what is actually said. When Thomas Nugent in the eighteenth century translated Montesquieu's *Spirit of Laws*, he completely missed the irony in a famous passage about slavery; so completely, that he felt called upon to add a footnote of apology for the great author who, although enlightened, still defended the institution. The apology should have been addressed to the great author who was being thus misrepresented. Such blunders inspired the Italian proverb *"Traduttore, traditore"*—"A translator is a traitor."

The Act of Carrying Over, *or Translation*

The researcher is of course doing his best to be the very reverse of a traitor. His motto is Fidelity first and foremost. But for lack of good advice and a sound tradition, fidelity has been misconstrued into Literalism. Literalism dismisses responsibility toward the original with an implied shrug—"that's what it says!" There is no "it." There is a foreign mind, and there is yours, charged with the duty of

[18]For an enjoyable lesson on this point, and the humor to be drawn from willfully forgetting it, read in Mark Twain's "Private History of the 'Jumping Frog' Story" the portion that gives in English his impression of the French version of the tale.

reexpressing what that mind thought. This second capacity depends upon your mastery of your own language. For unless you can discriminate between shades of meaning and turns of phrase in your native tongue, you will be blind and deaf to their counterparts in the text that is waiting to be transported into corresponding forms. If you cannot summon up half a dozen related expressions to render the spirit of the original, the letter of it will show through; you will be giving not a translation but a transliteration. At times, to be sure, you may want to tell your readers the exact word or phrase used by the author you are translating; this you do by reproducing it italicized in parentheses. But your prose should give his *thought*.

A rough way to define true translating would be to say that a certain sentence in a foreign language contained, over and above its cargo of information, eleven additional points or features—an alliteration, a play on words, a rhythmical halt, an allusion to a famous poem, a colloquial turn, a long learned word where a short common one was expected, and so on. The able translator, noting these points, will try to reproduce somewhere in his version each element or effect in his own language. Not until he has exhausted its resources—which really means *his* resources—will he consider the original sentence to have been carried over, that is, translated.

Some examples of successive attempts at this perfection of rendering will make the task and its method clear. Our first example will again be from the French, the language that, as translators agree, is of all the leading European languages the most unlike English in the movement of its thought and the most deceptively like English in its vocabulary. As such, it combines in the highest degree the two difficulties that must be met in every piece of translation. The following passage comes from a work which has been twice translated in our century, and which would benefit from a third effort that would retain the happy turns of the previous two. Here is the original:

Un des plus grands personnages de ce temps-là, un des hommes les plus marquants dans l'Église et dans l'État, nous a conté, ce soir (janvier 1822), chez Mme de M . . . , les dangers fort réels qu'il avait courus du temps de la Terreur.

"J'avais eu le malheur d'être au nombre des membres les plus marquants de l'Assemblée constituante: je me tins à Paris, cherchant à me cacher tant bien que mal, tant qu'il y eut quelque espoir de succès pour la bonne cause. Enfin,

les dangers augmentant et les étrangers ne faisant rien de'énergique pour nous, je me déterminai à partir, mais il fallait partir sans passeport."[19]

In 1915 this was translated as follows:

One of the most important persons of our age, one of the most prominent men in the Church and in the State, related to us this evening (January, 1822), at Madame de M——'s, the very real dangers he had gone through under the Terror.

"I had the misfortune to be one of the most prominent members of the Constituent Assembly. I stayed in Paris, trying to hide myself as best I could, so long as there was any hope of success for the good cause. At last, as the danger grew greater and greater, while the foreigner made no energetic move in our favour, I decided to leave—only I had to leave without a passport."[20]

A dozen years later an anonymous version, said to have been done under the supervision of the well-known translator, C. K. Scott-Moncrieff, appeared in New York and has since been reprinted in a popular series. It is on the whole less accurate than the first. Our passage comes out in this form:

One of the most illustrious persons of his time, and one of the foremost men in both Church and State affairs, told us this evening (January 1822), at Madame M's house, some of the very real dangers he had run at the time of the Terror.

"I had had the misfortune to be one of the most important members of the Constituent Assembly: I remained in Paris, trying to hide myself as best I might, so long as there was any hope of success for the good cause. At last, as the dangers were increasing and other countries were making no effort to help us, I decided to leave, but I had no passport."[21]

The meaning of the original is simple and the text presents no grammatical difficulty; the reader of the English "understands" it, as he thinks, through and through. Nevertheless some points are in doubt, since at those points the meaning has struck two pairs of

---

[19]Stendhal [Henri Beyle], *De l'Amour*, "Fragments Divers," (1822), 166.

[20]Translation by Philip and Cecil N. Sidney Woolf, London and New York, 1915, 329.

[21]Translation by H.B.V., New York, 1927; Black and Gold Edition, New York, 1947, 341.

translators rather differently. Quite apart from the resulting hesitation, the reader may feel that he would like to know what the "good cause" is which both translate literally. Could closer attention to nuance achieve greater fidelity? Let us try, adding explanatory comments and signposts as we go:

> One of the greatest figures [*not* "persons" and *not* "illustrious"] of this age ["his age" would conflict with what follows], *who is* [needed for the sentence to sound English] among the foremost men *in Church and State* [English idiom], told us at Madame de M's this evening (January 1822) [the natural English order for Place and Time is to put the shorter modifier first] *about* the very real dangers to which he had been exposed [one *runs* a risk but not a danger] during the Terror.
>
> "I had [the pluperfect is literal but throws us off] the misfortune of being *among the foremost* [phrase repeated from above, as in the original] members of the *National Assembly* [the more familiar name in English, little used in French]. I *hung on* in Paris [= the true force of the original], trying to hide [*not* 'hide myself,' which suggests children playing] *in one way or another* [*not* 'as best I could,' which goes without saying], so long as there was any hope of success for *our cause* [that is, the 'good cause' was naturally his own, but it is also that of the people he is addressing]. At last, the danger increasing [singular, since he is not counting but gauging] while the foreign powers [*not* 'countries,' which is weak, nor 'the foreigner,' which is vague] *were taking no strong action* in our behalf, I *made up my mind* ['decided' gives no sense of a gradual resolution] to leave—only, [comma essential; otherwise the sentence means 'no one but I'] I had to leave without a passport." [Here as elsewhere the second translator omits a whole idea.]

Now if ten quite simple lines are capable of improvement by the application of a little critical thought, it is easy to imagine how much attention long and complex passages require. Our shelves are full of works in "famous" translations that yet contain page after page of gibberish—the gibberish that comes of a "careful" literalism. For examples of this fatal fault, one has only to leaf through the two volumes of Henry Reeve's well-known translation of Tocqueville's *Democracy in America*. Here is the beginning of Chapter 2:

> A man has come into the world; his early years are spent without notice in the pleasures and activities of childhood. As he grows up, the world receives him when his manhood begins, and he enters into contact with his

fellows. He is then studied for the first time, and it is imagined that the germ of the vices and the virtues of his maturer years is then formed.[22]

The Necessity of Knowing English

This innocent nonsense should be enough to dispel the illusion that French is an "easy" language, to which almost anything vaguely intelligible is a good enough equivalent. No language is easy; all translation is hard. But both grow easier with practice and become an interesting challenge to the person who is, to begin with, eager to express his own thoughts with lucidity. For translation *is* writing your own thoughts. True, you have just borrowed them from another mind; you have overheard, so to speak, a secret spoken by a foreign agent. Your concentration upon it makes you aware of its effect as a whole and in parts—this depends on your knowledge of the foreign tongue. And the total awareness inspires you to reproduce somehow every one of the effects—this depends on your knowledge of your own tongue. It follows that one can translate faithfully only from a language one knows like a native into a language one knows like a practiced writer.

An example from the German, again comparing two translations, will show what the second requirement means. Goethe tells in his autobiography how in his eighth year he and his family were much excited by the outbreak of the Seven Years' War and the ensuing partisanship for or against Frederick the Great:

> *Und so war ich denn auch preussisch oder, um richtiger zu reden, Fritzisch gesinnt: denn was ging uns Preussen an? Es war die Persoenlichkeit des grossen Koenigs, die auf alle Gemueter wirkte. Ich freute mich mit dem Vater unserer Siege, schrieb sehr gern die Siegslieder ab, und fast noch lieber die Spottlieder auf die Gegenpartei, so platt die Reime auch sein mochten.*[23]

The "standard" translation, originally by John Oxenford reads as follows:

---

[22]Alexis de Tocqueville, *Democracy in America*, the Henry Reeve Text, as revised by Francis Bowen, further corrected and edited by Phillips Bradley, New York, 1945, 1:26.

[23]Goethe, *Dichtung und Wahrheit*, Book 2, paragraph 4.

So it was that my sympathies were on the side of Prussia, or more accurately, of Fritz; what, after all, was Prussia to us? It was the personality of the great King that impressed everyone. I rejoiced with my father in our conquests, willingly copied the songs of victory, and perhaps yet more willingly the lampoons directed against the other side, poor as the rhymes might be.[24]

The three people who had a hand in this did not satisfy at least one modern reader, who produced a new version during the Second World War. The passage occurs there in this form:

And so my views were Prussian, or, to speak more correctly, those of Frederick, for what did we care about Prussia? It was the personality of the great King which moved all hearts; I rejoiced with my father over our victories, most readily copied out the songs of triumph and almost more readily the lampoons against the other party, however poor the rhymes might be.[25]

In this pair of renderings almost the only part that seems assured is: "It was the personality of the great King." As for the rest, in either version, the least that can be said is that it does not come up to the jauntiness of the original. Here we have the old poet looking back on the first enthusiasm of his childhood, recalling a distant hero worship, half-political, half-poetical; how shall we express it when he has done it so well in the simplest, clearest German? We can only try—and very likely fail:

And so here I was, a regular Prussian, or to put it more exactly a Fritz man: for what did Prussia mean to us? It was the personality of the great King that captured the imagination. With my father I gloried in our victories. I eagerly made copies of the songs of triumph, and still more eagerly, perhaps, of the songs that mocked the other side, no matter how lame their verse.

So much for the goals of fullness and felicity. A peculiar danger the researcher must guard against when he has been plunged for some time in foreign sources is the inability to distinguish between the idiom he understands "like a native" and his own. This failing

---

[24]*Poetry and Truth*, a revised translation based on that of John Oxenford and A.S.W. Morrison, revised by Minna Steele Smith, London, 1913, 1:35.

[25]R. O. Moon, *Goethe's Autobiography*, Washington, D.C., 1949, 34.

overcomes even the best translators and produces those odd passages we encounter in scholarly and other books. For example, a writer on French political parties will speak of "the militants" who attended a meeting, meaning "the rank and file"; or again, a student of Italian culture will write "The Illuminism" instead of "The Enlightenment"; just as a reporter on contemporary German life may slip into the habit of piling up adjectives in front of his nouns ("an easy-to-suspect assertion") without noticing that in coining such expressions he is Germanizing at variance with the genius of the English language.

The safeguard against this excessive adaptability of the mind is to translate in three steps: (1) a rough draft, quickly made with the original at hand; (2) a second draft, some days later, with the original out of sight: if you find a strange combination of English words, a twisted idiom, replace it by what the sense and the language require; (3) a third and possibly final draft, for which you consult the original, phrase by phrase, to make sure that *all the ideas and implications have found a place somewhere in your version.* Then, perhaps, you have a piece of prose that may pass for a translation.[26]

[26]The mechanical problems of translating coinage and weights and measures, and of transliterating Russian, Chinese, and other proper names, are so special and varied that they cannot be taken up in a book dealing with fundamentals. Current practice, moreover, is chaotic. Whereas the Chinese have recently adopted *pinyin*, a sensible system of equivalent letters that show how to pronounce, say, Mao Ze-dong, our printers do not apply it to established former spellings, e.g., Chiang Kai-shek, which is sounded Jyung Kyshek. Lately, too, the familiar Koran has begun to appear as Qur'ān and Mohammed as Muḥammad, with a meaningless dot under the *h*. Names transliterated from Russian, Polish, Hungarian, and Turkish continue to defy reason, in deference to an imaginary accuracy which is nothing better than pedantry.

15

The Rules of Citing:
Footnotes and Bibliography

Types and Functions of Footnotes

An important double biography of Benedict Arnold and Major André was originally issued with an announcement to the purchaser: "Source references available on request from the publishers, in a pamphlet designed to be affixed to the book."[1] By mailing a postcard to the publishers, one received a booklet of twenty-five pages, a package of footnotes. Passing over the question of where the library reader of the book would seek its documentation when the booklet was mislaid or out of print, we turn at once to the larger question: What are footnotes for? Are they a standard accessory of every good work other than fiction or are they optional for both the writer and the reader?

Footnotes are of two kinds. The first explains an assertion in the body of your work and is therefore reading matter. This kind of footnote is used when the elucidation or elaboration of a remark in the text itself would break the thread of the story, or otherwise divert the attention of the reader. Such comments and sidelights are sometimes so numerous and full that they take more space than the

[1]James T. Flexner, *The Traitor and the Spy*, New York, 1953.

357

statements they supplement. This abuse should be avoided, for, as one facetious objector pointed out, "it is quite a chore to keep focussing up and down the page, especially if you have old eyes or a touch of astigmatism."[2] Yet it would be wrong to outlaw this form of running commentary. When skillfully used it serves to fill out the narrative with details that would clog the mainstream but that greatly enrich the understanding of leisurely and reflective readers.[3] There is no warrant for the maxim "if it's important, put it in the text; if it's not, leave it out altogether." The danger to avoid is that of writing, in a succession of long footnotes, a separate book or article running parallel to the first.

The form of the explanatory footnote is simple: it consists of declarative sentences, usually in a more conversational tone than the rest of the book, like a stage aside. For example, in the main text of *The Age of the Great Depression*, Dixon Wecter wrote that a new magazine named *Ballyhoo* "rocketed to a two-million circulation largely by debunking the specious salesmanship of the twenties."[4] To this neutral report of fact he added the footnote: "Its creator was a disillusioned Manhattan editor and artist, Norman Anthony, but the name which *Ballyhoo* made famous was that of a fictional high-powered advertising man, one Elmer Zilch. In a chapter called 'Jackpot!' Anthony gave the history of this magazine in *How to Grow Old Disgracefully* (N.Y., 1946)."

This note, plainly, is to give diverting information that seemed to the author too detailed to find room in a paragraph surveying the years 1929–1931. The author is in effect saying that he knows more about the subject under discussion than he can relate at the pace and on the scale of his main discourse, but if you will step outside, he will extend his remarks.

Although in such works as textbooks footnotes may be unwanted, they cannot arbitrarily be ruled out even there. You may, for instance, want to give comprehensible equivalents for foreign coinage or land measures, or supply the original words of quotations trans-

---

[2]Frank Sullivan, "A Garland of Ibids for Van Wyck Brooks," *New Yorker*, 17 (April 19, 1941), 15.

[3]See, for example, Lawrence A. Cremin, *The Transformation of the School*, New York, 1961.

[4]Vol. 13 of *The History of American Life*, New York, 1927–1948, 15.

lated in your text, or furnish evidence on a subject tangential to the theme of your chapter or book, such as a four-line "identification" of a little-known character whose name is mentioned in passing. If in any kind of work your footnote is important but in danger of becoming too long, metamorphose it into an appendix, where you can take all the space you require and more adequately serve both yourself and your reader. This is what James G. Randall did in *Lincoln the President* with his illuminating information on Lincoln's relationship with Ann Rutledge.[5]

The second kind of footnote is the source reference; it records the origin of, or the authority for, a statement in the text. Footnotes of this type are used for both direct and indirect quotations. They form the main part of the "apparatus" that is said to distinguish a "work of scholarship" from a "popular work." They give us confidence in the book that displays them by announcing to the world that the "report" is open to anyone's verification. They declare in their way that the author is intellectually honest: he acknowledges his debts; and that he is democratically unassuming: the first comer can challenge him.

The form of this kind of footnote demands special attention. Though its arrangement and abbreviations may puzzle the inexperienced reader, to the informed it is a shorthand intelligible at a glance. Most readers are aware from their own observation that no method has been universally agreed upon for writing reference footnotes. Often the publisher or editor to whom you submit your work will propose or require the style used by the firm. If he does not, you will find it convenient to follow one of two widely used systems: that codified by a group of learned societies and published by the Modern Language Association;[6] or that described in the University of Chicago manual,[7] which has found wide acceptance among writers and researchers. A paperbound digest of the Chicago rules has been published by Kate L. Turabian.[8]

[5]New York, 1946–1952, 4 vols., 2:321–342.
[6]*MLA Handbook for Writers of Research Papers*, 2nd ed., New York, 1984.
[7]*The Chicago Manual of Style*, 13th ed., Chicago, 1982.
[8]*A Manual for Writers of Term Papers, Theses, and Dissertations*, 4th ed., Chicago, 1973.

Whatever the style—and the variations from one publisher to the next are slight—the principle underlying all the forms is the same; it is implicit in the purpose of the reference footnote, which is to refer you to sources. The note must be so framed that the reader can tell unfailingly the type of source cited—a manuscript or a printed article, a newspaper or a book, a letter or a conversation. These distinctions are important, for in estimating evidence sources are weighed, not counted. Each kind of source impresses the reader in a different way. For example, a magazine article is generally written with more care than a newspaper column but probably with less than a book. Other things being equal, such as authorship and place of publication, the article will be judged on this comparative rating. Similarly, a conversation may, depending on how it was recorded, prove to be less convincing than a manuscript.

Form and Forms in Footnote Writing

All these varieties of source are indicated by the typographical form of the note. If a manuscript is being cited the footnote will begin with the abbreviation "MS" (or "MSS" to show the plural):

MS Diary of Edmund Ruffin, February 17, 1857.

If the manuscript has a title it is cited in quotation marks without the label "MS":

"Big Me," William Herndon's autobiography.

A magazine article is always cited in quotation marks followed by the title of the magazine in italics:

Mrs. Kermit Roosevelt, "F.D.R., Lady Churchill, and the Brussels Sprouts," *Harper's Magazine*, 213 (August 1956), 62–64.

As we have seen (p. 342), an absolute rule in modern research is that *any printed volume referred to in a footnote appears in italics* (in typescript, underlining is the equivalent of italics).

Apart from manuscripts, which are cited as we have just shown, the use of quotation marks around a title in roman type indicates that here is a *portion* of the source that follows—a printed source, since *its* title is italicized.[9] Thus it comes about that we cite articles in magazines as we do. Note that chapter and book bear the same typographical relation as article and periodical.

Because footnotes are for convenience, the most important datum generally appears first. Most often it is the author's name that greets the reader:

> Laurence I. Barrett, *Gambling with History: Reagan in the White House*, New York, 1983.

The title of the work may come first if it is deemed more important than either the author or the editor. This is true, for instance, of encyclopedias, dictionaries, anthologies, annuals, and the like:

> *Political Handbook of the World: 1982–1983*, ed. Arthur S. Banks and William Overstreet, New York, 1983.

Sometimes the name of the editor of a work, rather than the author, should come first. This is especially to be observed when two or more collections of a man's writings are being used and must be quickly distinguishable:

> Worthington C. Ford, ed., *The Writings of George Washington*, 14 vols., New York, 1889–1893.
> John C. Fitzpatrick, ed., *The Writings of George Washington*, 39 vols., Washington, D.C., 1931–1944.

Since the use to which the notes will be put by the reader is practical—to assess or verify an assertion in the source or to seek more information from it—footnotes should never be used as ornamentation or ballast for your text. The quality and extent of your scholarship are not measured by the number of notes or by their elaborateness. Though printed outside the narrative, they are a part of your presentation, and their handling should show this. For example, it is now common practice, when you name an author and his book in the text, to use the "split footnote," which merely completes

---

[9]In learning these conventions, be sure not to confuse "printed" with "published." Many printed works found in libraries were never published, but were circulated privately.

at the bottom of the page the information given above. Footnote 5 of this chapter illustrates the split footnote. Instead of repeating "James G. Randall" and *Lincoln the President*, it merely adds where and when the book was published and the number of volumes. Although this form is relatively new in scholarly writing, it is in keeping with the same desire to conserve space, time, and words that prompted the making of conventions in the first place.

The smaller "forms" and the rules to be followed within a footnote will become second nature as you follow the instructions of a style sheet throughout your manuscript. But be sure that you know the exact meaning of the signs and abbreviations from the first time you set them down. Remember, for instance, that a colon or semi-colon or, more rarely, a comma separates a title from its subtitle:

> Alden T. Vaughan, *American Genesis: Captain John Smith and the Founding of Virginia*, Boston, 1975;

that you must cite the volume of a magazine in Arabic numerals even if it appears in Roman numerals on the publication itself:

> *Notes and Queries*, 9th Series, 8 (July–December 1901), 97–98;

that you cite the name of a newspaper in italics but not the city, which is not considered part of the title:

> Cleveland *Plain Dealer*, August 11, 1984.

Sometimes, it is true, you will find:

> *New York Times*, January 21, 1985

in order to avoid confusion with *The Times* of London. Likewise, the state is given in parentheses when the town is obscure:

> Thibodaux (La.) *Minerva*, March 1, 1856.

Remember that you put in brackets the name of an anonymous or pseudonymous author when you wish to supply it:

> "Strix" [Peter Fleming], *My Aunt's Rhinoceros and Other Reflections*, London, 1956;

that you may omit the date and place of publication, and certainly the publisher's name, when you plan to furnish them in your bibliography:

Gustavus Myers, *History of Bigotry in the United States*, 18;

that, thanks to uniform scholarly texts, the citation of the ancient authors can be given in condensed fashion, by name (and work if more than one is extant), followed by two numbers—those of the "book" (chapter) and "chapter" (paragraph):

Herodotus, 3. 14.[10]

Every one of these footnotes will be understood at sight by any well-read person. More difficult—but just as rational—are the footnotes that refer to books cited earlier in the same piece of writing. Certain Latin words, abbreviated or in full, indicate these connec-

FIGURE 18   *Roman Numerals and Their Use*

I = 1	A smaller number in front of another is	
II = 2	subtracted:	
III = 3	IV = 4	XC = 90
V = 5	IX = 9	CD = 400
X = 10	XL = 40	CM = 900
L = 50	Number(s) following another is (are) added:	
C = 100	XII = 12	LXX = 70
D = 500	XIV = 14	MD = 1500
M = 1000	XVI = 16	MDCCC = 1800
	XXX = 30	MCM = 1900

Roman numerals are less often used than formerly, but you must learn to read and write them quickly and correctly. They still serve to designate Tables, Plates, and similar "extra" matter, especially if the numbers needed are fewer than 100. Until recently, moreover, it was common practice to cite the volume number of periodicals in Roman numerals. It is usual to number the pages of "front matter" (every page before page 1 of the introduction) in Roman numerals printed in lower case (small letters), not caps: *i, vi, xiii,* etc.

In old books that use Roman numerals to give the date of publication on the title page or elsewhere, the figure *IIII* may appear instead of *IV,* as on clock faces to this day.

[10] In citing poets the second set of numbers indicates the line(s): Lucretius, 2, 121.

tions.[11] Such repeating symbols, being in a foreign tongue, are often but not always italicized. The abbreviating is done not to puzzle the layman, but (again) to save space. The resulting fragments have become an international shorthand, like musical notation or typographers' marks, and they are pronounced as written: "e.g." is *ee gee*; "op. cit." is *opp sit*; and so on.

The most commonly used is *ibid.*, which is the abbreviation of *ibidem*, meaning "in the same place." That "place" is, *and can only be*, the book cited in the footnote *immediately preceding*. For example:

[2]Hajo Holborn, *A History of Modern Germany, 1840–1945*, New York, 1969, 795.
[3]*Ibid.*, 675.

If the next footnote, number 4, then refers to a different book, and footnote 5 harks back once more to Holborn's volume, you must write "Holborn, *op. cit.*," short for *opere citato*, and meaning "in the work cited." What we have, then, is this:

[2]Hajo Holborn, *A History of Modern Germany, 1840–1945*, New York, 1969, 795.
[3]*Ibid.*, 675.
[4]George F. Kennan, *Memoirs, 1925–1950*, Boston, 1967, 130.
[5]Holborn, *op. cit.*, 799.

The perfect clarity of this arrangement will not be affected by the fact that a page may be turned between notes 2 and 3, and several pages between notes 3 and 5. But you must guard against using *op. cit.* when you cite more than one book by the same author. Each citation must unmistakably tell the reader which is meant. Suppose that you switch back and forth between Beard's *An Economic Interpretation of the Constitution of the United States* and his *Economic Origins of Jeffersonian Democracy*. These long titles will clutter your page or text if you refer to them each time in full. The remedy is to

---

[11]Recent codifiers of scholarly usage tend to prefer repeating the short title to any use of the Latin abbreviations, and indeed there are indications that the whole apparatus is being simplified as well as Anglicized. But since thousands of books use the older systems dating back as far as the seventeenth century, it behooves the researcher to learn the classic symbols and usages.

use a "short title." In this way you make clear in which Beard volume the reference given as "6" is to be found:

Beard, Economic Interpretation, 6;

and later:

Beard, Economic Origins, 302.

Occasionally it is necessary to tell the reader that in a certain work he will find almost anywhere, and not on one page rather than another, the attitude or opinion in question. This signal is given by the word *passim*, meaning "here and there":

¹For the development of the antebellum political cleavage, see Allan Nevins, *Ordeal of the Union*, New York, 1945, vol. 2, *passim*.

It hardly needs to be pointed out that if one is going to cite at all, one must use *all* these symbols and abbreviations correctly.¹² Wrongly or vaguely used they will mislead as surely as they will perform their complicated task neatly when used with precision. Moreover, you should learn the meaning of those that are obsolescent, such as "cf." for the "see" as employed in our last example, or *supra* (above) and *infra* (below).¹³ Learn all the current forms by heart and treat them as technical terms. Go to the trouble of finding out that "e.g." stands for *exempli gratia* and means "for example." It says something quite different from "i.e.," which stands for *id est* and means "that is." The one offers a random illustration; the other states an identity. To sprinkle these letters about interchangeably is comparable to what a doctor would do if he thought that "grain" and "gram" were "pretty much the same thing." No one can hope to become a professional who does not first master the minutiae.

Footnoting: When, Where, How Much?

Though the modern writer is never entirely free from the necessity of accounting for his words through footnotes, it is not he who deter-

---

¹²The commonest are listed in Figure 19 overleaf.

¹³It is well to use English equivalents, but do not imitate the writer in whose book one continually reads "See me above"; "See me below."

FIGURE 19   *Common Abbreviations*

A.D.   in the year of our Lord
(preceding the date)
A.L.S.   autograph letter
signed
anon.   anonymous
B.C.   before Christ (following
the date)
bk.   book
c., ca.   about (in dating)
cap.   capital letter
cf.   compare or see
ch., chap.   chapter
col.   column
ed.   editor, edition, edited,
edited by
e.g.   for example
et al.   and others (of persons)
etc.   and so forth (of things)
et seq.   and the following
f., ff.   and the following
page(s)
fl.   flourished (of persons)
ibid.   in the same place
id., idem   the same as before
i.e.   that is
infra   below
ital.   italics
l., ll.   line(s)
l.c.   lower-case letter

loc. cit.   in the place cited
MS, MSS   manuscript(s)
n.   note, footnote
N.B.   please note
n.d.   no date
N.S.   New Series; New Style
(of dating, since 1752)
op. cit.   in the work cited
O.S.   Old Style (of dating,
before 1752)
p., pp.   page(s)
passim   here and there
q.v.   which (or whom) see
rev.   revised, revised by,
revision
rom.   roman letter or type
sc.   to wit, namely
sic   thus (to show that an
obvious error is an exact
reproduction of the
original)
supra   above
TK   copy still to come
(in a typescript)
tr.   translation, translator,
translated (by)
v., vide   see
v., vol.   volume
viz.   namely

Some abbreviations used in books may be readily understood from the context, but a writer has to know their exact meaning before he can use them accurately. A correct understanding, of footnotes particularly, requires one to distinguish between one term or symbol and another, just as the ability to read Roman numerals at sight is necessary for the quick and errorless hunting down of references.

mines the number and fullness of these notes, but the subject in hand and the audience whose attention he hopes to hold. To the extent that footnotes communicate a part of his meaning and attest his reliability, they are as important as any other part of his writing. Hence an author should develop judgment about when and what to footnote.

All quotations that are more than passing phrases or anonymous remarks require a footnote. So do all novel or startling assertions and all distinct elements in a demonstration or argument. Beyond this, a good rule is to write a note whenever you think an alert person might feel curiosity about the source of your remarks. Do not document notorious facts, such as the date of Columbus's discovery of America or that a British force reconquered the Falkland Islands in 1982. Do not write as if the reader were convinced that you are a liar. The reader is, on the contrary, a trusting beast—at least until you shock or betray him.

He will feel betrayed when he catches you repeatedly in error, and shocked when you go against his preconceptions. A new subject consequently requires many more footnotes than a familiar one. For example, when Walter Prescott Webb wrote *The Great Plains*,[14] he was attempting to show a correlation between the development of the Plains and certain inventions. He had to give, as we say, "chapter and verse," that is, footnotes, for a quantity of things such as arms manufacturing and barbed-wire design. His materials and the pattern he wove out of them were both original. Writers on the same subject since Webb have been able to do with fewer footnotes, for the simple and sufficient reason that they can now cite Webb.

These two phases of scholarship on one and the same subject illustrate an important point: in certain circumstances, *anything* may be a source—an ad in a newspaper, an old theater program, a throw-away in a political campaign. But once scholarship has begun to work upon such materials, the published results *must* be used and cited among others of the former kind.

Similarly with great books. You should now cite by preference the scholarly edition of Thoreau's *Works*, not the casual reprints of *Walden* that you can buy at the airport. This is both for the conve-

[14]Boston, 1931.

nience of the reader (who is better able to go straight to the standard edition in a library than to lay his lands on that same cheap reprint) and for the advantage you yourself will derive from the textual perfection or critical elucidations of the *Works*. But observe that if you cite, as you may,

Hazlitt, Works, 6:114

you should not only make sure that the reader knows whose edition you are citing, but also consult the reader's possible interest in knowing *which* work is being referred to. Much may hang on this and you should not skimp but write in full:

Hazlitt, Table Talk, Works (Waller and Glover), 6:114

This is but one of the questions that the character of the reader should play a part in deciding. Fortunate is the author who knows in advance who his reader will be. A man writing a history of Italian fascism, for example, will plan his work (including his footnotes and bibliography) in one way if he addresses his peers and in another if he is producing a work of popularization. If the former, he will assume that his readers know the outlines of Mussolini's life, are acquainted with the theory of the corporate state, and are familiar with the outcome of the war in Ethiopia. He will mention and even discuss these things but he will not *explain* them as to an entirely uninformed reader; the footnotes will therefore bear almost wholly on new or disputed points. The writer for the so-called popular audience, however, will have to give sketches of figures like Il Duce, Matteotti, and Badoglio, and may even have to retrace the origins of the word "fascism" itself. His footnotes will be of the commenting and amplifying kind, and will refer to sources only by way of suggesting additional readings. Logically, the scholar should write fewer footnotes than the popularizer; but usually the proportion is reversed and scholarship is hedged about with footnotes to a degree that often frightens off the overmodest reader.

This excess is a legacy from the 1870s and 1880s, when historians tried to become "scientific" and preferred being thought forbidding to being thought "literary." Now better judgment prevails. Footnotes are necessary but need not be obsessive. As we said earlier, they have wormed their way into popular writing and become familiar to all who can read. In books, the footnote is coming back into its own by recapturing the bottom of the page after a time of exile at the back of the book. Most trade publishers now accept without a murmur footnotes that are footnotes, not backnotes.

Still, circumstances occur in which the "backnote" (or end-of-chapter note) is called for. Sometimes the commentary notes are printed at the foot of the page and the reference notes elsewhere. Sometimes the two are mingled, at the foot, the end of the chapter, or the back of the book. What is in any case essential is to make it as easy as possible for the reader to find quickly the remarks that he should read right after the superior number (^{23}) in the text. For this purpose, one thing is indispensable: the section of notes at the back should not indicate merely "Chapter 4," "Chapter 6," before each group of twenty or thirty numbered notes. The reader has no idea in what numbered chapter he is. Repeat, therefore, the chapter heading, for he does know that he is reading the part entitled "Rolling Down to Rio." Better still, use that heading at the top of each page of notes belonging to that chapter (in which case it is called a "running head").

Another aid to the reader in finding his way through backnotes is to provide either page numbers or catch phrases or both. The page number indicates that on a particular page of the text there is a word marked with an asterisk (*) or dagger (†) or superior number (^{23}). The catch phrases serve to distinguish one note from another on the same page. Figure 20 shows two arrangements.

In essays, articles, or reports, the foot-and-back principle of dividing explanatory from reference footnotes is seldom used, though if the piece is over fifteen or twenty pages in length there is no reason not to separate the two kinds. The notes in a shorter paper will obviously be so few that it would be a nuisance to leaf back and forth.

The one exception to these allowable choices is the scientific or technical paper, in which it is customary to do without explanatory footnotes and to cite all references at the end. These citations (particularly in medicine, physics, chemistry, and mathematics) are brief, giving only last name and initials, the journal title, often abbreviated, and the volume and page numbers in bare figures. In the

FIGURE 20 *The Catch Phrase*

The Masterpiece

"What do we do now?" Glenn Weaver interview. Weaver to Humphrey, Oct. 31, 1967, PFPA, HP.
"Both are determined to move . . .": Humphrey to Johnson, Oct. 30, 1967, Box 937, HP. Herbert Beckington interview. Beckington to Van Dyk, Nov. 6 and 8, 1967, M u / p HP.

312. "Our business is to make history . . .": Transcript of Saigon speech, Oct. 31, 1967, Vietnam box 1965–71, M u / p, HP.
"our great adventure": Ibid. UPI bulletin, Saigon, Oct. 31, 1967.
"obscene, truthless, swine, totally dishonest . . .": *Ramparts*, Sept. 1968; *Rolling Stone*, Mar. 1972; New York *Post*, May 10, 1971.
"Our military progress is clear": Humphrey to Johnson, Nov. 7, 1967, Box 936, HP. Andreas to Humphrey, Nov. 6, 1967, CF68, HP. Watson to Johnson, Nov. 2, and 4, 1967, WHCF CF Exec, FG 440, Box 349, JL.

313. "very much upset": Humphrey to Johnson, Nov. 28, 1967, Vietnam box, 1965–71, M u / p, HP. McCarthy press release, n.d., Nov. 1967, Box 1064, HP. Humphrey to Miles Lord, Feb. 5, 1968, CF68 u / p, HP.
"I guess I have no influence . . .": Humphrey to Johnson, Nov. 28, 1967, Vietnam box 1965–71, M u / p, HP.
"Johnson's Baby Powder": *NYT*, Dec. 8, 1967. Douglas Bennet interview. Nov. 21, 1980.
"My dad was a grocer . . .": Humphrey memo for record, Nov. 21, 1967, WHM u / p, Box 48, HP.
"If the war in Vietnam is a failure . . .": Eisele, 255.

page
34 buzzing confusion. Pr. Psych., I, 488.
35 would be produced. Ibid., I, 24.
suggesters of these. Ibid., I, 20.
36 connected with it. Ibid., I, 347.
which they "know." Ibid., I, vi.
37 is metaphysics. Ibid.
in this book. Ibid., I, vii.
our farther knowledge. Ibid., 192.
38 is conscious of it. Ibid., 197; II, 171 n.
two things, not one. Ibid., I, 278–79.
39 it knows nothing. Ibid., I, 220.
mysterious sort . . . yet in sight. Ibid., I, 687.
systems, involve it. Ibid.
hypnotic trance. Ibid., II, 596.
41 individual minds. Ibid., I, 183.
in the brains of monkeys. See José M. R. Delgado, *Evolution of the Physical Control of the Brain,* American Museum of Natural History, New York, 1965.

The indicative words may come from the beginning of the sentence (or paragraph), from the middle if they are the dominating ones, or from the end. Words taken from the end are more easily remembered by the seeker of the source; they are the last he has read. The example on the left is from Carl Solberg, *Hubert Humphrey: A Biography* (New York, 1984); the one on the right is from Jacques Barzun, *A Stroll with William James* (New York, 1983).

text itself you will commonly find something like (Bohr, 1949), which means: "The statement just made rests on this author's article of that year which I cite in my bibliography below."

Bibliographies: Varieties and Forms

"Bibliography" is a rather loose term for research workers to be using, but there is no other that is as readily understood to mean "information about books." The first image in your mind is perhaps of a list of titles, grouped together at the end of a chapter or volume, after the text and before the index. This is the commonest meaning of the word.[15]

Since a bibliography in this sense cites a number of books, it may be looked upon as a collection of footnotes separated from their text and shorn of particular page references. In fact some writers make up their bibliographies—or at least fill them out—by picking up titles out of their own footnotes. Even when padding is not the aim, it remains true that bibliographies contain much the same information as reference notes, but arranged in a different way for a different purpose. The points of difference will strike the eye if the two forms are juxtaposed:

Howard Haycraft, *Murder for Pleasure: The Life and Times of the Detective Story*, New York, 1941, 139.

Haycraft, Howard, *Murder for Pleasure: The Life and Times of the Detective Story*, New York, Appleton-Century, 1941/1969.[16]

The first is a footnote; the second a bibliographical entry. In the second, the last name begins, so that the eye can quickly find it in its alphabetical place; the publisher is given as a help to finding or buying the book; and there is of course no page number. Some

---

[15]We saw in Chapter 4 that volumes containing lists of books organized by subject and flanked by criticism were also "bibliographies." But there are still other bibliographies, which consist of detailed descriptions and collations of rare or famous books, or which list and describe an author's complete works in all their printed forms. These bibliographies help to identify editions, establish dates, prove authorship, and the like.

[16]In giving the author's full name in the bibliography, avoid excess of zeal, especially with French names. See pp. 88–89 and n.

writers also give the total number of pages, but this, though sometimes helpful, is not compulsory. The two dates show original publication and latest reprint.

What then determines the amount of information to be given and the arrangement of the collection of titles? As before, as always, it is the particular use that the particular bibliography will most likely serve. The function of bibliographies is often misunderstood; to some writers and readers it is a device to cause wonder. One is supposed to think, "Good Heavens! Did he read all that?" But the real reason for a bibliography is to enable others to learn from it. Short or long, a bibliography should be drawn up to second the intention of the article or book it supplements. Three general kinds exist for you to choose from.

The first and most frequently used in books read by the general public is a single list arranged alphabetically by authors' names. This type is a catch-all for whatever has the slightest bearing on any part of the subject—articles, handbooks, interpretative works, newspapers, encyclopedias—everything. Too often this parade of print is a useless ritual. The writer indiscriminately shows off not only the books he has steadily used but also those he has casually looked into. Such a list gives the appearance but not the substance of learning.

Far preferable in this first class or type is the "select bibliography." This will help anyone working on your subject, because it excludes the worthless works and records only the valuable. One defect, however, in the "select bibliography" is that a student who independently comes upon a book that is relevant but unlisted does not know whether it has been rejected as bad or simply overlooked. Despite this disadvantage the researcher treasures the select bibliographies as embodying a deliberate and presumably thoughtful choice; with its aid he is one step ahead of the card catalogue.

Bibliographies of the second type are arranged according to the materials used, and may be called "classified bibliographies." Sometimes the division is simply between primary and secondary sources.[17] Sometimes it is only between manuscript and printed materials, or between books and periodicals. The subdivisions depend on the

[17]See p. 124n.

author's intention in writing the book and upon the variety of sources he has used. Keith Sward's *The Legend of Henry Ford* contains a bibliography broken down into: Books; Magazine and Newspaper Articles; Public Documents; and Legal and Quasi-Legal Actions—a division that fits the needs of most readers.[18] The last category was dictated by the contents of the biography, which narrates numerous and important patent suits.

Biographies almost always raise special problems because their subjects, so to speak, force the biographer's hand. The writer must follow where they lead. But to this guidance the author must add his own imagination. The subject of a biography has to be resurrected, and this requires the creation of a distinctive pattern. When C. Vann Woodward composed *Tom Watson, Agrarian Rebel*,[19] he was dealing with a Populist leader from Georgia whose career was full of puzzling paradoxes. The bibliography is worthy of the subject and fits it because its categories (all but numbers 5 and 6 in Figure 21) match the substance and significance of the life.

Compare such an arrangement with that in the biography of Admiral Mahan by William E. Livezey, where the subject's writings are listed not alphabetically but in the chronological order of publication between 1879 and 1931. Again, book and bibliography match, for this study of Mahan is a history of the development of a man's opinions about the role of sea power in history.

A third type of bibliography is the critical, which may take the form of an essay. This type is best suited to a large subject on which a whole library of books and articles is available. The critical remarks about each book mentioned enable future students to have the considered opinion of a scholar who has examined the literature, made a judicious selection from it, and balanced the virtues of various books into a comprehensive annotated reading list. It is usually convenient to divide this kind of bibliography by chapter. If the comments are appended to each book in an alphabetical list, they should be brief and in the literal sense "telling." There is little use in writing: "A thorough scholarly treatment, generally considered definitive." Say

[18]New York, 1948.
[19]New York, 1938.

FIGURE 21   *Components of a Bibliography*

---

1. Private Papers and Manuscripts (including unpublished letters)
2. Books and Ephemeral Publications (including books edited by ——)
3. Contributions to Books and Periodicals*
4. Published Correspondence
5. Broadcasts and Recordings (including taped conversations)
6. Misattributions
7. Biographies
8. Biographical Articles
9. Relevant Writings of Contemporaries
10. Special Studies and Unpublished Monographs

*Woodward listed in one category his subject's contributions to newspapers and other periodicals. Watson is remembered more as a politician than as an author, so the list records in one place the man's unmemorable writings.

Rarely will a work of scholarship (other than a bibliography itself) make use of all these categories, and in a given work any category may be subdivided. For instance, the first above might be split among Private Papers; Unpublished Manuscripts; and Unpublished Letters; and the last, if large, could list the two kinds of study separately. Number 5 reminds us that today, in place of the traditional *Life and Letters*, an author might write the *Life and Telephone Calls* of Senator X.

rather: "The only book that deals with all aspects of the subject with equal thoroughness and accuracy. Criticism has disputed but a few details."

Of late years the essay form of critical bibliography has sometimes been used as a substitute for footnotes, and has turned into a chatty interlude. Unless marked by critical judgment, its value to other researchers is small. Here is a sample of a useful one:

For Roosevelt's mannerisms while watching a movie see "The President," by Henry F. Pringle, the *New Yorker*, June 16, 1934, and "Roosevelt," an article by Geoffrey T. Hellman in *Life*, January 20, 1941. The quotation concerning lovely ladies is from *This Is My Story*, p. 319. That he never took women on cruises is in Tully, p. 3. Missy Le Hand's role in the appointment of Homer Cummings is mentioned in Edward J. Flynn, p. 126. See *This I Remember*, p. 49, and *My Boy Franklin*, p. 22, for details on Roosevelt's attitude toward money. The quotation about the six-dollar pair of trousers is from *Letters*, Vol. I, p. 303. . . .[20]

A bibliographical essay may be made readable but must be informative *and* critical. Note how simple and direct is the discussion of books in Richard Hofstadter, *The American Political Tradition and the Men Who Made It*.[21]

There is no satisfactory biography of Roscoe Conkling, but Donald Barr Chidsey: *The Gentleman from New York* (New Haven, 1935) is helpful, and the older eulogistic work by Alfred R. Conkling: *The Life and Times of Roscoe Conkling* (New York, 1889) has significant material. David Saville Muzzey's sympathetic *James G. Blaine* (New York, 1934) is the best study of the Plumed Knight; Charles Edward Russell's *Blaine of Maine* (New York, 1931) is more critical. . . .

Hofstadter's bibliography is arranged by chapter, and within each chapter by subjects, in the order in which they are covered in the text. The value of this organization and these judgments is clear to anyone who has found and used such a bibliography in a moment of need. Academic scholars will often turn to their colleagues for this sort of help, informally given, when venturing into unknown territory. Thus a specialist in nineteenth-century English literature working on Dickens's London might call upon a colleague in British history to ask what is the best book on the English Factory Acts. In a printed work, the critical bibliography makes of the author a colleague of the reader.

But the limitations of the device should be known before one chooses it. It is especially suited to biographical subjects where dozens of works have already appeared about every facet of a man's life and work. It is not suited to a subject on which the facts must be dug out of a quantity of scattered books and articles not readily found in libraries, or out of family papers and other manuscripts. Take for

[20] John Gunther, *Roosevelt in Retrospect*, New York, 1950, 388.
[21] New York, 1948, 365.

example the instructive work by Jeannette Mirsky and Allan Nevins, *The World of Eli Whitney.*[22] The printed sources on which it draws range from a history of Connecticut dated 1840 to a study of cotton processing published in 1944. Again and again these authors consulted only a page or so in one of a miscellaneous group of books: they were seeking or verifying but a single fact and had no need to read the work entire. A critical bibliography could not have been written after this type of research without a great waste of time and talent. And had it been done it would have been of use only to a person writing on *exactly* the same subject. Such a person should not exist.

The type of bibliography you ought to draw up for your book is therefore not something you can decide about before you are well past the midpoint of your research. You are called upon to decide so many questions in the writing of any piece of work that it should come as a relief to know that the form of your bibliography will be virtually dictated by your subject and to a lesser extent by your audience.

Taken together, footnotes and bibliography signalize our relation to the fragments of the written record that we have dredged up out of the sea of books, made our own, and reshaped in answer to our fresh questions.

[22]New York, 1952.

16

Revising for Printer and Public

Errors and Their Ways

to revise, means to rev isit, notin order to see thee sights again
but to tidy thme up

The sentence you have just read stands in obvious need of
grooming. Its grammatical form will pass, but its graphic form is
faulty and annoying. It does not pass; it stops you; the meaning is
dimmed because letters are transposed, words are run together, and
the punctuation is at odds with sense and syntax. The work of
grooming, of making presentable what you have to present, is revision
in the second degree. The first has brought your words and sentences
to a high point of clarity, ease, and force.[1] Now you have a typescript
that we hope will not be so liberally dotted with visual blemishes as
the opening sentence of this chapter. But no matter how careful your
typing or your typist, there will be such errors and you must scrub
your manuscript clean. This is equivalent to washing your face and
combing your hair before appearing in public. It is but common
courtesy, for a succession of small specks creates a large hindrance to
your reader's concentration and pleasure.

[1]See Chapters 2, 6, 12, and 13.

But you cannot be sure, at this stage of final revision, that all the errors will be small and, like transposed letters and misplaced commas, readily detected. Before you send your report to the board, your thesis to the department, your article to the editor, your book to the publisher, you must make one last cast for the important errors of fact and sense that have persistently hid from you as you pursued more visible game. Blunders, illogicalities, Irish bulls, contradictions between one page and the next, probably still lurk in the passages you think you have completely verified and polished. How can you unblind yourself to them?

To the knowing reader, any error in your text is an error, grave or slight; that is all there is to it. But to you who have committed it, the cause is important and will help you to spot it while there is yet time. Errors, you will find on reflection, are of several kinds, distinct in origin, and worth regarding theoretically in hopes of reducing their number. By becoming aware of the sort of misstep that your particular mind and hands are likely to make, you can often outwit them. Few people go in for every kind of mistake. It is elementary, of course, that you look over your citations to confirm titles, dates, and other figures, and over your quotations for the correct wording, punctuation, and the like. Few things are harder than to copy a long passage with absolute fidelity, and the more intelligent and quick of perception you are, the more likely you will be to make a slip. Your only hope is to use your quick perceptions to *verify* what your leaping eye or hand has misdone.

Similarly, you will have been prompt to note errors in any of your printed sources, and you will make a blacklist of books that may be valuable but are full of small errors.[2] Each borrowing from such books must be verified, in doing which you will often uncover a trail of error leading back to the original sin, trustingly copied through a dozen books.

This kind of error is annoying and sometimes damaging, but it is not at once comic and infuriating, like the Blunder. A blunder may be defined as a whopper, a lulu of such magnitude as to make the reader laugh, or howl—hence, a howler. The blunder, too, is due to misplaced quickness of mind rather than to ignorance. All blunders, as a student of the genre has remarked,[3] presuppose some knowledge, which has unfortunately been hooked up the wrong way. For example, when Victor Hugo in exile was beginning to learn English and also writing a novel laid in the British Isles, he had occasion to refer to the Firth of Forth. This he felt impelled to translate for his French readers as *le premier des quatre*—"the first of the four." It is clear that if he had known no English whatever he would have been incapable of producing this jewel.

The remedy is never to trust your first intuition of meanings, explanations, allusions, and references without letting the intuition cool and considering it from all sides, preferably with the aid of reference works. Put yourself in the place of a total ignoramus, and go over what you have written as if every portion of it was hard to understand and of doubtful meaning. *Apply this test especially to what you "know as well as your own name."* For example, you are convinced that the saying "God tempers the wind to the shorn lamb" is from the Bible and since it is so well known, you will not bother with an exact reference but will simply introduce it with "in the Biblical phrase. . . ." The misfortune is that the saying is not from the Bible at all, but was coined by Laurence Sterne.[4] In other words, what we have long misknown wears for us an air of certainty that leads to blundering.

More mysterious is the occurrence of blind spots that prevent our seeing the blunders that we could detect at sight in the works of another. Some years ago, for instance, a biography of Haydn appeared with a portrait of the composer bearing the caption: "Haydn in his Eightieth Decade." One can see how the confusion of ideas came about, but when one thinks of the number of times these ridiculous words were read by author, editor, printer, proofreader, and publisher's helpers before issuing in print, one is struck with wonder. And yet an experienced author will *not* wonder. There is about the texts that one is producing a sort of glare that blinds one to

---

[3]H. B. Wheatley, *Literary Blunders*, London, 1893, 2.

[4]In "Maria," *A Sentimental Journey through France and Italy* (first published 1768), paraphrased from Henri Estienne, *Prémices* (1594).

their obvious blemishes at the very time when one is toiling to perfect them. This resembles the facility with which we can say "Tuesday" for "Thursday" when we are most eager to make an appointment.

An error sometimes reveals far more than its physical magnitude or innocence would suggest, and knowing this will put you on your guard. Suppose, for instance, that the book before you refers to "General Pershing, Chief of Staff in the Second World War." A howler, yes, you may say, but after all, he *was* a military giant of the nation and still alive in the 1940s: a slip of the pen is quickly made—and it is only one word wrong. On the contrary, much more than that is wrong: to place Pershing in the later war means that the author lacks any kind of mental image of the man in his accoutrements and his generation. The figure to him is a name, not a body with a distinct aura. The error *resembles* that of making Alexander Hamilton's birthplace Jamaica instead of Nevis—an "intelligent" error of association between two islands of the British West Indies—but the "slip" about Pershing is as grievous a misstep as citing a book one has not read.

Judging Others' Trespasses

We must be charitable when we criticize one another's productions, because error is inevitable. Our own work should convince the reader that—as Sydney Smith put it—our errors have come "not in consequence of neglect but in spite of attention."[5] But in assessing the work of others for use in our own, we must not be blinded by self-righteousness. In scholarly book reviews the critic often devotes valuable space to listing small errors and thinks he has struck a blow for truth, while some readers mark down the book as untrustworthy.

Actually, the matter is more complicated. Experience shows that all the best books, whether original monographs or reference books, attain near perfection of detail only in their revised editions. The experienced editors whom we quoted earlier found in their work of verification that at least one footnote out of six contained an error.

[5]Letter to Francis Jeffrey, August 1802.

But though it is true that any mistake can mislead the reader, it is also true that some errors are trivial and others important. Albert Jay Nock in his *Jefferson* has made the point in words that cannot be improved upon:

> There are qualities that outweigh occasional and trivial inaccuracy, and Parton has them, while the other biographers of Mr. Jefferson, as far as I can see, have not; and the worth of his book should be assessed accordingly. Indeed, if one were condemning books on the strength of minor inaccuracies, Mr. Hirst himself would get off badly. I noticed more inaccuracies in one very casual reading of his book than I ever saw in my close readings of Parton. But Mr. Hirst's errors of fact, like Parton's, are not important enough that one should think of them. The thing to think of is that a foreigner and an Englishman should have done as well as Mr. Hirst has done with a subject of uncommon difficulty, even for a native critic. His book should be judged on the scale of its major qualities, and so, I think, should Parton's. "Let us never forget that we are all pedants," said Benjamin Constant to his literary associates; which may be all very well for those who live to read, but hardly for those who read to live.[6]

Judging a work "by its major qualities" is the lesson every researcher must learn if he or she is to make the best of the available literature. For although no work is absolutely free of errors, it would be a waste of time to go back to every indicated source to see if it had been misquoted or given a wrong page reference. To do so would negate the very aim of scholarship, which presupposes, as does science, that every worker helps another by "contributing" to knowledge. If nobody relies on previous work and starts afresh from the sources, the word contribution has no meaning.

But how to judge "major qualities"? That is an expertise which comes as one reads and compares. Clarity and precision of prose is the outermost criterion. It proves nothing but promises a good deal, since important errors can lurk in single words. Biographers, who should paint a portrait line by line, can produce a daub or a caricature by successive errors of vocabulary, saying (for instance) that their subjected *admitted* something when in fact he *declared* or *volunteered* it; that he *resented* something else when he only *objected* to it; that he

[6]New York, 1926, 333.

interfered in a situation in which he *intervened*, and so on. The cumulative effect of misnomers is doubly treacherous because it goes unnoticed—creeping falsehood. Yet reviewers who will pounce on a wrong middle initial will let pass the innuendos of careless wording.

A second criterion of quality is a certain fullness of treatment. On any given matter the author leaves no reasonable questions hanging. He foresees doubts and possibilities and discusses or settles them. This usually brings in the views or findings of other writers, who are quoted or paraphrased. The use of significant details enters in at this point, "significance" being gauged by what hangs on minute accuracy. For example, Henry James arrived at his brother William's house on June 16, 1905, and was there the next day when William wrote a certain letter referring to Henry, therefore, etc. The sequence of dates and Henry's presence are all-important.[7] But in a running narrative that says the family left on April 11 and landed in Queenstown ten days later, the mistake of writing eleven then ten, instead of ten then eleven, though regrettable, will most likely never be of consequence.

Far more deplorable errors are too commonly dismissed as not affecting truth. One of these is bad organization, whether on the large scale or the small. The researcher who throws his notes into print after a cursory sorting is at once substituting facts for truth and scrambling the reader's mind about that possible truth. It is no venial error—see again the example on pp. 272–273. Another grave error is to pass judgments that are absolute instead of comparative; that is, to apply present or local standards to actions or events remote in time or place.

False judgments of that sort are often slipped in by means of epithets, vague or definite: for example, *Victorian, romantic, medieval*; or *absurd, irrational, superstitious*. Thus, the practice of duelling has been scorned as "adolescent" through the failure to see that it replaced the older custom of the family feud at a lesser cost of blood. The feud itself was not seen as the logical outgrowth of tribal or clan war; rather it was total war, which our enlightened age has merely expanded into national or "axis" wars on the global scale.

[7]See Jacques Barzun, *A Stroll with William James*, New York, 1983, 226.

In judging reference books, ascertaining quality is relatively easier. The look—format, print, paper, and binding—gives an inkling of the type of publication: is it a quickie fashioned from other, larger works, or is it a well-conceived and well-edited undertaking? The second category usually lists a board of editors or advisers to the editor-in-chief, all of them with stated scholarly or scientific affiliations. Then one turns to entries one knows something about and finds out whether they are compact, clear, and full of relevant details well-organized. Here dates, names, spellings, relationships must all be correct; they are equally significant, since the compiler cannot know what use may be made of them. Some errors will be found, as we said earlier, but they must be few. Next, inclusiveness is essential. A *Dictionary of Theatrical Terms* that omits *upstage* and *downstage* or *O.P. side* is not worth space on the shelf.

Recently, a good many firms not before known as reference-book publishers have taken advantage of the computer to produce tomes that profess to supply knowledge in dictionary form on a wide variety of subjects. For example, one now finds such handy volumes as *The Harper Dictionary of Modern Thought; Twentieth-Century Culture: A Biographical Dictionary; Makers of Modern Culture: A Biographical Dictionary*; in addition to the systematic anthologies published by the Gale Research Company: *Shakespeare Criticism; Literary Criticism from 1400 to 1800; Nineteenth-Century Literary Criticism; Twentieth-Century Literary Criticism* (up to 1960); *Contemporary Literary Criticism* (1960 on); and *Contemporary Issues Criticism*.

Some works with alluring titles are mere lists—printouts in bound form. They are not edited in the true sense of the word; their reliability depends altogether on the knowledge and judgment of the original programmers, who may have compiled the list for a purpose quite other than research-reference. The contents of such a repertory may give a useful lead, but any substantive matter must be verified. This is especially true of books that supply abstracts; they may have been done hastily, haphazardly, sloppily. One abstract, for example, summarized Swift's *Modest Proposal* as suggesting that the Irish poor should raise babies and eat them. The irony was not pointed out and even worse, the proposal was misstated: Swift proposes that the Irish should relieve their poverty by raising babies *to sell to the rich* as a delicacy. The point lifts a crude idea of cannibalism to the height of savage satire and explains Swift's final sentence: he has no vested interest in the proposal, his wife being past childbearing.

The Craft of Revision: Maxims and Pointers

With experience in judging not only books, but also the many components of accurate reporting, one finds the task of revising more and more pleasurable, even though its purpose is the discovery of one's own failings. The ultimate effort is the stage that some artists find peculiarly satisfying: the "fixing" of a pastel or the final polishing of a precious gem or the casting of a piece of sculpture. It is exhilarating and exhausting and one should be prepared for both sensations.

The first thing needful is that you should allow enough time for thoroughness at a deliberate, not a hurried, pace. What "enough time" is will depend on the length of your article, thesis, or book, and on your own habits of work. But the penalty of frantic, last-minute patching is no secret from anyone—a low mark, whether it be given by a professor, an employer, or the public. Many a gifted piece of writing has been lost in the flood of print because it was hastily revised and hence bore the marks of an imperfection at once pitiable and insulting.

If your work is a book, you should revise it chapter by chapter. If it is an article, part by part. This division of the task compels you to see the work in its small rather than in its large aspects. Even if you are submitting your report to a restricted private audience, conduct your revision as if you were giving the script its last review before it goes to the printer. This will make you as attentive as he, who is trained to set type in any language, familiar or not. He therefore sees, not paragraphs or sentences or words; he sees only single letters. So should you. His instructions always are to "follow copy," that is, reproduce what is there, not what ought to be there. You, of course, must "follow copy" in a second sense, scanning not only single letters but also sentences, consistency—indeed, everything.

For although you have long since passed the rewriting stage, you cannot avoid rereading yourself as one interested in the meaning.

You will seize any chance to improve your diction or syntax or transitions. Like a cabinetmaker who uses ever finer grains of sandpaper until he has achieved a glasslike smoothness, a reviser usually makes no radical changes; he only rubs and writes and rubs again. More than once, probably, you have been from the outset dissatisfied with a word. It stands there plaguing you still, because you could not think of the right substitute: all the synonyms are equally wrong. But now you must make a move: *stet* or—what? Your move is usually no more dramatic than a line through the dubious word and its replacement with the least undesirable alternative.

Once in a while you cannot avoid making sizable changes. You suddenly read your words in a new light and discover that you have conveyed an entirely erroneous impression, or seemingly contradicted yourself, or left ambiguous what you are very sure about—all this due to "not seeing" and now caught by reseeing or revision. Take as a subject for a last-minute perception of ambiguity: "She had outlived her ambition without realizing it." This seemed to the writer entirely correct even after innumerable readings. Suddenly the ambiguity caused by the two meanings of realize became so clear the wonder was, how could it have been tolerated for so long?[8] The meaning required a change to: "She had outlived her ambition without achieving it."

Painstaking writers whose work looks effortless in its precision and right proportioning keep revising to the end. Even if your form is set in all particulars, the appearance of a new edition of an old work may necessitate a change in your text at the last minute. It is a good rule never to consider your revision complete until the presses have started to roll.

When you go over a typescript that will be read by strangers in that form and not in print, you will naturally be on the lookout for missing punctuation and misplaced capitals, figures or letters transposed, italics omitted, and the like. But see to it also that the words you have used are correctly spelled. Spelling is one of the decencies of civilized communication. No doubt there are reasons, physical and

---

[8]"Realize" in the sense of "recognize," "acknowledge," "become conscious of" deserves a place on a list of forbidden words. Almost every sentence where it occurs in that sense would be improved by its replacement.

psychological, for misspellings, but a reason is not an excuse. This is especially true if you are fond of treacherous words such as "corollary" and "supersede" and "apophthegm"; the least you can do is to learn to spell them. It is like paying for what you use instead of stealing and spoiling it. As to the commoner words, such as "receive," "benefited," "indispensable," and "consensus," it should be a matter of pride with you not to exhibit your work pockmarked with infantile errors. If you are adult in years yet still in doubt about any of these spellings, go after it and settle it once for all.

And while you are about the task of making your text fully presentable, a polished mirror of your mind, see to it that neither you nor your typist has made the annoying mistake of mixing the Roman and Arabic figures for 1. Volume Two of a work should be typed as II or 2, never as 11. Likewise, most typewriters have a zero; do not use the *O*, large or small. Again, leave a space after the comma or period before beginning the next word or sentence. Lastly, do not join by a hyphen what you mean to separate by a dash. The dash consists of two hyphens close together. Without the use of conventions such as these, the lump of words is unreadable; in any case, the misuse of letters, figures, and spaces is unprofessional. Reread the opening sentence of this chapter and imagine ten pages in that form, which is what some writers complacently proffer to their instructors or associates. Trivial departures from convention? Yes, but they stop your reader and make him think of your incompetence instead of your ideas.

In revising, it is always helpful to have the assistance of someone who will be, like you, attentive to details, and who, because of friendship for you or dedication to your subject, is willing to devote time and effort to assisting you. You will require this Jonathan to aid you in collating quotations (that is, comparing them word for word and point for point with the originals) or in verifying against the sources the statistics used in your tables. He should read aloud words or figures to you with a clear enunciation, so as to enable you to follow them easily in the printed copy and make corrections. If nothing else moves you, reflect that your reviewers will catch some of the errors you have missed and that the unfavorable comments may give the impression of a uniformly careless execution even if your work is 90 percent accurate and reliable.

The Craft of Revision: Technique and Symbols

In making changes and corrections you must write legibly, otherwise your reader or editor will not notice them quickly or follow your meaning smoothly. If you must insert a word or phrase, be sure that the point of insertion is clearly shown by a caret,[9] and that the added words are not only neatly written but also conveniently placed for the eye, between the lines, which have been double-spaced for this very purpose. Do not sprawl over the margins or in any way attract the eye to half a dozen manuscript corrections out of a whole typed page.

Some inserts are longer, amounting to a paragraph or more. If so, they should be typed and pasted where they belong. This is the rule for any manuscript submitted to a publisher or going ultimately to a printer. For a typist who will produce clean copy, you can simply staple your typed slips to the left-hand margin, using two staples and letting the free end cover a part of your text. Mark the slip "insert" (or "insert A" if more are to come), and at the right point of the text put a caret and write the word "insert" and A (or B, C, etc.) with a circle around them. If you have to attach more than two inserts, cut and paste to make the page manageable: a manuscript with little flags flying all over it is liable to tearing, misplacing of parts, and broken reading.

If inserts and additions lengthen the text beyond the limits of the original page, go on to a fresh one. All you have to do is number the run-over sheet the same as the original with the letter *a* added. If more than one page is needed, use *b*, *c*, and so on. Do not worry if, say, page 10a is only half-filled. Draw a vertical line from below the middle of the last line of text to the bottom of the sheet. The printer will "run in" page 11 to fill the space, for like Nature he abhors a vacuum.

Your lesser corrections, we have said, should be interlined, *above* the line to which they belong, never below. The margins are reserved for instructions to the printer, who will apply them to the word or words marked with the appropriate signs (caret, slash, underlining, dots, etc.) on the same level as the marginal comment ("cap.," "l.c.," "tr.," and the like). Do *not* draw guidelines from the

---

[9]For the caret and other conventional signs, see Figure 23, p. 402.

error in the center of your text to the comment in the margin. Always see your copy as it will look to a stranger who does not know your words by heart, yet must make out your meaning rapidly. Remember he is probably earning his living, not playing a puzzle game.

Enter the Word Processor

The combined electronic devices known as a word processor have charmed into purchase a good many people who write, and have tempted others who still withhold investment. If one can trust a friend who is a writer, "Ask the man who owns one." But it often happens that the question is not answered quite candidly, in part from the human urge to persuade and recruit, in part to save face if one has developed doubts. So a few pointers are in order as to the character of the machine itself.

A word processor permits the writer to make successive changes in his draft without having to proofread again and again the unaltered portions, notably quotations and footnotes. This relief aids speed of production, though it may not entirely improve the text, since changes and additions have a way of affecting the surrounding paragraphs, as when a new passage unwittingly repeats a word already used in the unchanged section. A careful writer rereads the whole after every important change.

A processor also affords the pleasure of seeing every change quickly inserted into an unencumbered text; it is like having a succession of clean proofs, giving a fresh look that inspires to further improvements. In the course of making changes, however, it is not possible to compare two or more pages on the screen; they must be run off on a "printer" and used like a typescript.

What may prove awkward—at least for some people—is composing the revision. On the typewriter or in longhand, one first crosses out, then above or after the deleted words one works out the new phrasing. On the processor, the earlier wording is eliminated; one cannot go back to it, or part of it; one must rethink it. And what one can revise is based on no more than 25 lines at a time, of 80 characters each—say a full page of typescript. The paragraphs above or below are out of reach.

As for hand revisions of the first satisfactory draft that one has "printed," they are easy to enter only if they are not numerous and intricate. Writers who rewrite a chapter four or five times will find that inserting a series of complicated changes taxes attention and requires long effort. Presented with a typescript averaging ten small and ten large changes a page, an experienced hand at word processing declared "It will be easier and quicker to redo the whole thing." The obvious conclusion is that before switching from a swift electric typewriter to a word processor and printer, one should take stock of one's ingrained writing habits. The processor will not make *writing* easier. True, it will help out uncertain spellers (though it may "correct" *unclear* to *nuclear*) and it will offer haphazard punctuators a choice of better ways. But it will not assist composition and it may hinder revision unless one's habits fall within the limitations of the machine.[10]

Besides, the very possibilities of its use call for conscious choices and moves. A writer who is not quick and sure in digitial maneuvers will probably not enjoy the full range of its benefits. And just as it is often true that a writer who has used longhand for composing is less fluent mentally when he uses a typewriter, so a longhand or typist composer will feel less fertile at the processor keyboard. The physical habits are associated with mental ones, and the mode of writing will work its magic or hindrance when it is familiar or strange.[11] No doubt, if processors are introduced to children in the first grade, a generation of writers will grow up who compose best in front of a green-eyed screen.

But here is a drawback too. Video screens are now known to pose health hazards. The strong green light is a strain on eyesight; the prolonged staring at a small area affects posture; and it is also possible—though not proved—that undesirable radiation occurs. The American authority on the subject is Dr. Milton Zaret, who studied the disabilities suffered by the staff that used processors at the United Nations. Indeed, the operators went on strike until their hours of work were reduced to allow long intervals of rest. It would

[10]See William Zinsser, *Writing with a Word Processor*, New York, 1983.

[11]See Erik Sandberg-Diment, "But Is It Writing?" (*New York Times*, June 26, 1984) as well as Derek Rowntree, *Do You Really Need a Home Computer?* (New York, 1985), section on Word Processors.

seem a wise precaution for writers and scholars not to spend as many hours at the word processor as they were used to at the desk or typewriter.

One other point needs notice. Common talk about word processors has included the attractive idea that by preparing a disk on one's machine, one might be able to hand a publisher a finished text that he could transmit to his offset printer and thus obtain the book or article at a great reduction of time and expense. Some authors even foresaw the possibility of increased royalties from the elimination of editorial costs.

But the assumptions behind this shortcut have so far proved contrary to fact, for two reasons. Skipping the stage of editing (which includes *copy* editing) is not really practicable. The publisher always suggests and usually obtains alterations in the author's work. House style and forms are imposed by the copy editor and can only be carried out by a professional compositor: the author lacks the training and practice. Finally, it has not so far been easy to link every type of disk with the font desired or available at the printing press. All these elements vary, and they make the straight path from author's mind to bound book a more rugged road than the imagination conceives; which is not to say that word processors may not be extremely useful machines in many sectors of the intellectual life, as they have shown themselves to be in business and government.

The Professional Touch

The minor virtue that you must adopt as a reviser is consistency. Every time you make the same sort of correction, indicate it in identical fashion. This is the only way you can conduct proper discourse with editor and printer. There are some small differences between the practice of authors who correct typescript for their colleagues or editors and that of the copy editor who prepares a text for the printer; but these variations need not concern you. Follow the present suggestions but remember the point: the convenience of not writing out instructions over and over again is the reason for the proofreader's, that is, the typesetter's, marks, which have become so widely accepted as to constitute an international sign language. A few may be mentioned as examples of a shorthand you should master for your advantage and others':

1. When you must change a whole word, draw a horizontal line through it. When it is only a letter you are altering, draw a vertical line through it. The vertical should project on each side in order to be clear; not so the horizontal.

2. When you have crossed out a word, and regret your decision to do so, you restore it by writing the word "stet" in the margin and putting a series of dots under the word. *Stet* is Latin for "let it stand."

3. Bear in mind that your editor expects your typescript to be marked up. An altogether clean one suggests that you have not taken the trouble to proofread your work. This is slacking, for there are never too many pairs of eyes engaged in hunting down "typos."

4. If your handwriting is uncertain, use print letters, shaping and spacing them carefully. Never try to patch up a typewritten word by writing over its constituent letters. Cross it out and put its replacement just above it.

5. The technique of correcting on a word processor is, as we have seen, different. The machine obliterates rather than strikes out visually and not all models permit the recovery of discarded text; the word *stet* is powerless against the disk (see above p. 388).

The reviser's awareness of the way error begets error makes him take as his golden rule: "Leave nothing to chance or to the guesses of editor and printer." Whoever the reader may be, never leave him in doubt about your meaning. If you are being edited before printing, revisions by several hands will have decorated your copy with a quantity of pencil marks, some full of purpose and meaning, others random and mysterious. It is usually the punctuation that suffers from the handling, both because people differ about it and because the marks are small and indistinct. One thing you can do to forestall confusion is to put a circle around a period, thus: ⊙ ; and a caret over or under other common marks: ʌ ʌ̂ v̌ v̈ v̌ and so on.

One of the most frequent of last-minute changes is in the paragraphing. Even the best of writers will discover that a sentence which seemed like an appropriate ending to a paragraph now strikes him as an excellent topic sentence for the next. If you change your mind about the right place to break the paragraph and decide to have none where one now exists, write "No ¶ " in the blank space in front of the indention and (for printers) draw a "run on" line from the word that closes the previous paragraph. Here is a set of markings for such a change of mind:

```
. . . If we think of the colonies as advance

outposts of the European powers, we have an

idea of how Europeans looked upon them.  Thus

they represented their sovereigns' strength

and prestige.

(no ¶)  The rivalry of the European countries was

reflected in the history of the colonies
                ¶
overseas.  Nothing illustrates this fact

better than the story of English–Dutch

relations in America.

(no ¶)  Holland occupied little territory but she

was located at the mouth of the Rhine. Like a

watchdog, she sat astride the trade routes that
            the        cies
led out of Germany o o o
```

If in typing, two words have been run together, draw a vertical line between them; otherwise you risk confusion or, even worse, misunderstanding through miscorrection. Suppose, for example, that your copy contains this sentence:

```
She greeted the crowd withoutstretched arms.
```

There is a chance that your editor may absent-mindedly divide the words after "without"; for the work of editing tends to concentrate the mind on visual detail at the expense of meaning and such a blunder can remain unseen through several readings. You save yourself the resulting absurdity by marking your copy in this way:

```
She greeted the crowd with#outstretched arms.
```

Conversely, the pieces of a word must sometimes be brought together. Here is the way:

```
The author's chief qualification was in sight.¹²
```

Another recurrent problem of revision is that of changing the capitalization. You have, let us say, cut a long sentence into smaller pieces and, like a cut earthworm, each segment now has a life of its own. To show a change from a small (or lower case) letter to a capital (or upper case), draw three small lines under the letter:

```
It was a blueprint for an elaborate

feudal society, and at the top of the pyramid

of government was the landed aristocracy.
```

¹²In typing, remember the injunction never to use capital *I* for *1* in any series of Arabic numbers, and especially not to combine the two styles, as in *12*. If your typewriter lacks the Arabic *1*, use the lowercase letter *l*. In referring to any part of an outline, say, *1 2 a*, space the figures and letters, to avoid even a momentary confusion with *12a*.

To reduce a capital to a small letter, draw a slanting line (slash) through it:

and

Life was harsh on the range, The cowboy

was a lonely figure.

The most common kind of alteration is the transposing of letters, words, or larger units. If two letters have been reversed they can be put right as follows:

pspecial

If two words are in the wrong order, do this:

Praz, Mario Machiavelli in Inghilterra,

Rome, 1943.

When a whole paragraph has to be moved to a new place, the simplest way is to circle it completely and draw a line from it up or down the margin to the caret that shows the point of insert. In a grafting operation of this kind, make certain that the broken edges will fit when brought together. The connecting words must be as appropriate as they were before the transplant. Sometimes the mood and voice of the verbs have to be changed. Sometimes you must find synonyms for words because the same ones are now repeated too near each other for euphony.

Occasionally there is need to remove a paragraph from one part of a chapter to a distant one. You have a choice of methods. One is to use the same device as that which serves on a single page: circle the paragraph that is to be moved to page 22 and write next to it: "Tr. to p. 22." (If more than one transposition is to be made, letter them all consecutively beginning with *A*.) Then mark page 22 with a caret to show where the traveling paragraph belongs and in the margin write: "Tr. from p. 8."

The alternative is to retype the paragraph and make of it an insert on page 22, crossing it out altogether on page 8. This is preferable when the gap is greater than the one between the page numbers just cited, for instance in a large book in which a portion of page 8 is removed to page 300. At the printer's the manuscript may be split up among several typesetters, or the early portion may be returned to the author with his first galley proofs, or be in some way hard of access when page 300 suddenly calls for the presence of page 8.

When your revising is finished to your satisfaction, go through the manuscript to make sure that the pages are arranged and numbered consecutively, including charts, graphs, and other illustrations. You have, of course, made an exact duplicate copy of your work showing every correction or instruction, even those made at the last minute before you turn in the original. If this main copy goes astray or is damaged, you can replace it immediately. Few of us could take calmly what happened to Carlyle when he entrusted the manuscript of the first volume of *The French Revolution* to John Stuart Mill, whose housemaid used it to light the fire. This was before the days of typewriters and carbon copies and copying machines, and Carlyle had to start afresh from his notes—an act of fortitude one shudders to think of.

After your editor has brought to your text the suggestions that occur to him, he sends back the altered copy for your approval.[13] His fresh eye and good judgment can be useful to you in improving the form and phraseology of your work. It is clear, however, that an editor can sometimes become so possessive about your text that his suggestions begin to do violence to your meaning and intent. Do not let him write his book over your name, and on no account let him dispatch your work to the printer with his changes unexamined by you. He is in good faith when he says they are "only minor," but you may not think them so, and the time and expense of discovering and changing them in proof should not be an added burden on you.

---

[13]At a book publisher's a manuscript is usually edited by two people in two different ways: the editor goes over it for sense, organization, and literary style; the copyeditor goes over it for spelling, grammatical niceties, and consistency of form.

In general—and this applies to friends or colleagues who help you by reading your manuscript ahead of publication—the criticisms and suggestions you receive must be interpreted in the light of *your* purpose, *your* plan, *your* style. This caution will make little difference in mechanical corrections; it applies to larger matters. Almost always, the word or passage that is questioned needs to have something done to it—it shows where the intelligent reader stumbled or jibbed. But this does not mean that *what* he or she suggests as an improvement is what you should accept as the right thing.

The Handle to a Writer's Works

It may come as a surprise that one of the very last acts of revision before printing is the putting of a title to the piece. Yet the common experience is that the title is written last more often than not. You may have thought of your report, article, or book in some descriptive phrase that fitted it very well. You have used this formula in telling your friends what you were working on, and again the phrase fitted the form of your spoken sentence. But the description was never a title. By itself it was unsayable. We know, for example, that Thackeray called his first great novel *Pen and Pencil Sketches of English Society*. The reason was that he had illustrated the book himself and that his earlier literary work had consisted of character sketches. Under that cumbrous rubric the work we now know as *Vanity Fair* had little chance of catching the eye or capturing the imagination of publisher or public. It lacked a handle.

When the piece offered to view is science or scholarship, the duty to provide a convenient handle to pick it up and hold it by is just as great. And baptizing the work once the chapters and parts have been named is always a ticklish business. The difficulty of titling is due to the fact that modern titles are not descriptions but tags. Publishing usage is not likely to permit one to write simply *A History of the United States*. Perhaps the label has been seen too often. So it must become *The Land of the Free*, supplemented by an explanation in smaller type, "A History of the United States." Within this allusive style there are fashions, and these it is well not to follow if one wants to avoid embarrassment a dozen years later, when the fashion has faded. At one time the titles even of serious works tended toward the flowery: *Poor Splendid Wings* (a study of the Pre-Raphaelites), *So Fell the Angels* (an account of Salmon P. Chase and his daughter Kate), *A Time for Angels*—angels are popular—a history of the League of Nations. Allusiveness continues to attract the author and publisher who want their joint product to stand out from the mass of printed books, but it should be held in check by common sense. *The Better Half* no doubt suggests its subject, disclosed in its subtitle, "The Emancipation of the American Woman," but it is a question whether *Fearful Symmetry*, even with the explanatory words "A Study of William Blake," is not too allusive for any but readers familiar with Blake's *Tyger*.[14]

A title should indicate what realm of thought or action the work treats of, and possibly also what contribution or assertion it makes. *Born Under Saturn* fails on both counts and is rather hackneyed besides.[15]

Such considerations need not keep a title from legitimately arousing curiosity. Marjorie Nicolson's *Newton Demands the Muse* does this admirably, and with economy and dignity. It tells us at once that science and poetry jointly form the subject, while the alluring image it raises is more vivid and true to the reality of the past than any pair of abstractions. When a title that is short enough to be easily remembered proves too general to fit the book closely, a subtitle performs that adjustment. Thus *The Flowers of Friendship* absolutely requires "Letters Written to Gertrude Stein." Simplicity, in titles as elsewhere, is a great virtue, and as elsewhere it is found only by hard work and self-control. The last thing one wants from a title is a glimpse of the author striking a pose.

The titles of chapters can be fuller, more descriptive than those of a book. A certain harmony among the names of chapters is a pleasing and useful thing, just as an artificial attempt to suggest

---

[14]The study of Blake is by the distinguished critic Northrop Frye; the study of American women is by Andrew Sinclair.

[15]Two excellent works hide under this designation—one a biography of William Hazlitt by Catherine Maclean and the other a study of the character and conduct of artists by Rudolf and Margaret Wittkower.

drama or "revelations" is futile and displeasing. Remember that readers browse before buying and judge the unknown by its outward features. Sometimes an excellent book is as it were mislabeled by its injudicious chapter titles. For example, Stewart H. Holbrook's sound and valuable *Story of the American Railroads*[16] fails to represent itself justly to the roving eye because its chapter headings lack harmony and attempt sensationalism. The first five are acceptable:

1. Panorama
2. The Prophets
3. Primeval Railroading
4. Railroad Fever
5. "The Work of the Age"

But then we fall on:

6. Forgotten Genius [which is a short digression about one man]
7. The Pennsy and the Central [which sounds as if out of chronological order in a book of thirty-seven chapters].

From then on the sense of progression and tone is broken by such headings as "War Comes to a 'Neutral' Line," "Locating the Route," "Out in the Wild and Woolly," "Up in the Cold and Icy," "The Carriers are Harassed," "Through the Dark Ages—and After," "The Fast Mail," "Spotters," "The Little Fellers," "News Butchers," and—unexpectedly sedate for the last one—"The Railroad in the Drama." After the colloquialism of the middle chapters, one's sense of fitness wants for that last topic something like "The Footplate and the Footlights"—a deplorable parallel, but at least one in keeping with the prevailing mood.

One test of the harmony we speak of is length. If you start out terse and dramatic with (1) "Hope"; (2) "Effort"; (3) "Power"; you cannot very well continue with (4) "There's Many a Slip Twixt the Cup and the Lip." In fact, it is best to avoid the monotony of a striking device repeated: make the harmony arise from tone and what the novelists call the "point of view." This often means naming your chapters in the same voice, form, or construction. For example, if you have (1) "The Outbreak of Revolution," and continue "The . . . of . . ." through (4) "The Rise of the Consulate and Empire," you ought not to switch to (5) "Napoleon Falls"; you have bound yourself to "The Fall of Napoleon."

Essay titles differ somewhat from chapter titles in that they do alone the work of catching and holding the glancing eye. But like chapter titles, they may be a little more explicit than book titles unaided by subtitles. This usually means deciding what the first impression is that you want to create in your reader's mind. The idea must be important yet not give the point away; it must be arresting without being an impudent nudge. An excellent example of just the right mixture is the title of an essay by Meyer Schapiro on Lewis Mumford's *The Culture of Cities*. It is called "Looking Forward to Looking Backward."[17]

The chance for such felicity is rare. Usually, one has to fall back on the simply declarative with "in," "and," "on," or the possessive case, as links between ideas: "Machiavelli's Politics," "The Education of Engineers in Russia," or "T. E. Lawrence on Leaders in the Middle East." The trouble with these titles is that they do not enable the reader to keep the memory of one such essay clear from another on the same theme. They do not state or evoke enough, what they say is not distinctive, they are not *telling*. A sharp, clear message is needed, even if the article is not the first to treat that subject. If Lionel Trilling, for example, had written "A Poet's Letters" or "Keats and His Letters," his memorable essay would be much less easily brought to mind than under its actual title: "The Poet as Hero: Keats in His Letters." Note how strongly affirmative this is, for all its quietness, and how vivid is the substitution of "*in* his letters" for the ubiquitous "and."

The lesson is plain: keep revolving ideas for your title from the moment you begin writing. Make lists of possible ones, and if you are lucky the ideal phrase will flash on you before it is time to part with your manuscript.

---

[17] *The Partisan Reader*, New York, 1946, 310.

Revision at a Distance: The Printer and You

At last you are going to be published—that is, if your essay or dissertation is workmanlike in form and mature and original in contents. Publishing, of course, means a fresh set of problems, but most of them are mechanical; and unless yours is an unusual case you will never see those who query you and ask for your last revises.[18] Though the typesetters of your text may be several, to you they will be "the printer"—an anonymous, collective function and dignity like "the firm" or "the house."

Before many weeks have passed the printer will send you evidence that he has not been idle: galley proofs. These are long sheets of paper on which your work has been printed. A galley (so named from the tray in which the type is held) will contain the equivalent of two or three pages of text. As you reread your words for perhaps the twentieth time, you will not escape the feeling that they are familiar, and yet they will seem new. This is partly because they now look clean, black, and definitive, partly because your old landmarks have vanished.[19] You associated a certain phrase with the top of page 8, and a certain paragraph looked long and sprawling. Now the phrase is lost somewhere and the paragraph has shrunk to a modest size. This is a pleasant discovery you should take advantage of: it allows you to read your text again with a fresh eye.

It may happen that you will come upon an egregious blunder even at this stage, but you must restrain yourself from wanting to redo whole passages under the inspiration of your own words. The changes you make in galleys are charged to you unless they are "printer's errors." At an increasing rate as computer typesetting becomes more sophisticated, changes can be an expensive indulgence, especially since substituting a single word for another sometimes necessitates resetting an entire paragraph. Often the author is

---

[18]When the printer's proofreader is in doubt, he will "query" ("?" or "Qy" in the margin) and suggest what seems to him right. When you have answered and he has made the change, the proof sent is a "revise."

[19]Nowadays, proofs of articles to appear in periodicals may not look "clean, black, and definitive." They may consist of a word-processor printout, where the letters made up of dots and the symbols scattered about to direct the computer typesetting make proofreading a trial.

FIGURE 22   *R.I.P.!*

The deceased, clearly, was an academic, whom the threat of "Publish or Perish" spurred to publication and earned him promotion, but did not save him in the end.

FIGURE 23   *The Proofreader's Marks*

MESSAGE TO PRINTER	MARK	INDICATION IN TEXT	CORRECTED TEXT
Remove letter or word.	ℐ	He read the boopk.	He read the book.
Insert letter.	t	She wrote a leter.	She wrote a letter.
Insert space.	#	We wenttogether.	We went together.
Change to capital letter.	cap	Pam asked bill.	Pam asked Bill.
Change to lower-case.	lc	Do Χou know him?	Do you know him?
Wrong font (type face).	wf	He mixed them up.	He mixed them up.
Broken letter. Replace.	X	Clear your type.	Clean your type.
Inverted letter. Turn.	⑨	It mnst be wrong.	It must be wrong.
Reset in italic type.	ital	Don't do that!	*Don't* do that!
Reset in roman (regular).	rom	What can it be?	What can it be?
Reset in bold-face (dark).	bf	The word was nor.	The word was **nor.**
Reset in small capitals.	sc	The sign said Stop!	The sign said STOP!
Transpose.	tr	but enough world and	but world enough and
Insert period.	⊙	Such is life	Such is life.
Insert hyphen.	/=/	Mr. Wycliffe Jones	Mr. Wycliffe-Jones
Insert comma.	⌄	That's all folks.	That's all, folks.
Insert apostrophe.	⌄	Dont look now.	Don't look now.
Insert quotation marks.	⌄⌄	Eureka, he said.	"Eureka," he said.
Insert inferior figure.	⌄	Water is HO.	Water is H_2O.
Insert superior figure.	⌄	E = MC	$E = MC^2$
Insert question mark.	?	What's going on here	What's going on here?
Paragraph.	¶	done? Now we must	done? Now we must
No paragraph.	no ¶	decided. Then they	decided. Then they
One em space.	☐	☐Call me Ishmael.	Call me Ishmael.
One-em dash.	/🇲/	had if only because	had—if only because
Move as indicated.	⊏	⊏Move left.	Move left.
	⊐	⊐Move right.	Move right.
Close up space.	◯	They had a break up.	They had a breakup.
Let stand as is.	stet	Which one did it?	Which one did it?
Straighten type.	=	Type can shift a bit.	Type can shift a bit.
Query to author.	?	A word overlooked.	A word was overlooked.

FIGURE 24   *The Copy Corrected: Proofreader's Marks in Use*

¶/ˌLet me begin by reminding youˌthat the possession of *of the facts*
ℒ/#/ ~~the~~ true thoughts⌿mean every◯where the possession ⊂/
ι̇ / of ɡnvaluable instruments of action; and that our
ℒ/ duty to gain truth⸗, so far from being a blaȼk com- n/
from◯/ mandˌout of ⟋the blue, or a "stuntˌselfˌimposed by our ⸜/=/
intellect, can account for itself by excellent ℱractical ℓc/
◯/ reasonsˌ

—ⅉames⟋William⟍ ⓒⓐⓟ/ⓣⓗ

Let me begin by reminding you of the fact that
the possession of true thoughts means everywhere
the possession of invaluable instruments of action;
and that our duty to gain truth, so far from being a
blank command from out of the blue, or a "stunt"
self-imposed by our intellect, can account for itself
by excellent practical reasons.

—William James

Copy editing requires exactitude and a prevision of how the corrected
copy will appear. Changes in spacing, vertical or horizontal, and in type style
(italic to Roman or boldface or the reverse) will usually be caught by the
proofreader before the author sees proof. Since several persons work on the
same proof, each should make his or her marks clear but modest in size,
especially queries; for if the query is to be answered equally clearly, adequate
space must be left for that answer. Nothing is less workmanlike than proof
margins filled with sprawling marks and comments.

asked to approve—without later opportunity for change—his typescript as edited by the publisher's staff. Then, omitting galleys
altogether, come page proofs, on which only the correction of typos is
permitted. Experience teaches that one may change one's mind about
a correction a few minutes after making it, or the next morning,
before the galleys have gone back to the printer. This dictates the
rule: *correct all galley and page proofs in erasable pencil.*

The full set of marks used by authors, copy editors, and printers to
indicate corrections or changes in copy. The first is an old "Greek" d, for
delete, and is often reduced in practice to a line with an o-loop in it: the⸍.

To communicate with the printer you use the same traditional signs referred to before. Study the list given in Figure 23 and make the symbols a part of your technical equipment like the alphabet and the multiplication table. When you correct galleys, it is convenient to use a red pencil for the printer's errors and one in another color for changes that depart from copy. This will make it easier to fix responsibility for costs later on. Always mark your changes in the margin next to the line being altered—the left for corrections nearest that side, the right for the other half of the line. The printer will be more surely guided thus, and will avoid compounding the original mistake.

If you can manage it, correct your proofs with the help of another person who "holds copy," that is, reads your manuscript aloud while you enter the corrections on galleys. Have him or her spell the proper names and read out every punctuation mark, paragraph break, and all deviations from lowercase Roman type, such as capitals, italics, and boldface. If you can arrange to read the proof a second time, preferably with a different person holding the copy, you will catch more errors than you now suppose possible. In this kind of collating you must try to see your work in its smallest portions and temporarily lose sight of its meaning. It is like scrutinizing a halftone picture in the newspaper so closely that you see only dots, instead of the different shadings that the eye puts together to make a likeness. In reading galleys all words are equally important.

The printer's marginal queries will draw your attention to some peculiarity in the text, some error in spelling, some ambiguity in your instructions, or some other equally cogent problem. Never let these queries go unanswered.[20]

After galley proofs only one chance of revising remains—the reading of page proofs. These proofs result from dividing the corrected galleys into page size and running off a new set of long sheets; two or three of the future pages appear on each sheet, with page numbers at the appropriate places. Changes, except of the most

[20]The printer may sometimes seek your help in solving a layout problem, such as three successive lines ending in a hyphen or three lines containing an identical word at beginning or end. Again, it is a tradition, apparently as old as printing itself, that the "typographical widow" must be killed at all costs. The widow is defined as less than a full line of type that ends a paragraph and begins a new page. You may be asked to oblige by adding a phrase or two to your text.

FIGURE 25   *An Author and His Proofs*

For seekers after perfection there is no end to revising. Here is a proofsheet of Balzac's famous novel *Eugénie Grandet*, which is a typical "revise" not only of this author's but of many others' in the nineteenth century: printing was cheap and printers were trained to follow this kind of copy. Today such extensive revisions must be made on the typescript—and much more clearly—long before it is turned over to the printer or "keyboarder."

minor sort, are now very costly, virtually prohibitive. You read page proofs only to make certain that in correcting the galleys the printer has not committed new errors in the lines he has reset. Even if you have absolute faith in your editor's ability and willingness to correct page proofs for you, you must also do it yourself.

The author's last duty before launching his work is the preparation of an index. Some few kinds of books do not call for them, such as the collection of literary essays, the casual anthology, and of course fiction generally. But all works for study and consultation need an index. By it their usefulness to the public is greatly increased, particularly if the index is well made.

Many a writer who is wanting in patience and energy will turn the tedious task over to a professional index-maker—or to his research assistant. This is a mistake unless the author is a bad bungler; for however competent the assistant or professional may be, the author has a special understanding of the book and its contribution to knowledge, which only he can accurately reflect in the index. The index is the book reduced to its essential themes and topics. Indexing these so that the reader can penetrate the work and find his way through it easily and with dispatch is a technical task that the beginner can learn by following step by step the instructions in Martha Wheeler's manual.[21]

The general principles are simple enough: with the page proof in hand, you take slips or cards of convenient size—3 × 5 will do—and you write on each the name or word that you consider sufficiently important to index. These are known as "entries." They are followed by the number of the page or pages on which the reader will find these topics treated. Subentries may be made in order to break up a large subject or indicate the aspect of it that is dealt with or referred to on a given page. The slips or cards are alphabetized as you go along, to facilitate the adding of later page numbers. When complete, the set of cards is either sent as it is to the printer, or pasted on sheets, or transcribed in typewritten pages like the remainder of your copy.

The degree of detail in an index varies not with your inclination

[21] *Indexing*, 5th ed., Albany, 1957. Also very helpful is Robert L. Collison, *Indexes and Indexing*, 3 rev. ed., New York, 1969. For computer indexing, see above, p. 104f.

but with your subject matter. A biography, for example, must contain, besides the names of persons and places, entries for the principal activities of the subject's life. But a collection of edited letters needs an even finer sorting of topics, because in the biography the table of contents leads to the data a researcher would seek, whereas the letters can in most cases be arranged only chronologically, and this tells us nothing about their contents. Since the editor cannot predict all the uses to which his work may be put, the index must by its completeness anticipate everyone's questions. *The New Letters of Abigail Adams: 1788–1801*, for instance, contains entries for "Bathing machine," "Bleeding and blistering," "Conechigo waggons," "Lyons: cloaks from," "Measles," "Newspapers: malice of," "Theophilanthropy," "Wine cellar: at Quincy."

To whatever kind your book may belong, make your index such as to prevent the reader's saying that he could not find again a choice passage he came across in its lively pages. At the least, an index will guide the reader to the proper names mentioned in the book. At the most, it will provide a clue to every single item of interest, from a total eclipse of the sun to a passing anecdote.[22] By the care of its preparation, the index shows the author's pride in his work and his regard for other researchers. Both it and they deserve better than to be slighted at his hands.

It may be that after all the pains you and others have taken to make your work an example of perfect printing, you will open your first author's copy and immediately fall upon a grievous typographical error. This will make you indignant for a day or so, while you imagine that every reader sees nothing but that ridiculously misspelled word. Console yourself, if you can, with the thought that in the five centuries of printing few works have been letter perfect. And before Gutenberg, it was the copyists who provided the absurdities, one at a time, by hand.

---

[22]In this regard, the indexes that Samuel Butler prepared for his works are models. One finds, for example, in *Evolution, Old and New*, "Day, Portrait of Mr." and also "Portrait, of Mr. Day." Indexes often tempt their makers to mild eccentricities and even jokes. In a work on economics privately printed in the 1890s, one finds under "Price": "of this book and where to obtain it." For other curiosities of indexing see H. B. Wheatley, *How to Make an Index*, London, 1902.

Speaking What One Knows

The researcher no doubt looks to the printed word as the means by which his learning will reach others. But nowadays speech has regained a Herodotean importance. Broadcasting is ubiquitous, and although teaching by lectures has declined and been widely replaced by the so-called discussion method, the amount of lecturing done by academic people (even in a discussion class) is still very great. Large introductory courses require lectures at least from time to time, and the professional in every field is called upon again and again to address either his fellows or his constituency or both together. A few words about teaching history will indicate attitudes and habits that are desirable in all teaching, most markedly so in dealing with any of the humanities.

Teaching history is no sinecure. This is true, first, because all effective teaching is hard work; and second, because history, like mathematics, meets in certain minds a resistance hard to overcome. History properly deals with the actions of men and women in particular circumstances of time and place. These elements must for the most part be recreated in one's imagination before the "story" becomes understandable, reasonable. For the student, the time is remote—"in those days"—and its customs seem *un*reasonable; as for the place, the child or youth has probably never seen it. And the actors or events are intelligible only when people's complex motives and shifting purposes are made vivid enough to engage the listener's sympathies.

To convey these facts, ideas, and *feelings*, the teacher must naturally possess them to begin with. Few textbooks supply anything but the facts and names, held together by generalities and conventional adjectives. With the aim of "covering" long periods, the author gives cold servings of information that would bore any intelligent adult and a fortiori a younger person. In any case, the student of history should have some notion of how men and women behave, what their economic needs are, and how their political emotions or ideas cause them to act—in a word, what a society and a government are like. It is useless to talk about "the forces of reaction" or "imperialistic greed" or "the conflict between nationalism and liberalism" until these abstractions evoke concrete images of human wants and aims. It is this series of links that the teacher must make vivid. The cant phrase is, "Mrs. X was a great teacher; she made history come alive." The meaning is clear enough but wrongly phrased: history *is* alive to start with and any true written history is as lifelike as a good novel. But for true history many textbooks and some teachers substitute dry-as-dust propositions that merely refer, from a great distance, to the tangible reality of the historical event.

The teacher who knows the danger of this substitution, this second-handness, is on the road to good teaching. The difference between the vivid and the perfunctory is what the teacher must learn and rely on. He or she must read the genuine history of the period, including some of its sources; must read several histories of the same events, several biographies of the same figures, and must keep on reading, with a view to feeling more and more at home with all that he expects to describe and discuss.

We may now return to the technique of lecturing at large.

The Lecture: Tonic or Sedative

The first and most important facts to ascertain before preparing any sort of talk are "how long am I expected to speak?" and "who and how many are expected to attend?" The first question determines the amount and kind of material to present; the second, the vocabulary, tone, and degree of complexity that are appropriate. Knowing the characteristics of your audience, you can pitch your remarks at the right level. If, for example, you are addressing the League of Women Voters you can count on a degree of political sophistication that allows you to present your ideas about this or that public issue with confidence that it will be listened to eagerly and with a ready grasp. The requirements of a freshman class at the beginning of the year, or of a mixed public audience seeking diversion will be understandably different. You must supply more detail and proceed step-by-step. Audiences quickly sense whether the speaker has taken the trouble to meet their needs. When a famous public figure, once an academic, was asked to address a noontime, half-hour student convocation at Berkeley and, having announced that he would discuss four points, reached the twenty-five-minute mark with the words "My second point is . . . ," he saw several hundreds of his listeners rise and depart. This legitimate rebuff was for his implied discourtesy—his neglect of the duty to prepare a balanced presentation fitting the terms of the invitation.

An academic lecture usually lasts fifty minutes, and a practiced lecturer will find that on any subject he knows well he can deliver, without looking at the clock, fifty minutes' worth of coherent information. The set lecture has at least the merit of fulfilling the tacit contract between speaker and listener, provided, of course, that the lecturer is not only practiced but also conscientious. This qualification means that (1) he has invariably prepared himself before lecturing; (2) he took special pains when he was a beginner; and (3) he has never ceased being self-critical after each of his performances. These three statements need concrete illustration.

"To prepare" includes carving out a subject that exhibits unity; assembling and organizing the relevant materials; writing out a text or notes, and measuring the time of delivery. This measurement may be made by rehearsing the speech with an eye on the clock, or by writing out every word and counting. A good rate of delivery is 125 words a minute.[23] It allows for variations of speed as well as pauses for rest or emphasis. But of course, a speaker must adjust any norm to his own temperament—within limits. Though the drawl native to Vermont or Texas probably cannot be hurried up, some people's breathless rush of words *must* be slowed if any ideas are to enter and survive in the audience's minds.

---

[23]The great English advocate Marshall Hall spoke, in at least one famous case, at the rate of 158 words a minute. His opponent, Rufus Isaacs, spoke 120 words a minute. (Edward Marjoribanks, *The Life of Sir Edward Marshall Hall*, London, 1929, 307–308.) These are perhaps the limits within which any speaking that occupies more than a few minutes ought to proceed. To be sure, other features of delivery matter equally. It is not enough, as someone put it, "to drone at the proper rate." The handbooks on public speaking list a dozen or fourteen other "factors," such as "specific words," "colorful words," "suspense and climax," and so on. But these enumerations are really of little use; they itemize too narrowly. No speaker can say to himself, "Now's the time for a colorful word. . . . Here goes for a little suspense." Those elements must spring naturally out of the movement of one's thought, or else develop gradually as a mental trait from critical dissatisfaction with one's mode of lecturing.

To carve out the subject, collect the facts, and set them down are interlinked operations. The big subject is defined by the occasion itself—the course, the conference, or the lecture series. If it is "Revolution in Europe: 1789, 1917," it is clear that the desired comparison will allow only a few points to be made. Only the self-centered lecturer with no judgment will spend his time trying hopelessly to give a full account of the French Revolution, apologizing at the last minute for ignoring 1917 and cheating his audience. But the moral applies even more generally: *all* lectures should limit themselves to a few points—six at the most. These points (ideas, conclusions, issues, questions) form the invisible structure of the performance. They are best announced near the beginning, mentioned as needed for cross references showing relationships, and restated—perhaps in combined form—at the end.

All this artifice is designed to make up for the unavoidable weakness of instruction by word of mouth: the listener cannot turn back the page, cannot request "please say that again," cannot stop and think over a new or difficult interpretation. On his side, the lecturer cannot help forging ahead—rattling on—so that if the interested listener is taking notes, an abyss of time and idea will quickly widen between them. Hence repetition, which gives the auditor a second chance to follow what all parties hope is consecutive thought.

Repetition will best enhance the presentation of facts and ideas under each main point when it is done with art, not mechanically. Once in a while a single pregnant statement may be said twice in the same words; but the device, overused, would irritate and insult. The subtler way is by words of linking. For example, the point has just been made that the Austrian Foreign Office did not in fact know that Serbian conspirators with official backing were responsible for the murder of the Archduke Francis Ferdinand; they merely suspected and hoped that it was so but asserted that they had proof. Repeating this important truth can then take the form of saying: "Yet *in this state of actual ignorance and deceit coupled with high expectancy,* the decision was made to issue an ultimatum." The italicized words would be redundant in a written text; they show skill and sense of form in a lecture.

The remaining part of preparation is to equip oneself with an aid to memory. It is all too easy to forget Point 3 when its time comes or to anticipate it at the wrong place, through a chance association of ideas. On formal occasions, conscientious lecturers bring a text fully written out.[24] They, and their audience as well, rightly consider improvisation a sign of disrespect. For of the many risks entailed by speaking without a text the greatest is the waste of time: it is not possible to avoid stumbling, backtracking, and repeating to no purpose. With a complete text the speaker says more in the same number of minutes and says it more exactly. The disadvantage of dullness through poor reading will be discussed in a moment.

For lecturing in courses, or on informal occasions, or again on subjects which frequent handling has rendered intimate, one lectures from notes. These may range from very brief to full. Full notes, whether they consist of complete paragraphs with gaps of thought between, or whether they follow the outline style of heads and subheads, should be typed in the clearest possible form, so that the lecturer can use them without bobbing his head up and down between the paper and the faces of the audience. The complete paragraphs need not be spoken word for word. They serve to launch the lecturer on each successive topic—they are "topic paragraphs," which he then enlarges upon extemporaneously out of his stock of learning. An outline does the same thing, but guides the thought down to the last item of the planned discourse. As for brief notes, they can be condensed so as to fit on a single 3 × 5 card bearing only the four or five main heads, or they may occupy four or five such cards, with hints under each point. Old-time after-dinner speakers used to jot down key words on their starched cuffs, from which grew the expression "to speak off the cuff"—without preparation.

The impromptu, off-the-cuff speaker can give himself and his hearers a special satisfaction, but only if he is fluent, clear, witty, and coherent. He then seems like a candid friend addressing each person in the audience intimately. He sounds spontaneous, unprepared, free of the constraint of a folder or stack of notes—even his cuff is not in

---

[24]In fact, the sponsors of the lecture are all too likely to ask for the full text a week or more before the lecture, in order to give it to the press, and they often want it for printing or excerpting afterwards.

sight. But such artistry is the fruit of much hidden preparation and long practice. And what goes into this practice is directly applicable to the deliberate lecturer as well.

To begin with, anyone who speaks much in public should learn to enunciate properly and steadily. Nothing is more annoying to a listener than to miss every tenth word, either because the speaker mumbles or because he drops his head and his voice at the end of every sentence. That terminal swallow sometimes coincides with what is meant to be a joke, or at least an ironic remark. It is tiresomely bad. And the same holds—though in a lesser degree—for all tricks of the hand, head, and limbs. Don't draw attention away from your golden thoughts by fiddling with objects, rocking on your feet, or clutching your chair, lectern, or elbows. Elementary—yes, but do not just approve the precept: make sure, by asking a friend in the audience, whether you act out your nervousness in any of these ways.

Next, make an habitual effort to speak in complete sentences, not just on the platform, but all the time. You will not succeed; it is virtually impossible, but any degree of success helps. The intent to "preview," as it were, the words you are about to say enhances ease, fluency, and clarity when you address your listeners more formally than in conversation. That effort will not make you talk like a book—which nobody wants; rather, it will eliminate the stumbles and substitutes for speech: "er-," "you know," "like," "zise saying," "right?," and even the less noticeable but equally unnecessary "now," "however," "well," "of course," with which speakers mechanically conceal the lack of the next word.

When a lecturer speaks from notes, the chances are good that he will utter fairly short sentences of simple form, that is, if his sentences have intelligible form at all. The threat to form and clarity will then come chiefly from the desire to throw in qualifying clauses one after the other, until he forgets how he started his simple sentence and so cannot find the exit door to its proper ending.

The lecturer who uses a written text for all or part of his speech runs a different risk. He is likely to use the sentence structure that he finds natural in what he writes and what he reads—the complex, periodic style which is so convenient and precise in printed prose. It is quite the wrong style for a lecture. The reason why audiences often dread seeing the lecturer pull out his typescript is not merely that some lecturers do not know how to read aloud, it is also that many written lectures are not lectures at all, but essays, which no actor or elocutionist could make attractive by speech. In short, there is a way to "write for the voice" which lecturers should learn.

The way is not difficult; it consists mainly of negatives. Do not write long sentences. Do not begin with your modifiers and qualifiers, but let them trail after. If you start with the "although . . . ," "since . . . ," or "whereas . . . ," which properly introduces a limitation on the idea that will follow the clause, the listener must hang on to that limitation for some time before he knows what to apply it to. When he finds out, he will probably have forgotten the point or force of the limitation. What was recommended about shaping sentences on p. 320 above is here disallowed, the purposes being opposite. And what applies to the complex sentence applies to the paragraph: don't begin "whittling away" before you have "built up." Affirmation(s) must come first and be thoroughly clear before you raise objections, make exceptions or concessions. Failing this awareness of the difference between understanding by ear and by eye, you will leave your audience confused—or thinking *you* confused.

To continue favoring the ear, don't use words that are or sound like technical terms in long strings connected by prepositions. They soon dizzy the mind with their abstractions and their similar endings in *-tion* or *ity.* Use concrete subjects and verbs of action—as in written prose—and vary the pace, alternating comment with information.

Again, do not go from one main point to another without a break and a remark. Use still more signposts than are necessary for print. Invite your audience to look back ("We have seen . . .") and forward ("Now we can turn to . . ."). The You-and-I (or we) attitude is much more desirable in the lecture form than in the essay. The audience likes to feel guided, which in no way implies that it must be talked down to. The assumption is always that the lecturer and his listeners are on the same plane, equals in their concern with the subject and in their courteous attention to each other. The lecturer's learning or string of degrees has nothing to do with the case. This rule must govern especially the question period or class period in which questions are asked.[25] The lecturer puts the best construction on all questions, overlooking impertinence as well as incoherence—usually signs of nervousness—and giving his best thought to answering what the questioner very likely has in mind and other listeners too.[26] And naturally the lecturer admits any errors of fact or statement that are brought to his notice.

The principle of civility holds as in conversation, for a lecture can hardly be effective if it does not arouse in the minds of the listeners a continuous response and a kind of silent conversing with the speaker. Only when this rapport obtains will a lecture instruct, let alone entertain. An experienced lecturer knows whether he has brought his audience to this condition of give-and-take, and an inexperienced one is apt to think that starting with a joke insures it automatically. That is a common error. Nothing is harder than telling a joke well; half the audience has heard it before, and if it has no bearing on the subject of the lecture, the hearers, after their dutiful laughter, are as cold as when the lecturer first opened his mouth. Begin seriously, then, having taken thought about the place *within the subject* where the collective mind probably stands. In a lecture course or series, gather the minds to that place by referring to the point where you left off the time before. Then carry on, with a dash of humor or wit if truly relevant and fresh. An audience commonly wants to be pleased and is therefore not hard to please; it wants to think well of the lecturer, and he is honor-bound not to defeat that generous impulse.

These truths suggest a last bit of advice, for the occasions when a lecture is to be read. We shall assume it was written *to be* read and clearly typed for reading, that is, in pica type and triple-spaced.[27] The sheets should be stapled (not clipped) together, or bound in a folder with spread fasteners. So secured, no loose pages will fly all over the

[25]It is not difficult to provide a question period from time to time in courses with large enrollments that are taught by lectures. Twenty minutes at the end of, say, every third lecture will suffice to answer important questions that the entire class is wondering about, even though only a few ask them. But the period must be handled with candor and judgment.

[26]This recommendation does not mean that he should be patient under heckling or insults. He should then, with an apology to the civil part of the audience, excuse himself from the place of turmoil.

[27]Some typewriters carry a font called "Orator," which is large and legible, being all capitals. See Figure 26.

platform when you make an unlucky gesture in the middle of your speech. (And check the sequence of pages before fastening.) If equipment is to be used in the lecture—a public address system or a slide projector—it is likewise the duty of the modern rehearser to make sure that they will work. It is surprising how often such machines are out of order and how carelessly the "management" assumes that turning on the switch will make them perform.

To read agreeably, your nose and chin must be visible to the audience for most of the time. If the nose is on the page and the chin on the chest, you are reading to yourself, not to the assembly. This fact of nature explains why your text must be legible at a distance of, say, eighteen inches. Only your eyes must look down, to catch the beginning of the next sentence while you are still speaking the preceding words. A little practice will make this coordination of functions seem natural, as in playing an instrument. The eyes are raised again while the greater part of each sentence is spoken, for the listeners understand with pleasure only what the living countenance delivers—that is why TV can afford to talk a great deal longer at a stretch than radio could.

It is obvious that if most of your words are to be spoken with the eyes off the text, those words must be familiar to you. Well, you have written them, revised them, and proofread them, and you must shortly before the lecture rehearse them. A convenient routine is to go over the phrasing of the delivery, that is, the natural pauses. Certain groups of words must be said in one breath, yet the end of the line (or page) cuts off, let us say, the last two: mark that false ending so that your delivery rolls on unbroken. Upright lines or double lines, short arrows, and underlinings for special emphasis are usually enough for all ordinary purposes. (See Figure 26.) You will find that the very effort of preparing this reading copy imprints on your mind the necessary information for giving a persuasive performance. Having marked, you have nothing more to do until an hour or two before the speech, when you go over it for possible changes or additions to the marking. Some lecturers actually rehearse aloud, others hear as they read silently. In either case, the preparation is complete. On the platform, or rather on the lectern, the "score" gives you absolute confidence, and you find that you do not so much "read a speech"—a heartless act—as give a recital of your ideas.

FIGURE 26   *Marking a Speech for Delivery*

AT OUR LAST MEETING,‖ MY PURPOSE ′ WAS TO GIVE YOU AN acc′t

A̶C̶C̶O̶U̶N̶T̶ OF THE RISE OF ART AS A RELIGION IN THE NINETEENTH⌒

CENTURY.‖ BY SHOWING HOW ÁRT CAME TO BE REGARDED ′ AS THE

SUPREME EXPRESSION OF MAN′S SPIRITUAL POWERS,‖ I WAS ABLE TO⌒

EXPLAIN HOW ′ AT THE SAME TIME ′ ÁRT NECESSARILY BECAME THE

(2)   (1)
ULTIMATE CRITIC OF LIFE AND THE MORAL CENSOR OF SOCIETY.‖‖

AT THE END OF MY LECTURE ′ I SAID I WOULD NEXT DISCUSS THE final

         (2)   (1)
F̶I̶N̶A̶L̶ PHASE OF THIS CLAIM AND THIS DUEL,↗ THE PHASE OF

  (2)   (1)   ‖
ESTHETICISM AND OF ABOLITIONISM WHICH FILLS THE QUARTER- century

---

Any convenient marks will do, provided they are used consistently. The vertical, short or long, suggest pauses of corresponding length—for emphasis or the separation of ideas. The horizontal indicate that the voice must hold up to the end, usually not visible all on one line. Numbers in reverse order show how many equal and matching parts occur in a series. The curved arrows point to the next phrase or line when necessary. The handwritten inserts at the end of a line that is incomplete prepare the mind for the broken or unguessable word in the next line or overleaf.

The Whole Circle of Work: Scholarly Editing

The ultimate test of a scholar's skill is *editing*. It is in fact the sum and application of all the mental and physical operations performed in research. That this art-and-craft is not generally acknowledged as high intellectual work shows how few of those who put their names on a title page as "editor" have understood what the undertaking demands: It would be good for scholarship and for culture generally if instead of requiring wordy dissertations that chiefly quote and para-phrase, the Ph.D. degree called for editing with thoroughness a text of modest size.

The editor has a double obligation, to his author and to his readers. The author's work must be presented faithfully and also intelligibly. This means recording variants, explaining allusions, identifying names, and clearing up apparent or real errors and contradictions. An able editor will also want to indicate sources and influences and offer a judgment on points that over the years have created controversies. The latest editor, in short, settles everything, for his author's sake. For that sake also, the intelligent editor produces a readable text. There is a modern practice favored by the show-off species of editor, which makes the apparatus overwhelm the work. Variants are stuck between brackets in the very middle of a sentence and a blizzard of notes and symbols blankets the discourse that they should unobtrusively assist the reader in following.

The truth is that the good scholarly editor must explain only what needs explanation and must dispose his myriad facts in the most artful way for use—such a way that the reader who does not need a particular identification can ignore it easily and the reader who does need it can find it just as easily. Variants, likewise, should not be placed where they destroy meaning and should be featured when they add to it. For a model of intelligent editing see Roy P. Basler's *Collected Works of Abraham Lincoln*, from which we gave extracts above on p. 333.

The editor, in effect, must be a layout artist, and a concise writer. For the composition of good footnotes is by no means easy. Identifying an obscure name, for example, calls for bringing to bear on the point of the text some fairly scattered facts: "Claude Ruggieri (fl. 1830) was descended from a large family of pyrotechnic experts who came to France under Louis XIV and who maintained their specialty through the ensuing regimes." Or again, about a source: "This supplement, dated 1867, does not occur in the National Edition of Mazzini's works, but only in the six-volume English selection from the writings. It is therefore given in the words of the English translator of that edition, who presumably was the only one to see the Italian original."

The compact presentation of such minutiae is an art that requires practice; as in any art, success depends on the selection and ordering of parts; for the editor in his search invariably turns up more than he can (or should) use, and having often had a hard time obtaining his information he may be tempted to unload his treasures on the reader. As to the painstaking of the search itself, hear the testimony of the latest editor of Pepys' huge *Diary*, Robert Latham, who among his other tasks had to identify some three thousand names. Here in his own words is one aspect of his adventure:

> It was fortunate, as I said, that Pepys was a Londoner. It was fortunate, too, that I also was a Londoner when doing most of my research, for the editor of the diary has to tackle a wide range of subjects—the history of politics, of the machine of government, of the navy, the Church, of music, the theatre and science, of food, drink and dress and so on—and his task is infinitely easier if he has easy access to London's institutions of learning—the British Library, the Public Record Office, the Institute of Historical Research and the rest. Splendid institutions—and almost without exception splendidly served by their staff who often spend hours of their time on readers' difficulties. The only exception I found—and I can be frank for things have now changed—was at Somerset House. There were kept the contemporary registers of the wills proved in the diocese of Canterbury—essential tools for biographical work. The registers are large and repulsive volumes—the heaviest and dirtiest books I ever came across in the course of my research. These it was the duty of the officials to carry from the stacks to the readers' desks. At one end of the reading room was an official (clerical grade) to whom one handed one's application slip (he was reading the *Daily Telegraph*): at the other end was an official (messenger grade) who fetched the volumes. (He was reading the *Daily Mirror*.) And it was the aim of each to go on reading his paper rather than get the volumes out. But, as I say, all that has now changed. The wills for my period are now kept in the Public Record Office, and the officers in charge at Somerset House, presumably, are left undisturbed with their newspapers.[28]

With such an example in one's memory, no ordinary task of research can seem arduous, beyond one's strength. To be sure, there will come to all of us moments of discouragement, when the serried ranks of notebooks, or even a small pile of "look-ups" can seem to be mountains. The image to conjure up at that point is the Chinese "drop of water which, falling day by day, pierces through rock." Tackle *one* notebook, do a *portion* of the items to verify, write the opening of that chapter. Keep at it and the handy fractions will in the end add up to the unity of the finished work.

[28]*Journal of the Royal Society of Arts*, 132, no. 5334 (May 1984), 395.

Afterword:
A Discipline for Work

You have now reached the end of a long course of advice, exhortation, and instruction. It may seem to you that you have been told too many things to be able to apply all of them at once to your research and writing; you have been made self-conscious about unsuspected traps, and this has damped your carefree mood. Or again, you may think that you have been told many useful things, but not the details you want for your present project. If either of these impressions is yours at the moment, your reading has not been in vain. You have been shaken out of your normal ways and made to reflect on your powers and responsibilities. The only alarming symptom at this point would be the feeling that now you know all there is to know and can apply it forthwith.

Such a belief would be dangerous for two reasons: first, because this book has given you but the principles of research and writing, with some illustrations; which means that you still have to make the adaptive transfer of the rules and suggestions to your work and your needs; and second, because no new knowledge can ever be grasped and made use of in one sweep of the mind. Time is needed to assimilate it by the formation of new habits. Time is also needed to go back to one or another topic in order to refresh the memory about what was actually said. In a word, now that you have finished reading or studying this book, you should begin to use it as a mentor at your elbow and as a work of reference on your desk.

This suggestion brings up a matter we have not yet discussed, one that is generally taken for granted, though perhaps without warrant—the matter of when and how to work. Some hints were given in Chapter 2 about the division of tasks in research, and we may repeat it here: you should keep your clearest stretches of time for the uninterrupted study of your main sources. Verifying dates, hunting down references, and, generally, all broken-field running should be reserved for occasions when you have a shorter time at your disposal or when you are feeling less alert or energetic than usual. Your best mind should go to what takes thought.

The same principle applies to writing, with variations and additions. Faced with the need to write, most people (including practiced writers) experience a strong and strange impulse to put off beginning. They would do anything rather than confront that blank sheet of paper. They start inventing pretexts for doing something else: they need to look up another source, they have not sufficiently mulled over the organization of the paper, they want to steep themselves in their notes once more. Or—what is really cowardly—there is some shopping that cannot wait, or again, the typewriter keys need a thorough cleaning. Let it be said once and for all: *there is no cure for this desire to escape*. It will recur as long as you live. But there are palliatives, and some of them are good enough to turn the struggle virtually into a game.

The palliative principle is that a regular force must be used to overcome a recurrent inertia: if you can arrange to write regularly, never missing your date with yourself, no matter whether you are in the mood or not, you have won half the battle. You do not have to be pleased with what you do, nor expect a set amount to be done by the end of the session, but *some* writing you must do on the morning or afternoon or evening that is kept sacred for the purpose. The writer's problem is the inverse of the reformed drunkard's. The latter must *never* touch a drop; the former must *always* do his stint. Skip but one writing period and you need the strength of Samson to get started again.

It goes without saying that these writing periods must be close enough together to create a rhythm of work, and that they must be chosen with an eye to the greatest convenience in your present mode of life. For example, if you possibly can, set aside one free morning or day for writing. The longer the free period, the better. A time with no fixed obligation at the end is preferable to one that will draw your eye to the clock halfway through, and so on. Similarly with the place. Do not try to write at home if you can hear your roommate's video tapes or the domestic symphony of kitchen and nursery noises; conversely, do not attempt to write in an office where the phone and your associates will interrupt every ten minutes.

In making your arrangements, consider that a likely cause of the distaste for beginning is that writing is for all of us an act of self-exposure. Writing requires that we create some order in our thoughts and project it outside, where everybody can see it. The instinct of self-protection, of shyness, combines with the sense of our mental confusion or uncertainty to make us postpone the trial of strength. Hence the desirability of being alone and uninterrupted. In silence our thoughts can settle into their proper shapes; they will be exclusively the thoughts bearing on our topic, and as soon as a few of them are down on paper they will draw out the rest. The momentum will increase until, after a time, the bulk of work done will set up a desire to keep adding to it. The hour or day set aside for writing will be waited for, and the work will truly be *in progress*.

Since the problem is best seen as one of inertia and momentum, other rules of thumb suggest themselves as corollaries:

1. Do not wait until you have gathered all your material before starting to write. Nothing adds to inertia like a mass of notes, the earliest of which recede in the mists of foregone time. On the contrary, begin drafting your ideas as soon as some portion of the topic appears to hang together in your mind.

2. Do not be afraid of writing down something that you think may have to be changed. Paper is not granite, and in a first draft you are not carving eternal words in stone. Rather, you are creating substance to be molded and remolded in successive drafts.

3. Do not hesitate to write up in any order those sections of your

total work that seem to have grown ripe in your mind. There is a moment in any stretch of research when all the details come together in natural cohesion, despite small gaps and doubts. Learn to recognize that moment and seize it by composing in harmony with your inward feeling of unity. Never mind whether the portions that come out are consecutive.

4. Once you start writing, keep going. Resist the temptation to get up and verify a fact. Leave it blank. The same holds true for the word or phrase that refuses to come to mind. It will arise much more easily on revision, and the economy in time *and momentum* is incalculable.

5. When you get stuck in the middle of a stretch of writing, reread your last two or three pages and see if continuity of thought will not propel you past dead center. Many writers begin the day's work by reading over the previous day's accumulation. But there are other ways of beginning, such as writing one or two letters, transcribing or expanding a few notes, making an entry in a diary, and the like. The common feature of such a wind-up or running start is that the chosen act is one of *writing* and that it is brief—a *few* notes or lines before tackling the main task.

6. Since the right openings for chapters or sections are difficult, special attention must be paid to them. As you collect your materials, be on the watch for ideas or facts or even words that would make a good beginning.[1] Remember that in any extended work you begin many times, not only at each new chapter, but often at each subsection. Supposing that writing a twenty-page chapter takes you three sessions, you may find it helpful to break off in the middle of, and not at, a subdivision. In this way you take up the story in midstream, instead of having to begin the day *and* the section together. Some writers make a point of breaking off the day's work just before they completely run down and while they still see ideas ahead. They scribble two or three final words to call these up at once on resuming work.

7. It will often happen that the opening paragraph of the whole piece (or of any of its parts) will on rereading seem quite alien to what follows. This calls for a pair of scissors. What has happened is that the first paragraph was simply the warming-up, and the true beginning

[1] See again p. 288.

was set down in the second. From this common experience you should infer that a slow sluggish start on Saturday morning is no reason for discouragement. You are priming the pump, coaxing the car, and the splutter is of no consequence.

8. A writer should as soon as possible become aware of any peculiarities and preferences regarding the mechanics of composing. He or she may like pen better than typewriter or vice versa, may favor a certain size or color of paper, may require a special disposition of the books and notes on the desk, and may even prefer a kind of clothes, of posture, or of lighting to another. In all these matters one is entitled to complete self-indulgence provided one remains faithful to one's choices. This is consistent with our underlying principle: indulge yourself so that you will have no excuse for putting off the task; and stick to your choice, so that the very presence of your favorite implements will elicit the habits of the good worker.

When the first draft is done the back of the job is broken. It is then a pleasure—or it should be one—to carve, cut, add, and polish until what you say corresponds reasonably well to what you know. The span of time and other conditions of revising are less rigorous than those of first drafting. If your manuscript has passed into typed form, you can use a spare half-hour to proofread it and mark the rough spots with little xs or wavy lines in the margin. You can be thinking about substitutions and additions until the next free hour when you can Revise with a big R, as against typographical revising with a small one—respectively the big operations described in Chapters 2, 12, and 13, and the lesser mentioned in Chapter 16.

Ideally, a report should be in progress in its entirety long before it is finished. The earlier parts will be well advanced while the last ones are still in the rough, the research for them not yet finished. Research will in fact continue to the end, which is, in the case of a book, indexing from page proofs. The revision at one time of different parts in different stages of perfecting is an excellent way of seeing one's construction as a whole and in detail. Each critical observation supplies hints to be carried out in other parts, and this evens out the advantages of experience gathered on the way. Follow this suggestion and your work will not seem better done in proportion as it approaches the end.

But it is a little premature to speak here of the end. Despite what was said at the outset of this section about having completed a sizable course with us, the reader is only at the beginning of real work. Whatever the enterprise—short report or extended monograph—let him take his courage in both hands and, by the application of mind, bring order and meaning out of the welter of facts. With the best will in the world, the work will not be free from error—so much it is safe to predict. But that part of it which is sound, clear, readily grasped and remembered will be a contribution, no matter how limited its scope, to that order among ideas which we call knowledge. For as Francis Bacon wisely observed in his *New Method*, "truth will sooner come out from error than from confusion."[2]

[2]*Novum Organum*, Book 2, 20.

For Further Reading

The list of books that follows is not a bibliography in the sense of a repertory comprising the works cited in the text or consulted in its preparation. Only a few such books are listed here. Instead, we are suggesting a small number of outstanding books related to the three parts of our work, so that readers may acquaint themselves with other points of view on the various topics we have taken up.

On the Historian's Work

Method

Altick, Richard D., *The Art of Literary Research*, 3rd ed. New York, Norton, 1982.

Elton, G. R., *The Practice of History*. London, Methuen, 1967.

Hancock, W. K., *Attempting History*. Canberra, Australian National University Press, 1969.

Renier, G. J., *History: Its Purpose and Method*. Macon, Ga., Mercer University Press, 1982.

Truth and Causation

Bloch, Marc, *The Historian's Craft*. New York, Vintage Books, 1964.

Dunning, William A., *Truth in History and Other Essays*. Port Washington, N.Y., Kennikat Press, 1965.

Hexter, J. H., *The History Primer*. New York, Basic Books, 1971.
Winks, Robin W., ed., *The Historian as Detective: Essays on Evidence*. New York, Harper and Row, 1970.

Modes of Historiography

Berlin, Isaiah, *Historical Inevitability*. New York, Oxford University Press, 1955.
Butterfield, Herbert, *Man on His Past: The Study of the History of Historical Scholarship*. Cambridge, Cambridge University Press, 1969.
Geyl, Pieter, *Debates with Historians*. Cleveland, World, 1964.
Löwith, Karl, *Meaning in History: The Theological Implications of the Philosophy of History*. Chicago, University of Chicago Press, 1957.
Lukacs, John, *Historical Consciousness*. New York, Schocken Books, 1985.
Muller, Herbert J., *The Uses of the Past: Profiles of Former Societies*. New York, Oxford University Press, 1957.
Nevins, Allan, *The Gateway to History*, rev. ed. Garden City, N. Y., Anchor Books, 1962.
Plumb, J. H., *The Death of the Past*. Atlantic Highlands, N.J., Humanities, 1978.
Sellar, W. C., and Yeatman, R. J., *1066 and All That*. New York, Dutton, 1958.
Stern, Fritz, ed., *The Varieties of History: From Voltaire to the Present*. New York, Random House, 1973.
Trevelyan, George Macaulay, *Clio, A Muse and Other Essays*. Folcroft, Pa., Folcroft, 1973.

The Great Historians

Barker, John, *The Superhistorians*, New York, Scribner, 1982.
Burckhardt, Jacob, *Judgments on History and Historians*. Boston, Beacon Press, 1958.
Clive, John, *Macaulay: The Shaping of the Historian*. New York, Knopf, 1973.
Cunliffe, M., and Winks, R., eds., *Pastmasters: Some Essays on American Historians*. Westport, Conn., Greenwood Press, 1979.
Gooch, G. P., *History and Historians in the Nineteenth Century*. Boston, Beacon Press, 1965.
Grant, Michael, *The Ancient Historians*. New York, Scribner, 1970.
Hofstadter, Richard, *The Progressive Historians: Turner, Beard, Par-*

rington. Chicago, University of Chicago Press, 1979.

Schmitt, Bernadotte E., ed., *Some Historians of Modern Europe*. Port Washington, N.Y., Kennikat Press, 1966.

Thompson, J. W., and Holm, B. J., *A History of Historical Writing*, 2 vols. Gloucester, Mass., Peter Smith, 1967.

The Sister Disciplines

Barzun, Jacques, *Clio and the Doctors: Psycho-History, Quanto-History and History*. Chicago, University of Chicago Press, 1974.

Berelson, Bernard, *Human Behavior*. New York, Harcourt Brace Jovanovich, 1967.

Gerth, H. H. and Mills, C. W., eds., *From Max Weber: Essays in Sociology*. New York, Oxford, 1946.

Harris, Marvin, *The Rise of Anthropological Theory: A History of the Theories of Culture*. New York, Harper and Row, 1968.

Heilbroner, Robert L., *The Worldly Philosophers: The Lives, Times, and Ideas of the Great Economic Thinkers*. New York, Simon and Schuster, 1961.

Jouvenel, Bertrand de, *The Art of Conjecture*, trans. by Nikita Lary. New York, Basic Books, 1967.

Landes, D. S. and Tilley, C., eds., *History as Social Science*. Englewood Cliffs, N.J., Prentice-Hall, 1971.

Merton, R. K. and Nisbet, R. A., eds., *Contemporary Social Problems*, 4th ed. New York, Harcourt Brace Jovanovich, 1976.

Mink, Louis O., *Mind, History and Dialectic*. Bloomington, Indiana University Press, 1969.

Petrie, W. M. Flinders, *Some Sources of Human History*. London, Society for Promoting Christian Knowledge, 1919.

Watson, P. J., LeBlanc, S. A., and Redman, C. L., *Explanation in Archeology: An Explicit Scientific Approach*. New York, Columbia University Press, 1971.

Woodworth, R. S., and Sheehan, M. R., *Contemporary Schools of Psychology*, 3rd ed. New York, Ronald Press, 1964.

On Writing and Composition

Diction and Style

Barzun, Jacques, *Simple and Direct: A Rhetoric for Writers*, rev. ed. New York, Harper and Row, 1985.

Follett, Wilson, *Modern American Usage*. New York, Hill and Wang, 1966.

Fowler, H. W., and Fowler, F. G., *The King's English*, 3rd ed. Oxford, Clarendon Press, 1934.

Gowers, Sir Ernest, *Plain Words: Their ABC*. Baltimore, Penguin Books, 1963.

Hull, Helen, ed., *The Writer's Book*. New York, Barnes and Noble, 1956.

Titles and Forms of Address: A Guide to Their Correct Use, 12th ed. London, A. and C. Black, 1964.

Weil, Benjamin H., *Technical Editing*. Westport, Conn., Greenwood, 1975.

Forms

Bond, John J., *Handy-book of Rules and Tables for Verifying Dates with the Christian Era*, New York, Russell and Russell, 1966. (Calendars of various eras and peoples.)

Chaundy, T. W., Barrett, P. R., and Batey, C., *The Printing of Mathematics: Aids for Authors and Editors and Rules for Compositors and Readers at the University Press, Oxford*. London, Oxford University Press, 1954.

The Chicago Manual of Style, 13th ed. Chicago, University of Chicago Press, 1982.

Collins, F. Howard, *Authors' and Printers' Dictionary*, 10th ed. London, Oxford University Press, 1956.

Deighton, Lee C., *Handbook of American English Spelling*. New York, Van Nostrand Reinhold, 1973.

Jarrett, James, *Printing Style for Authors, Compositors, and Readers*. London, Allen and Unwin, 1960.

Labaree, Leonard W., ed., *The Papers of Benjamin Franklin*. New Haven, Conn., Yale University Press, 1959, I, xxxiv–xlvii. (Document editing.)

Modern Language Association of America, *MLA Handbook for Writers of Research Papers*, 2nd ed. New York, 1984.

The New York Times Manual of Style and Usage, rev. and ed. by Lewis Jordan. New York, Quadrangle/The New York Times Book Company, 1976.

Summey, George, *American Punctuation*. New York, Ronald Press, 1949.

Turabian, Kate L., *A Manual for Writers of Term Papers, Theses, and*

Dissertations, 4th ed. Chicago, University of Chicago Press, 1973.

Wheeler, Martha Thorne, *Indexing: Principles, Rules, and Examples*, 5th ed. Albany, New York State Library, University of the State of New York, 1957.

Translation

Adams, Robert Martin, *Proteus, His Lies, His Truth: Discussions of Literary Translation*. New York, Norton, 1973.

Anderson, J. G., *Le Mot Juste: An Anglo-French Lexicon* (1932), rev. ed. by L. C. Harmer. New York, Dutton, 1938.

Barzun, Jacques, *On Writing, Editing, and Publishing*, Chapter 3. Chicago, University of Chicago Press, 1971.

Bissell, Clifford H., *Prepositions in French and English*. New York, Richard R. Smith, 1947.

Brueckner, John H., *A French Contextuary*, Englewood Cliffs, N.J., Prentice-Hall, 1975.

Chevalley, A., and Chevalley, M., *Concise Oxford French Dictionary*, Introduction and *passim*. New York, Oxford University Press, 1950.

Flood, W. E., and West, M., *An Elementary Scientific and Technical Dictionary*, 3rd ed. London, Longmans, Green, 1962.

Kastner, L. E., and Marks, J., *A Glossary of Colloquial and Popular French*. New York, Dutton, 1929.

Knox, Ronald A., *On Englishing the Bible*. London, Burns Oates, 1949. (The American edition is *The Trials of a Translator*, New York, Sheed & Ward, 1949.)

Koessler, M., and Derocquigny, J., *Les Faux Amis: les pièges du vocabulaire anglais*. Paris, Vuibert, 1949.

Levieux, M., and Levieux, E., *Cassell's Beyond the Dictionary in French*. New York, Funk & Wagnalls, 1967.

Postgate, J. P., *Translation and Translations: Theory and Practice*. London, Bell, 1922.

Smith, W. J., *A Dictionary of Musical Terms in Four Languages*. London, Hutchinson, 1961.

Von Ostermann, Georg, *Manual of Foreign Languages*, 4th ed. New York, Central Book Company, 1952.

Index

433

History writing (*Cont.*)
ancient, 44–46; aim of, 47, 48; verification in, 111–12; and journalism, 122; and attributions in, 122–24; demand for accuracy, 144; avoiding fallacies, 155–58; form in, 193–94, 195; selection in, 197–98; bias in, 198, 199–205; revisionism, 205–6; collective, 223–24; specialization, 231; *see also* Historian; Historiography
Hitler, Adolf, 227*n.*; "Diaries," 122
Hoaxes, 87–88, 117*n.*, 122, 141
Hoffmann, Banesh, 183*n.*
Hofstadter, Richard, 246; quoted, 375
Holbrook, Stewart H., 398
Holy Alliance, 13
Homer, 45, 89, 288
Honesty: in research, 57–58; and selection of facts, 190; intellectual, 200; in footnoting, 359
Hook, Sidney, 210*n.*
Hudson River School, 195, 196
Hugo, Victor, 156, 379
Humanism, 9, 54
Hume, David, 186, 219, 229, 268*n.*
Hypotheses, 57, 202; confirmation of, 174 archeological, 189*n.*; and bias, 198, 200; must fit old facts, 243

Ideas: in research, 19; relevance, 20; linking, 37, 287, 321; place in history, 44; communicated orally, 47–48; inherited, 56; facts and, 145–46, 194, 195, 284; defined, 147, 148; all history as history of, 148–49, 160–61; inferred, 149; perceptiveness about, 149; study of, 159–61; as causes, 190; as historical themes, 198; conflicts of, 208–9; of freedom, 221, 222, 223; gradual alteration of, 244; symbols for, 285; words and, 315, 316, 329; simplicity of, 327–28
Idiom: twisted, 296 (fig.), 297, 311 and *n.*, 312; and translating, 355–56
Iliad, 288
Images: ideas as, 147; loose coupling of, 155; in writing, 299–303, 304, 322; national, 232, 236; self-, 232, 238, 244; concrete, 409
Imagination: and notetaking, 24–27; enrichment of, 51; in research, 58–59, 68, 69, 113; value, 85; past falsified in, 179; failure of, 196; and right judgment, 203; of the real, 215; and one's own past, 246; no substitute for, 279; in writing, 317, 373

Index: cross, 22; of notes, 26, 30–31, 278, 281*n.*; in scholarly books, 72; to periodicals, 80 (fig.), 90, 94*n.*, 96*n.*, 100 (fig.); newspaper, 87; historical, 90, 96*n.*; by computer, 103–8; of finished work, 406–7; Samuel Butler's, 407*n.*
Individualism: religious, 208; in history, 209; in action, 225; European, 228
Industrial Revolution, 232*n.*
"In God We Trust," 127–28
"Interest": in history writing, 181–82, 199, 200, 206, 217, 238, 250–53; bias the extreme of, 207; in Man, 257
Interlibrary loans, 93
Ireland, conflict in, 201
Irony, 330, 331, 350, 383
Irredentism, 222
Italics: as a form, 272; in quotations, 342; for book titles, 342, 360; in footnotes, 360, 364
Italy: Hancock on history of, 203; unification of, 232; fascism in, 368

Jackson, Andrew, 11; and labor movement, 83; A. Kendall and, 138*n.*; applauded by Bancroft, 230; articles on, 234; Age of, 239
Jacksonian democracy, 232
Jacobins, The (Brinton), 197
Jacobites, 226
James, Henry, 59, 106, 382; mode of speech, 184, 185
James, William, 257, 382; quoted, 303 and *n.*, 403 (fig.)
Japan: opening of, 69; and "containment," 348*n.*
Jargon: computer, 101, 102–3; examples of, 154, 184, 324; political, 222; and abstractness, 267; a fault in writing, 296 (fig.), 297, 300, 301, 312, 325; origin and effects, 304–6; living without, 306–8; and images, 322
Jaurès, Jean, 225
Jefferson, Thomas, 11, 83*n.*, 146, 160; papers of, 125; as President, 148; and Hamilton, 232, 237; biographies of, 381
Joan of Arc, 90
Johnny Appleseed, 234
John Paul I, Pope, 122
Johnson, Lyndon B., 121–22
Johnson, Samuel: letter to Chesterfield, 177–78; 266
Jones, Casey, 234
Jones, John Paul, 251
Jordan, Elizabeth, 184*n.*
Journalism: and historical research, 7;

441

Musicology, as history, 8
Musset, Alfred de, 156
Mussolini, Benito, 124*n*., 227*n*., 368
Myths, 97, 117, 122; exploding of, 130–32

Nagel, Ernest, 188*n*.
Names: of persons, in research, 85–90;
    encyclopedias of, 88, 96; conventions,
    88–89; French usage, 88–89, 89*n*.; in-
    dexed by computer, 103, 105; verifica-
    tion, 122–24; transliteration, 356*n*.; *see
    also* Pseudonyms
Napoleon, I, 11, 13, 209, 230*n*., 241, 251
Napoleon III, 13
Narrative, as historical form, 253, 260,
    261, 263, 267, 268, 274, 280
Nationalism, 13; cultural, 54; intensified
    after 1789, 218–20; and history writing,
    221–22, 229–30, 232; the New, 237
National Trust for Historic Preservation,
    10
National Union Catalog, 76, 94 and *n*.; of
    manuscript collections, 124*n*.
Natural rights, 149
Natural selection, 149
Navigation Acts, 239
Nectarine (Smith), 69
Neologisms, 296 (fig.), 297
Nevins, Allan, 376
New Deal, 235
New Freedom, 237
Newspapers: indexes to, 87, 90, 93; on
    microfilm, 93–94; verifying reports in,
    110; fabrications in, 126–27; how to
    cite, 362
New Style: *see* Calendar
Newton, Isaac, 91, 117, 397
Nexis (data base), 108*n*.
Nicolson, Harold, 121
Nicolson, Marjorie, 397
Nietzsche, Friedrich, 148, 159, 212 (fig.),
    214
Nixon, Richard, 88; tapes, 11
Nock, Albert Jay, quoted, 381
Notebook: use of, 25 and *n*., 26, 278,
    281*n*.
Notes: on cards, 25, 26, 92, 278, 282
    (fig.), 283 (fig.); indexing of, 26, 30–31,
    278, 281*n*.; in composing, 280, 281 and
    n.; in outlining, 283 (fig.); lecturing
    from, 412, 413; *see also* Notebook;
    Notetaking
Notetaking, 24–27, 278, 311; on one side
    of card or slip only, 27; and thinking,
    27–31; abbreviations in, 28, 29, 30; and
    grasp of subject, 29

Noun plague, 299ff., 325, 414; *see also*
    Abstraction
Novel: resembles history, 8; historical,
    54, 250; the "New," 261
Numeration (statistics): where found, 96;
    see also Quantification

Obituaries, 87 and *n*.
Objective: meaning of term, 183–84,
    183*n*., 184*n*.; and politicization, 244
Old Style: *see* Calendar
Ologies, 256–57, 258, 263
Omaha Beach, 180, 181
Oman, Sir Charles, 25*n*.
Omnibus words, 309
Online Public Access Catalog (OPAC),
    64, 65
Openings: sentences, 320, 329–30;
    phrases, 327–28; chapter and para-
    graph, 424
Oral evidence: in research, 163–64, 166
    (fig.)
Oral history, 164*n*.
Order: in daily work, 56–57; in material
    gathered, 194, 195, 315; *see also*
    Arrangement; Organization; Pattern
Organization, 275–76; steps in, 276–80;
    words for, 299; in bibliographies, 375;
    errors in, 382
Origin of Species, The (Darwin), 73, 149
Orosius, 53, 255
Outline, 30, 281, 283 (fig.); from notes,
    282–83; for lecture, 412
Overtones, 150, 294, 311–12, 347

Page proofs, 403, 404–6
Palmer, R. R., 92
Pantelleria, 185
Paper: slips for notes, 26; disintegration
    of, 66; permanent, 66
Paperback reprints, 94
Paragraph(s): form, 281; unity, 291–92;
    revision, 392; transposing, 394–95;
    topic, 412; opening, 424–25
Parallelism, 321–22
Paraphrasing, 29, 349–50
Parkman, Francis, 268*n*.
Parody, 106, 129 (fig.)
Parrington, Vernon L., 246
Partisanship, 218–19, 221, 222–23, 226,
    227; *see also* Bias; Interest
Pascal (computer language), 102
Pascal, Blaise, 187
Pater, Walter, 97
Patience, need for, 85, 135
Patriotism, 221–22
Pattern, 193; chronological, 195; condi-

Publishing: growth of, 65–66; university press, 72; and quality, 71–72; "vanity," 86; reprint, 93, 94; *see also* Editing, copy
Punctuation, 362, 391

Quanto-history, 239–41, 254, 259–60, 262, 263, 264, 265–66
Quotation(s): dictionaries of, 80 (fig.), 83–85, 97, 98–99 (fig.); art of, 337; philosophy of, 338–41; rules of, 339; as illustration, 339, 344; merged, 339–40, 343; mechanics of, 341–44; marks, 342, 360–61; permission for, 343–44; translating, 344–56; and paraphrase, 349–50; footnotes for, 359, 367; collating, 386

Rabelais, François, 93
Race: Gobineau on, 211, 212 (fig.); intepreting history by, 211, 223, 240; Anglo-Saxonism, 220; and nationality, 256
Radiation: dating by, 167*n.*; dangers of, 389
Railroads, 206, 233
Rambaud, Alfred, 223
Randall, James G., 359
Ranke, Leopold von, 221, 231, 257
Reader: obligation toward, 32; clues for, 287; thought accessible to, 327; qualities desired by, 330
Readers' Guide to Periodical Literature, 80 (fig.), 100 (fig.)
Reading: part of research, 20; ease of, 38; foreign language, 83*n.*, 348, 349; difficult art, 84 (fig.); experience brought to, 150; clues in, 287; no good writing without, 312; one's own words, 384–86, 388, 400; for teaching, 409; a written text, 413–16, 417 (fig.)
Reasoning, 37, 112; bad, 156; circular, 171; *see also* Logic
Reconstruction period, 179
Record-keeping, 166 (fig.), 179*n.*, 233–34, 233*n.*, 251
Reductive fallacy, 156–57, 160, 215, 223
Reeve, Henry, quoted, 353–54
Reference works, 57, 65, 92, 143; how to use, 75–85, 90–93; general and specialized, 76 (fig.), 93; guides to, 79, 93, 97; types, 80 (fig.), 92; and disputed authorship, 133 and *n.*; dictionaries indispensable, 297–98, 297*n.*; judging quality, 383
Reformation (Protestant), 208, 219

Reform movements, 232
Regularities: and cause, 186; among events, 188, 207; in social behavior, 257; *see also* Pattern; Quanto-history
Reilly, Sidney, 120
Reischauer, Edwin O., 348*n.*
Reliability: in history writing, 17, 24; of source material, 72, 383
Relics, 166 (fig.), 176, 251, 252–53
Religion: in history writing, 207, 211–12 (fig.), 214–15, 255–56
Religious wars, 201
Renaissance, 54, 195
Repetition: hidden, 157; necessary, 287; awkward, 325; composition by, 340; in lecture, 411
Report(s): as a form, 3–6; presidential, 4; business, 4, 6, 35, 278–80, 287; sources for, 4–5, 14; history embodied in, 5–6, 34–35; book, 6, 290–91, 342*n.*; prerequisites, 17–21; intended audience, 31–32; rewriting, 36–39; oral, 45; putting life into, 49; verification, 109; false, 117–19; critical scrutiny, 178–82; arrangement, 290
Reporter: virtues of, 55–59, 149; sources protected, 120; fabricating news, 126–27
Reprint (publishing), 93, 94
Rereading: one's own work, 384–86, 388, 400
Revision (rewriting): need of, 36 (fig.), 36–39, 292, 293, 316; of published book, 72; of encyclopedia, 82; continuous, 82*n.*; self-questioning in, 334–35 (fig.); final, 377–407, 406 (fig.); through multiple editions, 380, 385; maxims and pointers, 384–86; techniques and symbols, 387–88, 390–95, 402 (fig.); with word processor, 388–89, 390, 391; consistency, 390–91; in preparing for printer, 390–96; punctuation, 391; paragraphing, 392; capitalization, 393; transposing, 394–95; to find a title, 396–99; in proofs, 400–403, 404–6, 405 (fig.); from part to part, 425
Revisionism: as knowledge increases, 190–91, 241–43; and the arts, 205–6; influence, 214; bias and interest in, 221, 243*n.*; and nationalism, 226; historical, 239
Revolution: American, 229–30; *see also* French; Industrial
Rewriting, *see* Revision; Revisionism
Rhodes, James Ford, 25*n.*
Rhodesia, 222*n.*

Whigs (British), 199
*Who's Who*s, 85ff., 96
"Widow," 404*n*.
William Rufus, 242–43 and *n*.
Williamsburg restoration, 10
William the Conqueror, 243
Wilson, James, 95
Wilson, Woodrow: medical history, 171–73; quoted, 203; peacemaker, 236
Wilsonline data base, 100 (fig.)
Winslow, Edward, 229
Witness(es): testimony of, 13, 167, 169, 170, 178, 179, 184, 185
Wittkower, Rudolf and Margaret, 397*n*.
Women: in nineteenth-century America, 236
Woodward, C. Vann, 373, 374 (fig.)
Word processor, 388–90, 391, 400*n*.
Words: key, 22*n*., 30–31, 285; your own, 28–29; choice of (diction), 37; reference books on, 83; vulgarisms, 83, 160; arrangement, 150; connotations, 150, 294, 311, 312; technical, 150–52, 153, 345, 365; study of, 154–55, 158, 294–95, 311; distorted meanings, 295–98; failure to distinguish, 296 (fig.), 297; vogue, 296 (fig.), 297; idiomatic, 296 (fig.), 297, 311 and *n*., 312; blurred meaning, 297–98; analysis of, 298–99, 301; images, 299–303; omnibus, 309; "dressing gown," 309, 312; circumlocution, 310; vernacular, 310; meaning, 315, 316; superfluous, 322, 323; transitional and qualifying, 323; and ideas, 329; "false friends," 346–49; play on, 351; Latin, 363, 364, 365; *see also* Jargon; Vocabulary; Writing
Wordsworth, Dorothy, 173–74

Wordsworth, William, 156, 173–74
Writing: part of research, 20; notes in one's words, 28–29; précis, 29; for professional journals, 32*n*., 33; faulty thinking and, 33, 35, 39; tautology, 35, 157, 305, 322, 324, 325; and rewriting, 36 (fig.), 36–39; analysis of, 37; clarity in, 38, 315, 316, 330, 332; style, 47, 316, 332–33; form, 271–76; organization, 276–80; transitions, 277, 284, 288; composing, 280–92, 328–29; plain words in, 293, 294–99, 296–97 (fig.); first draft, 293, 295, 310; purpose, 294; second draft, 295, 310, 327, 329; lazy, 298, 307; images, 299–303; avoiding pitfalls, 304–10, 312–13; fixed idioms, 311–12; qualities of, 315–18, 326–27, 332–33; syntax, 317; construction, 318–22, 327–30; tone, 319, 320, 330–33, 398; modern, 322–26; vagueness, 324, 325; economy in, 326; "fine," 331; questions to ask in, 334–35 (fig.); errors in, 377, 378–82; arrangement and pagination, 395; keeping duplicate, 395; how to begin, 422–23, 424; rules of thumb, 423–25; *see also* Historiography; History writing; Revision; Words

"Yankee," 236
Yeatman, R. J., 49*n*.

Zaharoff, Sir Basil, 120
Zaret, Dr. Milton, 389
Zeldin, Theodore, 265
Zilch, Elmer (fictional), 358
Zimbabwe, 222*n*.
Zinsser, William, 389*n*.